Palgrave Studies in Interna

Series editors
Mai'a Cross
Northeastern University
Boston, Massachusetts, USA

Benjamin de Carvalho
Norwegian Institute of International Affairs
Oslo, Norway

Shahar Hameiri
University of Queensland
St Lucia, Queensland, Australia

Knud Erik Joergensen
Department of Political Science
University of Aarhus
Aarhus, Denmark

Ole Jacob Sending
Norwegian Institute of International Affairs
Oslo, Norway

Ayse Zarakol
University of Cambridge
Cambridge, UK

Palgrave Studies in International Relations, published in association with European International Studies Association, provides scholars with the best theoretically-informed scholarship on the global issues of our time. The series includes cutting-edge monographs and edited collections which bridge schools of thought and cross the boundaries of conventional fields of study.

Mai'a Cross is the Edward W. Brooke Professor of Political Science at Northeastern University, USA, and Senior Researcher at the ARENA Centre for European Studies, University of Oslo, Norway.

Benjamin de Carvalho is a Senior Research Fellow at the Norwegian Institute of International Affairs (NUPI), Norway.

Shahar Hameiri is Associate Professor of International Politics and Associate Director of the Graduate Centre in Governance and International Affairs, School of Political Science and International Studies, University of Queensland, Australia.

Knud Erik Jørgensen is Professor of International Relations at Aarhus University, Denmark, and at Yaşar University, Izmir, Turkey.

Ole Jacob Sending is the Research Director at the Norwegian Institute of International Affairs (NUPI), Norway.

Ayşe Zarakol is University Lecturer in International Relations at the University of Cambridge and a fellow at Emmanuel College, UK.

More information about this series at
http://www.palgrave.com/series/14619

Maéva Clément • Eric Sangar
Editors

Researching Emotions in International Relations

Methodological Perspectives on the Emotional Turn

palgrave
macmillan

Editors
Maéva Clément
Institute of International Politics
Helmut Schmidt University
Hamburg, Germany

Eric Sangar
FNRS / University of Namur
Namur, Belgium

Palgrave Studies in International Relations
ISBN 978-3-319-88059-4   ISBN 978-3-319-65575-8 (eBook)
https://doi.org/10.1007/978-3-319-65575-8

© The Editor(s) (if applicable) and The Author(s) 2018
Softcover reprint of the hardcover 1st edition 2017
This work is subject to copyright. All rights are solely and exclusively licensed by the Publisher, whether the whole or part of the material is concerned, specifically the rights of translation, reprinting, reuse of illustrations, recitation, broadcasting, reproduction on microfilms or in any other physical way, and transmission or information storage and retrieval, electronic adaptation, computer software, or by similar or dissimilar methodology now known or hereafter developed.
The use of general descriptive names, registered names, trademarks, service marks, etc. in this publication does not imply, even in the absence of a specific statement, that such names are exempt from the relevant protective laws and regulations and therefore free for general use.
The publisher, the authors and the editors are safe to assume that the advice and information in this book are believed to be true and accurate at the date of publication. Neither the publisher nor the authors or the editors give a warranty, express or implied, with respect to the material contained herein or for any errors or omissions that may have been made. The publisher remains neutral with regard to jurisdictional claims in published maps and institutional affiliations.

Cover credit: GettyImages-534192281

Printed on acid-free paper

This Palgrave Macmillan imprint is published by Springer Nature
The registered company is Springer International Publishing AG
The registered company address is: Gewerbestrasse 11, 6330 Cham, Switzerland

Acknowledgments

This book is the result of a two-year collaborative process and would not have been possible without the advice and support of others.

The first impulse for this project came under the Sicilian sun at the European International Studies Association's conference in September 2015. Sarah Roughley, our editor at Palgrave, then expressed interest in our research on emotional narratives in the context of the international use of force. After considering a monography, we were excited about the idea of a book which would not only propose a narrative approach to emotions in international politics but present other methodologies and, beyond that, other ontological, epistemological, and theoretical positions. Sarah was excited about the idea of an edited volume on emotions and methodology and has accompanied our project from the first proposal to the final manuscript with sound advice and much patience.

We wish to thank all the contributors to this volume for their outstanding commitment throughout the project, despite many research commitments and sometimes heavy teaching activities. We greatly appreciated the constructive feedback and smooth cooperation. Our special thanks to Emma Hutchison and Roland Bleiker, who, despite many challenges, agreed to engage with the volume in the form of a critical conclusion.

Our special thanks go also to Thomas Lindemann, who worked closely with us in the early stages of the project, providing valuable advice and guidance on the volume's conceptualization and the book proposal. Furthermore, we are particularly grateful to Anna Geis and Thierry Balzacq for their useful comments on earlier versions of the introduction and for their support throughout the project. We extend our thanks to our colleagues and friends at the Helmut-Schmidt University, the University of Namur, and the Goethe University Frankfurt, who showed interest in our project and offered opportunities to discuss our ideas.

We would like to thank Katharina Höne for organizing the young researcher's workshop "IR's feelings: Avenues for theorising the processes that render emotions political" at the 2015 EISA in Sicily, which allowed us to meet a number of the contributors to this volume. We also thank the participants in the roundtable "IR's feelings: Critically Exploring Emotional Methodologies" at the 2016 BISA general conference in Edinburgh for their critical feedback and genuine interest in emotion research and opportunities for teaching.

We also wish to thank the anonymous reviewers of the first draft of our volume. Their insightful comments challenged us to deepen our arguments while at the same time making the volume accessible to a larger audience—the book has grown in depth thanks to them.

We would like to thank the students in our seminars and lectures for engaging with us on methodological debates and offering both genuine interest and challenging feedback.

This project was made much easier thanks to the financial contribution of several institutions. Eric would like to thank the Belgian Research Funds (FNRS) for his postdoctoral funding, which provided him with sufficient time and flexibility to devote to this project. Maéva is grateful for the travel grants of the Ile-de-France region (AMID) and the Franco-German-University (UFA/DFH) which allowed her to take part in several workshops alongside some of the contributors to the volume.

Finally, we are deeply grateful for the emotional and intellectual support we received from our families and friends. Maéva's and Eric's special thanks go respectively to Janusz Biene and Brigitte Mougin for their unwavering support and confidence throughout this project.

Last but not least, we would like to thank Samantha Snedden and the Palgrave staff for their hard work throughout the production process.

All remaining shortcomings and errors are solely our responsibility.

Contents

1 Introduction: Methodological Challenges and Opportunities for the Study of Emotions 1
Maéva Clément and Eric Sangar

Part I The Influence of Emotions on Actors and Politics 31

2 Eugene Gendlin and the Feel of International Politics 33
Erik Ringmar

3 Interpreting Affect Between State Leaders: Assessing the Political Friendship Between Winston S. Churchill and Franklin D. Roosevelt 51
Yuri van Hoef

4 More Rigor to Emotions! A Comparative, Qualitative Content Analysis of Anger in Russian Foreign Policy 75
Regina Heller

Part II Emotions Shaped by Powerful Actors and Institutions 101

5 Auto-ethnography and the Study of Affect and Emotion in World Politics: Investigating Security Discourses at London's Imperial War Museum 103
Audrey Reeves

6 A Plea for a Discursive Approach to Emotions: The Example of the French Airmen's Relation to Violence 129
Mathias Delori

7 The Formation of the 'Western' Strategic Gaze: A Case Study on Emotional Irrelevance in International Politics 151
Christophe Wasinski

8 Of Heroes and Cowards: A Computer-Based Analysis of Narratives Justifying the Use of Force 179
Eric Sangar, Maéva Clément, and Thomas Lindemann

Part III Discursive Agency and Emotions 207

9 Moving Images and the Politics of Pity: A Multilevel Approach to the Interpretation of Images and Emotions 209
Gabi Schlag

10 Political Emotions as Public Processes: Analyzing Transnational Ressentiments in Discourses 231
Reinhard Wolf

11 Emotions and Time: Approaching Emotions Through a Fusion of Horizons 255
Clara Eroukhmanoff and Bernardo Teles Fazendeiro

12 **Speaking from the Heart: Emotion Discourse Analysis in International Relations** 277
Simon Koschut

13 **Grasping the Role of Emotions in IR via Qualitative Content Analysis and Visual Analysis** 303
Sybille Reinke de Buitrago

14 **Methods and Methodologies for the Study of Emotions in World Politics** 325
Roland Bleiker and Emma Hutchison

Index 343

List of Figures

Chart 4.1	Anger curve Kosovo 1999	93
Chart 4.2	Anger curve Russian-Georgian war 2008	94
Picture 5.1	The Imperial War Museum (London)	106
Picture 5.2	The atrium of the Imperial War Museum, July 2014	115
Illustration 7.1	The 'genealogical tree' of the military cartographic narrative	158
Picture 7.1	Seventeenth-century schematic illustration of a fortification	163
Picture 7.2	Seventeenth-century cartographic illustration of an infantry formation	165
Picture 7.3	Eighteenth-century cartographic illustration of tactical battle movements	166
Picture 7.4	Twentieth-century geopolitical map 'The Natural Seats of Power'	170
Fig. 8.1	Codebook design	191
Fig. 8.2	Screenshot of coding software QDA Miner	195
Fig. 8.3	Relative frequencies of narrative roles in violent versus non-violent discourses	196
Fig. 8.4	Relative frequencies of narrative structures in violent versus non-violent discourses	197
Fig. 8.5	Comparison of relative frequencies of coded segments between statements by Bush and bin Laden	200
Picture 9.1	Graffiti Version of the Alan Kurdi picture, Frankfurt/Main	224
Fig. 11.1	Illustration of the fusion of emotional appraisals	272

List of Tables

Table 1.1	Overview of the types of research question, ontological position and method(s) per chapter	17
Table 1.2	Methodological approach, advantages and limits of each contribution	22
Table 3.1	Structure of the case studies	59
Table 3.2	Results of the case study	65
Table 4.1	The coding system	86
Table 4.2	Kosovo case search slots	89
Table 4.3	Georgia case search slots	89
Table 4.4	Search categories for contextualized text sampling within the predefined slots	90
Table 4.5	INTEGRUM query/search key example for contextualized document search	90
Table 4.6	Document-coding ratio	91
Table 8.1	Case selection	194
Table 8.2	Co-occurrences in speeches by Bush and bin Laden: absolute frequencies	198
Table 11.1	Applying affective stylistics to the study of emotional appraisals	265

CHAPTER 1

Introduction: Methodological Challenges and Opportunities for the Study of Emotions

Maéva Clément and Eric Sangar

Almost ten years ago, Bleiker and Hutchison observed in a widely cited article that it seemed "surprising" there were "hardly any sustained discussions about how to go about studying emotions in world politics" (2008, p. 124). Few researchers in international relations (IR) interested in emotions would have then disagreed with this diagnosis.[1] The nascent research on emotions focused on explaining why emotions matter conceptually, thereby having methodological debates take a backseat at the same time as these gained importance in the larger IR discipline. Even though emotion research in IR has started to address methodological issues more systematically, it is lacking consolidated insights discussing methodology in relation to the ontological, epistemological and theoretical debates on emotions in international politics.

This collective volume is the first of its kind to specifically address methodological considerations in doing empirical research on emotions in IR. It discusses the link between theoretical argument(s) and methodology

M. Clément (✉)
Helmut Schmidt University, Hamburg, Germany

E. Sangar
FNRS / University of Namur, Namur, Belgium

© The Author(s) 2018
M. Clément, E. Sangar (eds.), *Researching Emotions in International Relations*, Palgrave Studies in International Relations,
https://doi.org/10.1007/978-3-319-65575-8_1

by presenting research-practical insights from contemporary cases in international politics. In so doing, this volume encourages researchers interested in emotions in international politics to discuss methodological choices more explicitly as well as the opportunities and limits associated with these choices. The book is committed to a 'hands-on approach'. It emphasizes research-practical problems and solutions, thus providing an accessible and useful guide to students and scholars alike.

We define *methodology* as the way research is done, that is, how the researcher aims to gain knowledge with regard to his/her research question. It is a roadmap including—among others—selection principles, data collection procedures, decisions about the use of a specific research method or a combination of methods and, decisively, the justification for these specific choices. *Methods* are defined, for the purpose of this book, as tools, techniques and processes of data collection (interviews, surveys, archival work, etc.) and analysis (narrative method, content analysis, process-tracing, etc.). Their use is shaped by and codified in the researcher's methodology.

Against this backdrop, the volume pursues three specific objectives:

- It provides valuable insights into how emotions and affects can be operationalized. It thereby problematizes methodological path dependency, that is, the extent to which ontological positions and theoretical arguments imply specific ways of collecting and analyzing empirical material in concrete research projects. Since methodological choices vary from research project to research project, the authors of this volume write about methodology and methods within the context of their own research project. By reconstructing and making accessible how researchers translated complex theoretical frameworks into concrete empirical analysis, readers can draw practical inspiration for producing both empirically creative and methodologically founded research;
- The volume takes stock of several of the main methods currently used to produce empirical evidence on the role of emotions in IR. The volume does not claim to be exhaustive but focuses rather on the call for integrating tools from 'classical' social science with approaches from the humanities in the study of emotions in IR (Bleiker & Hutchison, 2008, p. 131);
- Each individual chapter deals with key challenges identified in the introduction and discusses limits and advantages with regard to the

specific method(s) presented. In this regard, the contributing authors remind us that no method is perfect and offer insights and suggestions on how researchers might overcome some of the limits that they identified in their own methodological approach.

In the following, we briefly discuss the current state of the art of research on emotions in international politics. While not aiming at providing an exhaustive review of this vibrant field, we pinpoint two major theoretical debates, discuss general methodological trends in the current scholarship, and present six key methodological issues that we deem particularly important for studying emotions empirically. In the second part, we explain the rationale of the volume and the didactic structure followed by each chapter. As the volume is designed both for research and teaching purposes, we highlight the two key aspects presiding over the volume: plurality and practicality. Finally, we present the volume's structure, followed by an overview table of the contributions, and introduce each individual chapter.

Overview of the State of the Art in Emotion Research

Until the late 1990s, among the central analytical categories of IR, emotions had occupied the role of a strange uncle who is invited to all family reunions but often sits isolated at the coffee table. 'Fear' in realist accounts of the international system (Freyberg-Inan, 2006), mutual sympathy in neoliberal conceptualizations of social capital (D'Aoust, 2014), 'pride' in constructivist accounts of recognition (Lindemann, 2014) and the influence of emotions on individual perceptions of rationality in actor-centric foreign policy analysis (Mercer, 2005) are just some examples of how implicit assumptions about emotions underline some of the most influential IR paradigms. This neglect is even more surprising given that both during and after the Cold War, emotions have played a central role in representations of conflict, with examples ranging from the transformation of 'enmity' into 'friendship' during the Franco-German reconciliation in the 1960s to the fear of a 'nuclear holocaust' within the peace movements of the 1980s or the media coverage of 'ethnic hatred' in the 1990s civil wars.

This changed at the turn of the twenty-first century, when several scholars began arguing that the presence of emotions in and their relationship to international politics should be analyzed in their own right (Bially Mattern, 2008; Bleiker, 2001; Crawford, 2000; Danchev, 2006; Lebow, 2005; Linklater, 2004; Marcus, 2000; McDermott, 2004; Ross, 2006; Saurette, 2006). In the past ten years, publications on the topic have been on constant rise, showing how much resonance this field of study is getting nowadays.

Emotions were long denied the status of a legitimate research object in IR. As a result, scholarly work in the 2000s mostly centered on showing that taking emotions into account was *worth it*, for one thing because they relate to real-world problems and for another because existing IR theories had been implicitly relying on them all along (Bleiker & Hutchison, 2007; Ross, 2006). This argument was further developed along epistemological and theoretical lines (Bially Mattern, 2011; Bleiker & Hutchison, 2008; Mercer, 2010; Sasley, 2011). Path-breaking contributions have been made in this regard, which provided increasingly sophisticated theories on emotions in international politics, opened up new fields of inquiry beyond the already well-established political-psychological accounts of decision-making processes (for instance Jervis, Lebow, & Stein, 1985), and which decentered the perspective away from the state (Brounéus, 2008; Fattah & Fierke, 2009; Ross, 2010; Solomon, 2015; Sylvester, 2012; Wright-Neville & Smith, 2009).

More recently, research on emotions has focused increasingly on specific aspects of international politics, such as—to take only two examples—the relationship between emotions and violent conflict (Åhäll & Gregory, 2015; Eznack, 2012; Fierke, 2012; Hall, 2011; Hutchison & Bleiker, 2007; Khalili, 2010; Mercer, 2013; Pearlman, 2013; Penttinen, 2013; Ross, 2013; Schut, de Graaff, & Verweij, 2015) or between emotions, norms and governmentality (D'Aoust, 2014; Jeffery, 2011; Ross, 2016). Some have also called scholars to question the role of emotion in their own research process, thus asking for more reflexivity regarding the extent to which emotions stabilize the discipline's own research practices (Ling, 2014; Soreanu & Hudson, 2008; Sylvester, 2011).

Two Major Conceptual-Theoretical Debates

Though it goes beyond the scope of this volume to provide a history of the scholarship on emotions in IR, we identify two major conceptual-theoretical debates in the literature: the differentiation between emotion and affect as analytical concepts and the theorization and conceptualization of emotions at the *international* level. This summary cannot replace already existing, extensive theoretical reviews (some sophisticated accounts are Åhäll & Gregory, 2015; Ariffin, Coicaud, & Popovski, 2016; Bleiker & Hutchison, 2007; Crawford, 2000; Hutchison & Bleiker, 2014; Ross, 2006).

Emotion as an analytical concept is particularly tricky. Researchers refer to three main terms—affect, emotion and feeling—whose definitions are contested and particularly fuzzy at times. In a simplified fashion, affect refers to non-reflective bodily sensations, which are situated before and beyond consciousness (Hutchison & Bleiker, 2014; Ross, 2006). In contrast, an emotion is said to refer to the "subjective experience of some diffuse physiological change" (Mercer, 2014, p. 516) and has "intersubjective, and cultural components" (Crawford, 2000, p. 125). Finally, a feeling can be defined as the "conscious awareness that one is experiencing an emotion" (Mercer, 2014, p. 516); though internally experienced, the meaning attached to them is cognitively and culturally constructed (Crawford, 2000, p. 125).

From these summary definitions, it becomes obvious how closely interrelated these concepts are. While some choose to "treat emotion and feelings as synonyms" (Mercer, 2014, p. 516), others argue that "only feelings […] are fully available to consciousness" and prefer to use the term affect while equating it to "corporeally mediated 'emotions'" (Ross, 2006, p. 216). The dividing lines between affect and emotions on one side and emotion and feelings on the other side thus seem rather porous. In her early work, Crawford defined emotions in a more integrative fashion as "the inner states that individuals describe to others as feelings, and those feelings may be associated with biological, cognitive, and behavioral states and changes" (Crawford, 2000, p. 125), thereby taking into account all three dimensions. In a similar fashion, Hutchison and Bleiker highlight that "affect and emotions can be seen as intrinsically linked, for affective states are subconscious factors that can frame and influence our more conscious emotional evaluations of the social world" (2014, p. 502).

Notwithstanding the diversity of conceptual uses for naming such phenomena, we use 'emotion' as an umbrella term, partly because 'emotion research' has become the most common term to designate the field, but also because each of the volume's chapter specifies the researcher's understanding of emotional phenomena on an affect-emotion-feeling continuum.

The second theoretical debate refers to the processes through which emotions acquire a collective and political character. This challenge rests at the core of our ability to account for the role emotions play in international politics. Are emotions actually 'private'? Under which circumstances do they become 'social', 'shared', 'public' and 'political'? Mercer contends, for instance, that the social character of emotion is linked to its "intrinsic importance to an actor in some relationship with an entity" (Mercer, 2014, p. 516). Against this backdrop, he calls for studying social (or 'group-level') emotions *through* identity, because "identification requires a feeling of attachment" to a group (understood in a broad sense).

At the other end of the theoretical spectrum, some reject the analytical distinction between individual and collective emotions altogether. Ross, for instance, stresses that "there is nothing inherently individual about the body and its affects" and warns against making a distinction "between social and individual dimensions of emotions" (Ross, 2006, p. 216). Analyzing the US response to the 9/11 attacks, he argues that one cannot pinpoint a precise collective emotion such as anger but rather a crystallization of "memories", "habits" and "public mood or moods conducive to militarist response", that is, a specific type of collective action. In a similar vein, Bially Mattern contends that private emotions are always collective at the same time (Bially Mattern, 2014).

In short, most IR emotion researchers broadly agree that emotions are historically, culturally and socially contingent, yet they disagree on how to account for emotional change. For example, why certain emotions become more relevant than others in specific political configurations (Bleiker & Hutchison, 2014), how the same emotion category—'anger' or 'fear'—come to be evaluated in a positive or negative light across time and space (Linklater, 2014), or how certain collective emotions become 'institutionalized' (Crawford, 2014). As much as these represent theoretical questions, they raise evident methodological issues, such as at which level(s) or site(s) emotions are to be empirically observed, or how the emergence and disappearance of politically relevant emotions could be traced over time. In this regard, the much-relayed call for increased methodological debate on how to empirically ground the 'emotional turn' in IR reflects *ongoing* theoretical controversies.

Emotions and Methodology: A Slow Coming Methodological Debate

The IR literature explicitly addressing methodological issues in the study of emotions remains relatively scarce compared to other disciplines, such as the sociology of emotions (Flam & Kleres, 2015; Stets & Turner, 2014). Most journal articles and books on the subject have focused on the theoretical challenges linked to the study of emotions in international politics. For the early publications, this is not all too surprising as the introduction of 'new' research objects requires establishing their theoretical relevance first. Yet 20 years on, it seems that methodology is still relatively under-discussed. So far, even case study-based publications have rarely provided insights into the researcher's method(s), let alone into his/her methodological approach. Too often, the choice of a specific method seems to rest on personal preferences rather than on a specific conceptualization of emotion. Beyond questions of transparency and scientific good practice, this deficit points to key methodological and disciplinary challenges. Hutchison and Bleiker thus point out that "questions of methods are crucial [...], not least because they explain why emotions remain understudied even though their political role has for long been recognized" (Hutchison & Bleiker, 2014, p. 494).

A brief overview of major publications since the 1970s provides some clues on methodological trends and shortcomings in IR emotion research. In the 1970s, the nascent political-psychological accounts of foreign policy provided cognitive accounts of emotions at the individual level, that is, the decision-maker. With the 'emotional turn' starting at the end of the 1990s, scholars debated ever more elaborated theoretical propositions, without actually offering suggestions on how to research emotions empirically (Bleiker & Hutchison, 2007, p. 4). Mercer already summarized the difficulties 20 years ago: "emotion is hard to define, hard to operationalize, hard to measure, and hard to isolate from other factors" (Mercer, 1996, p. 1). In order to develop theoretical arguments and in the absence of dedicated empirical studies, early IR emotion research has tended to overemphasize the insights gained from neuroscientific experiments. Though this trend seems less accurate today, Jeffery argues that emotion researchers still rely much "on recent findings in the neurosciences to bolster their arguments" (Jeffery, 2014, p. 584).

In this regard, many IR researchers have built on social scientific methods—from experiments to classical forms of discourse analysis—to account for emotions without completely breaking the discipline's focus on cognitive frames of analysis. More recently, following the call to "supplement social scientific approaches with modes of analysis stemming from the humanities" (Bleiker & Hutchison, 2007, p. 4), IR emotion research has seen a growing trend to turn to methodologies that borrow extra-disciplinary tools and techniques of data collection and analysis.

These developments represent opportunities to reflect on at least four questions:

- How can researchers create meaning around emotional phenomena?
- What aspects may be 'lost' in doing so?
- To what extent should researchers adapt available methods to the study of emotions? And which existing methods might be particularly appropriate?
- How much interdisciplinarity is necessary to capture the specific ontological character of emotions?

These issues relate in turn to fundamental questions about the kind of research scholars want to do, write, publish and teach. In this regard, this volume highlights the methodological challenges and opportunities resulting from diverging theoretical positions in concrete research projects as an avenue for stimulating an overdue scholarly debate.

IDENTIFYING SIX KEY METHODOLOGICAL CHALLENGES

Although a substantial debate on methodologies for the study of emotions is still nascent, it is useful to highlight the disagreements and problems current scholarship is facing. We identify six key methodological challenges, which relevance for the individual researcher may vary, depending on the theoretical and empirical scope of the concrete research project. The first two represent general methodological challenges referring to the forms of knowledge emotion researchers aim to produce: aiming for generalizability or the insider's view; and adapting traditional methods and/or borrowing methods from neighboring disciplines. The following four challenges refer to practical methodological issues linked to the operationalization of emotions: narrowing down the variety of emotional phenomena in a concrete research project; negotiating the mediated character of emotions; clarifying the level(s) or site(s) of analysis; accounting for emotions' different temporalities. While we distinguish these six issues for didactic purposes, yet they are closely interrelated. For each issue, we discuss the main scholarly positions and stress their implications in terms of research desiderata, opportunities and limits.

Generalizing Versus Accounting for the Insider's View

The first issue resides in the potential tension between two criteria: systematically generating knowledge on emotions in international politics *and* accounting for emotions as authentically as possible. The first criterion refers, for instance, to whether it is possible to *generalize*, that is, to extend research findings to a broader research context and/or transfer research findings from one research context to another (see Heller, Chap. 4 and Sangar et al., Chap. 8 in this volume). Generalizability rests on causal relationships and implies some degree of measurement and quantification. The social and cultural environment of the specific phenomenon under study is typically taken into account as a 'variable' which defines the characteristics of a whole class of objects to which statements from the specific phenomenon under study can be transferred. Conversely, the second criterion prioritizes capturing the intrinsic complexity of the emotional phenomenon at stake. It means being concerned with how to try and render the emotions of the researched as closely as possible. Beyond this, it also calls for self-reflexivity and transparency about the role of the researcher's emotions in the production of the research insights (see Reeves, Chap. 5).

The extent to which emotion research can—or even should—satisfy both criteria remains contested. Both positions are difficult to maintain in their ideal forms. For Bleiker and Hutchison, "emotions cannot be quantified, nor can they easily be measured, even in qualitative terms" (2008, p. 125). Similarly, authentic accounts of emotions might not be a realistic goal to achieve since "the inner feelings of a person cannot easily be known or even communicated authentically. The same is the case with emotions that are shared by communities" (Bleiker & Hutchison, 2008, p. 126). The challenge or opportunity here is thus to propose alternative criteria or standards of reference to evaluate the quality of empirical analysis in emotion research.

Adapting Traditional Methods Versus Borrowing Methods from Neighboring Disciplines

The second challenge relates to whether it is sufficient to rely on methods traditionally used in IR research, or if emotion researchers need to adapt and repurpose such methods, or if they need to borrow methods from other disciplines. After all, methods usually relied upon in IR research originated in studies that did not address emotions and/or were explicitly averse to their study. Moreover, the search for appropriate methods of data collection and evaluation is not merely a question of practical tools but is closely related to the researchers' conceptualizations of emotional phenomena. For instance, if one conceives of emotions primarily as affects of the individual body, which largely elude cognition, methods such as textual analysis—as useful as they might be for other approaches to emotions—would not have much methodological relevance, compared, for instance, to phenomenological or auto-ethnographical approaches.

The chapters discuss and problematize these links between ontological, epistemological and theoretical views on emotions and their empirical exploration. Most stress the need to at least adapt methods used traditionally in IR to render them more emotion-sensitive (see, for instance, Koschut, Chap. 12). Some argue that the study of emotions in IR requires incorporating methods of inquiry that were developed and are more common in neighboring disciplines, such as visual analysis (Schlag, Chap. 9), (auto)ethnography (Reeves, Chap. 5), historical-sociological analysis (Wasinski, Chap. 7) or psychoanalysis (Ringmar, Chap. 2). Others still present methodologies arguing for a combination of both, complementing traditional social scientific methods with humanities-oriented methods (van Hoef, Chap. 3; Heller, Chap. 4; Sangar et al., Chap. 8; Reinke de Buitrago, Chap. 13). The contributions thus present a variety of methodological options and illustrate best the extent to which the study of emotions will benefit from a lively debate on methodology alongside the effort to gain theoretical depth and sophistication.

Narrowing Down the Variety of Emotional Phenomena

The third challenge concerns how to capture *specific* emotional phenomena within a concrete research project. It is not realistic to account for all emotional phenomena that might come into play over a defined period or even in the context of a specific event. Consequently, emotion researchers select certain emotions to focus on and hence operate distinctions between emotion expressions across time as well as across cultural and social space. In this regard, some argue that it is useful to isolate specific or 'discrete' emotions (such as anger or joy) and observe them separately, for instance, to analyze their relationship to specific types of behavior (Bially Mattern, 2014; McDermott, 2004). Others contend that they cannot be isolated and should be treated, as Ross suggest, as 'mixed emotions', complex 'affective energies' or 'public moods' (Ross, 2006). Indeed, if one conceives emotional stimuli as mutually interdependent, it makes little sense to develop methodologies to empirically detect instances of specific emotions. Rather, holistic approaches would seem more appropriate to provide thick descriptions of emotional states, situated in time and space.

On the other hand, if the aim is to account for the potential impact of discrete (evolving) emotions within political processes, researchers might try, for analytical purposes, to disentangle emotional phenomena by creating ideal-typical categories of emotion (van Hoef, Chap. 3; Wolf, Chap. 10; Heller, Chap. 4). Though this means addressing difficult questions about the impact of specific emotions in causal processes (Bially Mattern, 2014), it allows researchers, for instance, to trace certain practices in international politics back to 'institutionalized emotions' (Crawford, 2014) or even to the institutional repression of emotions (see Wasinski, Chap. 7). In this regard, it might be particularly fruitful to increase triangulation through the use of multiple methods and/or of multiple materials in order to compare and potentially aggregate insights (Schlag, Chap. 9; Reinke de Buitrago, Chap. 13). Admittedly, triangulation might seem challenging in IR, when sources of empirical material are scarce and access to interviews and participant observation often limited. Yet researchers are considering increasingly diverse sources, from architecture, art, to social media (see the discussion by Reeves, Chap. 5).

Negotiating the Mediated Character of Emotions

Closely linked to this, the fourth challenge relates to the mediated character of emotions. Accessing emotions' authentic dimension might be a mirage, especially considering that the relationship between emotions and the 'rational mind' (Mercer, 2006) is not unequivocal. Emotions might frame what we perceive as our 'rational' interests (Fierke, 2006). In turn, the rational mind might to a certain extent re-orient emotional reactions. In other words, IR researchers cannot easily determine whether emotions are 'genuine' or 'filtered' through other—social or individual—instances (Fierke, 2014). For most authors in this volume, researchers thus ought to focus on what is displayed, communicated, represented and perceived by actors (see, for instance, the arguments by Delori, Chap. 6; Sangar et al., Chap. 8; Eroukhmanoff and Teles Fazendeiro, Chap. 11; Koschut, Chap. 12). In this regard, a focus on the interplay between the represented and the perceived or interpreted seems particularly promising.

Analyzing emotions via externally displayed behavior is not unproblematic though (Åhäll & Gregory, 2013). Ross, for instance, is skeptical about this research strand's capacity to "capture their [i.e. emotions] depth and intensity" (Ross, 2006, p. 201). Affect theorists sometimes even argue that affective phenomena are beyond representation (Hutchison & Bleiker, 2014). As immediate bodily experience and mediated representations of emotions may differ, some contributors in this volume try to integrate both perspectives and account for potential empirical differences between bodily experiences and representations.

Clarifying the Level(s) or Site(s) of Analysis

The next, related challenge consists in clarifying the level(s) or sites of analysis within a specific research project. If researchers cannot reduce the conceptual complexity of both collective emotional representations and their individual manifestations in and through the body (Ahmed, 2004), what are the best ways of capturing their interactions empirically? Should researchers approach this interaction as a 'top-down' dynamic, where powerful actors and institutions might shape collective and individual emotional representations, or rather as a 'bottom-up' dynamic, where emotional stimuli at the individual level shape protest and/or institutional politics (see the different positions by Schlag, Chap. 9 and Delori, Chap. 6)? Conceptualizations that consider emotions as co-dependent on individual and social dynamics need to either adapt hermeneutical approaches that have been developed in the humanities, or combine social scientific approaches with insights from (social) psychology and the neurosciences. Beyond this, some scholars invite to caution when operationalizing individual and group dynamics. McDermott rightly points out that it is not clear that individuals' identification with a group "renders [them] subservient to the group in the generation of emotions" (McDermott, 2014, p. 559). Researchers should also be cautious to avoid regarding all collectives in the same homogenizing light (Reus-Smit, 2014), as some collectives provide more conducive contexts and structures for the emergence of shared emotions than others (see, for instance, the argument by Sangar et al., Chap. 8, on patriarchal contexts).

Accounting for Emotions' Different Temporalities

Lastly, the temporal character of emotions constitutes a challenge that has not received enough attention in IR research so far. Should researchers think of emotions as only 'short-lived', as argued by Ariffin (2016, p. 2), and if this is the case, when do emotions change or disappear (Linklater, 2014)? Or do specific emotions display some continuity over time? Scholars working on resentment (Frijda, 2008; Petersen, 2002; Wolf, Chap. 10; 2015) and on trauma and reconciliation (Bell, 2006; Brounéus, 2008; Edkins, 2002; Fierke, 2006; Hutchison, 2010; Kelly, 2010; Resende & Budryte, 2014; Rosoux, 2014) point to the endurance of certain emotional phenomena. Moreover, certain emotions appear to be more strongly linked to specific representations of time than others. For example, Murphy has argued that feelings of humiliation result not only from present experiences but are linked to perceptions of 'stolen futures' (Murphy, 2011). In another vein, scholarship using visual analysis has come up with innovative insights about analyzing separately (and comparing) the immediate emotional impact of images and the medium- and long-term emotional effects that might follow from perceived reactions to images (and not the images themselves) being debated (Schlag, Chap. 9; Hansen, 2011). There is increasing work on how to access emotions' temporal character and longer term impacts (van Hoef, Chap. 3; Hom, 2016; Solomon, 2014), as well as on how to uncover emotional continuities over time which help reassess established accounts in IR scholarship (Wasinski, Chap. 7; Eroukhmanoff and Teles Fazendeiro, Chap. 11). Research on emotion is strongly event-oriented so far, which bears the question of how to account for emotional phenomena 'in-between' events or under changing circumstances.

The Volume's Guiding Principles: Plurality and Practicality

This volume does not provide definite answers to these key challenges but rather contributes to an open-ended debate on methodological limitations and opportunities. We expect increased attention to methodological issues to further establish emotion research as a dedicated field of study within the IR research community. In fact, earlier introductions of alternative paradigms in IR research have always been accompanied by a thorough debate about *which* phenomena should be studied and *how* they should be studied. The contributors to this volume believe that to further establish emotion as a research strand able to spark debate and produce cumulative knowledge, emotion researchers need to position themselves more openly as to whether the nature of emotional phenomena requires specific ways of producing knowledge.

Plurality

We believe that researchers produce substantially different insights on the role of emotions in international politics depending on the methodologies they design and the methods they use. Our volume does not aim to provide a representative canon of methods for the study of emotions in IR, neither does it rely on hierarchical assumptions about methodological validity and reliability. Rather, the methodologies presented in the volume correspond to current trends in emotion scholarship, focusing mainly on representations of emotions in social discourse.[2] The volume features methodological frameworks inspired by positivist and by interpretative traditions, using qualitative and/or quantitative methods of inquiry and situating the analysis in the interactions between micro, meso and/or macro levels. Furthermore, some chapters focus on the advantages and limits of specific methods, while others address the heuristic potential of interdisciplinary and mixed-methods frameworks. Finally, some chapters deal with classic IR themes, while others cover empirical phenomena going beyond traditional Western- and state-centric angles. The various methodological positions showcased in the volume are not necessarily compatible; the contributors' effort to spell out their varied epistemological, ontological, theoretical and methodological positions makes it possible to bring the chapters into discussion and offer a critique (see the concluding remarks by Bleiker and Hutchison, Chap. 14).

Furthermore, we expect the increased engagement with methodological issues to benefit the quality of teaching curricula on as well as students' self-engagement with emotions in international politics. Most of the contributors to this volume have taught courses on emotions in international politics and have been confronted with the extra difficulty to transmit methodology on a topic for which methodological practices are very little debated, much less codified. Students proved to be very open to and often instinctively attracted by theories emphasizing emotional dynamics in IR, yet were deeply frustrated with the all too often glossing over the concrete research steps that had been undertaken by researchers. Not to mention how most were at a loss when asked to outline potential methodological ways to go about researching emotions in their final essays. This volume should serve as a source of inspiration and guidance for both lecturers interested in including emotions in their curricula and students looking for practical illustrations on ways to approach emotions empirically.

Practicality

The methodological discussion within the volume unfolds in three ways: through the volume's organization, via the similar chapter construction and by means of a conclusion in the form of a critical assessment which builds bridges between the introduction and the chapters. In the following, we lay the emphasis on the chapters' common composition. All contributors followed a hands-on approach described in a uniform guideline. In each chapter, the contributors start by presenting their research question, epistemological background and theoretical argument, clarifying from the outset how they understand and conceptualize emotions in their research. As these have strong implications for methodological choices, the contributors explain *why* they opted for a specific method or combination of methods. Following this, contributors elaborate on the specificities of the method(s) they chose, thereby making explicit what research-practical consequences these have in terms of material, indicators, categories, etc. Contributors that chose to combine two methods also explain what synergic effects were expected and how these methods are articulated within their research framework. Thereafter, each contribution presents a concrete illustration or case study in order to exemplify the practical analytical steps deriving from the methodological framework. Finally, each chapter ends with a reflexive assessment of the advantages and limits of the proposed methodological approach. It points to what might be improved in further research and draws insights from this experience to present some recommendations for similar projects.

There is more than one way to read the volume, depending on researchers' and students' interests. Readers interested in specific methodological issues can consult the chapters referring to each of the six key issues flagged up in the introduction. To orient themselves more quickly, readers looking for a specific method can look up Table 1.1, which provides an overview of the chapters, as well as Table 1.2, which summarizes the advantages and limits of the method(s) used and some recommendation for future research. The short presentation of the chapters at the end of this introduction guides the reader towards specific case studies or material types.

Finally, the type of material analyzed in this volume is accessible to students. Its focus on accessibility makes the volume a precious resource to explore emotions in course exercises and research essays. Students are encouraged to be creative in the design of their own empirical analysis (e.g. by combining several tools), as well as rigorous in justifying their methodological choices. In this regard, lecturers can use the volume as a manual for a dedicated course on emotions in international politics, or individual chapters to stimulate methodological reflection in more general IR courses.

STRUCTURE OF THE BOOK AND OVERVIEW OF THE CHAPTERS

The volume's empirical chapters were grouped according to the research questions formulated by the authors, which can be subsumed under three generic types of research questions. The volume is thus structured in three parts, based on the analytical functions given to emotions:

1. Their presence or absence can help explain the occurrence of some other phenomenon, such as the formation of perceptions or decision-making outcomes. Researchers not only seek to account for the presence (or absence) of emotions at the individual or collective level but also to analyze whether this presence (or absence) results in change that would not have occurred otherwise.
2. They emerge or disappear following the actions and/or the discourses of powerful political actors or institutions, who/which contribute to impact the evocation or suppression of individual or collective emotional phenomena. Here emotions 'have to be explained' and the analysis focuses on power relations and institutionalized mechanisms of control.
3. They are inseparable from and hidden in larger dynamics of social discourse. Here, emotions are part and parcel of larger political discourses and have to be analyzed hermeneutically, in context with other phenomena of social discourse.

Table 1.1 provides an overview, for each individual chapter, of the analytical function given to emotions (generic types of research question), how emotions are conceptualized, and which specific method(s) is/are featured.

In the following, we present each chapter briefly, summarizing its main characteristics and arguments. The first section features approaches which build on the ontological assumption that emotions—individual or collective—have an independent influence on politics.

Erik Ringmar conceives emotions as distinctively situated affects in the individual body and ontologically separate from the cognitive mind. For

Table 1.1 Overview of the types of research question, ontological position and method(s) per chapter

Empirical chapter #	Author(s)	Analytical status of emotions in the chosen research question	Ontological focus in the chosen research question	Specific methods
2	Erik Ringmar	What effects do emotions have on other empirical phenomena (such as perceptions or behavior)?	Affect in and through the body	Psychoanalytical phenomenology
3	Yuri van Hoef		Affect in and through the body	Interpretative political science, biographical analysis
4	Regina Heller		Social discourse	Comparative qualitative content analysis
5	Audrey Reeves	Why and how are specific emotions used by political leaders and institutions?	Affect in and through the body/social discourse	Participant observation, auto-ethnography
6	Mathias Delori		Social discourse	Interview analysis, Foucauldian discourse analysis
7	Christophe Wasinski		Social discourse	Historical sociology, STS
8	Eric Sangar, Maéva Clément and Thomas Lindemann		Social discourse	Computer-assisted narrative analysis
9	Gabi Schlag	How to detect the inseparable yet partly hidden role of emotions within larger discursive dynamics?	Affect in and through the body/social discourse	Multimodal analysis, visual analysis
10	Reinhard Wolf		Affect in and through the body/social discourse	Discourse analysis
11	Clara Eroukhmanoff and Bernardo Teles Fazendeiro		Social discourse	Fusion of horizons, affective stylistics
12	Simon Koschut		Social discourse	Emotion discourse analysis
13	Sybille Reinke de Buitrago		Social discourse	Qualitative content analysis, visual analysis

him, emotions should be analyzed as phenomena *sui generis* and cannot be reduced to mere effects of social discourses. They can help us understand individuals' perceptions of their environment. Ringmar demonstrates the potential of combining phenomenological and psychoanalytical approaches to construe more accurately the interaction between emotions, affect and international politics. Ringmar relies on Eugene Gendlin's psychoanalytical notion of 'focusing' and shows how individuals develop a 'feeling' of the situation in which they find themselves, thus adapting their perception and resulting cognitive interpretations. He discusses the impact of such an approach for studying international politics.

Yuri van Hoef's contribution focuses on how affects resulting from personal encounters can modify the perceptions and behavior of individual decision-makers. His analysis centers on those interpersonal interactions between state leaders that are characterized as friendships. Defining friendship in international politics as an "emotional bond between individual politicians that influences their political actions", van Hoef argues that emotions should also be operationalized as an inter*personal* phenomenon: affection resulting from personal encounters of like-minded individuals can transcend distrust resulting from membership in different collective entities with diverging material interests. Using the relationship between British Prime Minister Winston Churchill and US President Franklin D. Roosevelt as an empirical case, van Hoef's methodology combines Bevir and Rhodes' interpretative political science with biographical analysis to detect the impact of interpersonal emotions on foreign policy decision-making.

Analyzing the influence of anger on Russia's foreign policy towards the West, Regina Heller is interested in how emotions resulting from perceived misrecognition influence institutional discourse and policy-making. Emotions are thus conceptualized as social phenomena produced in intersubjective discourse, which, in turn, has policy effects that cannot solely be explained by rational interests. In her contribution, she demonstrates the analytical potential of qualitative content analysis, which combines the sensitiveness of qualitative discourse analysis with the reliability of classical content analysis. She contends that by building dictionaries of emotional attributes, metaphors and other semiotic structures, emotions can be detected reliably across a large number of documents produced by several actors. Heller illustrates this with a comparison of representations of anger in discourses produced by several Russian institutions during the Kosovo crisis of 1999 and the war against Georgia in 2008.

The chapters of the second section conceptualize emotions primarily (albeit not necessarily exclusively) shaped by the actions and/or the discourses of powerful actors and institutions.

Audrey Reeves opens the section of contributions which focus on the extent to which and why emotions may be used by political leaders and institutions. She pursues this argument from a post-structural position, emphasizing self-reflexivity and the need for the researcher to question and expose his/her position as a subjective observer of social reality. Reeves argues that researchers should use their own emotional experiences in everyday life as a source of insight. Her methodology draws on autoethnography to explore how the Imperial War Museum in London produces specific emotional reactions to representations of war on visitors, and triangulates her observations with impressions collected on the social website TripAdvisor. These observations allow her to identify how architectural designs facilitate the stimulation of emotional support for political narratives about legitimate and illegitimate warfare.

Mathias Delori makes a plea for conceiving emotions as a strictly socially constructed phenomenon and indeed for interpreting them as the result of institutional discourses motivated by hegemonic political interests. In his contribution, he presents semi-structured interviews as a useful tool to observe how Western airmen represent their emotional reactions to the act of killing. He argues that said representations can only be understood via the impact of institutionally constructed frames that facilitate selective compassion due to differential framings of suffering and death. By connecting the hermeneutic analysis of interviews to larger discursive frames of liberal warfare inspired by Judith Butler, he shows that the airmen's bodily reaction to killing is thoroughly managed by institutional discourses disseminated through military doctrine.

Another perspective on how military institutions manage and manufacture emotions is offered by Christophe Wasinski. He shows in his chapter how military strategists have historically attempted to make emotions 'irrelevant' by promoting techno-centric representations of war through a 'strategic gaze'. He argues that in order to appear rational and to present feasible plans, strategists have removed emotional aspects from representations of war by employing specific cartographic narratives. By studying historical texts written by strategists over the last millennium and using a historical-sociological approach inspired by Social and Technology Studies, he shows that the comparative analysis of historical documents can help detect the century-old continuity and transnational diffusion of the cartographic narratives which facilitate the neutralization of emotions such as compassion, fear but also hatred—and, as a result, dehumanize warfare.

The contribution by Eric Sangar, Maéva Clément and Thomas Lindemann relies as well on an understanding of emotions as socially constructed phenomena. They aim to understand how political leaders inscribe collective emotions, especially anger and compassion, in elaborate narratives in order to justify the use of force. They introduce the 'hero-protector narrative' as a model to understand the relationship between collective emotions, morality and action. Their methodology consists in a computer-assisted narrative approach which combines narrative coding categories with systematic cross-case comparison. Drawing on a corpus of political speeches and statements around the 2003 invasion of Iraq, some advocating the use of force, others rejecting it, they demonstrate the cross-cultural relevance of the 'hero-protector narrative' in speech acts by actors seeking to gather support for the use of force.

The chapters in the third section follow an ontological approach which regards emotions as a phenomenon that is epistemologically interlinked with social discourse.

Gabi Schlag's contribution argues that while images do have an immediate emotional effect that goes far beyond the one resulting from texts, it does not mean that images alone can stimulate collective action and ultimately change political decisions. Drawing on a case study of the image of Alan Kurdi and its reception, Schlag argues that without analyzing the immediacy of a picture together with its embeddedness in a larger discourse which continues to be shaped by power interests, it is impossible to assess its widespread and yet contradicting reception. She illustrates the potential synergies gained by combining visual analysis and a multimodal approach. Schlag shows how and why images such as Alan Kurdi's may provoke strong individual emotions but nevertheless fail to mobilize large-scale political action at the institutional level.

Reinhard Wolf turns his attention to shared emotional attitudes which are reproduced in public discourse over time. Taking political *ressentiments* as a case in point, he shows that such negative emotional stereotypes have a typical pattern. Wolf argues that discourse analysis is well-suited to uncover the articulations of cognitions, affective arousals and action tendencies which form these patterns. He suggests a set of indicators to detect the emergence of resentment-based national discourses. He then illustrates his methodological reflection with a case study of the Syriza administration's discourse on Greek-German relations in the wake of the Greek sovereign debt crisis, focusing on *ressentiments* aimed at Germany.

Clara Eroukhmanoff and Bernardo Teles Fazendeiro explore how researchers could turn the methodological difficulty of seizing emotions' temporal character to their advantage. Combing Hans-Georg Gadamer's aesthetic theory with the analytical method of 'affective stylistics' developed by Stanley Fish, they suggest a methodology which allows to detect the underlying temporal specificities of emotional representations. In Gadamer's epistemological concept of a 'fusion of horizons', multiple temporal perspectives are placed in dialogue with one another, thus enabling the detection of hidden continuities in emotional representations, which would otherwise remain undiscovered by approaches focusing on specific events. Emotional representations are seen as being embedded in socially constructed, relatively stable traditions of discourse. Drawing on the US discourse on Afghanistan before and after the 9/11 attacks, the authors demonstrate the usefulness of this method as they uncover temporal similarities in the emotional representation of Afghanistan in the imaginary of US political leaders.

Simon Koschut's contribution also argues that emotions should be conceived as an integral part of discourse, the relevance of which is sometimes hidden. He calls for methodological innovation in textual analysis in order to account more accurately for such emotional dynamics integrated into discourse. He presents a methodological framework called 'Emotion Discourse Analysis', which includes tools to systematically map and compare discursive utterings of emotions. He subsequently applies this framework to the emotional underpinnings of NATO's discourse towards Russia after the annexation of Crimea in 2014. More than the 'cold' meaning of the chosen vocabulary, he argues that it is the subtle emotional associations in discourse that mark the profound shift towards an antagonistic representation of Russia.

Sybille Reinke de Buitrago's argument is about the intrinsic links between emotions in social discourse and the construction of self-identities and perceptions of the other. Looking at the construction of the perception of Iran within US security discourses around the 2015 nuclear agreement, she highlights the impact of emotions on US representations of the self and the other. Collective emotions shape representations at the societal level which in turn influence the perceptions of decision-makers. To empirically demonstrate the interdependence of societal and policy discourses, she combines visual analysis of cartoons with qualitative content analysis of official documents. She thus argues in favor of combining methods of qualitative analysis to assess the role of emotions in the making of collective representations in the policy-society nexus.

Table 1.2 summarizes each chapter's methodological proposition, its advantages, limits and how it could be further improved.

Table 1.2 Methodological approach, advantages and limits of each contribution

Ch. #	Type of research question	Method(s)	Characteristics	Advantages	Limits	Recommendations/lessons learnt
2	What effects do emotions have on other empirical IR phenomena (such as perceptions or behavior)?	Psychoanalytical phenomenology	Develop an understanding of the 'felt sense' of international actors	Takes bodily experiences and their unconscious impacts on behavior seriously	Difficult to apply to collective dynamics or to make causal prediction over a class of phenomena	Move beyond a purely intellectual exercise and focus on bodily aspects
3		Interpretative political science, biographical analysis	Engage with the interpersonal dimension of emotions	Conceptualization of the impact of interpersonal emotions via the concept of friendship	Limited potential for cross-case generalization; potential neglect of structural factors conditioning interpersonal emotions	Further research should extend to non-Western contexts and integrate relationships of enmity
4		Comparative qualitative content analysis	Offers a diachronic and synchronic approach to emotion dynamics	Generates much more information about the effects of emotions on decision-making than a single n-case investigation	Difficulty to delineate intrinsic appearances from instrumental uses of emotions; inter-coder reliability cannot be fully assured	Imperative to use native speakers as decoders; possibility to complement the analysis with process-tracing

(*continued*)

Table 1.2 (continued)

Ch. #	Type of research question	Method(s)	Characteristics	Advantages	Limits	Recommendations/lessons learnt
5	Why and how are specific emotions used by powerful political actors?	Participant observation, auto-ethnography	Make use of one's own affective and emotional experience	Aesthetic mode of apprehending world politics, from bodily movement to architecture; mobility between sites allows shifts in perspective	Risk of re-producing an Anglo-European perspective on world politics; difficult to challenge one's first impression of a site	Multiply field material to recreate the site experience and reinvestigate it later, i.e. with a video diary, panoramic photos, etc.
6		Interview analysis, Foucauldian discourse analysis	Reconstruct the impact of social frames of liberal warfare on individual emotional representations	Interview-based approach helps to discern how institutional socialization shapes individuals' emotional representations, while allowing for potentially contradictory evidence	Lack of differentiation between affects, feelings and emotions; no engagement with bodily conditions of emotional representation	Interview material may subsequently be analyzed via formal coding, thus enabling transnational comparison
7		Historical-sociological approach	Reconstruct the emergence of transnational narratives shaping specific emotional representations of war across long time periods	Possibility to reconstruct the transnational diffusion and institutional reproduction of visual narratives shaping emotional representations	Difficulty of assessing the effectiveness of the institutional narrative on individual representations during actual warfare	Institutional routines and discourses as essential resources to reconstruct how certain collective emotions can be made irrelevant
8		Computer-assisted narrative analysis	Analyze and identify transcultural narrative techniques of mobilizing collective emotions	Potential of reliable, cross-cultural comparison of complex narrative structures	Neglects contextual factors facilitating the justification of violence; Cannot detect the 'effectiveness' of identified narrative techniques	Can be potentially supplemented with visual analysis; qualitative coding takes time and the coding categories should be firmly defined and discussed prior to coding of actual discourses

(*continued*)

Table 1.2 (continued)

Ch. #	Type of research question	Method(s)	Characteristics	Advantages	Limits	Recommendations/lessons learnt
9	How to detect the inseparable yet partly hidden role of emotions within larger discursive dynamics?	Multimodal analysis, visual analysis	Analyze how emotions are constructed via several, simultaneously interacting media	Accounts for potentially diverse effects of verbal and visual communication on immediate and long-term emotional representations	Difficulty of isolating the larger social and political impact of the circulation of a single photograph and the discourses contextualizing it	To understand the emotional impact of pictures, a multimodal approach combining visual analysis with an analysis of the discursive context to understand why meaning and reception of images varies in time and space
10		Discourse analysis	Uncover how emotion dynamics affect the persistence and transformation of shared attitudes	Enhances our understanding of how antagonistic collective identities endure, i.e. how short-term emotions may have enduring affective consequences	Cannot determine the intensity or relative weight of an emotion in relation to other emotions, nor does it indicate the involvement of countervailing emotions	Can be supplemented with process-tracing and/or survey research
11		Hermeneutics, affective stylistics	Question the extent to which certain emotional appraisals are novel	Allows to account for intertwined emotional appraisals across time and to question one's own assumptions	Is limited to the representational dimension of emotions and to the researcher's own horizon(s)	Study the links between emotional appraisals and underlying ideas about how time is constituted
12		Emotion discourse analysis	Develop insights into the social nature of feelings	Traces the effects of emotional expressions in discourse, over time; offers generalizable patterns of emotional meaning	Approximates the type of affective phenomena founds in discourses; risk of homogenizing the emotions of groups	Triangulate using different materials; determine the dominant emotion meaning in a specific sociohistorical context
13		Qualitative content analysis, visual analysis	Decipher the importance of emotions in social constructions of the self and the other by combining the analysis of cartoons and policy discourses	Allows to stress the relationships between cultural, political and journalistic discourses in the production of emotional representations about social identities	Limited number of cartoons on specific empirical issues; need for cultural-specific knowledge to allow for contextual cartoon interpretation	Place the emphasis on the integration of the results of both types of analysis

Notes

1. As an interdisciplinary field of study, International Relations is understood here in its broadest sense. It does not merely refer to relations among states or political entities at large, but also to politics against or beyond the state which has transnational dimensions and impacts. Consequently, IR as a concept is used, throughout the volume, interchangeably with international politics, world politics and global politics.
2. While we recognize the insights gained through psychological experimentation (for instance, in the work of McDermott), the volume is made primarily for a broad readership for whom experimental work and the resources it demands is not a realistic option.

References

Åhäll, L., & Gregory, T. (2013). Security, Emotions, Affect. *Critical Studies on Security, 1*(1), 117–120.

Åhäll, L., & Gregory, T. (Eds.). (2015). *Emotions, Politics and War*. London and New York: Routledge.

Ahmed, S. (2004). *The Cultural Politics of Emotion*. New York: Routledge.

Ariffin, Y. (2016). Introduction. In Y. Ariffin, J.-M. Coicaud, & V. Popovski (Eds.), *Emotions in International Politics* (pp. 1–19). Cambridge: Cambridge University Press.

Ariffin, Y., Coicaud, J.-M., & Popovski, V. (Eds.). (2016). *Emotions in International Politics*. Cambridge: Cambridge University Press.

Bell, D. (Ed.). (2006). *Memory, Trauma and World Politics: Reflections on the Relationship Between Past and Present*. Houndmills: Palgrave Macmillan.

Bially Mattern, J. (2008). The Concept of Power and the (Un)discipline of International Relations. In C. Reus-Smit & D. Snidal (Eds.), *The Oxford Handbook of International Relations* (pp. 691–698). Oxford: Oxford University Press.

Bially Mattern, J. (2011). A Practice Theory of Emotion for International Relations. In E. Adler & V. Pouliot (Eds.), *International Practices* (pp. 63–86). Cambridge: Cambridge University Press.

Bially Mattern, J. (2014). On Being Convinced: An Emotional Epistemology of International Relations. *International Theory, 6*(3), 589–594.

Bleiker, R. (2001). The Aesthetic Turn in International Political Theory. *Millennium – Journal of International Studies, 30*(3), 509–533.

Bleiker, R., & Hutchison, E. (2007). *Understanding Emotions in World Politics: Reflections on Method*. Canberra: Australian National University.

Bleiker, R., & Hutchison, E. (2008). Fear No More: Emotions and World Politics. *Review of International Studies, 34*(S1), 115–135.

Bleiker, R., & Hutchison, E. (2014). Introduction: Emotions and World Politics. *International Theory, 6*(3), 490–491.

Brounéus, K. (2008). Truth-Telling as Talking Cure? Insecurity and Retraumatization in the Rwandan Gacaca Courts. *Security Dialogue, 39*(1), 55–76.

Crawford, N. C. (2000). The Passion of World Politics: Propositions on Emotion and Emotional Relationships. *International Security, 24*(4), 116–156.

Crawford, N. C. (2014). Institutionalizing Passion in World Politics: Fear and Empathy. *International Theory, 6*(3), 535–557.

D'Aoust, A.-M. (2014). Ties That Bind? Engaging Emotions, Governmentality and Neoliberalism: Introduction to the Special Issue. *Global Society, 28*(3), 267–276.

Danchev, A. (2006). "Like a Dog!": Humiliation and Shame in the War on Terror. *Alternatives: Global, Local, Political, 31*(3), 259–283.

Edkins, J. (2002). Forget Trauma? Responses to September 11. *International Relations, 16*(2), 243–256.

Eznack, L. (2012). *Crises in the Atlantic Alliance: Affect and Relations Among NATO Members*. New York: Palgrave Macmillan.

Fattah, K., & Fierke, K. M. (2009). A Clash of Emotions: The Politics of Humiliation and Political Violence in the Middle East. *European Journal of International Relations, 15*(1), 67–93.

Fierke, K. M. (2006). Bewitched by the Past: Social Memory, Trauma and International Relations. In D. Bell (Ed.), *Memory, Trauma and World Politics: Reflections on the Relationship Between Past and Present* (pp. 116–134). Houndmills: Palgrave Macmillan.

Fierke, K. M. (2012). *Political Self-Sacrifice: Agency, Body and Emotion in International Relations* (Vol. 125). Cambridge: Cambridge University Press.

Fierke, K. M. (2014). Emotion and Intentionality. *International Theory, 6*(3), 563–567.

Flam, H., & Kleres, J. (Eds.). (2015). *Methods of Exploring Emotions*. London and New York: Routledge.

Freyberg-Inan, A. (2006). Rational Paranoia and Enlightened Machismo: The Strange Psychological Foundations of Realism. *Journal of International Relations and Development, 9*(3), 247–268.

Frijda, H. N. (2008). The Psychologists' Point of View. In M. Lewis, J. M. H. Jones, & L. B. Feldman (Eds.), *Handbook of Emotions* (pp. 68–87). New York: Guilford Press.

Hall, T. H. (2011). We Will Not Swallow This Bitter Fruit: Theorizing a Diplomacy of Anger. *Security Studies, 20*(4), 521–555.

Hansen, L. (2011). The Politics of Securitization and the Muhammad Cartoon Crisis: A Post-structuralist Perspective. *Security Dialogue, 42*(4–5), 357–369.

Hom, A. R. (2016). Angst Springs Eternal: Dangerous Times and the Dangers of Timing the 'Arab Spring'. *Security Dialogue, 47*(2), 165–183.

Hutchison, E. (2010). Trauma and the Politics of Emotions: Constituting Identity, Security and Community After the Bali Bombing. *International Relations*, *24*(1), 65–86.
Hutchison, E., & Bleiker, R. (2007). Emotions in the War on Terror. In A. Bellamy, R. Bleiker, S. E. Davies, & R. Devetak (Eds.), *Security and the War on Terror* (pp. 57–70). London and New York: Routledge.
Hutchison, E., & Bleiker, R. (2014). Theorizing Emotions in World Politics. *International Theory*, *6*(3), 491–514.
Jeffery, R. (2011). Reason, Emotion, and the Problem of World Poverty: Moral Sentiment Theory and International Ethics. *International Theory*, *3*(1), 143–178.
Jeffery, R. (2014). The Promise and Problems of the Neuroscientific Approach to Emotions. *International Theory*, *6*(3), 584–589.
Jervis, R., Lebow, R. N., & Stein, J. G. (1985). *Psychology and Deterrence*. Baltimore: Johns Hopkins University Press.
Kelly, R. (2010). *Memory and Conflict Resolution*. London: Routledge.
Khalili, L. (2010). Gendered Practices of Counterinsurgency. *Review of International Studies*, *37*(4), 1471–1491.
Lebow, R. N. (2005). Reason, Emotion and Cooperation. *International Politics*, *42*(3), 283–313.
Lindemann, T. (2014). Interest, Passion, (Non)recognition, and Wars: A Conceptual Essay. *Global Discourse*, *4*(4), 483–496.
Ling, L. H. M. (2014). Decolonizing the International: Towards Multiple Emotional Worlds. *International Theory*, *6*(3), 579–583.
Linklater, A. (2004). Emotions and World Politics. *Aberystwyth Journal of World Affairs*, *2*, 71–77.
Linklater, A. (2014). Anger and World Politics: How Collective Emotions Shift Over Time. *International Theory*, *6*(3), 574–578.
Marcus, G. E. (2000). Emotions in Politics. *Annual Review of Political Science*, *3*(1), 221–250.
McDermott, R. (2004). *Political Psychology in International Relations*. Ann Arbor, MI: University of Michigan Press.
McDermott, R. (2014). The Body Doesn't Lie: A Somatic Approach to the Study of Emotions in World Politics. *International Theory*, *6*(3), 557–562.
Mercer, J. (1996). *Approaching Emotion in International Politics*. Paper Presented at the International Studies Association Annual Convention, San Diego, CA.
Mercer, J. (2005). Rationality and Psychology in International Politics. *International Organization*, *59*(1), 77–106.
Mercer, J. (2006). Human Nature and the First Image: Emotion in International Politics. *Journal of International Relations and Development*, *9*(3), 288–303.
Mercer, J. (2010). Emotional Beliefs. *International Organization*, *64*(1), 1–31.

Mercer, J. (2013). Emotion and Strategy in the Korean War. *International Organization, 67*(2), 221–252.
Mercer, J. (2014). Feeling Like a State: Social Emotion and Identity. *International Theory, 6*(3), 515–535.
Murphy, F. (2011). Archives of Sorrow: An Exploration of Australia's Stolen Generations and Their Journey into the Past. *History and Anthropology, 22*(4), 481–495.
Pearlman, W. (2013). Emotions and the Microfoundations of the Arab Uprisings. *Perspectives on Politics, 11*(2), 387–409.
Penttinen, E. (2013). *Joy and International Relations: A New Methodology*. London and New York: Routledge.
Petersen, R. D. (2002). *Understanding Ethnic Violence: Fear, Hatred, and Resentment in Twentieth-Century Eastern Europe*. Cambridge: Cambridge University Press.
Resende, E. S. A., & Budryte, D. (Eds.). (2014). *Memory and Trauma in International Relations: Theories, Cases, and Debates*. London: Routledge.
Reus-Smit, C. (2014). Emotions and the Social. *International Theory, 6*(3), 568–574.
Rosoux, V. (2014). Portée et limites du concept de réconciliation: Une histoire à terminer. *Revue d'études comparatives Est-Ouest, 45*(3–4), 21–47.
Ross, A. A. G. (2006). Coming in from the Cold: Constructivism and Emotions. *European Journal of International Relations, 12*(2), 197–222.
Ross, A. A. G. (2010). Why They Don't Hate Us: Emotion, Agency and the Politics of 'Anti-Americanism'. *Millennium – Journal of International Studies, 39*(1), 109–125.
Ross, A. A. G. (2013). Realism, Emotion, and Dynamic Allegiances in Global Politics. *International Theory, 5*(2), 273–299.
Ross, A. A. G. (2016). Exceptionalism, Counterterrorism, and the Emotional Politics of Human Rights. In Y. Ariffin & J.-M. Coicaud (Eds.), *Emotions in International Politics: Beyond Mainstream International Relations* (pp. 315–340). Cambridge: Cambridge University Press.
Sasley, B. E. (2011). Theorizing States' Emotions. *International Studies Review, 13*(3), 452–476.
Saurette, P. (2006). You Dissin Me? Humiliation and Post 9/11 Global Politics. *Review of International Studies, 32*(3), 495–522.
Schut, M., de Graaff, M. C., & Verweij, D. (2015). Moral Emotions During Military Deployments of Dutch Forces: A Qualitative Study on Moral Emotions in Intercultural Interactions. *Armed Forces & Society, 41*(4), 616–638.
Solomon, T. (2014). Time and Subjectivity in World Politics. *International Studies Quarterly, 58*(4), 671–681.
Solomon, T. (2015). Embodiment, Emotions, and Materialism in International Relations. In L. Ahall & T. Gregory (Eds.), *Emotions, Politics and War* (pp. 58–70). New York: Routledge.

Soreanu, R., & Hudson, D. (2008). Feminist Scholarship in International Relations and the Politics of Disciplinary Emotion. *Millennium – Journal of International Studies, 37*(1), 123–151.
Stets, J. E., & Turner, J. H. (Eds.). (2014). *Handbook of the Sociology of Emotions*. Heidelberg; New York; London: Springer.
Sylvester, C. (2011). The Forum: Emotion and the Feminist IR Researcher. *International Studies Review, 13*(4), 687–708.
Sylvester, C. (2012). War Experiences/War Practices/War Theory. *Millennium – Journal of International Studies, 40*(3), 483–503.
Wolf, R. (2015). Emotionen in den internationalen Beziehungen: Das Beispiel Ressentiments. In K.-R. Korte (Ed.), *Emotionen und Politik: Begründungen, Konzeptionen und Praxisfelder einer politikwissenschaftlichen Emotionsforschung* (pp. 187–212). Baden-Baden: Nomos.
Wright-Neville, D., & Smith, D. (2009). Political Rage: Terrorism and the Politics of Emotion. *Global Change, Peace & Security, 21*(1), 85–98.

Maéva Clément is a Research Associate and Teaching Fellow at the Institute of International Politics at the Helmut Schmidt University Hamburg. She is a doctoral researcher in the Department of Political Science at the Goethe University Frankfurt. Her research focuses on collective emotions, political violence and discursive and narrative methodology. In her thesis, she analyzes the role played by emotions in the turn to violence of several Islamist groups across Western Europe over the 2000s. She has previously published in *Political Psychology* and *Global Discourse*. She teaches courses on emotions in international politics, international relations theory and peace and conflict studies at several universities in France and Germany.

Eric Sangar is a FNRS Research Fellow based at the University of Namur and an associated researcher at the Centre Emile Durkheim of Sciences Po Bordeaux. In his personal research, he currently focuses on the theoretical and empirical links between collective memory, regimes of historicity and uses of history in contemporary armed conflicts. He holds a PhD from the European University Institute in Florence. His thesis entitled *Historical Experience: Burden or Bonus in Today's Wars?* was published in 2014. His research has been published in various journals in English, French and German language, including the *Journal of Strategic Studies*, *Political Psychology* and *Contemporary Security Policy*.

PART I

The Influence of Emotions on Actors and Politics

CHAPTER 2

Eugene Gendlin and the Feel of International Politics

Erik Ringmar

The social sciences have always had an anti-emotional bias. Emotions have been regarded as aberrations and as unfortunate deviations from a rationalistic norm; emotions are what women have, lower-class people or foreigners. Yet as we now know, everything we do is couched in terms of affect. Emotions are not an afterthought or an add-on, but they are there right from the start, coloring everything we do, setting the parameters for what we remember and plan and making each situation into a situation of a specific kind. Emotions tell us what things are and what they mean. International politics provides plenty of examples. People express love for their fatherlands, hate of their enemies, fear during wars, terror in the face of terrorist attacks and anxiety about the consequences of globalization. Take away the emotions, and there will be little international politics left (Bleiker & Hutchison, 2008, pp. 115–135; Crawford, 2000, pp. 116–156; Fierke, 2014; Hutchison & Bleiker, 2014, pp. 491–514).

However, acknowledging the importance of emotions is only the first step. We also have to say what emotions are and how they can be studied. We need theories and we need a methodology. Yet the vocabulary of affect

E. Ringmar (✉)
University of Lund, Lund, Sweden

© The Author(s) 2018
M. Clément, E. Sangar (eds.), *Researching Emotions in International Relations*, Palgrave Studies in International Relations, https://doi.org/10.1007/978-3-319-65575-8_2

is hopelessly confused. "Emotions" are often used interchangeably with "feelings" and with "moods," and there is little consensus among psychologists, physiologists, brain scientists and philosophers regarding what these terms refer to. The social scientists who have weighed in on the subject have added to the confusion by intimating that emotions are nothing but "social constructions." That culture has an influence on emotions is certain, but we know that they have a biological basis too. Emotions concern our bodies at least as much as our minds. Indeed, emotions are lodged in our bodies before they are registered by our minds and this is the very reason why they come to determine the perimeters for what we regard as the meaningful. At long last, yet so far with some trepidation, students of international politics are reaching the same conclusions (Brown, 2013, pp. 435–454; Neumann, 2014, pp. 330–350; Ringmar, 2016, pp. 101–125).

Phenomenology provides a specific way of investigating emotions and psychologists of a phenomenological bent address a range of conditions that involve affective states (Giorgi, 1970; Jager, 1989, pp. 217–231; Wertz, 2009, pp. 394–411). Emotions, to a phenomenologist, have their origin in the body and not in the mind; or rather, they originate in the interaction between our bodies and the situations in which they find themselves (Johnstone, 2012, pp. 179–200; Cf. Ringmar, 2017a). It follows that emotions only can be defined as an aspect of a person's experience of a particular environment. Indeed, emotions are not "things" and psychology is not about "the mental," since no distinction can be made between the thinking subject and the objective world. Such a holistic perspective, phenomenological psychologists will tell us, avoids many of the riddles—including the mythology of an "unconscious"—which traditional psychology has created. Regarding research methods, phenomenological psychology emphasizes precognitive, embodied, experiences—emotions arise as phenomena in our experience of being in the world.

One prominent example of a phenomenological psychologist is Eugene T. Gendlin. Born in Vienna in 1926, Gendlin received a PhD in philosophy from the University of Chicago in 1958, but he also worked closely with Carl Rogers, one of the founding fathers of American psychotherapy (Cf. Gendlin, 1988, pp. 127–128; Ikemi, 2005, pp. 31–42). Gendlin taught in both the departments of philosophy and psychology at Chicago until his retirement in 1995 and he also maintained a psychotherapy practice on the side. To the general public, he is best known as the person behind "Focusing," a program with distinct New Age overtones which currently is relied on by thousands of dedicated practitioners around the world.[1] The purpose of this chapter is to briefly introduce Gendlin's work and to show how it might help us think about the role of emotions in social life in general and in international politics in particular. What we will try to do is to put the actors of international politics on Gendlin's couch and make them talk about their emotions, following his phenomenological method.

Gendlin on the Felt Sense

Gendlin's phenomenology of affect is organized around a sharp distinction between feelings and emotions. Feelings are about how things feel. We feel things with our five senses to be sure, but we also have a generalized feeling for the whole of the situation in which we find ourselves. Gendlin calls this the "felt sense". The felt sense is not a result of an interpretation and it does not require conscious ratiocination. Instead, a felt sense is automatically and imperceptibly arrived at, and it is our bodies rather than our minds that are in charge. Think of it as "[a] bodily awareness of a situation or person or event. An internal aura that encompasses everything you feel and know about the given subject at a given time." Or "[t]hink of it as a taste, if you like, or a great musical chord that makes you feel a powerful impact, a big round unclear feeling" (Gendlin, 2003b, p. 32). In a lecture Gendlin provides an example (d'Orsogna, 2000). As a student at the University of Chicago, he participated in a study which asked questions about the impact that therapists have on their clients. The assumption was that this impact was strong, but preciously little evidence of the effects could be found using traditional survey methods. Then Gendlin thought about his own experiences as a client and remembered what took place as he was about to enter the room of his therapist. Standing outside the door, hesitant to knock, he gathered himself, prepared himself, set himself in a certain frame of mind. This, he came to realize, was where it all was happening. It was in this felt sense that the terms of the subsequent interaction between the therapist and the client were laid out.

It seems difficult to explain, Gendlin admits, but some way or another our bodies are able to make sense of situations without directly involving our conscious minds. There are a number of mechanisms at work here (Gendlin, 1991, pp. 15–29). Most obviously, our bodies are designed for interacting with their environment, and information about the environment is for that reason implicit already in our body's structure. From the bone of a prehistoric animal, one can infer not only the whole of its body but also the whole of its environment and what its body did in this environment. Our hands and feet are not only body parts but they have implications, as it were; there are things that they want to do. Besides, there are entire repertoires of largely instinctive behavior associated with basic activities such as feeding, sleeping, mating and child-rearing (Gendlin, 1991, p. 16). On top of these instinctive routines, there are habitual routines. In the course of our lives, our bodies develop ever better ways of coping with any number of standardized situations. Since our bodies are in charge, we do not have to explicitly think about how to walk upstairs, open doors and throw balls. So when unexpected situations occasionally come up, our habits can usually be adapted to fit the new circumstances (Gallagher, 1986, pp. 541–554; Noë, 2009, pp. 97–128). Put an ant on an oily surface and you will see instincts enabling the body to adapt to a new environment.

Recent work in neuroscience adds another mechanism. As the neuroscientist Antonio Damasio argues, everything that happens to us throughout our lives is given an emotional weight, a certain feeling tone. Damasio refers to these weights as "somatic markers" (Damasio, 1994, pp. 165–201). When we recall something, what we retrieve are not only the images associated with the event in question but also the feeling tones. Think about Marcel Proust eating his madeleines. Suddenly the spongy texture of a shell-shaped bun, together with a newly pressed sailor-suit, the dangling of tiny legs, the smell of coffee—combine to recreate the memory of a visit to a fashionable café as a child in the last century. Yet the memory not only *is* a certain way, it *feels* a certain way. Such madeleine effects, we can argue, are not necessarily the properties of individuals but can be shared by many individuals, even by societies at large. A culture contains all the associations that people in a society connect with a certain object, creature, place or situation; everything we ever read or heard said about an item; all the lore and the history; what we have seen in movies, newspapers and in nightmares (Gendlin, 1991, p. 16). All of these associations are stored away in the recesses of our minds, and although much of it is cognitive material, it is also labeled by somatic markers.

The result is that our bodies are far more knowledgeable than we are. Put in another way, we consist of far more than our conscious minds. Gendlin refers to this as an "excess" (Gendlin, 2004, pp. 127–151, 2009, pp. 147–161). There is an excess of embodied meanings which we usually never make explicit. No matter how long we talk or how fancy the metaphors we employ, the felt sense will not be exhausted. Somehow or another, words are simply the wrong medium for conveying feelings (Gendlin, 1992a, p. 344, 2003a, pp. 100–115). To some, this unsaid and unsayable surplus may be understood as a spiritual realm, and for Freudians it is the realm of the unconscious. For Gendlin, it is simply the inevitable consequence of the fact that we have bodies that have lived and are alive (Gendlin, 1978, p. 10). And yet, we still need words. After all, it is only with the help of words that we can talk about things. Psychological theories, drawn from any of the different schools that exist, provide an example. Psychologists like to talk and, as Gendlin implies, they often talk too much. While psychological theorizing is necessary, it leaves next to everything unsaid. "Feeling without further symbolization are blind, (and symbols alone are empty)" (Gendlin, 1978, p. 23).

The felt sense has a large number of implications, creating networks of entailments that spread far and wide. "A body isn't only an *is*; it is an is *and implies further*" (Gendlin, 1992b, p. 203; Gendlin in Heuman, 2011, p. 107). To feel hungry implies eating, and eating implies food, digestion and defecation; food, in turn, implies shopping and food preparation; food preparation implies kitchens, refrigerators and stoves ... and so on *ad infinitum* (Gendlin, 1973, pp. 371–372). In much the same way, our habits are stored in our bodies as sequences of actions which all imply each other (Cf. James, 1890, pp. 114–115). Thus if we start to do one thing, we will quite automatically go on to do the next. Some of these sequences can be very elaborate indeed—as when a violinist learns how to play an entire concerto by heart. Feeling tones imply each other, too. It is through the felt sense that things are associated in our minds, and the memory of one thing quite automatically triggers another.

By exploring these implications, a whole world can be deduced. But this is never a question of merely applying a set of preexisting rules. Instead, as we follow the implications of the felt sense, new and unexpected implications will come into view. "Our bodies can total up years of all kinds of experience, and at any moment give us something new, a new more intricate step" (Gendlin, 1992b, p. 206). Imagine, for example, that you are an artist working on a painting or a poet writing a poem (Gendlin, 1992a, p. 348). The work is not yet complete, something is missing. You add something, but you realize right away that it is not quite what you were looking for (Gendlin, 1992b, pp. 198–201). It does not feel right. So you try again, making new additions, until you are satisfied. When all the necessary implications have been deduced, and they all feel right, the painting or the poem is finished. Throughout this creative process, it is the felt sense which guides us. The felt sense is carrying us forward and allowing us to say something new.

This, Gendlin explains, is essentially a metaphorical process (Gendlin, 1995, pp. 1–2; Cf. Johnson, 1997). In a metaphor two systems of implications are suddenly, and perhaps unexpectedly, brought together. Metaphors are always literally false—a relationship, for example, is not really "at a crossroad" or "off the rails"—and yet we make sense of such language by letting the felt sense that we associate with relationships interact with the felt sense that we associate with journeys. By creatively exploring the connections between these two systems of implications, we come up with new ways of talking, but also with new ways of feeling. It is as though we have discovered a new world. Alternatively, we can explore the metaphors we take for granted, looking for unexpected implications. In this way, the felt sense can provide opportunities for criticism and political dissent (Levin, 1994, p. 350; Cf. Ringmar, 2007, pp. 188, 203–207).

This is how Gendlin's discussion of the felt sense takes him to a philosophy of language (Levin, 1997). The felt sense and language are closely related, he says, since language is based on the body. It is not that we make up words which we apply to the world but instead, language is inherent in the world, and as we explore the implications of the felt sense, this language is gradually revealing itself (Gendlin, 1978, p. 9). The body is the conduit of language, as it were. The implications demand to be spoken much as our hands and our feet demand to be used in a particular fashion. And what demands to be spoken, demands to be first verbalized and listened to (Cf. Hatab, 1994, p. 368; Johnson, 2008, pp. 86–110; Rosen, 2000). Many of these verbalizations may be obscure, and they may sound funny, and many people will not understand them, but, says Gendlin, since they clearly are related to existing ways of speaking, we will not misunderstand them either. When prompted by the quizzical looks of our interlocutors, we get a chance to say more (Gendlin in Heuman, 2011, p. 109).

On the Therapist's Couch: Feelings

Eugene Gendlin is not only a philosopher but also a practicing psychotherapist. He is not only interested in what feelings are and how they work, he also wants to help people deal with the problems that their feelings may cause. Often we simply do not understand ourselves and our reactions; we have problems dealing with situations and with other people;

we get stressed out for no reason, or anxious or depressed. What we need to do in these situations, Gendlin suggests, is to explore the felt sense. It is in the felt sense that all of our cognitive activities arise—our emotions, our reflections, plans, hopes and fears (Gendlin, 1992a, p. 347; cf. Stanghellini & Rosfort, 2013, pp. 3–8). For this reason, it is here that the solutions to our psychological problems can be found. Somehow or another the felt sense must be accessed and once accessed it must be rearranged.

Gendlin is well aware of the difficulties we run up against here. A felt sense is not the kind of thing which we can study explicitly or even pay direct attention to. In fact, a felt sense is not a thing. "People rarely have a felt sense," Gendlin admits.

> We usually act and speak sentiently, but without stopping to let that sentience come to us as a datum of inner attention. We attend to the people, and the things. Inwardly there are emotions, thoughts, images and memories, usually not a felt sense. (Gendlin, 1991, p. 16)

A felt sense is a medium, we might say, not a content. As such it allows our emotions, reactions, perceptions and thoughts to arise, but it is itself opaque. Much as the eye, the felt sense allows us to see but it cannot itself be seen. Yet we are not completely at a loss. There are techniques we can rely on, and the principal technique which Gendlin advocates is what he calls "focusing" (Friedman, 2003, pp. 31–42; Gendlin, 1991, p. 16; Heuman, 2011).

What you focus on above all is how you are feeling; that is, how your body finds itself in the world (Gendlin, 1978, p. 2). Yet the question "how do you feel?" is itself quite vague and it is not always clear how to answer. But if we go to our bodies, Gendlin suggests, there is bound to be something there, something worth exploring, however murky and indistinct. The body knows the whole of each situation, in far greater detail than our minds, and this embodied knowledge will present itself to us as long as we remain patient (Gendlin, 2003b, pp. vii–viii). Focusing is the method by which we gradually come to clarify this feeling and learn to follow its implications.

> For example, if you feel some excitement or some opposition or some discomfort, go to the quality. The first thing you get on this felt sense is just a quality, and you won't even know what to call it. You have to say it's "ugh" or it's uncomfortable, or it's "something important is happening in here and I don't know what, but I can feel it." (Heuman, 2011, p. 106)

Gendlin presents us with a focusing manual in six steps (Gendlin, 2003b, pp. 51–64). First we need to clear a space where we can sit quietly and return to our bodies. Next we try to get in touch with the felt sense, waiting for it, even if it takes time to appear. Then we look for what Gendlin refers to as a "handle"—a word or image which resonates perfectly with what the body tells us—perhaps something like "tight," "sticky," "scary," "stuck," "heavy," "jumpy." Next we test the accuracy of the handle by asking questions. Eventually the felt sense will stir and from this stirring answers will begin to appear (Gendlin in Heuman, 2011, p. 45). "Is this what the feeling is like?" asks the therapist. "No," says the client, "that is not quite it. What I meant to say is...." "I see," says the therapist, "but there might also be this and that, no?" "Yes," the client will acknowledge, "but you have to take into consideration that...." Prodded by the analyst in this fashion, the felt sense starts to speak, often in unexpected metaphors. Drawing one implication after another, we learn more and more, and all the while the client checks each step and statement against the felt sense . Eventually, with some luck, the client will experience a feeling of having arrived at a stopping point. The body shifts, it feels differently. The client exhales and says "OK, now I get it...."

At the same time Gendlin is careful not to present focusing as a full-fledged therapy. Instead it is best practiced together with other techniques (Gendlin, 1978, pp. 20–21). Actually, he suggests, it is through a process of focusing that all clients are helped regardless of whichever therapy they follow. Focusing helps since it allows us to lift a problem out of its old context and insert it into a new one. We put an issue in a place where it no longer hurts, where it no longer makes trouble for us or forces us to react in a strange and disruptive manner. Mere understanding is never going to be enough here; it is not enough to simply expose the problem and to put it into words. We must rebel against the dictatorship of cognition. In order to feel better, we need to feel differently. We must learn to explore new and unexpected implications, break old patterns of thought and acquire new habits. This is not a quick fix to be sure but the consequences are self-transforming. The self is transformed since its body feels different.

On the Therapist's Couch: Emotions

Let us think about emotions next. Emotions too, Gendlin explains, are a matter of feelings, but at the same time emotions feel quite differently than a felt sense. A felt sense, we said, is diffuse, vague and difficult to put into words, but emotions are only too obvious, not least since many of them take the form of visible physiological changes. Emotions make our hearts beat, our knees tremble, and they give us stomach cramps. Emotions are also far more focused, far narrower, than the felt sense. While the felt sense is broad and in the background, emotions make us zero in on specific details, blinding us to everything else. When we are emoting, we know it, and others do too since emotions are in your face and in the face of others.

Think about how animals react. Whether animals can be said to have emotions is debated but cats that fight certainly seem to be angry and cats that purr seem to be content. And yet, as far as we know, emotions in animals concern only a "readiness potential," a readiness, that is, to act in a certain fashion (Panksepp & Watt, 2011, pp. 387–396). What a human would call "anger" is thus an animal's readiness to fight, and what a human would call "fear" is an animal's readiness to flee. Human beings are animals too of course, and our emotions too have a readiness potential. For example: if we suddenly come upon a bear in the forest, we might quite automatically try to escape (James, 1994, pp. 205–210; Lange, 1922, pp. 33–92). We react instantaneously and before we have time to think about the matter, and it is only later, once we already are running, that we get scared. It is easy to see why such physiological immediacy has been favored by biological evolution.

When animals emote—if that is what they do—they always display the same, more or less identical, behavioral patterns, and the same can be said for humans, too, as long as we are talking about emotions understood as readiness potential (Gendlin, 1973, pp. 370–371). As most authors on the subject make clear, there is only a relatively small set of basic emotions. Although the list varies somewhat, the most commonly mentioned emotions are anger, fear, disgust, contempt, triumph, joy, sadness, jealousy, surprise and awe (Ekman, 1992, pp. 169–200; Russell, 1991, pp. 426–450). These basic emotions are expressed in a standardized set of behaviors, and the behavior we find in humans is in fact not that different from the behavior of animals. Thus, anger results in tense muscles, quickened breath and contorted facial muscles, and sadness implies tears, listlessness, downcast eyes and so on (Gendlin, 1973, p. 374). It is because the physical manifestations are standardized in this way that we can recognize emotions as the same from one person to the next, or across disparate contexts and cultures.

But—and this is crucial—in addition to these physiological changes, human beings represent emotions to themselves (Gendlin, 1973, p. 384;

cf. Lewis & Todd, 2005, pp. 210–235). This is not something animals do, and the representation is what turns the readiness potential into an emotion properly speaking. We represent the emotion by imagining scenarios for ourselves (Gendlin, 1973, pp. 373–377). The scenario describes ourselves, who we are and what we want, which situation we are in, the people with whom we interact and what our relations to them are. This scenario may apply to a situation which is right before us, but it can also apply to a situation that is remembered or as anticipated. We find ourselves not in a certain situation, rather in our representation of a certain situation, and it is in relation to this representation that we react. As a result, we are often in a position to repress our emotions or to express them in some alternative manner (Gendlin, 1973, pp. 375–377). We can also experience the emotion apart from the situation, and whenever we imagine the scenario, we are likely to experience the emotion again. These representations, says Gendlin, are constructed by means of the felt sense and they draw on its various implications (Gendlin, 1978, p. 10; Heuman, 2011, p. 45). People will represent things differently in their minds depending both on their personal experiences and on the society in which they live. As a result, although the readiness potential is expressed in much the same fashion across contexts and societies, emotions are expressed in culturally distinct ways, and also differently from one person to the other (Gendlin, 1973, pp. 379–380). Consequently, emotions come to feel quite differently too.

Our emotional reactions, or a lack thereof, are an important reason why we might seek the help of a psychotherapist. We react unpredictably and uncontrollably; we get angry, scared, anxious or sad for no reason or for reasons which we cannot quite understand. We seek professional help since we want to stop the emotional reactions from hurting us and from hurting others. This is where focusing comes in. It is by trying to uncover the felt sense that we can hope to understand why we imagine a certain scenario in a certain fashion. Focusing helps us lift out the emotion, as it were, and place it in a new context where it feels quite differently. Or perhaps focusing can help us create more robust routines that do not break down so easily and thereby never cause the emotion to arise in the first place (Gendlin, 1992b, p. 204). "Your body knows the direction of healing and life. If you take the time to listen to it through focusing, it will give you the steps in the right direction" (Gendlin, 2003b, p. 78).

The Feel of International Politics

International politics is next to always analyzed in rationalistic terms. It is discussed as a matter of the preferences, intentions and goals that guide policy-makers, or in terms of their interests, national or otherwise. Digging deeper, a student of international politics might ask about the perceptions of a politician, about her basic outlook on life, her *Weltanschauungen*, cognitive maps, or perhaps the psychological processes by means of which she perceives the world. Or we ask questions about identities and struggles for recognition. Digging deeper still, we might investigate matters of psychological makeup: what particular politicians think of their mothers, or what role emotions play in their lives. Yet none of this would be a primary concern of Eugene Gendlin's. To him, such cognitive and emotional material, interesting though it may be in its own terms, is a derivative of a felt sense. The felt sense comes first and everything else comes second. Thus, if we want to understand international politics, it is the felt sense we should investigate. No one has properly looked at this before or analyzed it in anything approaching the manner which Gendlin suggests. The prospects are exciting.

So let us imagine putting political actors on Gendlin's couch. How do they feel? How do they find themselves in the world? What is that murky, indistinct, sensation in the pit of their stomachs? Asking these questions, we suddenly recall a number of statements we have heard over the years: how president George W. Bush's claimed to have invaded Iraq based on a "gut feeling", or how Tony Blair insisted that he felt "the hand of history upon our shoulders" (Blair, 1998; Suskind, 2004). Or consider a Brexit supporter who argues that voting against British membership in the EU is a question of doing "what feels right", or Donald Trump's alleged ability to "speak directly to the gut, often bypassing the cerebral cortex altogether" (Freedland, 2016b). Students of international politics typically treat such statements as stock phrases to be ignored, but if Gendlin is right, the expressions point us towards a crucial experience. They are all references to a felt sense.

It is a mistake, in other words, to only listen to what political actors say or to only watch their actions. Instead we should be interested in body language. Watch the posture of the world leaders as they assemble in front of the TV cameras and listen out for any statements regarding the posture of the countries they represent. What we will find is that a "forward-leaning" country, such as that represented by Dick Cheney in 2003, is prone to act quite differently from a country which, like France in 1940, is "lying on her back" (Borger, 2003; Sartre, 1949, p. 51). Likewise, a leader such as Mao Zedong who has "stood up," is likely to behave quite differently from a leader, such as Nelson Mandela, who had "walked that long road to freedom," and who realizes that there still are many mountains to climb ("In His Own Words," 2013; Mao, 1949). It is from these bodies, no matter how metaphorical, that emotions arise—a desire for revenge, a sense of determination, feelings of shame, humiliation, pride, vulnerability, invulnerability and all others. "Is this what the feeling is like?," we can imagine ourselves asking the foreign minister or security advisor. "No," says our client, "that is not quite it. What I meant to say is…." "I see," we say, "but there might also be this and that, no?" "Yes," they will acknowledge, "but you have to take into consideration that…." Prodded in this fashion, the felt sense starts to speak, and drawing one implication after another, we learn more and more. Eventually, and with some luck, we will arrive at a stopping point; something has been revealed, a clearing has been made in the forest. The client exhales and says "OK, now I get it…."

So what was going on in George W. Bush's gut and in Tony Blair's shoulder? Why did the Brexit supporter feel the way she did and how is Donald Trump able to bypass a voter's cerebral cortex? Let's take Bush's gut first. It is easy to imagine his gastric acids acting up in the wake of the 9/11 attacks—an acute stomach cramp giving way to a persistent sinking feeling (Johnstone, 2012, pp. 179–200; Cf. Prinz, 2006). He had been asleep on his watch, betrayed his fellow Americans, and revealed himself and America as weak and vulnerable. The invasion of Iraq in 2003 was his way of relieving this sense of unease. Likewise, the weight of the hand on Blair's shoulder indicates his sense of being anointed by Fate, of being called by Providence, of being under scrutiny by History. Blair, by all evidence, often felt attended to by capitalized abstractions such as these, and this explains both the seriousness with which he took his responsibilities, and the momentousness of his mistakes (Owen & Davidson, 2009, pp. 1396–1406). As for the Brexit voter, her satisfaction stems from a feeling of finally having spoken up to the powers-that-be. After years of not being listened to, the referendum was her chance to get it all off her chest: her awkwardness in relation to things foreign, her growing anxiety with the sheer uncertainty of life, the way her well-established habits no longer seemed to be working. She wanted her country back and she wanted to regain control. This is how she felt, she felt it in her body

(Freedland, 2016a). The Trump voter surely shared many of these sentiments, yet in his case it was fear more than anything that dictated the choice. It is fear after all which most effectively bypasses the cognitive processes of the cerebral cortex: fear of being invaded by Mexicans, Muslims and Chinese goods, fear of black men with guns and impostor presidents with foreign birth certificates. He voted Trump since only Trump can make him feel secure.

Alternatively, to take another example, consider the case of a suicide bomber who kills himself together with a large number of his fellow human beings. Growing up as a regular child in the suburbs of a large European city, he became "radicalized" in his late teens. He began to pray regularly and attend mosque, to dress in a Muslim fashion and not eat certain food. He refers to the will of God as the reason behind these choices, but others say he was brainwashed by fundamentalist clerics. There are indeed reasons for what happened, the reasons have rational grounds and the rational grounds have further rational grounds, yet underneath all the rational grounds there is nothing but a felt sense. And it is against this felt sense that he constantly checks his choices. He does not fit into the society into which he was born; he feels discriminated and humiliated (Birzer & Smith-Mahdi, 2006, pp. 22–37; Gendlin, 1973, pp. 388–391). In response, he has set himself alternative standards, and these are the standards his actions are designed to uphold. Leaving for *jihad* in Syria suddenly feels right and, returning home, so does killing innocent civilians (Ash, 2006; Atran & Hamid, 2015).

Or take the case of a young American who decides to volunteer for the war in Iraq. Describing himself as "your normal North Carolina loser," he tells you about his disappointments in life: his father who left home and family way too soon, his bad grades in school, his occasional drug use and inability to hold down a permanent job (Wright, 2004, p. 235). These biographical facts can be described in sociological terms, or in terms of political economy, but they have a phenomenology too. There is a certain way of feeling to be poor, and given this phenomenology, joining the military feels like the right thing to do. There is a bodily posture to being a military man after all—standing to attention, standing tall, straight back and chest out. The military promised him a new start, to make something out of him, to make him feel proud. Economic incentives played a role in the decision to enlist and perhaps politics entered into it, too, but defending one's country feels right above all because it provides an opportunity to do one's duty. Doing one's duty is to stand up for what is right. Standing up feels good after years of slouching on a couch in North Carolina.

Consider, finally, the prospect of resolving conflicts and achieving peace. By investigating the felt sense, Gendlin suggests, we can explore the potential for reconciling opposing points of view (Gendlin in Heuman, 2011, p. 109; Cf. Rosen, 2000, pp. 1–14). The issue to be investigated here is not the interests that divide us or the hostile claims we make, and reconciliation is not a matter of negotiating or of somehow integrating contradictory positions. Instead we need to get back to the origin that interests, claims and positions have in a felt sense. A phenomenological sensation of unease, anxious twitchings in the legs, an existential tension of the jaw, a stomach cramp, can be relieved in a large number of different ways and thereby result in many contradictory actions (Ringmar, 2017b). But it is only by exploring the felt sense, in which all these experiences originate, that we come to see this common origin. Our respective bodies understand each other far better than our cognitive minds. This, Gendlin suggests, could be the beginnings of a mutual understanding.

Conclusion

Despite the trappings of a psychologist's couch and the confessional format of these engagements, you do not have to be a psychoanalyst to engage in this kind of research. Focusing, Gendlin explains, is ultimately not a psychoanalytical technique. Psychoanalysts analyze, that is obvious from their job title, but what is required here is not analysis or even thought. Instead we need to feel. The reason why we can understand the felt sense of other is not that we have the requisite training, or any particular insights, but instead that we have bodies as well. Likewise, we do not have to have a special training in the social sciences in order to understand the felt foundations of international politics. And if this sounds like an anti-intellectual point, it sounds that way because it is. International politics, at the very heart of it, is not an intellectual enterprise and to intellectualize it is to misunderstand it. Instead, international politics is a matter of how human beings, and the collectivities which they have created, find themselves in the world. We rely on our minds to find these places for ourselves but, as Eugene Gendlin explains, before anything else, we rely on our bodies.

Acknowledgments Thanks to Ross Crisp, Artie Egendorf and to the editors for comments on an earlier version of this chapter.

Notes

1. Gendlin, 2001, As presented in popular titles such as Gendlin, 2003b; See further "The International Focusing Institute," n.d.; Gendlin was an occasional lecturer at the Ensalen Institute in Big Sur, California, a leading center for the New Age movement. A personal account is Weisel-Barth, 2008, p. 386.

References

Ash, T. G. (2006). Islam in Europe. *The New York Review of Books, 53*(15), 32–35.
Atran, S., & Hamid, N. (2015, November 16). Paris: The War ISIS Wants. *New York Review of Books*.
Birzer, M. L., & Smith-Mahdi, J. (2006). Does Race Matter? The Phenomenology of Discrimination Experienced Among African Americans. *Journal of African American Studies, 10*(2), 22–37.
Blair, T. (1998, April 7). Statement to the Press on Arriving at Hillsborough Castle for the Northern Ireland Talks, 7 April 1998. In *Wikiquote*. Retrieved from https://en.wikiquote.org/wiki/Tony_Blair
Bleiker, R., & Hutchison, E. (2008). Fear No More: Emotions and World Politics. *Review of International Studies, 34*(Special Issue), 115–135.
Borger, J. (2003, July 17). The Spies Who Pushed for War. *The Guardian*. Retrieved from https://www.theguardian.com/world/2003/jul/17/iraq.usa
Brown, C. (2013). "Human Nature", Science and International Political Theory. *Journal of International Relations and Development, 16*(4), 435–454.
Crawford, N. C. (2000). The Passion of World Politics: Propositions on Emotion and Emotional Relationships. *International Security, 24*(4), 116–156.
d'Orsogna, S. (2000). *Eugene Gendlin Introduces Focusing* (Vol. 1). Toronto. Retrieved from https://www.youtube.com/watch?v=j7PEC5Mh5FY
Damasio, A. R. (1994). *Descartes' Error: Emotion, Reason, and the Human Brain*. New York: Penguin Books.
Ekman, P. (1992). An Argument for Basic Emotions. *Cognition & Emotion, 6*(3–4), 169–200.
Fierke, K. M. (2014). *Political Self-Sacrifice: Agency, Body and Emotion in International Relations*. New York: Cambridge University Press.
Freedland, J. (2016a, June 25). From Brexit to Trump? *The New York Review of Books*.
Freedland, J. (2016b, July 29). Donald Trump Speaks to the Gut – And Progressives Need to Do the Same. *The Guardian*.
Friedman, N. (2003). Eugene Gendlin's Theory and Practice of Psychotherapy: A Personal Account. *Person-Centered & Experiential Psychotherapies, 2*(1), 31–42.

Gallagher, S. (1986). Body Image and Body Schema: A Conceptual Clarification. *Journal of Mind and Behaviour*, 7(4), 541–554.

Gendlin, E. T. (1973). A Phenomenology of Emotions: Anger. In D. Carr & E. S. Casey (Eds.), *Explorations in Phenomenology* (pp. 367–398). Dordrecht: Springer. https://doi.org/10.1007/978-94-010-1999-6_18.

Gendlin, E. T. (1978). Heidegger and the Philosophy of Psychology. *Review of Existential Psychology and Psychiatry*, 16(1–3), 43–71.

Gendlin, E. T. (1988). Obituary: Carl Rogers (1902–1987). *American Psychologist*, 43(2), 127–128.

Gendlin, E. T. (1991). On Emotion in Therapy. *Emotion, Psychotherapy, and Change*, 15–29.

Gendlin, E. T. (1992a). The Primacy of the Body, Not the Primacy of Perception. *Man and World*, 25(3), 341–353.

Gendlin, E. T. (1992b). The Wider Role of Bodily Sense in Thought and Language. In M. Sheets-Johnstone (Ed.), *Giving the Body Its Due* (pp. 192–207). Albany: State University of New York Press.

Gendlin, E. T. (1995). Crossing and Dipping: Some Terms for Approaching the Interface Between Natural Understanding and Logical Formulation. *Minds and Machines*, 5(4), 547–560.

Gendlin, E. T. (2001). *Let Your Body Interpret Your Dreams* (Later Printing ed.). Wilmette, IL: Chiron Publications.

Gendlin, E. T. (2003a). Beyond Postmodernism: From Concepts Through Experiencing. In R. Frie (Ed.), *Understanding Experience: Psychotherapy and Postmodernism* (pp. 100–115). Abingdon, UK: Routledge.

Gendlin, E. T. (2003b). *Focusing: How to Open Up Your Deeper Feelings and Intuition*. London: Rider & Co.

Gendlin, E. T. (2004). The New Phenomenology of Carrying Forward. *Continental Philosophy Review*, 37(1), 127–151.

Gendlin, E. T. (2009). We Can Think with the Implicit, as Well as with Fully-Formed Concepts. In *After Cognitivism* (pp. 147–161). Berlin, Germany: Springer.

Giorgi, A. (1970). *Psychology as a Human Science: A Phenomenologically Based Approach*. New York: Joanna Cotler Books.

Hatab, L. J. (1994). Human Nature in a Postmodern World: Reflections on the Work of Eugene Gendlin. *Human Studies*, 17(3), 363–371.

Heuman, L. (2011). Focusing: An Interview with Philosopher/Psychologist Eugene Gendlin. *Tricycle Magazine*, (Fall), 40-46-109.

Hutchison, E., & Bleiker, R. (2014). Theorizing Emotions in World Politics. *International Theory*, 6(3), 491–514.

Ikemi, A. (2005). Carl Rogers and Eugene Gendlin on the Bodily Felt Sense: What They Share and Where They Differ. *Person-Centered & Experiential Psychotherapies*, 4(1), 31–42.

In His Own Words: The Inspiring Speeches of Nelson Mandela. (2013, December 6). *Express.co.uk*. Retrieved from http://www.express.co.uk/news/world/447158/In-his-own-words-The-inspiring-speeches-of-Nelson-Mandela

Jager, B. (1989). Transformation of the Passions: Psychoanalytic and Phenomenological Perspectives. In *Existential-Phenomenological Perspectives in Psychology* (pp. 217–231). Dordrecht: Springer.

James, W. (1890). *The Principles of Psychology* (Vol. 1). New York: H. Holt & Co.

James, W. (1994). The Physical Basis of Emotion. *Psychological Review, 101*(2), 205–210.

Johnson, M. (1997). Embodied Meaning and Cognitive Science. In D. M. Levin (Ed.), *Language Beyond Postmodernism: Saying and Thinking in Gendlin's Philosophy* (pp. 148–175). Evanston: Northwestern University Press.

Johnson, M. (2008). *The Meaning of the Body: Aesthetics of Human Understanding*. Chicago: University of Chicago Press.

Johnstone, A. A. (2012). The Deep Bodily Roots of Emotion. *Husserl Studies, 28*(3), 179–200.

Lange, C. G. (1922). The Emotions. In K. Dunlap (Ed.), *The Emotions* (Vol. 1, pp. 33–92). New York: Williams & Wilkins Company.

Levin, D. M. (1994). Making Sense: The Work of Eugene Gendlin. *Human Studies, 17*(3), 343–353.

Levin, D. M. (Ed.). (1997). *Language Beyond Postmodernism: Saying and Thinking in Gendlin's Philosophy*. Evanston: Northwestern University Press.

Lewis, M. D., & Todd, R. M. (2005). Getting Emotional: A Neural Perspective on Emotion, Intention, and Consciousness. *Journal of Consciousness Studies, 12*(8–9), 210–235.

Mao, Z. (1949, September 21). The Chinese People Have Stood Up! Retrieved June 24, 2010, from https://www.marxists.org/reference/archive/mao/selected-works/volume-5/mswv5_01.htm

Neumann, I. B. (2014). International Relations as a Social Science. *Millennium, 43*(1), 330–350.

Noë, A. (2009). *Out of Our Heads: Why You Are Not Your Brain, and Other Lessons from the Biology of Consciousness*. New York: Hill and Wang.

Owen, D., & Davidson, J. (2009). Hubris Syndrome: An Acquired Personality Disorder? A Study of US Presidents and UK Prime Ministers over the Last 100 Years. *Brain, 132*(5), 1396–1406.

Panksepp, J., & Watt, D. (2011). What Is Basic About Basic Emotions? Lasting Lessons from Affective Neuroscience. *Emotion Review, 3*(4), 387–396.

Prinz, J. J. (2006). *Gut Reactions: A Perceptual Theory of Emotion*. Oxford: Oxford University Press.

Ringmar, E. (2007). The Power of Metaphor: Consent, Dissent & Revolution. In R. C. M. Mole (Ed.), *Discursive Constructions of Identity in European Politics*. Basingstoke: Palgrave Macmillan.

Ringmar, E. (2016). How the World Stage Makes Its Subjects: An Embodied Critique of Constructivist IR Theory. *Journal of International Relations and Development, 19*(1), 101–125.
Ringmar, E. (2017a). Heidegger on Willpower and the Mood of Modernity. In A. Cerella & L. Odysseos (Eds.), *Heidegger and the Global Age*. Lanham: Rowman & Littlefield.
Ringmar, E. (2017b). Outline of a Non-deliberative, Mood-Based, Theory of Action. *Philosophia, 78*(2).
Rosen, S. M. (2000). Focusing on the Flesh: Merleau-Ponty, Gendlin, and Lived Subjectivity. *Lifwynn Correspondence, 5*(1), 1–14.
Russell, J. A. (1991). Culture and the Categorization of Emotions. *Psychological Bulletin, 110*(3), 426–450.
Sartre, J.-P. (1949). *Iron in the Soul*. London: Penguin.
Stanghellini, G., & Rosfort, R. (2013). *Emotions and Personhood: Exploring Fragility, Making Sense of Vulnerability*. Oxford: Oxford University Press.
Suskind, R. (2004, October 17). Faith, Certainty and the Presidency of George W. Bush. *New York Times*.
The International Focusing Institute. (n.d.). Retrieved July 25, 2016, from http://www.focusing.org
Weisel-Barth, J. (2008). A Response to Lynn Preston's Explication of Implicit Experience in the Work of Eugene Gendlin: An Appreciation. *International Journal of Psychoanalytic Self Psychology, 3*(4), 386–397.
Wertz, F. J. (2009). Phenomenological Currents in Twentieth-Century Psychology. In H. L. Dreyfus & M. A. Wrathall (Eds.), *A Companion to Phenomenology and Existentialism* (pp. 394–411). Oxford: Wiley-Blackwell.
Wright, E. (2004). *Generation Kill: The True Story of Bravo Company in Iraq – Marines Who Deal in Bullets, Bombs and Ultraviolence*. New York: Bantam Press.

Erik Ringmar teaches at the Political Science Department at Lund University, Sweden. He has a PhD from Yale University, taught for 12 years at the London School of Economics, and was, until 2014, Zhi Yuan Chair Professor of International Relations at Shanghai Jiaotong University, China. He has published some 40 academic articles and his latest book, *Liberal Barbarism*, discusses European imperialism in China in the nineteenth century. He is currently working on a book about the role of nomads in world politics.

CHAPTER 3

Interpreting Affect Between State Leaders: Assessing the Political Friendship Between Winston S. Churchill and Franklin D. Roosevelt

Yuri van Hoef

INTRODUCTION

> Our friendship is the rock on which I build for the future of the world so long as I am one of the builders.
> Churchill to Roosevelt, 17 March 1945 (Letter C-914 in: Kimball, 1984b, p. 574)

Within international relations (IR), the study of friendship has only recently gained traction (Koschut & Oelsner, 2014). However, the vast majority of friendship scholars are focused on theorizing friendly relations between states, rather than relations between individuals that could impact international relations (Berenskoetter, 2007, p. 653; Oelsner, 2007). Furthermore, friendship scholars have hereunto not dealt with the 'affective turn' within the social sciences: friendship as an emotional bond

Y. van Hoef (✉)
Utrecht University, Utrecht, The Netherlands

© The Author(s) 2018
M. Clément, E. Sangar (eds.), *Researching Emotions in International Relations*, Palgrave Studies in International Relations, https://doi.org/10.1007/978-3-319-65575-8_3

between individual political actors that influences their agency receives little to no attention, despite Byman and Pollack's famous appeal to bring 'the statesman back in' (Byman & Pollack, 2001). Analysing the role that friendship between state leaders plays offers an original contribution to the study of emotions, because emotions that result from personal encounters are neither completely individual nor a pure result of collective socialization. Furthermore, most research dealing with emotions has hitherto dealt with negative emotions (Löwenheim & Heimann, 2008; Sasley, 2011, pp. 453, 456; Scheff, 2000).

In addressing that gap in our understanding of IR, this chapter takes a distinctly interpretivist, anti-positivist approach. Therefore, this chapter is of particular interest to scholars who want to make sense of the role of personal relations in IR but find traditional IR theories and methods unsatisfactory. Friendship and the meaning and influence of it on and for individual political actors, cannot be measured by any traditional positivist methods. Because friendship has proven to be such an unfathomable phenomenon, the first section of this chapter offers a conceptualization of friendship that can be used by researchers who seek to study this bond. The following section shows how this theoretical framework can be practically applied by employing Mark Bevir and R. A. W. Rhodes' Interpretative Political Science (IPS) methodology as a tool for biographical analysis. Their antifoundational approach draws heavily upon various disciplines, including history, to offer an interpretivist toolkit for social scientists (Bevir & Rhodes, 2010). Most importantly, their methodology is not just compatible to my conceptualization of friendship, but it also adds additional intellectual depth. Finally, this methodology will be illustrated in the third section by applying it to the famous friendship between British Prime Minister Winston S. Churchill and US President Franklin D. Roosevelt (Meacham, 2003; Sainsbury, 1996). Applying my conceptualization of friendship in combination with IPS reveals that, in contrast to the prevailing sceptical view (Kimball, 1984a, pp. 4–5; Maney, 1992, pp. 190–191; Meacham, 2003), there (1) existed a genuine friendship between Churchill and Roosevelt and that (2) this friendship impacted international relations.

Crucially, the third section will discuss several weaknesses of IPS potentially hindering its practical use, as well as a number of challenges which come with studying emotional ties between actors. These include a number of traditional weaknesses of hermeneutics (Wachterhauser, 1986); further shortcomings that are revealed in the debate between interpretivism and critical realism (McAnulla, 2006a); and, following Sasley, the extent to which emotions constrain political actors (Sasley, 2010). Although several of these flaws are inherent to an interpretivist approach, IPS' value lies in its potential to challenge established interpretations which fail to illuminate the impact of emotional ties on political actors. Accordingly, the final section poses relevant questions to scholars that are inclined to employ, or dismiss, IPS. This chapter, then, differentiates itself from the current state of the art both in the studies of emotions and friendship in IR, by offering an approach to study friendship at the intermediary level, rather than at the individual or the collective level.

The case study reveals that, though the friendship between Churchill and Roosevelt has been highly romanticized, their mutual emotional affection at crucial moments influenced the relations between Great Britain and the USA. Throughout the analysis, the value of IPS as an analytical tool is exemplified, especially its ability to make sense of the past and provide an outlook on potential future ramifications. I argue that the 1956 Suez crisis can be interpreted as an unintended consequence of the Churchill-Roosevelt friendship. Thus, this chapter not only illustrates the negative and positive ramifications of friendship on state leaders and their decision-making, but also demonstrates the profound influence individual friendships have on IR.

Conceptualizing Friendship

> 'But when you talk about friendly relations in politics, it's not the friendship of schoolmates.'
> Mikhail Gorbachev (quoted in Heintz, 2004)

Friendship between state leaders shares a number of characteristics with friendships that ordinary citizens might have, but also differs in a number of important aspects. First, each and every friendship has a history, is a chronicle of a personal story between two or more individuals, and it therefore lends itself well to a more interpretive and historical approach. That means it consists out of the three elements of every story: a beginning, middle, and an end. Even a very specialized form of friendship such as the Special Relationship clearly 'describes and explains an end point' (Gardner Feldman, 2014, p. 124). Within the story there will be a foundational moment (Eznack & Koschut, 2014, pp. 74, 78–79), a pillar upon which the structure of the friendship rests, such as the famous 2001 meeting of George W. Bush and Vladimir Putin in Ljubljana. This shared experience could be a 'heroic act of reconciliation' (Vion, 2014, p. 113), such as between Helmut Kohl and François Mitterrand at Verdun in 1984, which precipitated their countries growing closer.

An interpretative analysis will focus on the progress of the relationships, paying specific attention to first impressions (the beginning), the way the relationship developed (the middle), and, if applicable, how the relationship ended. To illustrate, consider that Churchill and Roosevelt took an immediate disliking to each other when they first met, or that we would expect a friendship, in contrast to a partnership (Van Hoef, 2014, pp. 68–69), to outlast the terms of office. An example of the latter is the friendship between Mikhail Gorbachev and George H. W. Bush, exemplified by Barbara Bush's heartfelt eulogy for her dear friend Raisa Gorbacheva in *Time* Magazine in 1999 (Bush, 1999; Van Hoef, 2012b). These are very concise examples of how we can witness friendship between state leaders in the international arena.

When conceptualizing friendship, it is crucial to differentiate between indicators for, and key components of, friendship. Owing to the highly individualized nature of friendship, indicators can be very diverse, and include shared character traits, values (Smith, 2014, p. 36), virtues, opinions, and political agendas. They provide the fertile ground for a friendship to grow. For example, two presidents might share a deep religiosity, and in that recognize each other, as George W. Bush and Vladimir Putin did in Ljubljana in 2001. Another indicator, especially in the international arena, is the dissemination of the relationship. Friendship is not limited to the two state leaders, but the friendship will disseminate and affect others that are close to the two friends. Their romantic partners become friends as well; the children play together; the families go on joint holidays; circles of acquaintances and colleagues intermingle, and so on:

> Because friends [states] are embedded in a larger social environment—an international society—their world-building efforts not only create an exclusionary space that seals friends from criticism and creates bias, but also promote an idea of international order that affects others. (Berenskoetter, 2014, p. 67)

Yet indicators such as shared values and dissemination are present in other social relationships as well. Alone, they are not enough to differentiate friendship from relations such as that between client and supplier, employee and employer, or that between pupil and teacher. There is an astonishing amount of friendship literature and conceptualizations of friendship are many and varied.[1] However, it is possible to identify a number of key components that are present in the extensive friendship literature and which are applicable to a political friendship between two state leaders. First, friendship is a reciprocal relationship made up out of equal partners (Gardner Feldman, 2014, pp. 139–140; Roshchin, 2014, p. 99). Furthermore, from the classical philosophers onward a virtuous friendship involves a joint task: to help each other strive for the good (Stern-Gillet, 1995, pp. 49–50). This 'moral' and 'ethical task' (Smith, 2007, pp. 187–188) is also found in the works of Johan Galtung, founding editor of the *Journal of Peace Research*, who in his vision of positive peace held that the great task of positive peace is the project of 'human integration' (Galtung, 1964). Another important element of friendship is the idea of strong moral obligations, such as personal sacrifices for the sake of the other (Schmitt, 2007, pp. 77–78; Smith, 2014, pp. 40–41). Finally, there is an element of critical realism's emergent properties where the 'emergent properties of an entity are properties possessed only by the entity as a whole, not by any of its components or the simple aggregation of the components […]' (Mingers, 2011, p. 306). Friendship is indeed, then, 'a catalyst of change *in its own right* [my emphasis]' (Koschut & Oelsner, 2014, p. 202). Identifying these five key components leads to the following working definition of friendship:

> an (1) equal and (2) reciprocal bond between two or more individuals, which (3) imposes moral obligations upon them, has (4) emergent properties, and has at its foundation (5) a shared (grand) project.

With this definition, it is possible to study a political friendship, such as the famous friendship between Churchill and Roosevelt, while operationalizing it through the use of IPS adds an additional layer of analysis. This definition also strongly hints at the emotional level of friendship.

By approaching friendship as an affective emotional bond between political actors, studying friendship offers an interesting alternative to more traditional realist notions of self-interest (Berenskoetter and Van Hoef, 2017). It is no surprise that most research so far has focused upon negative emotions (Sasley, 2011, p. 456). Even though the study of friendship as a positive affective bond is on the rise, this traditional realist view can still be found in recent publications. Todd H. Hall has argued that emotions such as anger, sympathy, and guilt are strategically deployed by political actors as a means to an end (2015, pp. 2–3). Even though Hall is open to the possibility of friendship in politics, he remains sceptical because 'for leaders and diplomats, enacting camaraderie with their counterparts is both a form of individual emotional labor and part of a larger corporate performance of emotional affinity' (2015, pp. 188–189).

Friendship scholars in IR have been accused of making an ontological mistake in attributing an emotional bond such as friendship to nations, because states 'are ontologically incapable of having feelings' (Digeser, 2009, pp. 327–328; see also Keller, 2009). This argument has been countered by friendship scholars by positing that they 'mean decision makers acting as the state' when speaking of states being affectively attached to each other (Eznack, 2011, p. 242; see also Smith, 2014, pp. 38–40). Lucile Eznack has advocated a collective approach to studying emotions by holding that 'affect exists in close allies' relationships, under the form of affective attachment to the latter and to the group—in this case, the alliance—as a whole' (2011, p. 241; see also Koschut, 2014).

In contrast, studying friendship between state leaders considers friendship at an intermediary level, in the space between political leaders. It is in this space, in their interactions and their outward displays of affection, that the bond becomes observable. Studying friendship at this level also sidesteps the ontological accusation of attributing feelings to non-human actors. Finally, following Sasley, by defining affects as 'general valence feelings toward something' (Sasley, 2010, p. 3), studying friendship between state leaders focuses on the positive affect political actors hold for each other and the extent to which this positive valence affects their policies.

Interpretive Political Science

> [...] to understand actions, practices and institutions, we need to grasp the relevant meanings, beliefs and preferences of the people involved. (Rhodes, 2011, p. 202)

Mark Bevir and R. A. W. Rhodes' interpretive political science (IPS) approach offers an interpretivist toolkit for social scientists. This section shows that their approach moves away from structural constraints that are nowadays common in mainstream IR theory and gives centre stage to individual actors. Moving into IPS marks the next step in the development of my study of friendship, where I previously dabbled in positivism, but found fields such as Game Theory and Social Network Analysis wanting and incapable of studying the effects of friendship (Van Hoef, 2012a). Friendship, its meaning and influence on and for individual political actors, cannot be measured by any traditional positivist methods. Bevir and Rhodes offer a method that is especially appealing to those unimpressed by positivist efforts, deliberately choosing to base their approach not 'on modernist-empiricism but on hermeneutics and historicism; on Dilthey and Collingwood rather than Weber or Marx' (2010, p. 19). That is not to say that they deny the relevance of structures. On the contrary, although their 'procedural individualism asserts that meanings are always meanings for specific people', Bevir and Rhodes situate the agency of individual actors against these actors' backgrounds and traditions (2006, p. 399).

The concepts of traditions, dilemmas, practices and unintended consequences form the basis of their theory. The behaviour of actors can be interpreted by studying their specific traditions (their ideational background), dilemmas encountered by actors (experiences or ideas that conflict with their tradition), and finally their practices, a set of actions or patterns (Bevir & Rhodes, 2006, p. 400). These concepts allow friendship to be studied at an intermediate level, taking the power of statesmen as reflective active agents into account (cf. Vogler, 2016, p. 77). Especially revealing is the concept of dilemma, because it allows us to study moments of choice in a friendship where an actor has to decide between their ideational background and their friend. In other words, friendship has the power to force an individual to alter and/or challenge their individual tradition. Following our definition of friendship, for a political friendship to truly be considered a friendship, both reciprocity and equality should be a pattern in the relationship. There is one last interesting insight to be gained from Bevir and Rhodes, namely the concept of unintended consequences, which stems from systems theory (McAnulla, 2006b, p. 407).

Certain consequences might be unintended by an actor, but are nevertheless the result of their actions and form an emergent property of the actions of an actor. Note that our friendship definition also included the idea of emergent properties, 'the friendship being more than the sum of its parts'. Bevir and Rhodes illustrate this with the example of a great multitude of people who decide to cross the Golden Gate Bridge by car in the morning so they can arrive early at work, which results in an unintended traffic jam (2006, p. 401). Consider the supposed friendship between François Mitterrand and Helmut Kohl which, arguably, led to German Reunification and further European integration. What if the German Reunification and the European integration were unintended consequences of their friendship? This short example shows the additional theoretical depth that can be added by invoking the interpretive theory of Bevir and Rhodes, rather than opting for historical analysis or process tracing.

In sum, Bevir and Rhodes' methodology is largely compatible with the view of friendship developed in the previous section and offers extra methodological depth when analysing a specific friendship. When developing the case studies, illustrated by the Churchill-Roosevelt friendship in this chapter, it is crucial to identify the traditions and ideational background of the political actors to determine whether there are any indicators for friendship. Owing to the highly individualized nature of friendship, indicators can be very diverse, and include shared character traits, values (Smith, 2014, p. 36), virtues, opinions, and political agendas. By studying memoirs, biographies and autobiographies of state leaders, and of their close associates, we can identify their ideational backgrounds to find common characteristics that could indicate their capacity and receptiveness to friendship. While the accounts found in these primary sources offer personal recollections of affects, the observations of the relationship in the accounts of friends, colleagues, and associates are just as vital. The latter offer the researcher the ability to verify and falsify the account of the actors themselves. However, even though these indicators are important, they can only suggest that two individuals were or were becoming friends.

For a political friendship to be present, the five key components (equality, reciprocity, moral obligations, emergent properties, and (grand) political projects) must be identified. Friendship then should be observable as a practice, with discernible patterns of reciprocity and equality. Moral obligations will be most readily observable in the dilemmas the actors face in their relationship. The bond becoming more than its parts, its dissemination and emergent properties can be found in IPS' unintended consequences. Table 3.1 illustrates how the four different elements of such a case study (Story; Challenges; Patterns; Unintended Consequences), correspond with the four components of IPS and the five key elements of friendship.

Table 3.1 Structure of the case studies

	Case study	IPS	Friendship
1	The story	Ideological background	(5) Grand project
2	Challenges	Dilemmas	(3) Moral obligations
3	Patterns	Practices	(1) Equality and (2) reciprocity
4	Unintended consequences	Unintended consequences	(4) Emergent properties

The red thread running through the story, challenges, and patterns of the friendship is the presence of reciprocal emotional affection of the friends for each other. Some overlap between the key components is possible. It might well be, for instance, that the grand political project previously formed a dilemma between the two actors. Such was the case with the issue of German Reunification between Helmut Kohl and François Mitterrand, which first divided the two friends before bringing them closer together (Van Hoef, 2014, pp. 73–74). Meanwhile, when presenting the story of the friendship, the researcher will also encounter the other elements of the relationship. Therefore, it is important to analyse the challenges, patterns, and unintended consequences of the relationship after the story is presented. The final section of this chapter will illustrate this approach by applying it to the friendship between Churchill and Roosevelt.

CASE STUDY: ASSESSING THE CHURCHILL-ROOSEVELT RELATIONSHIP

I had a true affection for Franklin. (Churchill, 1964, p. 128)

This case study elaborates on a previous study of the Churchill-Roosevelt relationship (Van Hoef, 2010, pp. 25–34) and illustrates how the proposed conceptualization of friendship can be operationalized using Mark Bevir's and R. A. W. Rhodes' methodology of Interpretative Political Science (IPS). This analysis is divided into four parts: (1) the story, (2) challenges, (3) patterns, and (4) unintended consequences. Each of these sections corresponds to one of IPS' concepts: ideological background (the story), dilemmas (challenges), practices (patterns), and unintended consequences. Finally, as illustrated in Table 3.1 on the previous page, the four parts of the analysis also correspond to the five key components of friendship. Within the story we look for indicators for friendship, but also for the presence of a grand project (5). Challenges call upon the moral obligations (3) friends have to each other. Reciprocity (2) and equality (1) can be observed as patterns, while the final part is devoted to the unintended consequences of the specific friendship.

Introduction

Winston S. Churchill (1874–1975) certainly had a capacity for making friends, with several studies having been devoted to his friendships alone (Meacham, 2003; Young, 1966). His friendship with US President Franklin Delano Roosevelt (1882–1945) is the stuff of legends. Warren F. Kimball, editor of the monumental *Churchill & Roosevelt: The Complete Correspondence*, identified five phases in their relationship but Churchill and Roosevelt only met intensively in the period from 1940 to the summer of 1943 (Kimball, 1984a, pp. 6–18). Following Kimball, one would expect to find signs of friendship mostly within that period. However, my analysis reveals that the history of their relationship both preceded and outlasted this period.

The Story

Famously, Roosevelt and Churchill did not get along when they first met in 1918, many years before they would both reach the pinnacle of political office (Meacham, 2003, p. 5). Roosevelt's dislike would waver when the two statesmen found themselves in the minority concerned about the rise of Nazi Germany. In 1938, Roosevelt predicted 'an inevitable conflict within five years' and started corresponding with Churchill, who had impressed him with his stalwart opposition to Germany (Black, 2003, pp. 480–481). Roosevelt saw a potential ally in Churchill: 'I'm giving him attention now because there is a strong possibility that he will become the prime minister and I want to get my hand in now' (Berthon, 2001, p. 25).

This was clearly a partnership then (Van Hoef, 2010, p. 69), born out of opposing a mutual adversary. It was not until Pearl Harbor on December 7, 1941 that the USA joined the war. The instrumentality of the partnership is revealed in Churchill's responses to the attack: 'This certainly simplifies things' (Meacham, 2003, p. 130), and, when one of his advisors cautioned him to maintain consistency in his diplomatic approach: 'Oh! That is the way we talked to her [America] while we were wooing her; now that she is in the harem, we talk to her quite differently!' (Kimball, 1984a, p. 289).

Now that the USA was fully part of the war, a series of personal meetings between the two leaders took place in which they grew attached to each other. This worried their advisors: the Americans feared the impressive Churchill was gaining too much influence on Roosevelt, while the British feared that Churchill worshipped Roosevelt as a living hero (Black, 2003, p. 695). These meetings led to unprecedented historical decisions, such as British and US forces under a single commander (Kimball, 1984a, p. 9).

However, near the end of the war, the Soviet Union had supplanted Britain as the USA's most important strategical partner, while Churchill found himself increasingly at odds with Roosevelt on geopolitical and post-war visions. Churchill wanted Great Britain to play a leading role in a post-war world in which colonial powers would provide stability. Roosevelt advocated self-determination for the colonies (Meacham, 2003, p. 118). Edward Stettinius, US foreign Secretary at the time, mentions that Roosevelt's 'early fascination with [Churchill] had declined, and there was an increasing divergence in their desires for the postwar world' (Black, 2003, p. 1085; See also: Sainsbury, 1996, pp. 3–4).

Their diverging worldviews might have come into play but that question has become purely academic since Roosevelt died two months after the Yalta Conference, on April 12, 1945. Churchill had been very worried about Roosevelt's health and had requested Foreign Affairs to alleviate his workload because he worried it cost his friend too much energy (Charmley, 1993, p. 630). Churchill reflected upon the last time he saw Roosevelt: 'The president seemed placid and frail. I felt that he had a slender contract with life. I was not to see him again. We bade affectionate farewells' (Black, 2003, p. 1085).

One of the great mysteries surrounding the Churchill-Roosevelt relationship is that Churchill did not attend his friend's funeral. He seemed to intend to but came up with the rather weak excuse that too many British ministers were abroad at that time (Churchill, 1964, pp. 132–133). It seems more likely that Churchill feared to be too emotional at a public funeral: he cried at a later memorial service and reflected that he was 'overpowered by a sense of deep and irreparable loss' (Churchill, 1964, p. 137). A visit to America would not only have allowed him to pay his respects to a valued partner, and, by his own words, a dear friend, but would have also allowed him to meet Roosevelt's successor: postponing this meeting cost Churchill valuable diplomatic time (Black, 2003, p. 1115). Churchill reflected upon his affection for Roosevelt in letters sent to Eleanor Roosevelt and Harry Hopkins, Roosevelt's adjutant (Churchill, 1964, p. 128).

Born out of political necessity, the Churchill-Roosevelt friendship began as a partnership *pure sang*. Both recognized the threat of Nazi Germany and therefore sought each other out. Instrumentality was at the core of their early relationship, which is clearly evidenced by the way Churchill described the early stages of the relationship: the USA was not a friend, but a partner to be seduced. It is also clear that both state leaders held very different worldviews. Yet, though instrumentality was at the core of their nascent friendship, they sought each other out for a shared grand project, i.e. defeating Nazi Germany. They also show clear affection towards each other during their personal encounters, as evidenced in their letters, by the worries of their advisors that they are becoming too impressed by each other, and, finally, by Churchill's absence at Roosevelt's funeral, his crying at a later memorial service, and his heartfelt letters of condolences.

Challenges

There are two dilemmas in the 1941–1943 period that are intriguing. First, in a letter dated February 25, 1942, Churchill revealed to Roosevelt that British intelligence succeeded in decrypting codes used by US diplomats. This is a strange revelation, especially considering the way Churchill delivered the message: he had the British ambassador bring it himself 'by hand, to be delivered into yours personally' and requested that Roosevelt burned the letter after reading it, which indicates the highly confidential nature of the message (Letter C32/1 in: Kimball, 1984a, p. 371). Although it is possible that Churchill worried that the Americans would inevitably find out and that this would hurt bilateral relations, or that he was genuinely concerned there was a security risk (Letter C32/1 in: Kimball, 1984a, p. 371), this does not explain why Churchill chose to reveal very sensitive information to Roosevelt in such a delicate and personal manner.

A second interesting dilemma was the fall of Tobruk on June 21, 1942, where twenty five thousand allied soldiers were taken captive, which resulted in a vote of no confidence (easily defeated) in Churchill, and which led Roosevelt to send him one of his shortest letters: 'Good for you.

Roosevelt' (Letter R-160 in: Kimball, 1984a, p. 517). Roosevelt went much further though than just offering verbal support, he provided Churchill with 300 tanks and 100 pieces of artillery (Freidel, 1990, pp. 450–451). This was no empty gesture and it left a lasting impression upon Churchill (Letter C-146 in: Kimball, 1984a, p. 592). In a letter dated March 17, 1945, Churchill reflects on their friendship and refers to Tobruk as well:

> [...] Our friendship is the rock on which I build for the future of the world so long as I am one of the builders. I always think of those tremendous days when you devised Lend-Lease, when we met at Argentia, when you decided with my heartfelt agreement to launch the invasion of Africa, and when you comforted me for the loss of Tobruk by giving me the 300 Shermans of subsequent Alamein fame. I remember the part our personal relations have played in the advance of the world cause now nearing its first military goal. (Letter C-914 in Kimball, 1984b, p. 574)

Both the cracking of the US diplomatic codes (25 February 1942) and Roosevelt's aid after the fall of Tobruk (21 June 1942) illustrate Churchill's personal affection for Roosevelt. Both are clear instances of a moral obligation being fulfilled: Churchill warning Roosevelt, and Roosevelt offering military aid. It is only by discarding their emotions that it is possible to offer a more sceptical realist account: Churchill might have feared the potential backlash had the USA found out that their British allies had cracked their codes and it does not take much of imagination to posit that the USA had much to gain from providing Churchill with military material after Tobruk. Note that there were two potential future challenges: Britain becoming the junior member in the alliance and Churchill and Roosevelt's diverging worldviews. Roosevelt's early death prevents from speculating further on these matters. After all, a potential obstacle is not an actual obstacle.

Patterns

Throughout the friendship there are three patterns that are worth further consideration. Churchill consciously playing the part of the wooer is a recurring pattern. As noted above, Churchill's (assumed) romanticizing of the relationship has led scholars, including Warren F. Kimball, to be highly sceptical of the friendship. Second, there is also a pattern of the diminishing importance of the relationship, the cause being the Soviet Union's growing importance to the alliance, which hints at a possible future inequality between the friends. Finally, there is a pattern of mutual appreciation, even fondness, between the two state leaders, evidenced by their letters and the observations of their close associates.

Unintended Consequences

As noted above, the post-war world and how to approach it would have formed a major obstacle not just between the two countries but between Churchill and Roosevelt themselves. The friendship between Churchill and Roosevelt heralds the Special Relationship between Great Britain and the USA and the Special Relationship itself might be the most obvious of the unintended consequences of their wartime partnership. Though their diverging worldviews did not lead to a conflict during Roosevelt's lifetime, these diverging worldviews most clearly came to the front in the 1956 Suez Crisis. As one might wonder whether the Churchill-Roosevelt friendship would have outlived their post-war worldviews, one might also wonder if an earlier clash would have prevented the Suez Crisis from happening. Interpreting the Suez Crisis as an unintended consequence remains a tentative suggestion here, but this idea certainly merits future research. Others have interpreted the Suez Crisis as an example of friends simply disagreeing (Eznack, 2011, p. 254).

Conclusion

Kimball soberly argues that '[...] the Churchill-Roosevelt relationship has been much over-romanticized by historians, largely through Winston Churchill's own efforts' (Kimball, 1984a, pp. 4–5). An ulterior letter to Eisenhower reveals as much (Van Hoef, 2010, p. 64).

My analysis shows that there is a clear instrumentality to their early relationship, more akin to a partnership than a friendship (Van Hoef, 2014, p. 69). As the USA gets drawn into the war, the relationship intensified and the two state leaders were also drawn to each other. They enjoyed a reciprocal and equal bond, which focused upon a grand project (defeating Nazi Germany). The friendship also contained emergent properties: the story of their friendship became a legend on its own and heralded the Special Relationship. The letter from Churchill to Eisenhower shows how keen

Churchill was to maintain the unique bond that had developed between the two countries. This is an effect of the Churchill-Roosevelt friendship. The fifth key component, their moral obligations, is hardest to pinpoint.

Here, IPS' concept of dilemmas proves enlightening. First, there is Roosevelt's offer of assistance after Tobruk. Churchill's professed gratitude, at multiple occasions, shows that for him this was a seminal gesture on Roosevelt's part. The most interesting dilemma is the moment Churchill went out of his way to reveal the decryption of the US diplomatic service to Roosevelt, a move potentially harmful to British intelligence services. Churchill's careful phrasing in the letter, hand delivered by the British ambassador to Roosevelt, implied that he was aware of the sensitivity of the situation. This is a further example of a moral obligation being fulfilled for a friend. Since each of the five key components of our conceptualization of friendship are present in the Churchill-Roosevelt relationship, the claim that their friendship has been romanticized is unfounded (Table 3.2).

It is in their different ideological backgrounds that the seeds for future conflict can be found. The (unverifiable) claim that their friendship would not have survived World War II is connected to their divergent views on what the post-war world would have to look like. Clearly, Churchill's imperialism would have found itself at odds with Roosevelt's ideal of self-determination for the colonies. In this regard, the idea of the Suez Crisis as an untended consequence of the Churchill-Roosevelt relationship sheds an interesting light on the possible ramifications of close relations between state leaders. The story of a political friendship does not end with the friendship itself; the possible ramifications the unintended consequences of such relationships offer an exciting field for future research.

Table 3.2 Results of the case study

Case study	Results	Friendship?
1 The story	Diverging views; defeating Nazi Germany	• Grand project
2 Challenges	Tobruk; cracked codes	• Obligations fulfilled
3 Patterns	Equality; reciprocity; mutual fondness	• Equal and reciprocal
4 Unintended consequences	Suez Crisis; Special Relationship	• Emergent properties

IMPLICATIONS FOR FUTURE RESEARCH

Affective attachments [...] order priorities for leaders. (Sasley, 2010, p. 7)

The Churchill-Roosevelt case study brings several advantages and disadvantages of IPS to light. These include a number of traditional weaknesses of hermeneutics (Wachterhauser, 1986), further shortcomings that are revealed in the debate between interpretivism and critical realism (McAnulla, 2006a), and, following Sasley, the extent to which emotions constrain political actors (Sasley, 2010). This section will outline some of the lessons that can be learned from the latter two. The friendship definition proposed in the first part of this chapter contains the concept of emergent properties, which is found in critical realism, while Sasley's findings on the role that emotions play serve to further deepen the analysis of emotions in this chapter.

Bevir and Rhodes' interpretivism shares critical realism's critique of a fully positivist empirical approach to our field of study and both focus on the role actors have. However, critical realism does not share the crucial role that IPS lends to actors and stresses how social structures can both impede and allow for the agency of actors (McAnulla, 2006a, pp. 135–136). In an IPS perspective, Churchill and Roosevelt's different post-war worldviews are part of their traditions and their differences form a dilemma, to either be overcome (one or both change their ideological backgrounds) or to be an obstacle. As seen in the preceding part, an IPS analysis stresses the agency of the actors to effect change, while critical realism would stress the inhibiting role of their backgrounds. Adopting IPS therefore amounts to take position in the agency-structure debate. For those researchers that wish to focus in on the role of social structures, critical realism offers a different, yet akin approach. The case study showed how the relationship eventually disseminated and came to mean much more than just the bond between two individual state leaders. The extent to which the friendship between Churchill and Roosevelt came to have meaning for their successors, in both the immediate and distant future, illustrates the theoretical depth that Bevir and Rhodes' approach offers.

One of the main criticism that can be addressed to IPS is its neglect of the actions of preceding actors - and their influence - on present actors, thereby forgetting that 'current activity and acts of reflexivity always take place within a pre-structured context' (McAnulla, 2006a, p. 121). I have answered that critique by making critical realism's concept of emergent properties one of the five key elements of friendship. Assigning emergent properties to the actions of past and present actors gives them a form of agency that is lacking in IPS' tradition (McAnulla, 2006a, p. 121), which assigns all agency to the actors (Bevir & Rhodes, 2003, p. 2). That friendship is more than the sum of its parts is mirrored in the concept of emergent properties, because friendship is a social system and as such: 'involves interactive, coordinative, and synergistic dynamics that create emergent group-level properties not reducible solely to individual attributes' (Bandura, 2006, p. 166). Following from Albert Bandura's social cognitive theory of triadic reciprocal causation, 'personal agency and social structure operate independently' and 'human agency operates generatively and proactively on social systems, not just reactively' (Bandura, 2000, p. 77).

By focusing on the role of individual state leaders, this chapter took an approach which bears ressemblance to Foreign Policy Analysis.[2] However, analysing the role of friendships of individual state leaders contributes, more importantly, to understanding the role emotions play at the intermediate level in IR. Both Roosevelt offering material aid to Britain after Tobruk and Churchill revealing to Roosevelt that US diplomatic codes were deciphered are instances of political action being taken out of personal affect for the other. While most research focuses on negative emotions (Sasley, 2011, p. 456), a study of friendship focuses on the positive affects that actors have for each other and the extent to which these affect their policies (Sasley, 2010, p. 3). Furthermore, by considering friendship at the intermediary level, an additional layer of analysis is offered next to the individual (cognitive) and the collective (national/transnational) level that has so far been left unexplored. While this case study's main concern was the question whether a friendship existed between Churchill and Roosevelt and whether it had an effect on the relations between the USA and Great Britain, the analysis contains examples of clear expressions of affect. Future studies focusing solely on the different ways state leaders express affect, as well as towards which objects (cf. Wissenburg, 2014), could further account for the role friendship plays in IR. Finally, while the idea of friendship in IR has been gaining traction (Koschut & Oelsner, 2014), its opposite, enmity between state leaders, is an unexplored field altogether.

Studying friendship connects to a number of current research projects in IR. It is a particularly enticing field because at the heart of its subject matter is something that has an important and different meaning to each and every one of us. By carefully conceptualizing friendship, scholars do not only contribute to the growing scholarship on emotions on IR, but also engage with a subject that can count upon societal interest.

Conclusion

By conceptualizing friendship and operationalizing it through the use of Bevir and Rhodes' Interpretive Political Science (IPS), this chapter makes a case for studying the extent to which friendship between state leaders matters to international relations. This is an emotional bond present at the intermediary level, i.e. between the individual and collective level. Friendship is defined as a reciprocal, equal bond between two or more individuals sharing a (grand) project. It is a bond that is more than the sum of its parts, because it disseminates and affects others outside the relationship, and it carries with it important moral obligations, such as the ideal of self-sacrifice for the sake of the friend. In other words, friendship holds both promises and threats to international order. It brings to the fore important questions such as whether friends might privilege their friendship over the states they represent.

Bevir and Rhodes' IPS offers a fruitful framework for the analysis of relationships between actors because the key concepts of their method, and the philosophies underlying their approach, form a natural structure for researching the history of a relationship. Their approach offers additional depth compared to a process tracing or traditional historical analysis. This is especially evident when considering their concept of unintended consequences in a relationship and the ramifications those might have on the international order.

Analysing the friendship between Winston S. Churchill and Franklin D. Roosevelt served as an illustrative case study of using IPS. In contrast to many historical analyses of their relationship, which hold their friendship to be idealized and romanticized, this analysis showed that their friendship adheres to each of the key components of friendship we have identified. Two findings stand out. First, there are multiple instances of Roosevelt and Churchill fulfilling moral obligations towards each other, which further validates their relationship being a true friendship. Second, there are multiple instances of their friendship being more than the sum of its parts. There are both positive and negative examples of this dissemination, of which the Special Relationship and the Suez Crisis form the most vivid examples. Finally, throughout their friendship there were multiple instances of clear emotional affection. These are most prominently displayed by Churchill, both in contemporary letters and observations by his advisors.

This chapter offered an approach for studying friendship between political actors. There is room for future studies that delve more deeply into the ways state leaders express ties of affection and to what extent they describe personal friends and foes differently. Future research could also tap into ties of enmity between actors. Finally, this case study offered a Western conceptualization of friendship: non-Western conceptualizations of friendship are still very much unexplored (Devere, 2014, pp. 194–195) and offer fruitful ground for future research to further conceptualize friendship.

Acknowledgement I am grateful for the guidance of the editors, Maéva Clément and Eric Sangar, and the feedback provided by two anonymous reviewers. Further valuable comments on this chapter were provided to me by participants of the CEEISA-ISA 2016 Joint International Conference at the University of Ljubljana, particularly Brent J. Steele, Jelena Subotic, and Felix Berenskoetter. Finally, this chapter would not have existed at all without Katharina Höne inviting me to her expertly organized workshop *IR's feelings* at the 2015 EISA Pan-European Conference at the University of Catania, where I received treasurable feedback that allowed me to explore the role of emotions on an entirely new level.

Notes

1. In-depth overviews can be found in Simon Koschut and Andrea Oelsner's (Koschut & Oelsner, 2014) *Friendship in International Relations* and Barbara (Caine, 2014) *Friendship: A History*.
2. For an analysis of the role of friendship in Foreign Policy Analysis, see: Berenskoetter and Van Hoef, 2017.

References

Bandura, A. (2000). Exercise of Human Agency Through Collective Efficacy. *Current Directions in Psychological Science, 9*(3), 75–78. https://doi.org/10.1111/1467-8721.00064.

Bandura, A. (2006). Toward a Psychology of Human Agency. *Perspectives on Psychological Science, 1*(2), 164–180. https://doi.org/10.1111/j.1745-6916.2006.00011.x.

Berenskoetter, F. (2007). Friends, There Are No Friends? An Intimate Reframing of the International. *Millennium – Journal of International Studies, 35*(3), 647–676. https://doi.org/10.1177/03058298070350031501.

Berenskoetter, F. (2014). Friendship, Security, and Power. In S. Koschut & A. Oelsner (Eds.), *Friendship and International Relations* (pp. 51–71). Basingstoke: Palgrave Macmillan.

Berthon, S. (2001). *Allies at War: The Bitter Rivalry Among Churchill, Roosevelt, and De Gaulle* (1st Carroll & Graf ed.). New York: Carroll & Graf Publishers Inc.

Bevir, M., & Rhodes, R. A. W. (2003). *Interpreting British Governance*. London: Psychology Press.

Bevir, M., & Rhodes, R. A. W. (2006). Disaggregating Structures as an Agenda for Critical Realism: A Reply to McAnulla. *British Politics, 1*(3), 397–403. https://doi.org/10.1057/palgrave.bp.4200019.

Bevir, M., & Rhodes, R. A. W. (2010). *The State as Cultural Practice*. Oxford, UK: Oxford University Press.

Black, C. (2003). *Franklin Delano Roosevelt: Champion of Freedom* (New ed.). New York: PublicAffairs.

Bush, B. (1999). Eulogy. Raisa Gorbachev. *Time Magazine, 154*(14), 43.

Byman, D. L., & Pollack, K. M. (2001). Let Us Now Praise Great Men: Bringing the Statesman Back In. *International Security, 25*(4), 107–146.

Caine, B. (Ed.). (2014). *Friendship: A History*. London. Oakville, CT: Routledge.

Charmley, J. (1993). *Churchill: The End of Glory: A Political Biography* (1st US ed.). New York: Harcourt.

Churchill, W. S. (1964). *The Second World War. Part 12: Triumph and Tragedy*. London: Cassell.

Devere, H. (2014). Friendship in International Treaties. In S. Koschut & A. Oelsner (Eds.), *Friendship and International Relations* (pp. 182–198). Basingstoke: Palgrave Macmillan.

Digeser, P. E. (2009). Friendship Between States. *British Journal of Political Science, 39*(2), 323–344. https://doi.org/10.1017/S0007123408000525.

Eznack, L. (2011). Crises as Signals of Strength: The Significance of Affect in Close Allies' Relationships. *Security Studies, 20*(2), 238–265. https://doi.org/10.1080/09636412.2011.572687.

Eznack, L., & Koschut, S. (2014). The Sources of Affect in Interstate Friendship. In S. Koschut & A. Oelsner (Eds.), *Friendship and International Relations* (pp. 72–88). Basingstoke: Palgrave Macmillan.

Freidel, F. (1990). *Franklin D. Roosevelt: A Rendezvous with Destiny* (1st ed.). Boston: Little, Brown.

Galtung, J. (1964). An Editorial. *Journal of Peace Research, 1*(1), 1–4.

Gardner Feldman, L. (2014). German-Polish Ties: Special Relationship, Friendship, or Reconciliation? In S. Koschut & A. Oelsner (Eds.), *Friendship and International Relations* (pp. 123–143). Basingstoke: Palgrave Macmillan.

Hall, T. H. (2015). *Emotional Diplomacy: Official Emotion on the International Stage*. Ithaca: Cornell University Press.

Heintz, J. (2004, July 6). Gorbachev Recalls a Friend Who "Loved Life." *The Boston Globe*. Retrieved from http://www.boston.com/news/nation/articles/2004/06/07/gorbachev_recalls_a_friend_who_loved_life/?camp=pm

Keller, S. (2009). Against Friendship Between Countries. *Journal of International Political Theory, 5*(1), 59–74. https://doi.org/10.3366/E1755088209000329.

Kimball, W. F. (Ed.). (1984a). *Churchill & Roosevelt: The Complete Correspondence I: Alliance Emerging: October 1933–November 1942*. Princeton, NJ: Princeton University Press.

Kimball, W. F. (Ed.). (1984b). *Churchill & Roosevelt: The Complete Correspondence II: Alliance Forged: November 1942–February 1944*. Princeton, NJ: Princeton University Press.

Koschut, S. (2014). Emotional (Security) Communities: The Significance of Emotion Norms in Inter-allied Conflict Management. *Review of International Studies, 40*(3), 533–558. https://doi.org/10.1017/S0260210513000375.

Koschut, S., & Oelsner, A. (Eds.). (2014). *Friendship and International Relations*. Basingstoke: Palgrave Macmillan.

Löwenheim, O., & Heimann, G. (2008). Revenge in International Politics. *Security Studies, 17*(4), 685–724. https://doi.org/10.1080/09636410802508055.

Maney, P. J. (1992). *The Roosevelt Presence: A Biography of Franklin Delano Roosevelt*. New York: Twayne [u.a.].

McAnulla, S. (2006a). Challenging the New Interpretivist Approach: Towards a Critical Realist Alternative. *British Politics, 1*(1), 113–138. https://doi.org/10.1057/palgrave.bp.4200013.

McAnulla, S. (2006b). Critical Realism, Social Structure and Political Analysis: A Reply to Bevir and Rhodes. *British Politics, 1*(3), 404–412. https://doi.org/10.1057/palgrave.bp.4200029.

Meacham, J. (2003). *Franklin and Winston: An Intimate Portrait of an Epic Friendship* (1st ed.). New York: Random House.

Mingers, J. (2011). The Contribution of Systemic Thought to Critical Realism. *Journal of Critical Realism, 10*(3), 303–330. https://doi.org/10.1558/jcr.v10i3.303.

Oelsner, A. (2007). Friendship, Mutual Trust and the Evolution of Regional Peace in the International System. *Critical Review of International Social and Political Philosophy, 10*(2), 257–279. https://doi.org/10.1080/13698230701208061.

Rhodes, R. A. W. (2011). Thinking On: A Career in Public Administration. *Public Administration, 89*(1), 196–212. https://doi.org/10.1111/j.1467-9299.2011.01898.x.

Roshchin, E. (2014). Friendship and International Order: An Ambiguous Liaison. In S. Koschut & A. Oelsner (Eds.), *Friendship and International Relations* (pp. 89–106). Basingstoke: Palgrave Macmillan.

Sainsbury, K. (1996). *Churchill and Roosevelt at War: The War They Fought and the Peace They Hoped to Make* (Reprinted with Alterations). Houndmills [u.a.]: Macmillan.

Sasley, B. E. (2010). Affective Attachments and Foreign Policy: Israel and the 1993 Oslo Accords. *European Journal of International Relations, 16*(4), 687–709. https://doi.org/10.1177/1354066110366055.

Sasley, B. E. (2011). Theorizing States' Emotions. *International Studies Review, 13*(3), 452–476. https://doi.org/10.1111/j.1468-2486.2011.01049.x.

Scheff, T. J. (2000). *Bloody Revenge: Emotions, Nationalism and War* (Reprint). Lincoln, NE: Authors Guild Backinprint.com Ed.

Schmitt, C. (2007). *Theory of the Partisan: Intermediate Commentary on the Concept of the Political.* New York: Telos Press Publishing.

Smith, G. M. (2007). Kierkegaard: Responsibility to the Other. *Critical Review of International Social and Political Philosophy, 10*(2), 181–197. https://doi.org/10.1080/13698230701207964.

Smith, G. M. (2014). Friendship, State, and Nation. In S. Koschut & A. Oelsner (Eds.), *Friendship and International Relations* (pp. 35–50). Basingstoke: Palgrave Macmillan.

Stern-Gillet, S. (1995). *Aristotle's Philosophy of Friendship.* Albany: State University of New York Press.

Van Hoef, Y. (2010). *Friendship or Partnership? A Theory to Interpret the Role of Friendship Between Heads of State. With a Closer Look at the Relationships Between Churchill and Roosevelt, Kohl and Mitterrand, and Bush and Putin.* Thesis, University of Groningen, Groningen.

Van Hoef, Y. (2012a). *The Friendship Factor: An Investigation into the Potential of Social Network Analysis and Game Theory to Assess the Influence of Friendship in Politics on Historical Actors.* Thesis, University of Groningen, Groningen.

Van Hoef, Y. (2012b). Vriendschap en vijandschap. De relaties tussen Amerikaanse en Russische staatshoofden. In S. de Hoop (Ed.), *Erfenis van het verleden, geopolitiek en nieuwe dreigingen* (pp. 43–64). Groningen: Instituut voor Noord- en Oost-Europese Studies.

Van Hoef, Y. (2014). Friendship in World Politics: Assessing the Personal Relationships Between Kohl and Mitterrand, and Bush and Gorbachev. *AMITY: The Journal of Friendship Studies, 2*(1), 62–82.

Vion, A. (2014). Franco-German Friendship: A Dynamic Perspective. In S. Koschut & A. Oelsner (Eds.), *Friendship and International Relations* (pp. 109–122). Basingstoke: Palgrave Macmillan.

Vogler, G. (2016). Power Between Habitus and Reflexivity – Introducing Margaret Archer to the Power Debate. *Journal of Political Power, 9*(1), 65–82. https://doi.org/10.1080/2158379X.2016.1149309.

Wachterhauser, B. R. (1986). *Hermeneutics and Modern Philosophy.* Albany, NY: SUNY Press.

Wissenburg, M. (2014). Human-Animal Amity and Reciprocity. *AMITY: The Journal of Friendship Studies, 1*(2), 4–17.

Young, K. (1966). *Churchill and Beaverbrook. A Study in Friendship and Politics*. London: Eyre & Spottiswoode.

Yuri van Hoef is a lecturer of International Relations at the Department of History at Utrecht University, and a doctoral researcher at the University of Leeds. Previously, he held a lectureship in International Relations at the University of Groningen. His research examines the role of friendship in politics. Several of his publications deal with this subject, including 'Friendship in world politics: Assessing the personal relationships between Kohl and Mitterrand, and Bush and Gorbachev' for *AMITY: The Journal of Friendship Studies* (2014), and, co-authored with Felix Berenskoetter, '*Friendship and Foreign Policy*', edited by Cameron Thies, for the *Oxford Research Encyclopedia of Foreign Policy Analysis* (Oxford University Press 2017).

CHAPTER 4

More Rigor to Emotions! A Comparative, Qualitative Content Analysis of Anger in Russian Foreign Policy

Regina Heller

INTRODUCTION

Constructivist approaches to researching emotions in international relations usually apply discourse analysis or related interpretative methods that aim at exposing emotion-laden semantic patterns in the representations, mainly language, of social subjects in order to show how emotions construct the social reality. In the epistemological rationale of constructivism, this is fully legitimate. I share the basic constructivist view on and approach to emotions, understanding language as a key through which we gain access to emotions and their constitutive social function. However, such purely interpretative approaches produce problems. The classical interpretative approach via discourse analysis sometimes appears methodologically arbitrary and unsystematic. Furthermore, most scholars who study the discursive character of emotions prefer single-n case studies. Their results, therefore, remain a snapshot and cannot be generalized any further.

R. Heller (✉)
Institute for Peace Research and Security Policy at the University of Hamburg (IFSH), Hamburg, Germany

Finally, the interpretation of language and discourse is insufficient if we want to understand how emotions precede, form and sustain identity, for example: what function do emotions have in the social structure in which they are communicated and what effects they produce on international relations.

I suggest that we can only make full sense of the role and effects of emotions in international relations by integrating them into a broader and more systematic picture of time and space, with comparative elements and a more longitudinal perspective. Furthermore, we need to be more discriminate with emotional agency when analyzing the role of emotions. Not all utterances and displays of emotions necessarily need to have a constitutive function. We must ascertain who these 'subjects' are that enact emotions in international relations. Thus, I propose deviating from the conventional methodology in constructivist emotion research and adapting it. I propose a way of moving beyond these shortcomings by introducing a comparative, qualitative content analysis (QCA) of semantic patterns of emotions. I see two advantages in this approach: First, constructivist research can move from mere description to a more stringent 'testing' of the theoretical assumption that emotions are embedded in and shape social structures. Second, such an approach provides more robust insights about the actual impact of emotions on social structures and political behavior, hence on the interplay between emotions and international policy.

I illustrate this with an analysis of post-Soviet Russian foreign policy towards the West. I have identified semantic emotional patterns across a large corpus of documents produced by different Russian officials and institutions, thereby enabling me to compare them over time and issue area. Russian foreign policy towards the West is an insightful empirical case for studying the effects of emotions on political behavior and international relations. I have particularly concentrated on emotional responses to perceived disrespect of the country's international status. The idea that Russia is or must remain a great power in international relations exerts a strong identity-building power among the domestic political elite (Forsberg, Heller, & Wolf, 2014) and the concern over that self-defined great power status has strongly influenced Russian foreign policy strategy formulation since the mid-1990s (Russian Federation, 2000, 2008, 2013). Challenges to this status, therefore, are likely to infringe upon the Russian collective identity and, in a social psychological perspective, is likely to trigger emotions (Haidt & Joseph,

2004). It is a common view in Moscow today that Russia unrightfully holds a minor rank in international relations (Frolov, 2016), and that it is 'the West'—as the 'significant other' against which Russia traditionally measures its status—that is responsible for this status degradation. At the same time, we have seen Russia becoming increasingly assertive vis-à-vis the West over the years, thereby openly stressing discontent over Western conduct in this relationship. It is, therefore, plausible to assume that Russian policy shifts and changes, both temporary and more constant, are not exclusively the result of material considerations and extrinsic motivations but, to a significant extent, intrinsic and influenced by emotions, particularly by anger over Western status deprivation. My research interest lies in this longer-term change in the character of the Russian-Western relationship and I suggest that it is influenced by this socio-emotional factor.

I analyze the assumed link between status concerns and anger in Russian foreign policy towards the West by systematically identifying and comparing discursive representations of anger in official Russian speech in the context of two historical cases where a status conflict became obvious: in the context of the North Atlantic Treaty Organization (NATO) intervention in Kosovo in 1999 and in the context of the Russian-Georgian war in 2008. Document coding and comparative analysis was supported by an electronic program for qualitative content analysis (MAXQDA). With regard to the results, I have indeed found status-related anger markers in both cases; however, the substance of anger representations and their interplay with 'real' political behavior differ greatly. This leads me to conclude that the emotion anger in the two cases follows a different inner logic and serves different functions. The findings suggest that the applied method clearly enhances the researcher's ability to more rigorously investigate the discursive character of emotions as well as their impact on foreign policy and international relations and helps generate more reliable results in interpretative research designs.

Theory: Anger, Status and State Behavior

Anger, in its most simple psychological definition, is a negative emotional, individual reaction to a negative external stimulus. Kassinove (1995, p. 7) defines anger as a 'negative phenomenological (or internal) feeling state associated with specific cognitive and perceptual distortions and deficiencies (for example misappraisals, errors, and attributions of blame, injustice, preventability, and/or intentionality), subjective labelling, physiological changes, and action tendencies to engage in socially constructed and reinforced organized behavioural scripts'. Anger, as any emotion, is therefore strongly linked to the human body and it is of a highly subjective character. However, and in order to study the link between status concern/deprivation and anger in international relations, and Russian foreign policy in particular, we need to first clarify a couple of questions:

- Why is anger assumed to be the prevalent emotion in the status conflict between Russia and the West?
- What is anger and how can it be captured?
- Whose anger are we actually talking about and what is the level of analysis one has to consider?
- If, from a constructivist point of view, language is the key to identifying emotions, how can we get access to and find evidence of anger and angry behavior through language?

Anger in International Status Conflict

Social psychologists such as Mackie, Smith and Ray (2008), Stets and Burke (2000), Tajfel (1978) or Miller (2001) have added to the general definition mentioned above that anger stems from a feeling of frustration over failed verification of a positively distinctive identity. Thus, anger must be understood as a reactive attitude to perceived deliberate harm, unfair treatment, or disrespect aroused on behalf of or in defense of the self (Gould, 2003; Kelman, 1965; Rosen, 2005; Tiedens, 2001). Being respected in one's self-defined identity, therefore, is socially *and* emotionally important as it demonstrates that others attribute a specific rank and role—status—to somebody in a social relationship (Lindemann, 2000, p. 3; Wolf, 2008, p. 5, 2011, p. 106). Consequently, anger is indirect evidence of concern over status (Rosen, 2005, p. 50). Transferring this insight from social psychology to the international sphere, van Kleef et al. (Van Kleef, van Dijk, Steinel, Harinck, & van Beest, 2008, pp. 13–14) argue that anger is 'perhaps the most prominent and pervasive' emotion arising in social conflicts, be it between individuals, groups, organizations or nations, and, therefore, it is also potentially one of the most essential emotions in the study of international relations. Indeed, we know from the status-related literature in IR that states that care about status and see their status challenged seek to enhance it to a level they deem appropriate to their own role definition. This also makes them more dangerous as they are willing to 'resolve uncertainty around their status by competing more aggressively [...] to create larger roles for themselves in international affairs' (Volgy, Corbetta, Grant, & Baird, 2011, p. 11). Status attribution (recognition) by others is just as important as the possession of material status capabilities (ibid.). So status in international relations is not only a matter of material facticity but also to a large extent of perceptions of status consistency and inconsistency. Thus, it is subject to socio-emotional factors, which, as far as analytical approaches are concerned, have been greatly overlooked in the Russian-Western status conflict for a long time.

Facets of Anger

Kassinove's definition of anger points to at least two dimensions: The first relates to the *emotional experience* (*input*), that is, the feeling of anger over perceived unfair treatment, insult, provocation or verbal or physical aggression by others. The second dimension covers the emotion-induced *responses* triggered by these feelings, that is, the angry reactions (*output*). Anger triggers a number of typical responses—action tendencies—all of which have the function of coping with the emotion anger (Averill, 1983; Novaco, 1986) and in social psychology terms of restoring status. Action tendencies when angry are: open (anger) and covered (resentment) aggression, obstruction of or retreat from existing cooperation and/or display of autonomy through own initiatives. Kassinove's definition, moreover, shows that anger-induced individual reactions can be located on three different levels: an affective, a cognitive and a behavioral one. The affective dimension of anger is characterized by the inner tensions leading to spontaneous, mostly non-controllable arousal of the emotion of anger. On the cognitive level, anger triggers changes in moral judgments and evaluations: about the situation, the causer, his/her intentions, but also possible responses and their consequences. Finally, on the behavioral dimension, anger brings together the inner-individual affective and cognitive dynamics and transfers them towards specific, yet highly diverse action tendencies (Novaco, 1986). Averill's famous study on anger, for example, links it to aggression, although he objects that 'not all anger is aggressive, nor can all aggression be attributed to anger' (1983: preface). Furthermore, research on social conflict shows that anger tones down the desire for cooperation (Allred, Mallozzi, Fusako, & Raia, 1997) and even triggers obstruction of or total retreat from cooperation, or spurs more competition in social interaction (Butt, Choi, & Jaeger, 2005). Of course, this differentiation between affective, cognitive and behavioral levels only holds true for analytical purposes, as all three can go hand in hand. Angry verbal incitement is often accompanied by a specific physical activity, which can be oriented outwardly or inwardly, through aggression or withdrawal from social interaction (Isbell, Ottati, & Burns, 2006; Lerner & Keltner, 2000, 2001). Alternatively, a desire for retaliation may remain on a verbal or a symbolic level rather than being carried out, as they reflect upon the perceived frustration rather than the urge to respond with 'real' action (Averill, 1983, p. 1147; Mackie et al. 2008). Finally, when people change their evaluations under the influence of anger, they might also change the assessments regarding their self-interest which then leads to a change in behavior, thereby even breaking with established practices and behavioral norms of interaction (McDermott, 2004, p. 15). Research has proven that when angry, decisions are taken based on shorter notice, biased perceptions and information neglect, thereby accepting risks, consequences and losses higher than usual (Kahnemann & Tversky, 1979). The researcher is confronted here with the problem of equifinality, meaning that a behavior which resembles anger can well be the result of another rationale. It appears crucial to correlate the behavior under inspection of the mental representations—justifications and argumentations—that accompany them. This enables the researcher to better (although maybe not fully) identify genuine anger.

Anger must also be differentiated along temporal lines. Anger in a narrow understanding is a spontaneous and usually short-lived, episodic emotion that occurs in reaction to a specific event and then usually disappears again (Scherer, 2005). Cognitive and behavioral elements of anger are also episodic, although it might take a while until an individual reevaluates judgments about a situation that were formed under the influence of anger or is willing to adjust behavior. Yet, there are also longer-term conceptualizations of anger or emotional concepts with negative valence closely related to or overlapping with anger. Resentment is one of them. It is a long-term 'affective disposition' (Frijda, 2008, p. 73) that is enduring and describes an affective attitude towards somebody or something, even when there is no acute reason for being or turning angry (Deonna & Teroni, 2012, p. 8). Unlike an acute anger episode, affective dispositions do not interrupt cognitive processes or behavioral sequences (Fries, 2008,

p. 297). Resentment mainly puts the attention on subjectively perceived undeserved status inconsistencies based on moral categories (Feather & Nairne, 2009). How do anger and resentment interact? Decision-making when angry tends to be judged on the basis of resentment and ignores objective information. Vice versa, when the cause of frustration that triggered the anger endures and attention is constantly drawn towards the negative stimulus, including the negative feeling evoked (Bushman, 2002), rumination over unfair treatment starts and anger may connect with, integrate into and be activated from deeper layers of mental processing, thereby changing the organization of information processing substantially. Cathartic release from anger becomes impossible and instead 'avoidance coping' takes root, which is 'the intrusion into consciousness of autonomic failure-related thoughts elicited by the failure or by other external or internal stimuli' (Mikulincer, 1996, p. 203). When episodic anger turns into resentment, it carries a feeling of powerlessness against the provoker. Moral arguments become more important and the desire for revenge becomes more implicit and covered.

To sum up, when the emotion moves from acute anger to rumination and resentment, it is reflected in a modified use of speech and variances in the representations that stem from the cognitive, affective and behavioral level of anger. In the analysis we should therefore expect to see changes in the emotive pattern of anger. Any analysis of anger in Russian foreign policy, therefore, must take multidimensionality into account, both with regard to input and output, anger levels and their temporality. Methodologically, the three anger levels must be reflected and systematized in the coding scheme and translated into respective analytical categories according to their emotional logic.

Level of Analysis: Anger Agents and Their Speech

It is still not fully clear how an essentially bodily human experience can be translated onto a state. Can states really 'feel' anger concerning status deprivation? Can emotions such as anger be 'collectivized' and assigned to a nation? While it is true that 'states do not have a coherent body capable of feeling anything' (Hall, 2011, p. 532), states are made up of people and individuals who represent the state and share individual emotions. Through this process they generate collective identities, shared habits and interests, practices and preferences (Druckmann, 1993; Sasley, 2011). It is the state's representatives who identify with the state and through which a state 'feels'. Other authors suggest that we need to think of the state as a composite actor or 'institutionalized field', in which the individuals display certain similarities in their social configuration and share a number of social premises, so that a unified and collectively shared cognitive and emotional foreign policy disposition (Bourdieu, 1994, p. 9)—a specific mentality and habitus—becomes visible. When maintained by these authorized speakers in interactional-discursive contexts, such a mentality certainly influences a state's demeanor in international relations (Pouliot, 2010, p. 87).

Nevertheless, collective agents act in the most diverse environments, and therefore the potential or dynamic of collectivization of emotions can vary. For instance, in an environment such as in Russia where the policy process is far from transparent or is not a process of pluralistic bargaining and negotiation, we tend to be dealing with a smaller group of political decision-makers for which a shared identity can be more easily identified. This is even more so when no other 'corrective' influence, for instance a strong public as is (ideally!) the case in participation-oriented democracies, is rooted in the political culture of a country (e.g. Czempiel, 1998). Under such conditions, foreign policy elites are relatively free to transfer their social and emotional dispositions unto the national as well as the international scene. Emotional language, thus, represents both—it expresses the feeling state of the emotional agent and displays justifications of emotion-driven behavior. Through language, a speaker not only gives introspective emotive information about changes in his/her appraisal of the situation, the alleged causer, and the feelings triggered, but also comes up with new justification for non-cooperative, even confrontational action or other anger-induced, potentially costly, self-harming or intersubjectively unacceptable (deviant) behavior (Fries, 2008). With regard to methodology, therefore, I argue that it is essential to define the environment and agents of emotions. In the case of Russia, the political elites and their public speeches, rather than the discourse within the broader public, constitute the decisive spheres where empirical occurrences of anger and its impact on policy should be observed and studied.

Method: Studying Anger in Russian Foreign Policy

How have I proceeded methodologically in order to show the presence and influence of anger in Russia's foreign policy towards the West? I searched for evidence of anger by cumulating indicators of its input and output dimension in Russian-Western status conflicts. The centerpiece of the analysis was a qualitative content analysis (QCA) of statements and speeches from officials from the Russian foreign policy environment, understood here as authorized speakers, agents and administrative bodies who are carriers of the state's emotions. The research methodology included four main elements/steps: First, the selection of two cases of status conflict between Russia and the West; second, the development of the codebook, which includes the operationalization of anger in language and the development of semantic indicators of anger over status deprivation in Russian official language; third, the generation of the text corpus to be coded; and fourth, the actual coding process of the text corpus.

Case Selection

In order to test the assumption that socio-emotional factors, in particular perceived disrespect, are influential to Russian foreign policy behavior in its relations with the West, and shape or change the dynamic of the relationship over a longer period of time, I selected and juxtaposed two status conflict cases for the empirical analysis: the NATO's self-mandated intervention in Kosovo in 1999 and the Russian-Georgian war in August 2008. The choice of these two conflicts appealed to me for a several reasons: Firstly, it promised to provide cross-temporal insights about Russian anger patterns. The Kosovo issue took place in the late 1990s, that is, the pre-Putin era, when the stability of the political system had not yet come to rely so much on the domestic evocation of Russia's great power status and the relations with the West were still in a more cooperative rather than conflictive mode. The Russian-Georgian war, on the contrary, occurred at the height of the grievances over the West ignoring Russian interests, combined with an accelerated dynamic of domestic nationalist mobilization, which both triggered the most severe provocations in the relationship since 1991, with emerging narratives of a 'New Cold War'.

Secondly, although the Russian-Georgian war was not an issue directly related to Russian-Western relations, many observers have put forward the hypothesis that NATO's Kosovo intervention in 1999 and Russian conduct against Georgia in 2008 are highly interconnected. The former had created a 'perception among Russia's political elite that, rather than upholding liberal democratic values', NATO's intervention was not a necessary act to end human rights violations against Albanians, but rather 'constituted a selective defence of the interests of the leading Western powers and an act which bypassed 'traditional' international law and sidelined Russia in order to promote a particular vision of the European security order' (Averre, 2009, p. 575). A comparison of the two cases appears fruitful to analyze whether this shift in perception had an emotional basis and can be traced back to earlier status conflicts.

The Coding System

The coding system was developed deductively.[1] Deductive categories were mainly taken from the psychological and linguistic literature on anger and its manifestations in language (as presented above) and were structured along the three dimensions of anger: cognitive, affective, and behavioral (Table 4.1).

Cognitive Level (Code Category A)

On the cognitive level, I developed the analytical categories along Wierzbicka's linguistic model of an 'emotional scene' (1995). Emotional scenes describe the cognitive, hence reflected dimension of anger as it materializes in the verbalized mental representations of a speaker. In the given case, I took into account all verbalized mental representations that are evidence of a perceived mismatch between the speaker's status expectations and the policy of the Western interaction partners. Such verbalizations carry in themselves an implicit cognitive appraisal (*moral judgment*) by the speaker (*causer*) of who is responsible for a specific incident or in what way the West has deprived Russia of its status (*status-related problem/cause*) and how this negatively affects Russia's international status (*moral belief*). Mental representations are not reduced to one word or expression, but consist of 'frames', which are more complex constructions that 'identify problems and causes and provide solutions' (Benford & Snow, 2000).

Behavioral Level (Code Category B)

Wierzbicka's model of emotional scene includes two more categories of mental representations: (a) expressions of disappointment or frustration about an interacting partner's conduct (*condemnation*), and (b) reflections about what the speaker, who feels deprived of status, could/must do to stop the offender and why a specific reaction to the offense is or was necessary (*action required*). I have subsumed these indicators under behavior, because they represent what psychology describes as anger action tendencies. Such anger-induced (re)actions must be justified. As I expect speakers to justify their behavior as 'rightful', in particular when it deviates from or contradicts given interaction patterns, another analytical category for anger is '*action justification*'. Also derived from psychology is the category *impression management*, which coresponds to the obvious attempts by the speaker to rhetorically engage in positive, status-consistent self-descriptions.

Affective Level (Code Category C)
Under the influence of anger, language is additionally filled with spontaneous expressions of strong emotional subjectivity that more concretely reflect the feeling of anger. Such 'emotion-signifying' and 'emotion-expressing' words produce emotional impressions and attitudes and reflect the emotive attitude of the speaker. In line with Schwarz-Friesel (2007, p. 134ff), I subsume intensifications, interjections and modal particles under emotion-expressing lexical items; and direct and indirect (metonyms, metaphors and other rhetorical means) expressions of anger under emotion-signifying lexical items. Between the cognitive and the affective level, there are connotations. Connotations are cognitive attributions combined with affective representations. Connotations inform us about the speaker's affective position or attitude towards an object. Under the influence of anger, lexical items usually have a negative connotation ('He died' vs. 'He bit the dust'). Negative connotations tend to be represented by clichés, degradation and negative stereotypes, but also through more neutral words, which generate negative or positive feelings due to the historical or cultural emotive knowledge connected to them (for instance, 'Auschwitz'). Connotations evaluate but also simplify and dramatize. Simplification comes through binary codes (good-bad, right-wrong, we-them, friend-foe), self-fulfilling prophecies ('we knew this would happen'). Negative stereotyping is more typical and prominent under resentment. Stereotypes are mental representations in the long-term memory, which characterize objects, people, and groups, strongly simplify and distort their initial characteristics, thus leading to 'wrong conceptualizations' (Schwarz-Friesel 2007, p. 341). Linguistics points out that it is also largely a matter of culture whether and how a lexical item is attributed under the influence of anger.

Table 4.1 The coding system

Code category A (cognitive)		
Code group	Code	Semantic indicators/question for qualitative text analysis
A1 problem	A1.1 problem identification	In what way is Russia's status endangered or damaged?
	A1.2 problem attribution[a]	How is the damage to status characterized?
	A1.3 moral beliefs touched	What 'should' the status structure be?
A2 causer	A2.1 causer identification	Who is responsible for status damage?
	A2.2 causer attribution	How is the causer characterized?
	A2.3 causer objective	Why is the causer acting this way?

Code category B (behavioral)			
Code group	Code	Sub-code	Semantic indicators/questions for qualitative text analysis
B1 reaction impulse	B1.1 resentment	B1.1.1 'hidden' revenge desires	Rhetorical signs of spitefulness
		B1.1.2 inferiorizations	Rhetorical signs of indignation at the other
		B1.1.3 feelings of injustice	Expressions of displeasure about unfair treatment
	B1.2 condemnation	B.1.2.1 expressions of disapproval	Expressions of dissatisfaction with the other's conduct
		B1.2.2 demanding rectification of the wrong	Rhetorical demands towards the other
	B1.3 action required	B1.3.1 action type	What is the character of the suggested action?
		B.1.3.2 action justification	Why is an action necessary?
B2 impression management			What status image of Russia does the speaker construct?

Code category C (affective)		
Code group	Code	Semantic indicators/questions for qualitative text analysis

(*continued*)

Table 4.1 (continued)

C1 direct expressions of emotion		All lexeme that directly express state of emotionality—*obida, trevoga, vozmushhenie, ozabochennost', razocharovanie, priskorbno*, etc.
C2 dramatization	C2.1 interjections	Lexeme such as <u>hey!</u>, <u>ey!</u>, expressing sudden feelings of anger—*nu, uvy*, etc.
	C2.2 intensifying words	Lexeme such as <u>very</u> [angry] which intensify the expressed emotional state of mind—*krajne, sovershenno, ochen', absoljutno*, etc.
	C2.3 modal particles	Lexeme such as <u>unfortunately</u> (*k sozhaleniju*), <u>apparently</u> (*verojatno*) which concretize the speaker's attitude towards the content of his/her message
	C2.4 analogies	Indirect, metonymical descriptions of the experienced feeling of anger through comparisons, i.e. <u>as or like</u> (*tak zhe kak, huzhe chem*)
C3 simplification	C3.1 stereotyping/ historical analogies	Negative attributions and 'wrong' historical comparisons
	C3.2 binary codes	Contrasting <u>'good-bad'</u> juxtapositions
	C3.3 self-fulfilling prophecy	Positive or negative expectations or predictions about the other's behavior
C4 other rhetorical means	C4.1 sarcasm	Expressions of bitterness
	C4.2 appeal	Speaker directly addresses the audience
	C4.3 exclamation	Outcry of the speaker (exclamation mark indicative)
	C4.4 repetition	Repeating of words or sentences
	C4.5 metaphors	Figurative speech
	C4.6 rhetorical question	Answer is already implicitly given or not expected
	C4.7 irony	Saying the opposite of what is meant
	C4.8 rupture	Interruption of sentence, concealing the message
	C4.9 non-chained speech	Enumeration without conjunction
	C4.10 iteration	Use of a number of conjunctions where not necessary
	C4.11 colloquial speech	Ordinary, everyday speech
	C4.12 embedded story	Speaker tells a 'story' within his/her speech

[a]Note that there is a strong overlap between cognitive attributions (A1.2) and their affective representations in speech (C3.1). A double coding was conducted here

Text Sampling

The third step consisted in the selection of relevant texts for each case. The texts were mainly sourced from the Russian database INTEGRUM which covers not only primary documents from Russian political institutions but also includes broad media coverage (e.g. radio and television transcripts). Complementary material was identified on the internet. I defined the relevant foreign policy environment as a set of actors including the executive (the Russian president and the presidential administration, the foreign ministry and ministry of defense as well as the Russian prime minister), the legislative (the Russian parliament—Duma and Federation Council) and other figures of the foreign policy establishment (foreign policy scholars or eminent individuals), in as far as they commented on status-relevant issues.

Usually, when identifying relevant official speech in qualitative content analysis (also in discourse analysis), the point of departure is the definition of a set of key words according to which the text search is conducted. A search along simple key words created a number of problems in this case, because neither the notion 'status' (*status*) nor the notion 'disrespect' (*neuvazhenie*) produced sufficient results. There were also no reliable dictionaries available to capture all discursive representations of anger and status in Russian language. The overall search strategy was therefore adapted and refined. A contextualized search strategy was developed, combining predefined, status-relevant, thematic slots (see Tables 4.2 and 4.3) and issue-specific as well as actor-specific characteristics with notions from the semantic fields of 'status' and 'anger' (see Table 4.4).

Particularly in the INTEGRUM database, texts can be searched by means of specific operators (search keys) (Table 4.5).

In the Kosovo case, 80 texts were found through the contextualized text search; in the case of the Russian-Georgian war, 52 texts.

Coding Process

The coding process was supported by the qualitative data analysis software MAXQDA. Coding with MAXQDA has several advantages, the main one being that it can help handle large quantities of texts and generate a more comprehensive codebook. Moreover, documents can be coded qualitatively but also categorized along formal, predefined and self-defined variables attached to each document, such as *document date*

Table 4.2 Kosovo case search slots

Slot name	Slot description	Events/impulses for Russian anger (±2)[a]
'NATO option'	Russian counterpleas and reactions to incidents where the West urges for an increased role of NATO in the solution of the Kosovo crisis	May–December 1998
NATO bombings	Russian reactions to the unauthorized NATO bombings	22 March–end of August 1999
KFOR deployment	Russian verbal and substantial reactions to influence the path of the international post-conflict peacekeeping efforts in Kosovo	February–August 1999
Bringing Russia 'back on board'	Reactions from Russia to the West's efforts to integrate Russia into international peacekeeping and diplomacy in Kosovo	April 1999–August 1999

[a]The thematic slots were sub-specified both time and event-wise; as a corrective, the temporal parameters for the text search within each slot were expanded for two months. This way, text could be found close to an event as well as texts that were produced independent of an event

Table 4.3 Georgia case search slots

Slot name	Slot description	Events/impulses for Russian anger
Reintegration enforcement	Russian reactions to Georgian efforts to enforce reintegration of renegade regions Abkhazia, Adzharia and South Ossetia	January 2004–July 2008
Escalation of violence in Georgian separatist republics	Russian reactions to escalation of violence in Georgian separatist republics	June/July–August 2008
Russian military intervention	Russian justifications of military intervention in Georgia	8 August 2008–19 August 2008
Independence	Russian justifications of its recognition of South Ossetia and Abkhazia independence	26 August–end September 2008

(date of production), *document type* (statement, interview, media coverage or the like), *speaker* (executive, legislative, military, other), or *audience* (domestic, international). This way, MAXQDA facilitated the cross-case comparison of the results.

The text coding was performed manually, whereby at least 50 per cent of each case was coded by two coders in order to guarantee inter-coder reliability. The two coders regularly verified and discussed their codings and, where necessary, adapted the codebook. Through this process, the coding team inductively derived the code contents and developed additional ones. Codes and sub-codes with less than two coded segments were eliminated; and other categories with high content similarity were merged, where applicable, at a higher abstract level. MAXQDA provided tools for comprehensive analytical operations within each case and comparisons across the cases such as analyses of selected coded segments along defined categories (e.g. speaker group, date/time periods or proximity of two or more codes).

Table 4.4 Search categories for contextualized text sampling within the predefined slots

Search category	Search words (in Russian)
Actor	President, foreign minister, prime minister, minister of defense, representative, deputy, Putin, Medvedev, Ivanov, Lavrov etc.
Institution	Government, Kreml, Duma, Federation Council, foreign ministry, ministry of defense, NATO-Russia Council etc.
Context	Meeting, press-conference, summit, note, interview etc.
Interaction	West, United Nations, NATO, OSCE, United States, international community etc.
Activity	Reaction, measure, countermeasure, step, action, policy, move, diplomatic talks, initiative, meeting, protest etc.
Master frame 'status'	Semantic field status (and lack thereof)
Master frame 'anger'	Semantic field anger

Table 4.5 INTEGRUM query/search key example for contextualized document search

Slot	Impulse/event	INTEGRUM search key
'NATO option'	June 1998: U.S. Foreign Minister Albright introduces the idea of a NATO intervention if necessary without a UN mandate	(министр или премьер-министр или "Председатель Правительства" или "министр иностранных дел" или Президент или Ельцин) (Кремль или правительство или дума или "совет федерации" или парламент или МИД или "министерство иностранных дел" или "внешнеполитическое ведомство" или министерство) ((НАТО или США или запад) (вмешательство или интервенция или посредничество) Косово) (06.1998! д)

Analysis and Results

Did the methodology live up to its promises? What results did the comparative qualitative content analysis produce? In what way does the proposed methodological approach contribute to interpretative research on emotions?

A Systematic Picture of Anger Patterns in Russian Official Speech

In each case, the analysis produced a systematic and comprehensive picture of semantic anger patterns in Russian official language. The document-coding ratio, that is, the average number of coded segments (codings) in one text, shows that Russian status representations are largely filled with anger markers. The document-coding ratio in the Kosovo case in 1999 is 29, in the case of the Russian-Georgian war, it is 40 (Table 4.6). This is a strong argument in favor of the initial hypothesis that status issues in post-Soviet Russian foreign policy are highly embedded in and subject to emotions, independent of the current ruling elite or group.

The systematic qualitative analysis shows that anger over the lack of and the desire for social recognition is directed at different aspects of Russian status. The analysis points at least to three major fields where Russian leaders are concerned about external, particularly Western recognition: (a) approval of centrality (recognition of Russia's central role in the formulation and application of the international system's norms and rules); (b) approval of equality (recognition of Russia's right to consultation on and participation in major, mainly European, security arrangements); and (c) approval of primacy (recognition of Russia's historically cultivated, 'privileged' role in the post-Soviet region). Security issues also play a frequent role and appear to be a status-related anger point. However, the analysis suggests that we should not treat security concerns and concerns over social status as separate, but rather as strongly interrelated issues which have their foundation within Russian identity and display strong

Table 4.6 Document-coding ratio

	Documents	*Coded segments*	*Document-coding ratio*
Kosovo 1999	80	2299	29
Georgia 2008	52	2107	40

emotional overlap. Particularly with regards to the Russian-Georgian war in 2008, I noticed a strong emotional overlap between primacy-concerns and security frames. The conviction that Russia plays a prime role in its region, and that this mode of commanding produces security, mainly materializes in the speakers' moral beliefs, not in the problem identification. The idea that security interests are exclusively or predominantly motivated extrinsically should be reconsidered and researchers should be more sensitive towards seemingly competing frames and motives.

Varying Emotion Curves: Acute Anger, Resentment and the Link Between the Two

The anger patterns in 1999 and 2008 differ greatly in their substance and emotional function. The Kosovo case is a showcase for an acute anger episode, where the typical anger-induced, spontaneous logic of the action tendencies can be traced in the language as well as in behavior. Typically, all anger reactions were short-lived, including sporadic withdrawal from cooperation with the West. The Russian political elite returned to the usual level of cooperation and rhetoric, even in the domestic political environment, in which ultra-nationalist forces in the State Duma were still pushing and spreading Anti-Western narratives and perceptions. This was clearly conducive to further emotionalization of Russian foreign policy and potentially to aggravating tensions with the West. From August 1999 onwards, after the initial euphoria among the Russian establishment over Russian status 'achievements' had died down, and particularly after the resumption of cooperation with NATO and Russian inclusion into the G8, both post-evaluations and policy shifted back to 'normal' (Heller, 2014) (Chart 4.1).

In contrast, anger patterns in 2008 followed a resentment-logic rather than an acute anger episode. The analysis detected rumination over status issues up to a year before, starting with the imminent Western recognition of an independent Kosovo. This process triggered an actualization of status concerns and latent feelings of disrespect, and it significantly fostered the cognitive evaluations, affective rhetoric and behavior of the speakers during the five-day war with Georgia. Anger patterns in 2008 were constructed to a large extent along moralization logics, whereas in 1999, the speakers' condemning rhetoric had revealed surprise and disbelief about

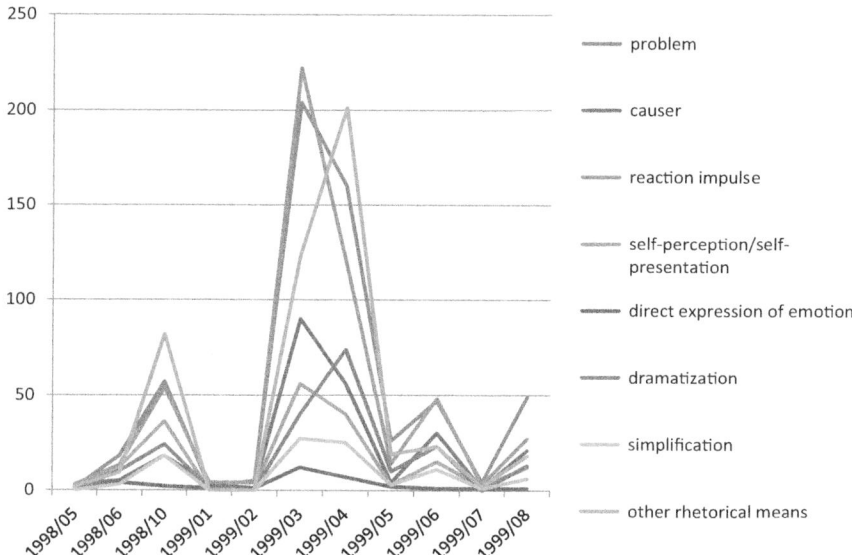

Chart 4.1 Anger curve Kosovo 1999

the West's conduct. These results clearly show that when the emotion moves from acute anger to rumination and resentment, this is also reflected in changes in the emotive patterns of the texts (Chart 4.2).

What Role Do Anger Agents Play?

The comparative analysis also gives more insights about who actually communicated anger and in which situations. Interestingly, despite a high fragmentation of the political spectrum in 1999, all speakers at that time were consistent and aligned in their general emotional attitude towards the NATO intervention. The ultra-nationalists in the State Duma, on the other hand, relied much more on anti-Western narratives and stereotypes, mainly drawn from World War II experiences and the antagonistic struggle of the Cold War period, than did officials from the executive. The latter seemed to deliberately avoid anti-Western agitation. The picture changed dramatically in 2008: Executive officials drew heavily on anti-Western stereotypes, although the knowledge that created these stereotypes had its foundation in the (perceived) status asymmetry and US

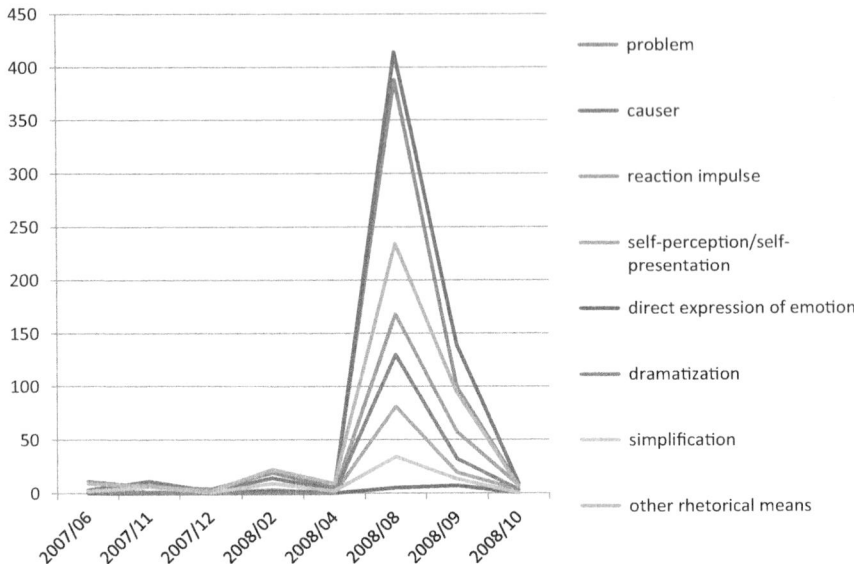

Chart 4.2 Anger curve Russian-Georgian war 2008

primacy of the Post-Cold War era, manifesting itself in liberal interventionist practices and Western-dominated changes in the normative foundations of the international system. Political synchronization (the elimination of opposition forces) in the ruling elite simulated unity in the assessment of and conduct regarding the events. In 2008, the Russian executive seemed much more determined to risk a confrontation with the West and to bear the consequences of this policy. Also, in the aftermath of the conflict, no reassessment of the course of action took place. The combination of resentment-rhetoric and the more substantial departure from cooperative and amicable relations with the West indicates that the perceived gains from such a course of action seemed to be greater than reconciliation.

Is There an Emotional 'Learning Curve'?

The findings suggest that the Russian establishment has undergone an emotional 'learning curve', that is, that rumination over perceived Western disrespect has reshaped the affective disposition towards the West over the years, thereby morphing initially intrinsic (social status) motivations to defend self-esteem into emotional foundations that inspire strategic power calculation. However, the analysis at hand cannot consistently show the processes through which initial anger over Western disrespect has intruded into the consciousness of Russian decision-makers and has turned into new patterns of anti-Western resentment over the years. One way to highlight this process and how it feeds into preferences, interests and strategic power calculations, would be to add more cases to the picture, trace and compare the emotional constants and changes therein, and complement them with more explicative methods such as process-tracing and a more systematic cost-benefit analysis.

Conclusion

The methodology suggested here—a comparative qualitative content analysis—helped me make sense of the changes in Russian foreign policy towards the West throughout the last 25 years and the more recent shift towards more assertiveness in the relationship. This diachronic (longitudinal) and synchronic (comparative) approach revealed the dynamics and effects of emotions on Russian decision-making and on Russian-Western (international) relations in a more systematic way than a temporally tightly defined, single-n case investigation of emotional discourses would have done. However, the findings are still only a small part of a much bigger picture, and in the Russian case, the researcher is well advised to broaden the object of investigation to a higher number of cases, such as NATO expansion, the European missile defense, the conflict over Ukraine and the Syria issue—all of which represent a latent or manifest status conflict.

The methodology could not solve one major problem that emotion research faces in general: the question of delineating intrinsic from instrumental uses of emotions in world politics. Therefore, some caution is advised in dealing with emotions in texts: We know that emotions can be strategically and instrumentally used by policy-makers in order to trigger specific reactions. I do not exclude that this is the case here as well. From my findings, I would suggest that emotions in the Russian context are primarily intrinsic and identity-driven, but they can and are indeed used instrumentally to reach a strategic domestic (strengthening regime legitimacy at home) or foreign polical (de-legitimizing specific Western norms and practices) goal. Materially, the Russian leadership is currently succeeding in increasing the basis of its international status, both domestically and internationally. Evoking emotions and creating and spreading anti-Western resentment represent important assets to this end.

Regarding the research process, a sensitive handling of different subjective understandings of emotions by each coder is important. Although the research group tried to ensure inter-coder reliability, a fully consistent understanding of the emotive value of the coded texts and segments is difficult to produce as one and the same passage resonates differently on an individual emotional level. What affects me does not necessarily move you. Finally, it appears indispensable to use native speakers as decoders. Emotions are more than simple information. In language, they reach deep into collective memories and are filtered by cultural dispositions as well as linguistic traditions. These last two points underline something fundamental about emotions, which reaches well beyond the scope of the methodology presented here: Emotions are definitely social, but, to a significant extent, they attain meaning only through individual experience.

Acknowledgment This article was written in the course of the research project "Claiming respect. Tracing the socio-emotional dimension of Russia's relations with the West" funded by the German Research Council (DFG).

Notes

1. Some codes were developed inductively, particularly those within C4.

References

Allred, K. G., Mallozzi, J. S., Fusako, M., & Raia, C. P. (1997). The Influence of Anger and Compassion on Negotiation Performance. *Organizational Behavior and Human Decision Processes, 70*(3), 175–187.

Averill, J. (1983). Studies on Anger and Aggression. *American Psychologist, 38*(11), 1145–1160.

Averre, D. (2009). From Pristina to Tskhinvali: The Legacy of Operation Allied Force in Russia's Relations with the West. *International Affairs, 85*(3), 575–591.

Benford, R. D., & Snow, D. A. (2000). Framing Processes and Social Movements: An Overview and Assessment. *Annual Review of Sociology, 26,* 611–639.

Bourdieu, P. (1994). Rethinking the State: Genesis and Structure of the Bureaucratic Field. *Sociological Theory, 12*(1), 1–18.

Bushman, B. J. (2002). Does Venting Anger Feed or Extinguish the Flame? Catharsis, Rumination, Distraction, Anger, and Aggressive Responding. *Personality and Social Psychology Bulletin, 28*(6), 724–731.

Butt, A. N., Choi, J. N., & Jaeger, A. M. (2005). The Effects of Self-Emotion, Counterpart Emotion, and Counterpart Behavior on Negotiator Behavior: A Comparison of Individual-Level and Dyad-Level Dynamics. *Journal of Organizational Behavior, 26*(6), 681–704.

Czempiel, E.-O. (1998). *Friedensstrategien. Eine systematische Darstellung außenpolitischer Theorien von Machiavelli bis Madariaga.* Opladen: Westdeutscher Verlag.

Deonna, J. A., & Teroni, F. (2012). *The Emotions. A Philosophical Introduction.* Abingdon and New York: Routledge.

Druckmann, W. (1993). *Personal Identity, National Identity and International Relations.* Cambridge: Cambridge University Press.

Feather, N. T., & Nairne, K. (2009). Effects of Observer's Own Status on Reactions to a High Achiever's Failure: Deservingness, Resentment, Schadenfreude, and Sympathy. *Australian Journal of Psychology, 60*(1), 31–43.

Forsberg, T., Heller, R., & Wolf, R. (2014). Introduction: Russia and the Quest for Status. *Communist and Post-Communist Studies, 47*(3–4), 261–268.

Fries, N. (2008). Die Kodierung von Emotionen in Texten. Part 1: Grundlagen. *Journal of Literary Theory, 1*(2), 293–337.

Frijda, N. H. (2008). The Psychologist Point of View. In M. Lewis, J. M. Haviland-Jones, & L. Feldman Barrett (Eds.), *Handbook of Emotions* (pp. 68–87). New York: Guilford Press.

Frolov, V. (2016). Govorit Moskva: chto Putin predlozhit miru v novoj mjunhenskoj rechi. Slon: Retrieved January 14, 2016, from https://slon.ru/posts/62473

Gould, R. V. (2003). *Collision of Wills: How Ambiguity About Social Rank Breeds Conflict.* Chicago: University of Chicago Press.

Haidt, J., & Joseph, C. (2004). Intuitive Ethics: How Innately Prepared Intuitions Generate Culturally Variable Virtues. *Daedalus, 133*(4), 55–66.

Hall, T. (2011). We Will Not Swallow This Bitter Fruit: Theorizing a Diplomacy of Anger. *Security Studies, 20*(4), 521–555.

Heller, R. (2014). Russia's Quest for Respect in the International Conflict Management in Kosovo. *Communist and Post-Communist Studies, 47*(3–4), 333–343.

Isbell, L. M., Ottati, V. C., & Burns, K. C. (2006). Affects and Politics. Effects on Judgments, Processing, and Information Seeking. In D. P. Redlawsk (Ed.), *Feeling Politics. Emotion in Political Information Processing* (pp. 57–86). New York: Palgrave Macmillan.

Kahnemann, D., & Tversky, A. (1979). Prospect Theory: An Analysis of Decision Under Risk. *Econometrica, 47*(2), 263–291.
Kassinove, H. (1995). *Anger Disorders. Definition, Diagnosis and Treatment.* London: Routledge.
Kelman, H. C. (1965). *International Behaviour. A Socio-Psychological Analysis.* New York et al.: Holt, Rinehart & Winston.
Lerner, J., & Keltner, D. (2000). Beyond Valence: Toward a Model of Emotion-Specific Influences in Judgement and Choice. *Cognition and Emotion, 14*(4), 473–493.
Lerner, J., & Keltner, D. (2001). Fear, Anger and Risk. *Journal of Personality and Social Psychology, 81*(1), 146–159.
Lindemann, T. (2000). *Die Macht der Perzeptionen und Perzeptionen von Mächten.* Berlin: Duncker & Humblot.
Mackie, D. M., Smith, E. R., & Ray, D. G. (2008). Intergroup Emotions and Intergroup Relations. *Social and Personality Psychology Compass, 2*(5), 1866–1880.
McDermott, R. (2004). *Political Psychology in International Relations.* Ann Arbour: The University of Michigan Press.
Mikulincer, M. (1996). Mental Rumination and Learned Helplessness: Cognitive Shifts During Helplessness Training and Their Behavioral Consequences. In I. G. Sarason, G. R. Pierce, & B. R. Sarason (Eds.), *Cognitive Interference. Theories, Methods, and Findings* (pp. 191–209). Hillsdale, NJ: Lawrence Erlbaum.
Miller, D. T. (2001). Disrespect and the Experience of Injustice. *Annual Review of Psychology, 52*(1), 527–553.
Novaco, R. (1986). *Anger as a Clinical and Social Problem. Advances in the Study of Aggression.* New York: Academic Press.
Pouliot, V. (2010). *International Security in Practice: The Politics of NATO-Russia Diplomacy.* New York: Cambridge University Press.
Rosen, S. P. (2005). *War and Human Nature.* Princeton and Oxford: Princeton University Press.
Russian Federation. (2000). The Foreign Policy Concept of the Russian Federation. Approved by Vladimir Putin, President of the Russian Federation on June 28, 2000. Retrieved from http://fas.org/nuke/guide/russia/doctrine/econcept.htm
Russian Federation. (2008). The Foreign Policy Concept of the Russian Federation. Approved by Dmitry A. Medvedev, President of the Russian Federation, on 12 July 2008. President of Russia Official Web Portal. Retrieved from http://archive.kremlin.ru/eng/text/docs/2008/07/204750.shtml
Russian Federation. (2013). Concept of the Foreign Policy of the Russian Federation, Approved by President of the Russian Federation V. Putin on 12 February 2013, The Ministry of Foreign Affairs of the Russian Federation

Official Site, Retrieved from http://archive.mid.ru//brp_4.nsf/0/76389FE C168189ED44257B2E0039B16D

Sasley, B. E. (2011). Theorizing States' Emotions. *International Studies Review*, 13, 452–476.

Scherer, K. R. (2005). What Are Emotions? And How Can They Be Measured? *Social Science Information*, 44(4), 695–729.

Schwarz-Friesel, M. (2007). *Sprache und Emotion, 2. Volume*. Tübingen and Basel: Francke.

Stets, J., & Burke, P. J. (2000). Identity Theory and Social Identity Theory. *Social Psychology Quarterly*, 63(3), 224–237.

Tajfel, H. (1978). The Psychological Structure of Intergroup Relations. In H. Tajfel (Ed.), *Differentiation Between Social Groups: Studies in the Social Psychology of Intergroup Relations* (pp. 27–98). London: Academic.

Tiedens, L. (2001). Anger and Advancement Versus Sadness and Subjugation: The Effect of Negative Emotion Expressions on Social Status Conferral. *Journal of Personality and Social Psychology*, 80(1), 86–94.

Van Kleef, G., van Dijk, E., Steinel, W., Harinck, F., & van Beest, I. (2008). Anger in Social Conflict: Cross-Situational Comparisons and Suggestions for the Future. *Group Decision and Negotiations*, 17(1), 13–30.

Volgy, T. J., Corbetta, R., Grant, K. A., & Baird, R. G. (2011). Major Power Status in International Politics. In T. J. Volgy, R. Corbetta, K. A. Grant, & R. G. Baird (Eds.), *Major Powers and the Quest for Status in International Politics: Global and Regional Perspectives* (pp. 1–26). New York: Palgrave.

Wierzbicka, A. (1995). The Relevance of Language to the Study of Emotions. *Psychological Inquiry*, 6(3), 248–252.

Wolf, R. (2008). Respekt. Ein unterschätzter Faktor in den Internationalen Beziehungen. *Zeitschrift für Internationale Beziehungen*, 15(1), 5–37.

Wolf, R. (2011). Respect and Disrespect in International Politics. The Significance of Status Recognition. *International Theory*, 3(1), 104–142.

Regina Heller is a Senior Researcher at the Institute for Peace Research and Security Policy at the University of Hamburg (IFSH), Germany. Her research interests include Russian foreign and domestic policy, Europe and the post-Soviet space, normative change and norm competition as well as peace and conflict studies. Throughout the last years, Regina Heller has been conducting a DFG-funded research project on status and emotions in Russian foreign policy vis-à-vis the West. She contributed a chapter entitled *Subjectivity matters. Reconsidering Russia's Relations with the West* to the volume *Russia and European Security* edited in 2011 by Roger E. Kanet and Maria R. Freire. She co-edited a special issue on status and emotions in Russian foreign policy in *Communist and Post-Communist Studies* (2014).

PART II

Emotions Shaped by Powerful Actors and Institutions

CHAPTER 5

Auto-ethnography and the Study of Affect and Emotion in World Politics: Investigating Security Discourses at London's Imperial War Museum

Audrey Reeves

INTRODUCTION: THE SOCIAL RESEARCHER AS AFFECTIVE AND EMOTIONAL SUBJECT

This chapter demonstrates how auto-ethnography enables researchers to use their own affective and emotional experiences in prominent political spaces, such as national war museums, to generate fuller understandings of the (re)production of transnationally influent security discourses. Scholarship on emotions and world politics increasingly draws attention to scholars' own emotional experiences as influencing and shaping the research process (Jauhola, 2015; Parashar, 2015; Sylvester, 2011). Simultaneously, the method of auto-ethnography, the use of the lived experience of the researcher as a methodological resource, is gaining traction in the study of world politics (Brigg & Bleiker, 2010; Dauphinee,

---

A. Reeves (✉)
Cardiff University, Cardiff, UK

© The Author(s) 2018
M. Clément, E. Sangar (eds.), *Researching Emotions in International Relations*, Palgrave Studies in International Relations,
https://doi.org/10.1007/978-3-319-65575-8_5

2010; Doty, 2010; Fitzgerald, 2015). In this contribution, I build bridges between bodies of research on affect/emotion and auto-ethnography. My reflection starts from the epistemological perspective that social research never achieves the ideal of objectivity or value-neutrality prescribed by positivist models of research: it is always historically, culturally, and politically situated. Acknowledging the researcher as an affectively and emotionally constituted subject makes the research process and outputs more reflexive by drawing attention to the subjectivities, biases, and assumptions constituted and expressed in our affective and emotional experiences. I show how auto-ethnography provides space for acknowledging and critically investigating our affective and emotional experiences, which in turn can generate innovative understandings of the importance of affects and emotions in world politics.

The research question that led me to conduct auto-ethnography is the following: How do affective and emotional experiences at London's Imperial War Museum (hereafter IWM) participate in the (re)production and transformation of security discourses? Before considering why I chose auto-ethnography and how it helped me answer this question, it is worth addressing three theoretical and conceptual points: (1) Why a museum? (2) Why affective *and* emotional experiences? (3) How are affects and discourses connected?

As Christine Sylvester notes, International Relations (IR) has often overlooked the close relationship between museums and international politics, deeming it too 'trivial' (2015, p. 1). Trivialising museums, and treating them as irrelevant to international relations, reproduces the intuitive but problematic assumption that sites of leisure/peace and zones of danger/war mutually exclude one another (Lisle, 2000, 2013). Although this assumption is common in global discourses of security, we should question it for at least three reasons. First, terrorist attacks in areas frequented by tourists from Bali to Paris compellingly undermine it. At a time when global media routinely shows images of tourism hotspots struck by violent attacks, it becomes increasingly difficult to defend the claim that tourism and security 'naturally' belong to different realms and social scientific disciplines. Second, fully understanding world politics requires curiosity for spaces and places dismissed 'as merely "private," "domestic," "local," or "trivial"' (Enloe, 2000, p. 3). As noted by feminist and postcolonial theorists, these places often naturalise global inequalities of gender, race, and class, amongst others, most seamlessly and thus most insidiously, and are therefore worthy of critical investigation.

Third, and most relevant to the topic of this volume, war museums and memorials provide interesting places to study the role of affect and emotion in world affairs. In heritage studies, war museums and memorials are well-known as sites for the circulation and reproduction of ideas about national identity. They provide places where citizens—particularly cultural and economic elites—gather to build common narratives about the nation-state's engagement in past wars and its identity as a security actor within a broader world order. In the British context, the IWM has acted as a central public depositary of memories of post-1914 wars waged by Britain for a century. The IWM is the flagship branch and headquarters of the broader IWM family,[1] founded by the UK government and to a large extent financed by it (Imperial War Museums, 2014a). Since their establishment in 1917, these museums commemorate wars involving the UK and its former empire from 1914 onwards.

In addition to their importance at the national level, prominent commemorative institutions like the IWM (see Picture 5.1) are also sites of public diplomacy and transnational communication about warfare. The Imperial Museum is a popular tourist attraction in the world's most visited city. It attracted 1.1 million visitors in 2015 (ALVA, 2016), a number expected to grow in coming years. In 2013–2014, forty per cent of visitors to the five IWM attractions came from overseas (Imperial War Museums, 2014b, p. 23); a percentage undoubtedly higher in the London branch, located in the most internationally visited city in the world. Through the years, the IWM has therefore instructed millions of home and foreign visitors into the histories of wars waged by the UK from World War I to the present, and thus it participates in shaping international public opinion about the national identity of the UK and its involvement in world affairs, including through military means. The instruction of visitors into distant and recent memories of 'Britain at war', far from a dry history lesson, is done in such a way as to deeply move visitors and leave a lasting impression: as I will show, it involves the engineering of both affect and emotion.

Affects and emotions, it is worth clarifying, are related but 'follow different logics and pertain to different orders' (Massumi, 2002, p. 27). Affects include visceral reactions (such as laughter, tears, and screams) that we associate in everyday speech with emotions (such as joy, sadness, and fear), but they specifically relate to the corporeal, somatic, embodied, and sensorial dimension of human experience (Deleuze & Guattari, 1980). The analytical distinction between emotion and affect can be summarised

Picture 5.1 The Imperial War Museum (London). Source: Wikipedia Commons, https://upload.wikimedia.org/wikipedia/commons/a/a8/Imperial_War_Museum_Front.JPG (Public domain licence by picture author, Alkivar at English Wikipedia)

along three axes: conscious/unconscious; subjective/pre-subjective; and representable/non-representable. For the sake of clarity, I illustrate each with reference to experiences you may have when visiting the IWM.

To start with, emotions are conscious, and affects typically unconscious. Museum visits involve a myriad of affective stimulations that most of us do not register in a conscious way. The IWM's upper floors host a permanent exhibition dedicated to the commemoration of the Holocaust. It would be impossible to consciously register the hundreds of material details that make the Holocaust Gallery affectively powerful, yet all contribute to an atmosphere heavy with death and atrocity. In this constricted, dark, tunnel-shaped space, affects include the sensuous pressure of the low ceiling and narrow passageways, a quiet and gloomy soundtrack, the sight of harrowing photos of bodies piled into mass graves and of women lying naked on the street after having been raped by soldiers; concentration camp uniforms on display; concrete floors and walls; sleek metallic surfaces; and glass display cases. In a room dedicated to Auschwitz, survivors' stories play from speakers placed at a low level in front of a three-dimensional reconstitution of the concentration camp. You must sit and place your ear close to the speaker to hear the recording distinctly, which gives the impression of hearing a ghost whispering secrets. At this point of my visit, I took out my fieldwork notebook and wrote down arising emotions: I felt 'loneliness and despair' in face of the horrors depicted before me. I was conscious of feeling these emotions (as evidenced by the notes in my notebook), although certainly not of the full extent of affects circulating in the gallery, which even several pages of notes could not fully or accurately describe.

In addition to being consciously experienced, emotion is easily verbally represented, whilst affect often eludes representation. This is why some refer to affect theory as non-representational theory (Thrift, 2008). It is easy for me to put words on how I felt in the Holocaust Gallery: 'loneliness'; 'despair'. It is much harder to convey the full detail and complexity of how the gallery is constructed as a space, and how it felt to be in it. To an important extent, it is impossible to represent in words the experience of walking through that gallery. The elusiveness of affect is an epistemological and methodological challenge for the social researcher. How can we study something that resists representation? If words do not easily represent affect, they can evoke it. Have we not all at some point been moved by a novel, a poem, or a letter from a loved one? I borrow from the writing genre of the travelogue to evoke affect. As a literary genre, the travelogue occupies a liminal space between the 'real' (it factually describes how one got from a place to another) and the 'artistic' (it uses metaphors and embellishment in an attempt to captivate the reader) (Lisle, 2006b, pp. 27–30). Its intermediary status between the description of movement and its aestheticisation provides an opportunity to capture the museum experience as a 'visceral encounter between the flesh of the body and the flesh of the world' (Fullagar, 2001, p. 172). Although the travelogue's primary material is the lived experience of the museum, its production involves 'artistic' decisions on what to include/exclude and what narrative form to adopt to produce a personal text that grips and moves the reader. This writing method does not, of course, provide an exact or full rendering of the IWM experience; not only is the account selective, but the experience will vary depending on the visitor and the day of the visit. However, affects are too politically important to let their elusiveness discourage us from interrogating them.

Affects are politically important because, while emotions are subjective, affects are pre-subjective and participate in the constitution of subjectivities we inhabit, such as the tourist, the citizen, or the researcher. Emotions are subjective in that they are 'owned' by the individual subject (Massumi, 2002, p. 28). Emotion is what you find when you look within yourself and find you have been moved into a state of mind that you can label and recognise as 'yours', if temporarily. 'Loneliness' and 'despair' are personal and subjective interpretations of how *I* felt in the gallery. In contrast, affects fluidly circulate in social space around and through us. At the Holocaust Gallery, visitors adopted stooped postures, slow and silent movements, drawn features, and quiet tones of voice. These bodily dispositions spread almost instantly from one visitor to the next, and contributed to the dark mood and atmosphere of the space as a whole. Affect, therefore, is most usefully conceptualised as circulating through people, and not as living within them. In this process of circulation, it shapes us physically by altering our postures and movements, but also socially. At the Holocaust Gallery, affect is essential to convey in a powerful way the moral abjection of the genocide of Jewish people and other minorities between 1933 and 1945. For students of world politics, the pre-subjective character of affect is crucial because it attunes us to thus far overlooked channels through which public and private institutions such as museums shape what poststructuralists refer to as 'security discourses'.

By security discourses, I mean relatively stable constellations of linguistic and non-linguistic practices that organise the (re)production of knowledge and meaning in the field of 'security' (Foucault, 2002 [1969], pp. 34–43; see also Hall, 1992, p. 291 in Wetherell, Yates, & Taylor, 2001, p. 72). They are the 'paradigms, policies, and practices' (Cohn, 2006, p. 91) around which people in a given social space 'speak' and 'do' security. Discourses become hegemonic when they succeed in fixing meaning and knowledge in such a way that they become 'common sense' (Laclau & Mouffe, 2001); discourses that are not hegemonic are often described as 'alternative'. Despite their relative stability, hegemonic discourses never remain closed and fixed as alternative discourses continuously challenge them. They evolve in such a way that yesterday's common sense (e.g. racial segregation in the US military, still widespread at the end of World War II) eventually transforms itself into something new (e.g. the normalisation of racial integration in the US Armed Forces from the 1960s onward).

Discourses make themselves accessible to people through texts, which include 'anything which we think has meaning, in one way or another *for us*' (Carver, 2002, p. 50). This comprises written texts, pictures, objects, movies, conversations, built spaces, and patterns of bodily movement, inter alia. Poststructuralist IR has a long history of analysing texts (often written documents, but increasingly non-linguistic forms as well) through which hegemonic security discourses are established, (re)produced, and challenged (e.g. Campbell, 1998; Doty, 1993; Hansen, 2006; Weldes, 1999).

As suggested by Ernesto Laclau (2004, p. 326), 'something belonging to the order of *affect* has a primary role in discursively constructing the social'. As the Holocaust Gallery example suggests, museum and memorial designers, curators, and architects purposefully choose affectively activating architectural designs to move us physically and emotionally and, in this process, construct meaning about warfare and security. IR literature has not yet fully investigated what lies at the intersection of affect and discourse (Solomon, 2015, p. 66). It is true that some have drawn attention to the manipulation of affect in situations of crisis such as the attacks of 9/11 (Holland, 2015; Holland & Solomon, 2014; Massumi, 2005; Ross, 2006). However, the global implications of the 'staging of affect' (Thrift, 2008) in everyday life situations such as war museums and memorials remain under-explored (for an exception see Hatch, 2014).

The rest of this chapter unfolds as follows. First, I explain what auto-ethnography is and why it provides a useful method to explore the political role of affect and emotion at a world-renowned war museum. Second, I detail how I deployed this method during my visits at the IWM in 2014–2015 and during the analysis that followed these visits. In this process, I explain how I reached the conclusion that came out of this research process: that the staging of affect at the IWM constructs the UK as a conductor of 'Just Wars', which obscures questionable aspects of the violence perpetrated by the UK and its allies in past and present military interventions. Third, I explain how confronting my own emotions of comfort and ease at the IWM productively pushed the theoretical development of my argument to include dynamics of consumption and class reproduction at the museum. Fourth, I conclude by tracing the limits of my auto-ethnography and lessons learned on its use in the context of this project.

Auto-ethnography as Method: What Is It and Why Choose It?

Like traditional ethnography, auto-ethnography immerses the researcher in the social environment under study—here, the IWM. Auto-ethnography encompasses elements of traditional ethnography in that it creates data from the observation and analysis of the behaviour and speech of other social actors, such as other visitors and museum personnel at the IWM. However, auto-ethnography distinguishes itself by calling on the researcher's own body 'as a site of scholarly awareness and corporeal literacy' (Spry, 2001, p. 706). Although auto-ethnography is sometimes at risk of becoming an exercise in 'navel gazing', narcissism, and vanity (see also Brigg & Bleiker, 2010, p. 789; Inayatullah, 2011, pp. 7–8), it is first worth noting that it is a priori not a personal investigation of the self, but a 'technique of social investigation conducted *through* the self' (Wakeman, 2014, p. 708, original emphasis). The self is not the object of the research but a 'methodological resource' to make sense of a particular social phenomenon (Brigg & Bleiker, 2010, p. 788).

My deployment of auto-ethnography at the museum entails, in the first instance, anchoring my consciousness into the museum as a material and sensorial environment, a basic mindfulness technique. I notice the feel of contact between the body and the ground, surrounding sounds, visual cues, floating smells, and so on. This grid of analysis addresses all five senses, as well as somatic awareness (consciousness of moving parts of the body, e.g. lifting an arm) and proprioception (the sense of one's movements in relation to the environment, such as going up or down). I document my affective experience of the museum in fours ways: (1) written notes taken during and immediately after the visits; (2) audio recordings of ambient noise, music, or my own narration of what was on display; (3) photos and sketches drawn on the spot; (4) documentation such as promotional flyers, maps, and restaurant menus, and artefacts such as items bought at the gift stores. I pay special attention to interaction between bodies and space, noting down sensations and patterns of movement generated by large brightly lit rooms and dark and constricted tunnels, by gloomy soundscapes and the chattering of cafés, by the humming buzz of a dense and excited crowd in the great hall and the solemnity of closely monitored galleries dedicated to commemorating the darkest memories of war.

I came to use auto-ethnography primarily because, due to its emphasis on the researcher's embodied, and thus affective, experience, this method provides a potent complement to existing discourse analytic and traditional ethnographic approaches, as well as other traditional qualitative research methods like interviews, surveys, and textual analysis. Auto-ethnography does justice 'to the importance of felt experience, and even to strange and hitherto excluded bodily and emotional sensations' in the creation of knowledge, in a way that IR as a discipline does not often recognise (Brigg & Bleiker, 2010, p. 795). In 2012, when I started researching museums, traditional methodological advice in IR did not offer much to help me understand how to make political sense of affective experiences at museums. The discipline inherits this blind spot from a philosophical tradition that treats the mind as superior to the body in its capacity to produce reliable knowledge (Büscher, Urry, & Witchger, 2011, p. 3; Yanow, 2014, p. 369). Conventional social scientific wisdom holds that physical distance, rather than proximity, between the researcher's body and the object of research favours an intellectual distance conducive to objectivity. As a result, investigations in IR and social sciences generally privilege the ocular as a way of accessing truth. Observing can be done at arm's length; it allows for a physical distance between the researcher and the object of research (Jonas, 2001 [1966], p. 135). In contrast, touching, tasting, or smelling the object of research involves a more intimate physical contact deemed detrimental to objectivity. Thus, traditional methodological advice focuses on the collection of 'observations' and 'evidence' (from the Latin *videre,* to see) and the building of *theory* (from the Greek *theoria,* looking at) (Kavanagh, 2004; Levin, 1999, p. 2).

Observation, however, is not politically neutral. Foucault has famously theorised the gaze as an instrument of power (Foucault, 2012 [1977]). Feminists have also denounced the equation between sight and objectivity as masking the reproduction of unequal power relations between an active masculinised observer and a passive feminised observed (Mulvey, 2006 [1975], p. 346). As Donna Haraway (1988, p. 581) argues, the idea of a neutral gaze is dangerously deceptive: it conveys the misleading illusion that the social scientist is disembodied and god-like, 'seeing everything from nowhere' (1988, p. 581). If it remains disembodied, the act of observing easily becomes a 'conquering gaze', one that arrogates itself 'the power to see and not be seen' (1988, p. 581). Auto-ethnography insists on 'the particularity and embodiment of all vision'; it allows the observer to be observed back (Haraway, 1988, p. 582). Performing auto-ethnography involves noticing and analysing not only what you see, but also what you feel. The principle runs against the assumption that reason—coded masculine in Western thought—must dominate the feminised realm of sensation and emotion as a way to create knowledge. Auto-ethnography invites us to let go of the mind/body, reason/emotion, masculine/feminine dichotomies, and use *both* our bodies and minds to sense and make sense of world politics.

Given the limited (but growing) extent to which IR offers instances and discussions of auto-ethnography, human geographers with an interest in affect and emotion provide a useful source of inspiration. They have convincingly argued that 'approaches associated with being and doing, with participation and performance, with ways of knowing that depend on direct experience' offer a privileged access to 'the world as mediated by feeling' (Anderson & Smith, 2001, p. 9; see also Pile, 2010, p. 6). Derek McCormack justifies focusing on his own subjective experience when researching Dance Movement Therapy, another social phenomenon saturated with affect and emotion, rather than interviews because the latter

> tended to get people to provide some interpretive, after-the-event sense to something that, as it was playing out, did not seem to require such sense to happen. It seemed that while ... it was movement that was the important thing, the sense of this movement disappeared when one tried to capture it through meaningful reflection. (2003, p. 493)

In other words, auto-ethnography allows a sense of intimacy and proximity (Pile, 2010, p. 10) that lends itself to a focus on affective flows that circulate in a given space more than traditional approaches, more often focused on seeing than feeling.

Much like dance, wartime heritage visits produce meaning through lived experience (Crang 1994 in Waterton & Watson, 2014, p. 61). Multisensorial stimulation in war museums include artefacts, photos, films, colours, and staff attires; music, sound effects, audio guides, and other visitors' voices; flight simulators, video games, touchscreens, and interactive exhibits; as well as souvenirs at the gift shop, and food and drinks at the cafe. Museum curators and designers carefully craft the spatial and temporal flow of such sensuous intensities through what Nigel Thrift calls 'the staging of affect, most of which revolve around *generating engagement* through the manipulation of mood' (2008, p. 245). Auto-ethnography provided a way of capturing the staging of affect at the museum in a deeper and more subtle way than other available methods.

Different lifestyles and interests hone different affective sensitivities that researchers can creatively put to use during the research process. A painter or photographer may pay more attention to colours and lighting; a musician to soundscapes and music; a chef to smells and tastes in the museum cafés. We do not need to be professional artists to draw on these alternative resources; all of us have developed in various circumstances such embodied ways of knowing, although they will vary based on past experiences and life trajectories. During fieldwork, I used affective sensitivities developed through fifteen years of training in contemporary ballet, to compensate for the silence of methods textbooks on how to research affect. For most people, in daily life, the continuous repositioning of the body in relation to the physical and human environment happens unconsciously. For instance, elevator riders usually stand as far from the other passengers as they can without any conscious effort. Performance artists, unlike the elevator riders, learn to *consciously* move in relation to an environment (e.g. the theatre) that is both human (other performers, the audience) and non-human (lighting, sets, costumes, props, music, and so on). The training I received as a dancer led me to notice that, just like a theatre stage, a war museum deploys affective stimuli that choreograph movement in space, such as the sorrowful bodily movements of visitors at the Holocaust Gallery, in ways that produce meaning.

Would another researcher with different affective sensitivities find similar insights? Such a question leads to another: is auto-ethnography anything but one person's perspective? How are we to handle concerns with the validity, reproducibility, and generalisability of the findings? The first step towards an answer is that auto-ethnographies do not pursue objectives of knowledge creation in the same way that more scientifically inclined projects do. It starts from the premise that the knowledge created is not absolute but relational: a relationship between the writer and the reader. The objective is not to prove a hypothesis, but to invite the reader to adopt a different theoretical outlook, and convince them that this outlook has something positive to contribute to our way of knowing 'international politics'. In this context, research is valid when it offers a perspective that is innovative but believable, relevant, convincing, and helpful to the reader in making sense of the world (Ellis, Adams, & Bochner, 2010, para. 34) and in 'open[ing] up new perspectives on political dilemmas' (Brigg & Bleiker, 2010, p. 779). Brigg and Bleiker usefully draw attention to the relationality of all knowledge production, making auto-ethnography less different than it seems at first, as it is like other research evaluated by a peer group (2010). I accept this last argument with one caveat: it obscures the writer's authority as expert of their topic and sites—especially the author who has gone to extra length to show how intensely they inhabited the site. Why should a reader unfamiliar with the topic and sites be expected to produce an informed judgment and critique my interpretation?

As one solution to this problem, I have chosen to embed auto-ethnography, the primary source of data creation, in a broader discourse analysis. I triangulate auto-ethnographic findings with accounts found in texts published by museum curators and architect firms. In addition, I compare my own affective and connected emotional reactions with visitor reviews on TripAdvisor. This triangulation buttresses auto-ethnographic claims and demonstrates that they reliably illuminate an intersubjective phenomena. In so doing, I provide more convincing evidence that although affective experiences may be fluid and diverse at the IWM (and indeed in many other museums) they circulate in patterned and structured ways with political effects. Prominent national institutions like the IWM adopt highly sophisticated designs that curators develop with expert skill and didactic purpose, which results in a generally high degree of narrative and aesthetic coherence. Although visitors, of course, read the museum experience through distinct affective and intellectual lenses that make each experience unique, the museum strives to reliably offer a satisfying and coherent experience of 'Britain at War' that involves the transmission of specific messages and ideas. Therefore, to conclude on the question of reproducibility, each researcher's unique affective sensitivities may draw their attention to different dimensions of the staging of affect, but I would not expect them to come to wildly different conclusions about how the museum constructs understandings of 'Britain at war'.

Case Study: Affect, Emotion, and the 'Liberal War' Discourse at the IWM

On a mild and cloudy day of October 2014, I exit Lambeth North tube station in South London and walk my way towards the IWM. As I step inside the grand neoclassical colonnade that frames the entrance to the building (formerly, a part of the Bethlem Royal Hospital), I am overtaken by a buzz of noise and activity. I walk past the cloakroom and two gift shops busy with school groups and families with young children. I then reach the central atrium (see Picture 5.2). Bathed in daylight flowing in from a skylight, military aircraft and missiles hang above my head. As I will later read on the website of the firm responsible for the museum's recent refurbishment, the atrium's architecture does not only favour the principle of 'clarity', distributing natural light through the atrium and the

Picture 5.2 The atrium of the Imperial War Museum, July 2014. Source: Wikipedia, https://en.wikipedia.org/wiki/File:IWM_2014_5760.jpg. Licenced by picture author Ashley Pomeroy under the Creative Commons Attribution-Share Alike 4.0 International

surrounding galleries, but also 'circulation' (Foster + Partners, 2016). The atrium works as the museum's beating heart, pulsing flows of people from the main entrance to the galleries and various facilities via an open staircase and lift, and back out again.

The museum architecture follows a third principle: 'chronology' (Foster + Partners, 2016). Wrapped around the central atrium, galleries are dedicated to (going from the basement to the third floor): World War I; World War II; post-war peace and security from 1945 to the present; and temporary exhibitions (which at the time focussed on the recent war in Afghanistan). The open structure nonetheless gives the impression of all galleries being part of a single unified space. They wrap around the central, sunbathed atrium in such a way that visitors constantly have the ground- and first-floor shops and cafés within eyesight and hearing distance. As a result, whilst we walk amongst World War II tanks, Cold War missiles, and artwork inspired by the Iraq War, the sound of explosions, sirens, and military fanfares coming from wartime archival footage overlaps with chatter arising from the other levels, children crying and playing chase, cutlery clicking and tills beeping in the café. In the central staircase that connects the different floors and galleries, sleek and bright announcement boards advertise the café, tearoom, bookshop, and upcoming paying exhibitions. Upon closer attention, the museum's architecture resembles a shopping centre, with flying bombs, rockets, military aircraft, and a car wrecked by a terrorist attack replacing the central fountain or playground.

In a radically different atmosphere, and cut away from all this agitation, the third and fourth floors host the sombre gallery dedicated to the Holocaust, mentioned above. The passage that leads to this gallery signals a transition into a darker space. I cross a white bridge that hangs above the atrium, bathed in white light falling from the skylight. I reach a black door. As I cross it, I leave a world of white light and white noise to plunge, literally and metaphorically, into a hole of darkness. The Holocaust exhibition's tunnel shape successfully isolates it from light, noise, children's ears and eyes (under-fourteens are not allowed in), and certain behaviours such as taking photographs (forbidden in this gallery only) and buying souvenirs (all shops are located on other floors and hidden from view). As I recounted in the introduction, the staging of affect favours reactions of horror and sadness to harrowing stories that accompany the display of artefacts documenting the persecution and mass murder of Jewish people such as piles of shoes, rag dolls, and clothes sewn with the yellow star of David. Like me, other visitors are moved by the exhibit, described as 'very sobering' and 'extremely moving' (Ben, 2016; roger_cook45, 2016). Online reviews confirm the effectiveness of the gallery, which 'truly does show man's inhumanity to man' in a way that leaves one with 'no words' (shropshiretraveller9, 2016).

Days after my first visit to the IWM, I am back at my work desk, trying to put some initial thoughts on paper. Examining floor plans, I am puzzled by the spatial separation of the Holocaust Gallery from the World War II Gallery: why break with the principle of chronology applied elsewhere in the museum, and claimed by the architectural firm as a leading design principle? Going back to my notes, drawings, and recordings, I notice the stark contrast between the dark austerity of the Holocaust gallery, and the brighter design and mood of galleries commemorating wars waged by Britain between 1939 and 2014. Drawing on the poststructuralist idea that discourses create meaning through the articulation of oppositional binaries, I start seeing a connection between the IWM's use of spaces that are either dark or light, quiet or loud, constricted or open, and a narrative about illegitimate and legitimate warfare. By isolating the Holocaust Gallery's in a closed, dark, constricted gallery, the IWM sets the Holocaust apart from other wartime events: it poignantly situates the Shoah as the ultimate example of *illegitimate* and *illiberal* warfare.

On the one hand, the Holocaust Gallery draws its affective poignancy from the contrast it offers to the rest of the museum. In this darkest of spaces, visitors feel the mix of 'terror and awe' that Debbie Lisle argues makes good war exhibitions productively destabilising (Lisle, 2006a, p. 843). One father reports that his son and him 'both came away with a mixture of awe and also sadness at the truly awful things that people can do to each other' (roger_cook45, 2016). As Lisle explains, the simultaneous instigation of terror and awe can generate a zone of productive ambivalence which 'might be the key to mobilising alternative narratives of war' (Lisle, 2006a, p. 844). Alternative narratives to the liberal war discourse might include pacifist convictions (e.g. all wars lead to horrible human rights abuses) or critiques about liberal democracies' role in facilitating the perpetration of genocide (e.g. by rejecting large numbers of refugees coming from continental Europe) or their own deliberate targeting of civilians during warfare (e.g. by dropping firebombs over German cities).

On the other hand, the architectural isolation of the Holocaust in a space of darkness constructs the other wartime events commemorated in the museum as comparably 'bright'. Rather than destabilising visitors, this promotes the comfortable belief that, in contrast to a fascist state like Nazi Germany, Britain wages 'Just Wars'. This in turn (re)produces the hegemonic 'liberal war' discourse, based around the belief that liberal democratic states like the UK wage liberal wars—that is, wars ostensibly waged to globally uphold democracy and human rights and 'proselytize the attitudes and behaviours that liberal states deem to reflect acceptable as opposed to unacceptable ways of life' (Duffield, 2010, p. 57). Reproducing the common tendency to 'commemorate suffering experienced [e.g. by the persecuted Jews of continental Europe, or British soldiers in the trenches during the First World War] rather than suffering caused [by the UK Armed Forces]' (Sybil Milton cited in Lisle, 2006a, p. 853), the IWM represents military violence perpetrated by the UK against foreigners or its own citizens (as in the case of the execution of objectors of conscience) in ways that do not generate the distress and upset experienced in the Holocaust gallery. As I walk through the World War II gallery, I cannot dissociate my encounter with artefacts of war from the surrounding affective environment: a party of ladies noisily enjoying tea and pastries a few feet below at the museum café, the continuously moving crowd around me, the brouhaha of conversations in more languages than I can recognise, and the lovely remembrance-themed souvenirs in the shop a few metres away. I am in the midst of a hypermobile and high-energetic environment conceived to draw me to attractive consumption opportunities all around. This atmosphere does not easily lead to emotional upheaval or critical reflection.

Advocates of the IWM might answer that some displays do invite uncertainty around the hegemonic 'liberal war' discourse. The 1945–2014 exhibit features abstract artwork by the artist Bruce McLean that 'challenge[s] the politics of the Falkland conflict … [and] attack[s] the flag-waving bias of the media's reporting of the war' (museum label, 2014). A few metres away, posters by the 'Stop the war coalition' against the 2003 intervention in Iraq similarly bear witness to the contested nature of these wars. Giving us the choice to decide whether we think military interventions by the UK government from Northern Ireland to Iraq were legitimate or not contains elements of a productive, critical approach. However, compared to the harrowing Holocaust exhibit with its life-sized photographs of mass graves and half-naked rape victims, and its arresting ghostly whispers, none of the artefacts representing the UK's war efforts invites a deep affective provocation. On the whole, the staging of affect never pushes or destabilises visitors on the question of the UK's own abuses of military violence, which remain hypothetical, invisible, or tame through the visit. As a result, the staging of affect facilitates the construction of the UK as a wager of just, liberal wars, and discourages critical attitudes towards the wars waged by the UK and other liberal democracies.

BACK TO EMOTIONS: THE RESEARCHER'S EMOTIONS AS METHODOLOGICAL DEVICES

I have so far focused on affect, but auto-ethnography also contains an opportunity to critically examine our emotional relationship with the things and people we study. Examining our emotions is a way to enhance reflexivity, that is, 'a theoretical reflection … on the process of knowledge production, scholars themselves, and political agents and their practices more generally' (Amoureux & Steele, 2015, p. 3). Reflexivity involves curiosity for how our emotions for the research object change during the research process. In this context, it is useful to think of emotions as 'appraisals or value judgments, which ascribe to things and persons outside the person's own control great importance for that person's own flourishing' (Nussbaum, 2003, pp. 3–4). Emotional reactions towards our object(s) of study and the normative judgements they entail come out of our particular location (not least in terms of gender, class, and ethnicity) in a given historical, cultural, and political context. Experiences of self-doubt and unease, in particular, can be productively troubling because they often reveal an ambivalent relationship with the research object (Eriksson Baaz & Stern, 2013, 2016, pp. 117–118). They provide moments when one realises, '*I don't know what I think I know*, or that *what I think I know is not so*' (Dauphinee, 2010, p. 808). At this point, it can be productive to question the researcher's own subjectivity and how it limits and frames one's encounter(s) with the research object.

Questioning my experiences of ease and unease at the IWM and other war museums led to a more nuanced account of the politics of affect at war museums and memorials. The light bulb moment happened shortly after visiting the IWM's elaborate gift shop, which offers a range of war-themed souvenirs. As I walk through displays of RAF wallets and spitfire cufflinks, vintage fashion books and a World War II-inspired 'beauty as duty' range of accessories, a collection of decorative items commemorating the centenary of World War I catches my eye. A set of notebooks ornamented with poetry and delicately interwoven flowers, birds, bees, and herbs, in the style of the late-nineteenth-century Arts and Crafts movement, instantaneously bewitch me. I buy the set of three—feminine, delicate, so small and thin they fit in my pocket. I also buy the assorted tea towel. Its floral design, the soft blue tones, the linen fabric, make a perfect fit for my mom's kitchen. Finally, I purchase a vintage recruitment poster for the Women's Royal Naval Service for an academic friend. I genuinely like these items. However, as I unpack my souvenirs on my journey back on the train, I am aware that I am being drawn into a discourse that turns World War I casualties into a theme for interior decoration.

Upon realising that the IWM and its attractive consumption opportunities wooed me and I ended up 'engrossed in ethnographic seduction' (Robben, 1995, p. 83), I find myself suddenly uneasy, but also puzzled. At Pearl Harbor and other American sites, I had found souvenirs on sale, such as Top Gun baseball caps, 'military wife' cookbooks, and military dog tags, unappealing and off-putting. On one occasion, I had reluctantly bought a Rosie the Riveter pencil, having forgotten to take a pen to take notes. I suddenly wondered, why would the same consumptive activities feel so pleasant and satisfying at the IWM? As the descendent of French-Canadian and Irish ancestors who were violently colonised by the British, should I not have found consumption at a British museum of war even less appealing? 'What made the US shops uncomfortable, and the British one so comfortable?', did I write in my fieldwork diary: 'The US shops felt tacky and kitsch', did I answer candidly to myself, 'while the IWM shop is more subtle, elegant, and tasteful'. As soon as I put these words on paper, I realised that my unease at the US naval ships was a form of snobbery and class performance. I had felt alienated but superior at US sites, strong of my privileged education spread between my relatives' upper-middle class homes in Québec and France, and my time spent in universities in Switzerland and the UK. In contrast, I read IWM consumption offers as appealing and valuable, and the museum experience as a whole felt more 'cultured' and 'sophisticated'—probably because the IWM deliberately targets an upmarket, cosmopolitan, and international elite audience. Moreover, as argued by Pierre Bourdieu and Alain Darbel (1969), in the European context, museum visits have long provided cultural elites a means to distinguish themselves from the lower classes and build symbolic capital. In short, the IWM seduced me by reaching out to me as a consumer belonging to the economically privileged, hyper-mobile, and highly educated classes.

Realising that my unease at American war museums was largely an effect of my privileged class position and consumer subjectivity generated a fair amount of anxiety and shame, but also a productive theoretical moment. By actively interrogating my sense of ease and unease and the classed subjectivity from which these emotions came from, I enlarged my intellectual perspective to include questions of everyday political economy. By acknowledging the economic importance of museums as sites of tourism and consumption, I developed a fuller understanding of the staging of affect at wartime heritage sites, one that acknowledges the interconnections between museums' political and financial objectives.

To make sense of the economic dimension of the staging of affect at war museums, I draw on the work of geographer Nigel Thrift. Thrift takes interest in the staging of affect as expressed in multinational corporations' use of polished advertisement campaigns and evermore engaging, immersive, and captivating consumption environments such as shopping centres and multidimensional entertainment centres. In these contexts, the staging of affect involves sensorially stimulating the customer with attention to customer intelligence involving 'detailed maps of what might be called susceptibility to particular affective cues' (Thrift, 2008, p. 246). At a time of neoliberal reforms in the heritage and cultural sector, the IWM and other war museums and memorials increasingly adopt growth-oriented management strategies that imitate shopping malls, theme parks, and other sites of consumption. The effective staging of affect partly serves the purpose of making the IWM competitive in London's thriving market of consumable 'experiences' available for locals but also for international tourist audiences. The economic importance of tourism for London's heritage sector is such that promotion agencies describe international visitors as 'the leading driver for growth across London's cultural attractions, accounting for the majority of visits' (London & Partners, 2015). As a result, transnational consumer subjectivities now importantly inform museum design.

The staging of affect in support of the liberal war discourse at the IWM is thus not 'merely' an exercise in public diplomacy; it also responds to commercial imperatives. The IWM proposes war stories that support a comforting view of liberal democracies at war because it markets itself to a large extent to European and North American visitors who are citizens of other liberal democracies. The ambivalence that emerges of some of the IWM exhibits provides a way to satisfy consumers with a variety of political opinions (pacifists and militarists alike) as well as those who are more interested in 'a good day out' than in intense reflection on matters of war and peace (Powell & Kokkranikal, 2015, p. 169). Finally, the circulation of an upbeat, leisurely, and touristic feel provides reassurance, encourages onsite spending at the shop and café, and leads to positive online reviews with titles like 'great fun' (Charlotte, 2016). In other words, highlighting the destructive costs of war without exposing liberal democracies as involved in such destruction in sometimes legally and morally questionable ways pleases customers looking for an experience in cultural tourism and feeds spending and economic growth without challenging the economic and political status quo. Thus, although the staging of affect may achieve the important goal of intensifying engagement in international spaces of reflection about the nature and legitimacy of war (as shown by the rapidly growing numbers of visitors), it appears necessary to ask whether it does not inhibit critical thinking about liberal warfare.

Conclusion: Advantages and Limits

In this chapter, I have argued that auto-ethnography enables researchers to use their own affective and emotional experiences as methodological devices in the study of world politics. Despite its many strengths and advantages, auto-ethnography remains in its infancy as a research method in IR. I thus seize this conclusion as an opportunity to reflect on the benefits and challenges encountered in its deployment.

First and foremost, auto-ethnography involves the advantage of enhancing creativity in the research process. Activating alternative affective sensitivities in the research context favours the deployment of 'an aesthetic mode of apprehension' that opens space for new imagining ways of thinking world politics (Shapiro, 2013, p. 9). In my case, it awakened a curiosity about the role of bodily movement and architecture as affective channels in world politics.

Auto-ethnography nonetheless entails the risk, connected to the challenge of 'narcissism', of re-centring a privileged Anglo-European perspective on world politics. The IWM is firmly anchored in European or 'Western' heritage. Moreover, given the structures of privilege that underlie access to academia, focusing on my experience of the museum reinforces an already existing focus on the lives of a wealthy, highly educated, white minority of 'elites' in the field known as International Politics. There is something to be said about the need to expose such privileged perspectives as suffusing institutions that (re)produce hegemonic discourses, such as the liberal war discourse, in thus far unacknowledged way. However, I do hope that as auto-ethnography becomes more widely known and used, it also becomes a channel for less privileged perspectives to come to the fore.

A second set of benefits and challenges arises from the transnationally mobile nature of the auto-ethnography performed in this project. Mobility enabled me to notice how different sites were more successful at engaging me affectively when they allowed me to perform consumer subjectivities that felt familiar and rewarding. Mobility thus favoured theoretically productive shifts in perspectives.

Mobile auto-ethnography was nonetheless limiting in two ways. Most problematically, it made it difficult to challenge my first impression of a site. I would struggle to 'revisit' the data in order to check that I had not omitted something important. For instance, I realised after completing fieldwork that I had often paid insufficient attention to visitors' resistance, and it was often logistically impossible for me to re-investigate the sites. Moreover, the more time passed after the visit, the harder it became for me to write about it in an affectively evocative manner. Detailed field notes, recordings, and photos did not quite succeed at recreating the experience of the site. For future auto-ethnographic work, I would recommend a greater use of longer audio and video recordings, panoramic photos, and a video diary. Although written diary entries help with tracing emotions (which can be verbally labelled), a video diary would more easily allow to reconnect with the affective experience, given the presence of sound and image in addition to words. In the absence of these, I resorted to publicly available online resources such as museums' online presence (many offer a 'virtual tour'); other visitors' videos on YouTube and other social media; and the 'street view' function of Google Maps. I found these useful, if imperfect ways to re-immerse myself in the research environment and would recommend them to other auto-ethnographers.

Notes

1. The IWM also comprises the Churchill War Rooms and HMS Belfast, also in London, as well as two other sites located outside London, the IWM Duxford, which considers itself 'the European centre of aviation history' (IWM, 2014) and IWM North in Manchester. This chapter only considers the IWM headquarters.

References

ALVA. (2016). 2015 Visitor Figures. Retrieved July 26, 2016, from http://alva.org.uk/details.cfm?p=606

Amoureux, J. L., & Steele, B. J. (Eds.). (2015). *Reflexivity and International Relations: Positionality, Critique, and Practice*. Abingdon, Oxon and New York: Routledge.

Anderson, K., & Smith, S. J. (2001). Editorial: Emotional Geographies. *Transactions of the Institute of British Geographers, 26*(1), 7–10.

Ben, K. (2016, July). War Museum – Imperial War Museum, London Traveller Reviews. Retrieved July 28, 2016, from https://www.tripadvisor.co.uk/ShowUserReviews-g186338-d187674-r397559382-Imperial_War_Museum-London_England.html#CHECK_RATES_CONT

Bourdieu, P. & Darbel, A. (1969). *L'Amour de l'art, les musées d'art européens et leur public*. Paris: les Éditions de minuit.

Brigg, M., & Bleiker, R. (2010). Autoethnographic International Relations: Exploring the Self as a Source of Knowledge. *Review of International Studies, 36*(3), 779–798.

Büscher, M., Urry, J., & Witchger, K. (2011). *Mobile Methods*. Abingdon, Oxon and New York: Routledge.

Campbell, D. (1998). *Writing Security: United States Foreign Policy and the Politics of Identity*. Minneapolis: University of Minnesota Press.

Carver, T. (2002). Discourse Analysis and the "Linguistic Turn". *European Political Science, 2*(1), 50–53.

Charlotte, Y. (2016, July). Great Fun – Imperial War Museum, London Traveller Reviews. Retrieved July 29, 2016, from https://www.tripadvisor.co.uk/ShowUserReviews-g186338-d187674-r398050345-Imperial_War_Museum-London_England.html#CHECK_RATES_CONT

Cohn, C. (2006). Motives and Methods: Using Multi-sited Ethnography to Study US National Security Discourses. In B. A. Ackerly, M. Stern, & J. True (Eds.), *Feminist Methodologies for International Relations* (pp. 91–107). Cambridge: Cambridge University Press.

Dauphinee, E. (2010). The Ethics of Autoethnography. *Review of International Studies, 36*(3), 799–818.

Deleuze, G., & Guattari, F. (1980). *Mille Plateaux*. Paris: Éditions de minuit.

Doty, R. L. (1993). Foreign Policy as Social Construction: A Post-positivist Analysis of U.S. Counterinsurgency Policy in the Philippines. *International Studies Quarterly, 37*(3), 297–320.

Doty, R. L. (2010). Autoethnography – Making Human Connections. *Review of International Studies, 36*(4), 1047–1050.

Duffield, M. (2010). The Liberal Way of Development and the Development—Security Impasse: Exploring the Global Life-Chance Divide. *Security Dialogue, 41*(1), 53–76.

Ellis, C., Adams, T. E., & Bochner, A. P. (2010). Autoethnography: An Overview. *Forum Qualitative Sozialforschung/Forum: Qualitative Social Research, 12*(1).

Enloe, C. (2000). *Bananas, Beaches and Bases: Making Feminist Sense of International Politics*. Berkeley: University of California Press.

Eriksson Baaz, M., & Stern, M. (2013). *Sexual Violence as a Weapon of War?: Perceptions, Prescriptions, Problems in the Congo and Beyond*. Uppsala: Nordiska Afrikainstitutet; London: Zed Books.

Eriksson Baaz, M., & Stern, M. (2016). Researching Wartime Rape in the Democratic Republic of Congo: A Methodology of Unease. In A. T. R. Wibben (Ed.), *Researching War: Feminist Methods, Ethics and Politics* (pp. 117–140). Abingdon, Oxon and New York: Routledge.

Fitzgerald, J. (2015). Why Me? An Autoethnographic Account of the Bizarre Logic of Counterterrorism. *Critical Studies on Terrorism, 8*(1), 163–180.

Foster + Partners. (2016). Imperial War Museum. Retrieved July 28, 2016, from http://www.fosterandpartners.com/projects/imperial-war-museum/

Foucault, M. (2002 [1969]). *Archaeology of Knowledge*. London and New York: Routledge.

Foucault, M. (2012 [1977]). *Discipline and Punish: The Birth of the Prison* (A. Sheridan, Trans.). New York: Vintage.

Fullagar, S. (2001). Encountering Otherness Embodied Affect in Alphonso Lingis' Travel Writing. *Tourist Studies, 1*(2), 171–183.

Hansen, L. (2006). Research Designs: Asking Questions and Choosing Texts. In *Security as Practice: Discourse Analysis and the Bosnian War* (pp. 73–92). London: Routledge.

Haraway, D. (1988). Situated Knowledges: The Science Question in Feminism and the Privilege of Partial Perspective. *Feminist Studies, 14*(3), 575–599.

Hatch, W. (2014). Bloody Memories: Affect and Effect of World War II Museums in China and Japan. *Peace & Change, 39*(3), 366–394.

Holland, J. (2015). Constructing Crises and Articulating Affect After 9/11. In *Emotions, Politics, and War* (pp. 167–181). London and New York: Routledge.
Holland, J., & Solomon, T. (2014). Affect Is What States Make of It: Articulating Everyday Experiences of 9/11. *Critical Studies on Security, 2*(3), 262–277.
Imperial War Museums. (2014a). About IWM London. Retrieved October 28, 2014, from http://www.iwm.org.uk/visits/iwm-london/about
Imperial War Museums. (2014b). *Annual Report and Account 2013–2014*. London: Her Majesty's Stationery Office.
Inayatullah, N. (2011). Falling and Flying: An Introduction. In N. Inayatullah (Ed.), *Autobiographical International Relations: I, IR* (pp. 1–12). Abingdon, Oxon and New York: Routledge.
IWM. (2014). About IWM Duxford. Retrieved May 14, 2015, from http://www.iwm.org.uk/visits/iwm-duxford/about
Jauhola, M. (2015). On "Being Bored": Street Ethnography on Emotions in Banda Aceh After the Tsunami and Conflict. In *Emotions, Politics and War* (pp. 86–99). Abingdon, Oxon and New York: Routledge.
Jonas, H. (2001 [1966]). *The Phenomenon of Life: Toward a Philosophical Biology*. Evanston, IL: Northwestern University Press.
Kavanagh, D. (2004). Ocularcentrism and Its Others: A Framework for Metatheoretical Analysis. *Organization Studies, 25*(3), 445–464.
Laclau, E. (2004). Glimpsing the Future. In S. Critchley & O. Marchart (Eds.), *Laclau: A Critical Reader* (pp. 279–328). Abingdon, Oxon and New York: Routledge.
Laclau, E., & Mouffe, C. (2001). *Hegemony and Socialist Strategy: Towards a Radical Democratic Politics*. London: Verso.
Levin, D. M. (1999). Introduction. In *Sites of Vision: The Discursive Construction of Sight in the History of Philosophy* (pp. 1–68). Boston: MIT Press.
Lisle, D. (2000). Consuming Danger: Reimagining the War/Tourism Divide. *Alternatives: Global, Local, Political, 25*(1), 91–116.
Lisle, D. (2006a). Sublime Lessons: Education and Ambivalence in War Exhibitions. *Millennium – Journal of International Studies, 34*(3), 841–862.
Lisle, D. (2006b). *The Global Politics of Contemporary Travel Writing*. Cambridge and New York: Cambridge University Press.
Lisle, D. (2013). Frontline Leisure: Securitizing Tourism in the War on Terror. *Security Dialogue, 44*(2), 127–146.
London & Partners. (2015, May 20). London Welcomes 17.4 Million International Visitors in Another Record-Breaking Year for Tourism. Retrieved May 21, 2015, from http://www.londonandpartners.com/media-centre/press-releases/2015/150520-london-welcomes-174-million-international-visitors-in-another-recordbreaking-year-for-tourism
Massumi, B. (2002). *Parables for the Virtual: Movement, Affect, Sensation*. Durham: Duke University Press.

Massumi, B. (2005). The Future Birth of the Affective Fact. Presented at the Genealogies of Biopolitics.

McCormack, D. P. (2003). An Event of Geographical Ethics in Spaces of Affect. *Transactions of the Institute of British Geographers, 28*(4), 488–507.

Mulvey, L. (2006 [1975]). Visual Pleasure and Narrative Cinema. In *Media and Cultural Studies* (pp. 342–352). Malden, MA, Oxford, Carlton: Blackwell Publishing Ltd.

Nussbaum, M. C. (2003). *Upheavals of Thought: The Intelligence of Emotions.* Cambridge: Cambridge University Press.

Parashar, S. (2015). Anger, War and Feminist Storytelling. In T. Gregory & L. Ahäll (Eds.), *Emotions, Politics and War* (pp. 71–85). Abingdon, Oxon and New York: Routledge.

Pile, S. (2010). Emotions and Affect in Recent Human Geography. *Transactions of the Institute of British Geographers, 35*(1), 5–20.

Powell, R., & Kokkranikal, J. (2015). Motivations and Experiences of Museum Visitors: The Case of the Imperial War Museum, United Kingdom. In V. Katsoni (Ed.), *Cultural Tourism in a Digital Era* (pp. 169–181). Athens: Springer International Publishing.

Robben, A. C. G. M. (1995). The Politics of Truth and Emotion Among Victims and Perpetrators of Violence. In *Fieldwork Under Fire: Contemporary Studies of Violence and Survival* (pp. 81–104). Berkeley and Los Angeles, CA; London: University of California Press.

roger_cook45. (2016, July). Great Day Out...– Imperial War Museum, London Traveller Reviews. Retrieved July 28, 2016, from https://www.tripadvisor.co.uk/ShowUserReviews-g186338-d187674-r396863513-Imperial_War_Museum-London_England.html#CHECK_RATES_CONT

Ross, A. A. G. (2006). Coming in from the Cold: Constructivism and Emotions. *European Journal of International Relations, 12*(2), 197–222.

Shapiro, M. J. (2013). *Studies in Trans-disciplinary Method: After the Aesthetic Turn.* London and New York: Routledge.

shropshiretraveller9. (2016, July). Lots to See and It's Free! – Imperial War Museum, London Traveller Reviews. Retrieved July 28, 2016, from https://www.tripadvisor.co.uk/ShowUserReviews-g186338-d187674-r397227183-Imperial_War_Museum-London_England.html#CHECK_RATES_CONT

Solomon, T. (2015). Embodiment, Emotions and Materialism in International Relations. In L. Åhäll & T. Gregory (Eds.), *Emotions, Politics and War* (pp. 58–70). London and New York: Routledge.

Spry, T. (2001). Performing Autoethnography: An Embodied Methodological Praxis. *Qualitative Inquiry, 7*(6), 706–732.

Sylvester, C. (2011). The Forum: Emotion and the Feminist IR Researcher. *International Studies Review, 13*(4), 687–708.

Sylvester, C. (2015). *Art/Museums: International Relations Where We Least Expect It.* Abingdon: Routledge.

Thrift, N. (2008). *Non-representational Theory: Space, Politics, Affect*. London and New York: Routledge.

Wakeman, S. (2014). Fieldwork, Biography and Emotion: Doing Criminological Autoethnography. *British Journal of Criminology, 54*(5), 705–721.

Waterton, E., & Watson, S. (2014). *The Semiotics of Heritage Tourism*. Bristol and Buffalo: Channel View Publications.

Weldes, J. (1999). *Constructing National Interests: The United States and the Cuban Missile Crisis*. Minneapolis, MN: University of Minnesota Press.

Wetherell, M., Yates, S., & Taylor, S. (2001). *Discourse Theory and Practice: A Reader*. London and Thousand Oaks, CA: SAGE.

Yanow, D. (2014). How Built Spaces Mean? A Semiotics of Space. In *Interpretation and Method: Empirical Research Methods and the Interpretive Turn* (pp. 368–386). Armonk, NY: M.E. Sharpe, Inc.

Audrey Reeves is a Lecturer in Politics and International Relations at Cardiff University and an Honorary Research Associate at the University of Bristol. Her research interests include critical security studies, international political sociology, and feminist international relations, with a focus on affect in international politics.

CHAPTER 6

A Plea for a Discursive Approach to Emotions: The Example of the French Airmen's Relation to Violence

Mathias Delori

INTRODUCTION

Many International Relations (IR) scholars are reluctant to study emotions. This diffidence does not stem from the view that emotions play no role in international politics. Indeed, history teaches us that emotions often impact on international politics. Think, for instance, of the weight of revengeful feelings in the century-old Franco-German antagonism (Delori, 2015) or the role of hatred and racism in many genocides (Mosse, 2000). In fact, the reason why many IR scholars have reservations about studying emotions seems to be more epistemological than empirical: they conceive of emotions as important but impalpable phenomena. This assessment often goes along with an individualistic representation of the body. The latter is presented as an envelope which separates the individual 'self' from the social space. Following this approach, those emotions that 'move'[1] human bodies are said to come from within, and the social context can only influence their expression. Hence, emotions are

M. Delori (✉)
CNRS/Sciences Po Bordeaux, Bordeaux, France

© The Author(s) 2018
M. Clément, E. Sangar (eds.), *Researching Emotions in International Relations*, Palgrave Studies in International Relations,
https://doi.org/10.1007/978-3-319-65575-8_6

seen as good objects of study for psychologists and biologists but not for social scientists and, *a fortiori*, not for scholars of international politics.

The argument developed in this chapter is that the reluctance to study emotions disappears if one admits—following the recent Foucauldian turn in the study of emotions (Butler, 2004, 2010; Fassin, 2005; Fausto-Sterling, 2000; Fierke, 2013; MacLeish, 2013; Weizman, 2012)—that emotions are pure socio-historical constructs. Judith Butler has put forward this idea by arguing that emotions are not 'pre-discursive' (Butler, 2010, p. 7), meaning that they are fashioned by the intersubjective 'frames' which constitute social reality. This Foucauldian approach to emotions is an invitation to go beyond the dualism between nature and culture, body and soul, feelings and emotions,[2] etc. (Foucault, 1971). It has one fortunate practical consequence: the realization that one does not need to study emotions *per se*—i.e. the actual biological phenomena which move human bodies—to understand their power and effectiveness. A parallel can be drawn with those sociologists of memory who do not study memory *per se* but, rather, the 'social frames' (Halbwachs, 1975 [1925]) which constitute it: history books, memorials, personal objects which carry family memories, etc. (Lavabre, 1994).

I will substantiate this point by relying on an empirical study of the emotional relation to violence of French fighter-bomber jet airmen. The work of Western airmen has changed since the development of the 'new Western way of war' (Shaw, 2006). They fly at altitudes where their enemies have no chance to inflict any damage on them. To a certain extent, their job is not very different from the job of drone operators: they kill at a distance. Hence, the first objective of my study was to understand what emotions 'move' their body as they perform this peculiar act: killing people outside any logic of 'self-defence' (Kaufman, 2009).

Following Butler (2010), I will call 'frames of war' those fragments of 'discourse' (in the Foucauldian sense of the term) which fashion and regulate the airmen's emotional relation to violence. I will show that two frames of war impact on their emotional relationship with violence: the language that they use when talking about their lethal actions, and the routinized procedures that they use when they drop bombs and kill.

I will argue, more precisely, that these frames of war fashion an original emotion/violence nexus. Contrary to soldiers in the First World War (Audouin-Rouzeau, 2008), these pilots and navigators do not really hate the people that they kill. In this sense, the paradigm of racist violence hardly applies. Nor do they fully reify their victims, as in the famous paradigm of bureaucratic violence popularized by Arendt in her study of the Eichmann trial (Arendt, 1963). Rather, they remind one of a character pictured by Tocqueville in *Democracy, Revolution and Society*: Madame de Sévigné. Tocqueville argues that Madame de Sévigné does not hate anybody and that she is not indifferent to the suffering of distant others either. Madame de Sévigné's specificity lies in the fact that she cannot experience compassion on a democratic basis. In Tocquevilian terms, she is driven by a selective 'economy of pity' (Tocqueville, 1980 [1835], p. 105). In other words, she grants some positive value to all lives (in the sense that she does not hate nor reify anybody) but cannot experience as much pity, sympathy, or compassion for a peasant or a bourgeois as for a fellow aristocrat. Now, my point is that fighter-bomber pilots are like Madame de Sévigné. They neither hate nor despise anybody. However, they do not grant the same (positive) value to all lives. Consequently, they calculate that it is sometimes necessary to 'kill' or 'let die' some people so that some other people with greater value can 'live' (Foucault, 1997 [1976], p. 214). I will draw upon two Foucauldian scholars researching contemporary Western wars—Eyal Weizman and Judith Butler (Butler, 2010; Weizman, 2012)—in order to make this point.

The argument proceeds as follows: The first section presents in greater detail my theoretical argument on the 'discursive' nature of emotions. The rest of the chapter narrates how I conducted the inquiry. I proceeded in three steps. I collected data on the discursive elements which mediate the airmen's emotional relationship to violence. I did so by interviewing about 40 airmen and members of the military staff (first step). The interviews helped me to identify two important vectors of discourse (and emotions): the language that these airmen use when they talk about their victims (second step) and the routinized procedures which precede their lethal actions (third step). I conclude this chapter with some remarks on the relevance and the limitations of this approach to emotions.

A Discursive Approach to Emotions

The Foucauldian notion of 'discourse' has led to many misinterpretations. Foucault does not use the term 'discourse' in a literal way, in the way that one terms a social actor's speech or writings 'discourse'. Foucault uses the notion of 'discourse' in a metaphorical way. The metaphor opposes 'language'—the medium that allows us to make an infinite number of statements—to 'discourse', the finite number of statements that are actually made (Foucault, 1969, p. 41). This leads him to observe that the reality we live in—i.e. all that seems natural to us (our beliefs, the things we say or do, the instruments we use, etc.) are made up of 'statements', i.e. words or things which carry social meaning. Methodologically, this entails identifying and interpreting the semiotic elements entailed in both 'discursive' (words, sentences, etc.) and 'non-discursive' practices (technologies, human artefacts, routinized actions, etc.).

Foucault did not explicitly link this notion of discourse to the question of emotions. However, he took a step in this direction when he reflected on the human body. In 'Nietzsche, Genealogy, History', Foucault points out that the postulate on the historical and social construction of reality does not only apply to ideas and practices but also to the human body itself (Foucault, 1977). By extension, Foucault argues, against 'constructivists', that human beings do not 'construct' culture upon a given (transhistorical) nature. The whole of reality is a social construct, including the human body itself.

Several biologists (Fausto-Sterling, 2000) and social scientists (Fierke, 2013; MacLeish, 2013) have illustrated the interest of Foucault's discourse theory for the study of emotions. In what follows, I will draw upon the work of two authors who have applied this framework to the more specific question of violence in current Western war: Judith Butler and Eyal Weizman (Butler, 2004, 2009, 2010; Weizman, 2012). As we shall see, their approaches not only nicely complement Foucault's, they also complement each other.

Firstly, Butler's approach is useful in understanding the social dimension of the 'frames' which fashion our emotional relation to violence. In her collection of essays entitled 'frames of war', she points out that one can experience the power of these frames when thinking about one's differential reactions towards distant suffering. She observes, for instance, that many Westerners reacted with horror to the attacks of 9/11 whilst showing little compassion for the (far more numerous) victims of US and Western wars in Afghanistan and Iraq. According to her, this shows that some powerful meaning structures operate behind what appears, at first sight, as 'natural' feelings: 'as long as we remain against interpretation in such moments, we will not be able to give an account of why the affect of horror is differentially experienced' (Butler, 2010, p. 49). She calls 'frames of war' the aforementioned meaning structures (or fragments of discourse) which move actors' bodies in war contexts and divide the world in two categories: the 'grievable' lives one identifies with and those which remain excluded from what might be called, after Tocqueville, the modern 'economy of pity'.

Secondly, Butler's approach helps us understand the political character of these frames. She notes, in this respect, that 'frames of war' are like photographic frames. They cannot grasp reality in its entirety. They entail a particular perspective, some arbitrary choices in terms of zooming, etc. In other words, they are 'always throwing something away, always keeping something out, always de-realizing and de-legitimating alternative versions of reality, discarded negatives of the official version' (Butler, 2010, p. xi). The selective nature of the frames which fashion social compassion has few political consequences when applied to natural deaths. Thus, the fact that we do not sympathize with the thousands of unknown people who die every day is of little political consequence. When applied to war, however, the selective nature of the frame becomes highly political. The selective 'economy of pity' is what legitimates and naturalizes warlike violence on both sides. This is why Butler has proposed redefining war as this social activity that 'divides populations into those who are grievable and those who are not' (Butler, 2010, p. 38). In the case of current Western wars, the power of the frame lies in its ability to naturalize the representation that a certain violence—the violence perpetrated by the liberal secular state—is more human than the so called 'terrorist' or 'criminal' violence, regardless of their respective performances in terms of innocent victims (Butler, 2010, p. 20).

The second (Foucauldian) author on whom I have massively drawn is Eyal Weizman (Weizman, 2012). In his recent essay on 'humanitarian violence', Weizman also argues that selective compassion has become a greater driving force for violence than hatred or indifference. This does not imply that racist and reifying dynamics are completely absent in the new Western way of war. For instance, it is clear that racialization contributes towards naturalizing the practice of using two different means of fighting 'terrorism': elite troops on the ground when 'terrorists' are located in Western territory and air power when they are located in the non-Western world (Delori, 2016a). Besides, it is clear that new technologies of war introduce more distance between combatants, thus helping to reify the victims of Western war violence. However, Weizman's framework helps us understand that a third form of logic operates alongside the two aforementioned ones: the logic of 'humanitarian violence'.

Humanitarian violence differs from racist violence and bureaucratic violence in the sense that it neither grants negative nor null value to its victims. As humanist subjects, perpetrators of humanitarian violence do not experience joy or indifference when they kill people. They grant some positive value to all lives and know that violence is evil. Yet they consider that it is sometimes necessary to do some evil in order to avoid a greater one. In other words, they reject the old Manichean view that situations are either right or wrong. They assume that good and evil can be measured, calculated, and weighted. Hence, their key idea is the 'principle of the lesser evil'. Weizman defines this rationale as follows.

The principle of the lesser evil is often presented as a dilemma between two or more bad choices in situations where available options are—or seem to be—limited. The choice made justifies harmful actions that would otherwise be unacceptable, since it allegedly averts even greater suffering (Weizman, 2012, p. 6).

Weizman gives several illustrations of this lesser evil principle. At the micro level, the most obvious example is the modern (non-sadistic) justification of torture. Memoranda released by the Bush administration in 2002 legitimized 'coercive interrogation methods' (a euphemism for torture) by referring to this principle of the lesser evil. These memos acknowledged that inflicting suffering on a defenceless body is morally wrong. In this sense, they acknowledged (to a certain extent) the humanity of the prisoners (they did not frame them as pure objects of hatred or indifference). However, the memos highlighted that this action (of inflicting suffering on a defenceless body) was acceptable if, firstly, it enabled useful information to be gathered (if it would help to prevent future 'terrorist' attacks) and if, secondly, the pain did not exceed a certain threshold. In practice, this threshold was very high. Indeed, as pointed out by Richter-Montpetit, 'in the post 9/11 lawfare the Bush administration juridically codified that abuse just short of killing a prisoner was considered permissible suffering' (Richter-Montpetit, 2014, p. 48). What matters is not the actual volume of violence but the very project of moderating it.

At the macro level, the most obvious illustrations of the lesser evil principle are 'humanitarian wars'—i.e. those wars that are supposed to stop or impede massacres, genocides or some other 'greater evils'. Partisans of humanitarian wars acknowledge that they cause some evil when they wage war and kill civilians. However, they consider that this constitutes a lesser evil as it has helped to prevent 'mass murder' and, perhaps, 'genocide'. M. Shaw's justification of the NATO war in Kosovo in 1999 provides a classic illustration of this rationale. Shaw calculated that NATO aircraft killed about 3000 innocent Serbian people in 1999. As a non-racist person, Shaw does not frame the killing of innocent Serbian people as a positive thing. As a humanist, Shaw is not indifferent to the fate of the victims of the NATO war. However, he considers that these 3000 innocent victims constituted a lesser evil as they meant that worse massacres were avoided (Shaw, 2006, p. 22).

Weizman adopts a critical stance towards the lesser evil principle. Following Arendt, he notes that 'politically, the weakness of the argument has always been that those who choose the lesser evil forget very quickly that they chose evil' (Weizman, 2012, p. 27). The problem does not only lie in the existence of some cognitive bias which may lead to a faulty assessment of both evils (as in the case of the disastrous 'humanitarian' war in Libya, for instance[3]). The problem is deeper and has something to do with the non-democratic (hidden) face of modern humanism. Contrary to what it claims, and contrary to what the greatest thinkers of humanism predicted (Elias, 2000 [1939]; Tocqueville, 1981 [1835]), modern humanist liberal discourse does not grant equal value to all lives. Rather, human lives have 'differential value (…) in the marketplace of death' (Asad, 2007, p. 94). This differential value does not only depend upon the racial and geographical distance between the humanist/liberal subject and the potential object of compassion. For instance, many modern humanist liberal subjects experienced compassion with the (geographically and racially remote) Afghan women oppressed by the Taliban, and this emotion contributed to naturalize the invasion of Afghanistan in 2001 (Ayotte & Husain, 2005). In humanist/liberal discourse, the differential value of human lives depends, rather, on each life's distance from the standard of the humanist/liberal 'good life'.

All this illustrates how Weizman and Butler converge when assessing the characteristics of the emotion/violence nexus in contemporary Western wars. They agree in rejecting classical approaches couched in terms of racist or bureaucratic violence. They argue that the greatest driving force of Western war violence is neither the arousal of negative emotions nor the neutralization of positive ones. Conversely, violence has its roots in compassion or, rather, the fact that humanist/liberal subjects experience more compassion for some than for others.

What can we say, finally, about the methodological implications of this framework? The first implication is this: from a discourse theory perspective, it is pointless to try to study emotions *per se*. This holds even more true for an interview-based inquiry. A scholar trying to analyse the emotions displayed by the actor during an interview would probably grasp just one thing: the emotions provoked by the social situation called an 'interview'. Hence, it is preferable to leave the actual emotions (the biological phenomena which move actors' bodies) aside and focus on discourse instead. The two authors I have presented above have done so in different ways. Butler—who is a professor of rhetoric—has analysed the role of language in the social construction of the mainstream approach to violence. Weizman—who is an architect—has investigated the material manifestation of contemporary frames of war: what he calls, after Ophir (2002), 'moral technologies'. I have tried here to combine both approaches: the approach focussing on the frames' ideational manifestations and the approach which analyses concrete technologies and concrete practices.

First Step: Interviewing the Relevant Actors

This study investigates the current emotion/violence nexus by looking at one particular case: the French bombing campaigns in Afghanistan (2001–2011), Libya (2011), and Mali (2013). The choice of France as a case study stems from the fact that France, along with the United States and Britain, has been one of the group of most warlike countries since the end of the Cold War. Additionally, I have chosen to focus on airmen because of the centrality of air power in the 'new Western way of war' (Shaw, 2006). This centrality emerges from the fact that several Western wars have taken the form of pure air bombing campaigns (Kosovo 1999, Libya 2011, Islamic State since 2014, not to mention President Obama's drone wars), and that air power played a central role in most other military operations, in particular in Afghanistan in 2001 and Iraq in 2003. My objective was to identify the actors' 'frames of war', i.e. those meaning structures which constitute their emotional relation to violence.

I did not start the research with any preconceived idea concerning the 'frames' that I would find. Indeed, the literature on this issue is dominated by two equally normative sets of arguments. Firstly, some essayists and anti-war activists have argued that new Western technologies of war such as remote control systems and computers have strong de-humanizing effects. Following this line of thought, Western combatants are said to develop a 'play-station mentality' (Cole, Dobbing, & Hailwood, 2010). They thus behave like the character of Eichmann depicted by Hannah Arendt in her famous essay (Arendt, 1963): they kill without realizing the practical consequences of their actions—the deaths, the suffering, the destruction, etc.

This view has been challenged by some 'defence intellectuals'[4] who have argued, on the contrary, that Western fighter-jet pilots and drone operators are so 'humane' and so 'empathetic' that they develop 'post-traumatic stress disorders' when they kill civilians. As pointed out by Chamayou, this contrasting literature is equally normative and political. It reproduces a central trope of Western war propaganda: the orientalist (Barkawi & Stanski, 2013; Said, 1979) narrative which opposes two mirror characters: hateful/fanatical 'terrorists' and compassionate/reasonable Western combatants (Chamayou, 2013, p. 147). In other words, in embarking on this study I was convinced of the need for a more scientific approach to the question of the emotion/violence nexus in current Western wars.

Data gathering consisted of conducting interviews with the relevant actors. The interviews took place between December 2012 and March 2013 on French military bases. I interviewed two groups of people. Firstly, I conducted ten interviews with high-ranking officers of the French naval and air forces (one Air Force general, one admiral, and four colonels in both forces). These interviews were aimed at learning about the concrete aspects of contemporary French air wars: the strategies, the doctrines, the rules of engagement, and the technologies used by French air and naval forces. Indeed, a key assumption of this study is that the soldiers' frames are like all elements of 'discourse': they do not float in the air. They are mediated by instruments, procedures, routinized practices, and apparatuses that both carry and fashion meaning (Holmqvist, 2013; van Veeren, 2014).

Secondly, I conducted interviews with those who actually drop bombs, i.e. the pilots and navigators (33 interviews). I was introduced as a 'CNRS researcher who is carrying out an independent study'. This introduction proved to be important in clarifying that I had not been commissioned by the military organization to learn about their qualities or potential weaknesses. I wanted to elicit their personal war experiences, not their capacity to present themselves as the 'best' pilots or navigators. For the same reason, I also laid great stress on the fact that the interviews would be anonymized.

The interviews took the form of dialogues where the interviewees were asked to talk freely about their personal experience of war. I structured the interviews around three main issues: (1) how they make sense of the act of killing and the risk of being killed, (2) how they perceive their enemies or the people that they kill (so-called 'collateral damage'), and (3) what they think about the new technologies of war which allow them to kill from a distance.

Each interview lasted between one and two hours. I recorded them and analysed them by using the old Weberian interpretivist method. This means, in effect, that my approach was mainly 'qualitative'. I paid little attention to word counts, simply calculating the number of occurrences of some key words such as 'terrorist', 'jihadi', etc.). For the rest, I tried to 'understand by interpretation'—to use Weber's famous expression (*deutend verstehen*)—how they perceive the battlefield, how they represent their enemies, and how they make sense of the practice of war. This also means that I did not try to analyse the emotions that the airmen displayed during the interviews. I did not want to understand what it feels like to narrate one's war experiences after the events in the specific social interaction of the interview. Rather, I wanted to identify what they feel when they drop bombs. To do so, I tried to be as empathetic as I could. I tried to understand what Boudon calls the actors' social 'dispositions' and 'position', i.e. their social background, the influence of military training, what it means to be a fighter-bomber pilot/navigator, the concrete technologies which mediate their experience of war, etc. (Boudon, 1986).

The interviewees talked easily about their lethal actions. They did not know exactly how many people they had killed. Some said 'three or four'. Others said 'dozens, maybe one hundred'. One thing seems clear though: the airmen have no difficulty in giving meaning to the violence they perpetrate. Indeed, I did not observe any clear case of 'frame breaking', in Goffman's (1974) term. One interviewee explained that he suffered from PTSD. However, these 'stress disorders' had nothing to do with the question of killing. This person had been traumatized by an explosion which had occurred whilst he was in a military base in Afghanistan. Another interviewee experienced some difficulty in making sense of an action which resulted in the death of a child. However, this case appears in many ways as an exception. He killed the child by accident and, as we shall see, accidents do not constitute the main cause of civilian deaths in the new Western way of war.

To put it differently, the first finding of my study is that most pilots and navigators enjoy going on 'opex' (*operations extérieures*, external operations). They often compete against one another to obtain the 'hottest' (*chaud*) missions, i.e. those where they drop bombs. This made the literature on the PTSD syndromes of drone operators completely irrelevant. The French airmen that I have interviewed have no difficulty in killing and making sense of it. I interviewed one member of the psychiatric department of the French Air Force. He had conducted hundreds of interviews with pilots and navigators. He confirmed that he had not met one single person suffering from PTSD linked to killing operations.

The second finding of my study was that the literature on the 'play station mentality' is equally irrelevant. Although they do not know exactly how many people they have killed, the airmen know what they are doing. They know that their bombs kill both enemy combatants and civilians. They simply have no problem making sense of this for a number of reasons on which I will elaborate further down.

Second Step: Understanding What Ideational Frames Fashion the Actors' Emotional Relation to Violence

I wrote above that 'frames of war' take both ideational and material forms. After the stage of data gathering, the second phase of my study consisted of analysing their main ideational manifestation: the very language airmen use when talking about their victims. To do so, I followed the example of Judith Butler in her studies of the language used by the Western mainstream media in the context of the 'war on terror' (Butler, 2004, 2009, 2010).

Butler has analysed how the Western mainstream media have depicted two groups of victims: the Western victims of the 'terrorist' attacks of 2001 on the one hand, and the non-Western victims of Western anti-terrorist wars on the other. In the former case, Butler argues, the mainstream media published the obituaries of the victims so that the public could learn about their names and stories. In the latter case, the mainstream media found no words other than 'collateral damage' or 'human shield'. She observes that this last expression—'human shield'—is probably the most reifying as it suggests that 'those children are not really children, are not really alive, that they have already been turned to metal, to steel, that they belong to the machinery of bombardment, at which point the body of the child is conceived as nothing more than a militarized metal that protects the attacker against attack' (Butler, 2010, p. xxvii).

Unsurprisingly, the airmen that I have interviewed drew on elements from both languages—the sensitive and the reifying—depending on the people they were talking about. Thus, they expressed great concern for some populations: the people of Paris or New York who might be killed, in the future, by 'terrorists', the Libyan population oppressed by Gaddafi forces, and the Malian population under the threat of jihadists. These people have something in common: in French mainstream war narratives, they are the people that the French bombs are supposed to save or to 'make live' (Foucault, 1997 [1976], p. 214).

The interviewees use a complete different language when talking about the people they kill. Their language made me think about what Carol Cohn has called 'techno-strategic', i.e. the mathematical and abstract language used by the US defence intellectuals who fashioned the deterrence theories current at the end of the Cold War. Cohn shows that the massive use of abstract periphrases had one important consequence: it erases the humane dimension of war and euphemizes the perception of violence (in her case, nuclear bombing). Cohn tested the power of this language on herself: 'the more conversations I participated in using this language, the less frightened I was of nuclear war' (Cohn, 1987, p. 704).

Now, the airmen I have interviewed make extensive use of this 'techno-strategic' language when talking about enemy forces. For instance, they use the word 'killing' hardly at all. They explain, instead, that they 'deal with' (*traiter*) or 'neutralize' their 'targets'. This leads them to experience 'little pity' for the referents of these signifiers, i.e. the people who die when their bombs explode. Some airmen even show reflexivity about the ease with which they perpetrate this particular act: 'Honestly, I was preoccupied by this question before [my first killing]. I thought that it would be psychologically difficult to live with it. I happen to believe in God, so I may have a particular approach to this question. I talked a lot about this with my family when I joined the military. Now, here is what strikes me the most: it left me completely indifferent (...). And this disturbs me a little'[5].

Despite and because[6] of the precision weapons that they sometimes use (see below), Western airmen kill many civilians. For instance, the economist M. Herold has calculated that the Western bombing campaign directly killed between 7948 and 9312 civilians in Afghanistan between 2001 and 2010, i.e. before the 'surge' of 2010 (Herold, 2012, p. 49). Although this is a small fragment of the US-led air war on terror, this figure reveals that these air wars 'have already resulted in massive losses of life that immeasurably exceed anything terrorists have managed to do' (Asad, 2007, p. 93).

Among the 36 airmen I have interviewed, only one expressed second thoughts about the killing of civilians. The event had taken place in Afghanistan. The aircraft was flying at a low altitude. For some reasons which remain unclear (probably a weaponry test), the pilot dropped a decoy device, i.e. a device which is intended to deflect the trajectory of possible anti-aircraft missiles. The decoy accidently fell into the middle of a village and killed a child. The pilot talked about this event in the following terms: 'Yes, this affected me a little. That was in Afghanistan during a 'show of presence' (in English during the interview) (…). The child picked up one of my decoy devices. It tore away his hand and he died afterwards (…). So yes, this was a hard time… However, it was an accident. If I had to do it again, I would'.[7]

The other interviewees who mentioned having killed 'non-combatants' expressed no second thoughts. The following interview extract resembles many others:

INTERVIEWER: Have you ever had second thoughts about the bombs you dropped?
AIRMAN: I kill terrorists. I do not target civilians. The guys we killed in Mali and Libya were no gentlemen farmers. They were planning terrorist attacks. When I kill somebody who plans to leave a bomb in the subway in Paris, I save lives. When I destroy a missile battery which bombs a market in the middle of Benghazi, I save Libyan lives.
INTERVIEWER: Indeed. But the bombs you drop also kill civilians.
AIRMAN: [silent] Yes, but if the amount of collateral damage—sorry, I do not like this word—if the number of civilian casualties is inferior to the number of people I save, it is fair to shoot. I know that this is not always easy to hear. Yet reason has to be opposed to emotion. I wish I had other means with which to neutralize them. Believe me. But I don't.[8]

This interview extract is interesting in many respects. Firstly, it illustrates that the airmen are fully aware of the lethal consequences of their actions and that they have no problem making sense of it. They know that they kill civilians, and this fact does not impinge upon the pleasure they take in going to war and fulfilling their missions. Secondly, this extract reveals the key to understanding the interviewed airmen's approach to violence. In contrast to the racist soldiers depicted by several historians of past wars (Audouin-Rouzeau, 2002; Barkawi, 2004), they do not hate the people they kill. Nor do they fully reify them as the paradigm of bureaucratic violence would suggest (Arendt, 1963). As 'humanist' or 'liberal' subjects, they acknowledge that it is wrong to kill civilians. However, they consider that it is acceptable to kill X if it allows to save Y, provided that the killing of X constitutes a lesser evil than the killing of Y. As we shall see in the next section, they have some 'good intersubjective' reasons to frame their violence in such a way: their relation to violence is mediated by technologies which embody this very idea.

THIRD STEP: CHECKING THE FRAMES' MATERIAL MANIFESTATIONS

I wrote above that almost no airmen expressed second thoughts concerning the killing of civilians. To understand this, one must remember or uncover an important dimension of the Western way of war: airmen are socialized and trained to consent to killing civilians. Admittedly, the practice of carpet bombing has diminished. With the notable exceptions of the United States in Iraq (Olsson, 2012) and Israel in Lebanon and Gaza in 2008/2009,[9] Western air forces have ceased to target civilians in order to 'terrorize' the population or undermine its morale. Since the mid-2000, they have become good students of international humanitarian law in the sense that: (1) they do not target civilians per se (in accordance with the discrimination principle); and (2) they control the violence that they perpetrate (in accordance with the proportionality principle). This does not mean, however, that current Western air doctrines exclude the killing of civilians. On the contrary, the killing of civilians is accepted in principle and, furthermore, measured and calculated. Concretely, current military doctrines state that the killing of civilians is acceptable provided that it does not exceed a given threshold. I will illustrate this by presenting an important element in current Western air wars: the 'Non-Combatant Casualty Cut-Off Value' or 'NCV'.

At first sight, the NCV appears as one of these numerous military acronyms that have little resonance with most people's lives. In reality, the NCV has important human consequences. It refers to a simple reality: the number of civilians that airmen are allowed to kill, or to put at risk, every time they drop a bomb. The NCV varies, in practice, between 0 and 30 (rarely more). An NCV = 0 means that that the airmen should not put any 'non-combatant' at risk. An NCV = 30 means that they are allowed to open fire if they estimate that they will not kill more than 30 civilians.

The airmen learn this number before taking off, yet it really becomes real when they arrive near their target. When this happens, they must follow a procedure called 'PID-CDE-ROE'.

- PID stands for 'positive identification'. It consists of checking whether they have identified the right target: the 'jihadist', the 'terrorist', the 'ammunition dump', etc.
- CDE means 'Collateral Damage Estimate'. It reminds pilots and navigators that they must calculate the number of 'non-combatants' that they will put at risk if they drop the bomb. Concretely, they estimate this number by counting the civilians that they see. At this stage, they ask the following questions: is this person a male or a female? Is this a child or a dog? How far are they from the military target (distance to military targets is central in the military definition of combatants).
- ROE stands for 'Rules of Engagement'. It invites airmen to check whether the amount of probable 'collateral damage' (i.e. number of civilian deaths) is lower than the NCV stated by the rules of engagement. If this is the case, they open fire. If not, the decision to open fire (or not) is taken at a higher level of the chain of command.

It is not exactly known which members of the military staff or government determine the NCV. What is known, however, is that it depends on several factors. First, it depends on some subjective and arbitrary assessment of the 'value' of civilians. In this respect, the most important variable is geographical or/and racial. When a terrorist attack occurs on the territory of a Western state, the NCV used by policy and military forces is close to zero, meaning that they do not want to put at risk any French/Western civilians. When they operate in the non-Western world, however, the NCV rises significantly. This is why Western forces use different instruments when they operate in Western territory or outside the West: elite commandos on the ground in the former case, armed drones and fighter-bomber jets in the latter.[10] Elite commandos can be used to 'neutralize' terrorists without causing 'collateral damage'. Air bombing structurally kills civilians.

Secondly, the NCV depends on a subjective and arbitrary assessment of the value of the military target. During the US war in Iraq, for instance, the US ROE stated that the NCV was 29 for each 'high-value military target' (Weizman, 2012, p. 129). This meant, concretely, that the pilots were allowed to kill up to 29 civilians in order to eliminate a high-ranking member of Al Qaida or a senior official of Saddam Hussein's regime. When the target is a low-ranking enemy combatant, the NCV declines significantly. This not only means, to return to Asad, that human lives have 'differential value (…) in the marketplace of death' (Asad, 2007, p. 94). It also means that these differential values are relational. When a person becomes a 'high-value military target', the value of all those people located nearby breaks down. Their killing becomes a 'lesser evil', a necessary means of achieving a greater end: the elimination of a 'high value military target'. This is why the 'securitization' of terrorism plays a central role in the death toll of current Western wars. The social construction of terrorism as an existential threat naturalize actions—such as the bombing of foreign cities—which would appear nonsensical otherwise.

Despite their obvious arbitrary character, the airmen involved rarely challenge the frames constructed by the rules of engagement, in particular the key notion of the NCV. Several factors explain this uncritical stance. Firstly, and unsurprisingly, they have faith in the state and the military organization they serve. In this sense, the old Weberian argument that the state has managed to 'monopolize the legitimate use of physical force' appears relevant.

Secondly and more importantly, several technologies contribute towards naturalizing the implicit interpretive schemes associated with the rules of engagement. A retired pilot told me that current fighter-bomber jet pilots behave like 'robots'. This is probably hyperbolic. However, it is clear that complying with the ROE has become one of the most important tasks assigned to fighter-bomber jet pilots and navigators. In the absence of enemies who would be able to retaliate or simply 'com-bat' (fight with), complying with the ROE is what determines the failure or the success of the 'mission'. Another concrete element reinforces this logic: pilots and navigators are among the many victims of new public management. Concretely, they are spied by their managers/commanders. The latter scrutinize the radio and video recordings of their missions so that pilots have potentially to account for their every act and everything they say. The consequence of this is simple: if they do not want to lose their job, they must accept the rules of the game. Within their social field, the rule is the following: drop as many bombs as you can but never infringe the rules. Although the violence that they perpetrate creates many more civilian victims than the 'terrorist' or 'criminal' violence that they fight, they see themselves as 'moderators of violence'. For instance, 7 out of the 40 interviewees spontaneously compared their job to that of first aid doctors or firemen. This is why I argued that their relation to violence resembles Madame de Sévigné: they do not really hate or despise anybody. They represent themselves as compassionate subjects. They 'kill' enemies and 'let civilians die' because they want the people who meet their definition of the 'good life' to live.

Conclusion

This chapter aimed to illustrate the interest of a Foucauldian discursive approach to emotions. I took the example of an investigation into French fighter-bomber pilots in order to make the point that one does not need to study emotions directly in order to understand how they operate. Since emotions are what discourse feels like within the social actors' bodies, it is possible to understand their power by studying discourse. In the case under investigation here, I found that neither hatred nor (absolute) reification are central motors of violence. Rather, violence takes on meaning within a framing which consists of granting different (positive) values to human lives and assuming that it is necessary to erase some lives so that others may be saved.

Like all frames of war, this one is underpinned by power structures of some considerable weight. In the case under investigation here, these power structures naturalize the use of 'sovereign' instruments (the bombings) within a discursive framework whose key notion is the preservation of life. In this sense, they illustrate the 'necropolitical' (Allinson, 2015; Mbembe, 2003) dimension of our humanitarian present (Fassin, 2010).

Methodologically, I came to these insights in three steps. Firstly, I gathered data about the fragments of discourse or 'frames of war' which constitute the actors' emotional relation to violence. Secondly, I analysed an important frame of war: the very words that the actors use when talking about their victims. Thirdly, I tried to confirm my interpretations by investigating the concrete semiotic elements which mediate these actors' relationship to violence, i.e. the procedures that they use before dropping bombs.

So far, I have stressed the potential of my approach. What can I say about its limitations? To start, this approach says little about the classical distinction between feelings (thought of as personal), emotions (thought of as social), and affects (thought of as corporal and, therefore, neither personal nor social). As MacLeish puts it in a Foucauldian fashion, these distinctions become pointless if one accepts that everything is discourse, including our very corporal and sensorial experiences (MacLeish, 2013, p. 14). Also, this approach will not speak to researchers who understand emotions as natural or personal phenomena. In other words, this discursive approach is unable to state whether human beings are 'naturally' sadistic or whether they are 'naturally' averse to violence. But then again, the entire history of violence seem to suggest that ordinary human beings easily learn to become violent (Arendt, 1963; Browning, 2002), or to cease to be violent (Delori, 2016b).

Acknowledgements I am grateful to Maéva Clément and Eric Sangar for their comments on a previous version of this text.

Notes

1. The words 'emotion' and 'move' have the same etymological roots.
2. Some authors who take for granted the aforementioned dualism conceive of emotions as social expressions of personal feelings.
3. House of Commons, Foreign Affairs Committee, Libya: Examination of intervention and collapse and the UK's future policy options, Third Report of Session 2016–2017.
4. The notion of 'defence intellectual' refers to scholars who work for think tanks or university departments sponsored by the industrial–military complex.
5. Interview no 19 with a pilot, March 2013.
6. So-called 'smart bombs'—that is, bombs equipped with guidance systems—have ambivalent effects on the fate of civilians. On the one hand, they enable targeting of specific sites which are, sometimes, empty of civilians. On the other hand, they rarely miss their target, meaning that they often fall in the middle of a city. In this sense, they differ from the 'blind' bombs of the Second World War which often fell in the sea or in no man's land. The consequence of this is simple: 'smart bombs' structurally kill a calculable number of civilians. I elaborate more on this idea in the last section.
7. Interview no 13 with a pilot, March 2013.
8. Interview no 3 with a pilot, December 2012.
9. See the famous Goldstone report published by the UN Human Rights Council, 12th session, agenda item 7, "Human rights in Palestine and other occupied Arab territories? Report of the United Nations Fact-Finding Mission on the Gaza Conflict", 25 September 2009.

10. It is important to highlight, in this respect, that the choice between both security instruments does not stem from technical considerations. As the assassination of Bin Laden illustrates, Western government do not hesitate to put elite troops on the ground when they deem it necessary. The preference for air bombing outside the West simply stems from the fact that they do not want to put their military personnel at risk and prefer 'transferring risks' to non-Western civilians (Shaw, 2006).

References

Allinson, J. (2015). The Necropolitics of Drone. *International Political Sociology, 9,* 113–127.
Arendt, H. (1963). *Eichmann in Jerusalem: A Report on the Banality of Evil.* New York: Viking.
Asad, T. (2007). *On Suicide Bombing.* New York: Colombia University Press.
Audouin-Rouzeau, S. (2002). La violence du champ de bataille. In S. Audouin-Rouzeau, A. Becker, C. Ingrao, & H. Rousso (Eds.), *La violence de guerre* (pp. 73–97). Paris: Editions Complexe.
Audouin-Rouzeau, S. (2008). *Combattre, Une anthropologie historique de la guerre moderne (XIXe-XXIe siècle).* Paris: Seuil.
Ayotte, K. J., & Husain, M. (2005). Securing Afghan Women: Neocolonialism, Epistemic Violence, and the Rhetoric of the Veil. *NWSA Journal, 17,* 112–133.
Barkawi, T. (2004). Peoples, Homelands, and Wars? Ethnicity, the Military, and Battle Among British Imperial Forces in the War Against Japan. *Comparative Studies in Society and History, 46*(1), 134–163.
Barkawi, T., & Stanski, K. (2013). *Orientalism and War.* New York: Columbia University Press.
Boudon, R. (1986). *L'idéologie ou l'origine des idées reçues.* Paris: Fayard.
Browning, C. R. (2002). *Des hommes ordinaires: le 101e Bataillon de réserve de la police allemande et la solution finale en Pologne.* Paris: Les Belles lettres.
Butler, J. (2004). *Precarious Life: The Powers of Mourning and Violence.* London and Brooklyn: Verso.
Butler, J. (2009). *Krieg und Affekt.* Berlin: Diaphanes.
Butler, J. (2010). *Frames of War. When Is Life Grievable?* London, Brooklyn: Verso.
Chamayou, G. (2013). *Théorie du drone.* Paris: La Fabrique.
Cohn, C. (1987). Sex and Death in the Rational World of Defense Intellectuals. *Signs, 12*(4), 687–718.
Cole, C., Dobbing, M., & Hailwood, A. (2010). *Convenient Killing: Armed Drones and the 'Playstation' Mentality.* Oxford: The Fellowship of Reconciliation.
Delori, M. (2015). *La réconciliation franco-allemande par la jeunesse. La généalogie, l'événement, l'histoire.* Bruxelles: Peter Lang.

Delori, M. (2016a). Brüssel bombardieren! Einige Widersprüche im Krieg gegen den Terrorismus. *Berliner Debatte Initial, 27*(1), 94–99.
Delori, M. (2016b). *La réconciliation franco-allemande par la jeunesse. La généalogie, l'événement, l'histoire (1871–2015)*. Paris; Berlin; Bruxelles: Peter Lang.
Elias, N. (2000 [1939]). *The Civilizing Process. Sociogenetic and Psychogenetic Investigations*. Oxford: Basil Blackwell.
Fassin, D. (2005). Compassion and Repression: The Moral Economy of Immigration Policies in France. *Cultural Anthropology, 20*(3), 362–387.
Fassin, D. (2010). *La raison humanitaire*. Paris: Seuil, 2010.
Fausto-Sterling, A. (2000). *Sexing the Body: Gender Politics and the Construction of Sexuality*. New York: Basic Books.
Fierke, K. M. (2013). *Political Self-Sacrifice. Agency, Body and Emotion in International Relations*. Cambridge: Cambridge University Press.
Foucault, M. (1969). *Archéologie du savoir*. Paris: Gallimard.
Foucault, M. (1971). Nietzsche, la Généalogie, l'Histoire. In S. Bachelard (Ed.), *Hommage à Jean Hyppolite* (pp. 145–172). Paris: Presses universitares de France.
Foucault, M. (1997 [1976]). *Il faut défendre la société Cours au Collège de France. 1975–1976*. Seuil: Gallimard.
Foucault, M. (1977). Nietzsche, Genealogy, History. In D. F. Bouchard (Ed.), *Language, Counter-Memory, Practice: Selected Essays and Interviews*. Ithaca, NY: Cornell University Press.
Goffman, E. (1974). *Frame Analysis*. Boston: Northeastern University Press.
Halbwachs, M. (1975 [1925]). *Les cadres sociaux de la mémoire*. Paris: Mouton.
Herold, M. W. (2012). The Obama/Pentagon War Narrative, the Real War and Where Afghan Civilian Deaths Do Matter, *Revista Paz y Conflictos* (Granada, Spain) No. 5: 44–64. Retrieved December 5, 2016, from https://paulcollege.unh.edu/faculty/herold
Holmqvist, C. (2013). Undoing War: War Ontologies and the Materiality of Drone Warfare. *Millenium: Journal of International Relations Studies, 41*, 535–552.
Kaufman, W. (2009). *Justified Killing: The Paradox of Self-Defense*. Lanham: Lexington Books.
Lavabre, M.-C. (1994). *Le fil rouge: sociologie de la mémoire communiste*. Paris: Presses de la FNSP.
MacLeish, K. T. (2013). *Making War at Fort Hood. Life and Uncertainty in a Military Community*. Princeton and Oxford: Princeton University Press.
Mbembe, A. (2003). Necropolitics. *Public Culture, 15*(1), 11–40.
Mosse, G. (2000). *La Brutalisation des sociétés européennes. De la Grande Guerre au totalitarisme*. Paris: Hachette littérature.
Olsson, C. (2012). *De la pacification coloniale aux opérations extérieures. Retour sur la généalogie "des cœurs et des esprits" dans la pensée militaire contemporaine*. CERI, Questions de Recherche/Research in Question, 39.

Ophir, A. (2002). Moral Technologies: The Administration of Disaster and the Forsaking of Lives. *Theoria veBikoret, 23.*
Richter-Montpetit, M. (2014). Beyond the Erotics of Orientalism: Lawfare, Torture and the Racial-Sexual Grammars of Legitimate Suffering. *Security Dialogue, 45(1),* 43–62.
Said, E. W. (1979). *Orientalism.* New York: Vinage Book.
Shaw, M. (2006). *The New Western Way of War: Risk Transfer and Its Crisis in Iraq.* Cambridge: Polity Press.
Tocqueville, A. d. (1980 [1835]). *On Democracy, Revolution, and Society.* Chicago: University of Chicago Press.
Tocqueville, A. d. (1981 [1835]). *De la démocratie en Amérique.* Paris: Flammarion.
van Veeren, E. (2014). Materializing US Security: Guantanamo's Object Lessons and Concrete Messages. *International Political Sociology, 8(1),* 20–42.
Weizman, E. (2012). *The Least of All Possible Evils: Humanitarian Violence for Arendt to Gaza.* London: Verso.

Mathias Delori is a political scientist and historian. He worked at Sciences Po Grenoble, France, the European University Institute of Florence, Italy, and the Université de Montréal, Canada. He has been working since 2011 as a CNRS research professor (chargé de recherche CNRS) at the Centre Emile Durkheim of Sciences Po Bordeaux, France. His research interests straddle the fields of critical peace and critical war studies. He published a monography on the reconciliation between France and Germany (Peter Lang, 2015). He is currently finishing a manuscript on the liberal way of war.

CHAPTER 7

The Formation of the 'Western' Strategic Gaze: A Case Study on Emotional Irrelevance in International Politics

Christophe Wasinski

> *The starkest reality of war is that the enemy is never really a monster, never inhuman. Warriors have often tried to reduce their foes to sub-humans to prop up their denial, but the fact is the enemy is someone who dreams, someone who loves, someone who just needed a job, someone who is just wanting for a break to take a leak or eat his supper: a full-fledged human just like us.*
> Stan Goff (US Army, retired) (2004, p. 38)

The analysis of material factors (be they military manpower, defense budgets, and/or weapons available in armed forces arsenals) and/or balances of power is not sufficient to decipher the war puzzle. In order to understand war, it is necessary to take into account the existence of social representations, especially those contributing to hush up 'positive' (empathic) emotions toward the Other. Illustrations of such representations are

---

C. Wasinski (✉)
Université libre de Bruxelles, Brussels, Belgium

© The Author(s) 2018
M. Clément, E. Sangar (eds.), *Researching Emotions in International Relations*, Palgrave Studies in International Relations,
https://doi.org/10.1007/978-3-319-65575-8_7

(sadly) relatively easy to find. For example, in an autobiographical book account, an American sniper explains that a marine, who had been interviewed by a journalist about what he had felt when killing, ironically answered 'Recoil' (LeBleu 2009, np). In another autobiographical narrative, an American infantryman deployed in Iraq compares the explosions he witnessed at night with the images of Walt Disney's 'psychedelic' cartoon *Fantasia* (Buzzell, 2005, p. 350). Black humor and aestheticization certainly helped these soldiers maintain emotional distance from the tragic and destructive effects of military violence. In spite of their importance and of their recurrence among soldiers, these dehumanizing discourses are not institutionally codified.

This is not, however, the case of the cartographic narrative of war(fare) which is key to generating both rationalization and dehumanization in military institutions. This narrative can be found in headquarters where officers plan and conduct operational or strategic actions using maps on which they picture their enemies by red symbols and their own troops in blue dots (since the 1980s approximately, they began to do the same on digitized maps used both for training purposes and actual operations). This narrative is also present in military academy lectures during which it is used to teach operational art. Likewise, it can be found in the tactical and operational doctrinal documents relying on maps to describe how to act on the battlefield. Such narratives can also be found in campaign studies contained in 'classical' military historians' books and in the geostrategic-geopolitical analyses using cartographic representations inspired by those in circulation in the armed forces to describe international dynamics. Media are also fond of using this narrative when they want to illustrate the operational evolution of contemporary conflicts. The iconography of contemporary wars provides further illustrations of the importance of the cartographic narrative. This type of narrative is mirrored in popular culture as well. Indeed, operational maps are sometimes reproduced on postcards which can be bought on touristic places where important battles took place in the past (*e.g.* the beaches of Normandy). Finally, widely sold board games like Risk© are also based on militarily inspired maps as are some computer games (re-)enacting past, present, or future wars.

Taken together, these illustrations point towards ow institutionally supported discourses, devices, and practices frame war as a geographic and cartographic phenomenon. It gives birth to a broad strategic narrative that generates an 'unemotional' gaze.[1] Among other things, this gaze produces a rationalized representation of the use of force. War(fare) looks much more organized on operational maps than in reality; the chaos of combat tends to 'magically' disappear. Another important consequence of this narrative is its dehumanization of human beings (Wasinski, 2011). In brief, the cartographic narrative at the core of the (geo)strategic gaze transforms human beings, taken individually or in groups, into pawns that can be sacrificed on battlefields for the maintenance of a certain world order. This narrative therefore participates in the neutralization of emotions towards human beings.

Depending on their nature, emotions refer to two broad categories of consequences in the context of armed conflicts. On the one hand, there are 'positive' emotions that foster recognition of Others' humanity. These empathic emotions must be controlled and hushed by the military institution in order to ease the recourse of violence against the Other (a good historical example is given by Ashworth, 1968). On the other hand, there are 'negative' emotions that encourage the use of force against the Other. These emotions can be at the origin of more or less spontaneous and violent emotional mobilizations (for an anthropological-historical illustration, see Corbin, 1993). Sociologist Wolfgang Sofsky even wrote about the existence of emotional communities that are described as confraternities of destruction welded together by feelings of cruelty (Sofsky, 2003). The attitude of the armed forces regarding emotions and emotional communities is ambiguous. From time to time, armed forces either tolerate or explicitly support them; this is for example the case during Marine Corps boot camps during which enemy hatred is instilled in young recruits. However, from a military technical standpoint, such emotions may lead to a 'waste' of resources and produce 'excessive' violence, i.e. violence not useful to attain operational goals in the field (Bataille, 1991). From a strictly military standpoint, the cartographic narrative of war has the advantage to silence all kinds of emotions. Soldier's fears, anxieties, feelings of disgust, hatred, revenge, or guilt are simply irrelevant for this narrative that serves to guide military action. In other words, dehumanizing processes are not only produced through description of enemies as 'savages' or 'barbarians', they are also the outcome of the absence of information related to emotions.

In a nutshell, this chapter focuses on the following research question: *Why and how did the (geo)strategic gaze—that makes empathic emotions irrelevant; encourages resort to violence against 'Others'; symbolically transforms 'own troops' into reified entities that can be sacrificed, and thus facilitates war-waging—emerge?* As shall be seen, in order to explain how this gaze developed, it is necessary to study knowledge production, the evolution of the military organization, and changes in the political and socio-economic structures in Europe (and to a lesser extent in the United States), since the end of the Middle Ages, through a historical sociological perspective. Here, emotions and their expressions are apprehended as dependent variable which presence rests on the absence of the dehumanizing geographic and cartographic narrative of war.

Studying Emotions and Dehumanization in War(fare)

'Classical' approaches in the field of international relations and strategic/security studies have traditionally shown little interest in emotions as a research topic. They have mostly put emphasis on material factors, balance of powers' configurations, and supposedly rational states and bureaucracies to explain the outbreak of wars (Vasquez, 1992). They have been less inclined to investigate non-material factors influencing conflicts, nor to tackle the issue of 'meaning construction' related to the use of violence. Even research stemming from the fields of 'peace research' and 'conflict resolution' have not been overtly concerned by the effects of emotions.[2]

Actually, military historians specialized in the social dimensions of contemporary wars and anthropologists researching military violence were the first to seriously consider this problem. Their case studies were based on the qualitative analysis of media products, political speeches, official reports and personal testimonies. They have demonstrated that the deployment of military violence was often connected to the existence of emotionally loaded representations of enemies, i.e. racist and/or dehumanizing images and speeches describing enemies as 'animals' or 'barbarians' to be eliminated. They have shown that such representations, appealing to emotions rather than to rationality contributed to fuel violence during both World Wars, in the colonies, and among American soldiers deployed in Afghanistan and in Iraq over the 2000s (Bartov, 1991; Brown, 2008; Brown & Lutz, 2007; Dower, 1987; Jeismann, 1997; Liulevicius, 2000; Renda, 2001). As a matter of fact, most of this scholarly work does not pretend emotions and racism are directly causing war. Rather, 'negative' emotions are seen as a cause engendering 'excessive' violence, i.e. violence deemed not necessary to accomplish operational goals (e.g. violence committed against prisoners and civilians).

In some conflicts however, racist and animalizing representations were/are few. This can even be the case during high-intensity conflicts. For example, historians have asserted that American and Soviet soldiers didn't systematically frame German soldiers along racist and animalizing lines during the Second World War, although the fight against them was bitter to say the least (Doubler, 1994, p. 258; Meridale, 2005). According to another strand of research based on either ethnological or archival and documentary analysis, violence is rather facilitated by dehumanization provoked by cold technical representations.[3] In other words, 'technostrategic discourses' (Cohn, 1987), 'organizational frames' (Eden, 2004), 'military cultures', or 'institutional routines' (Cameron, 1994; Hull, 2004; Sherry, 1989) also produce dehumanization by turning human beings into 'things' that can or should be destroyed by weapons. Also known as 'reification', this process works through 'omission, abstraction, classification, and disembodiment' (Eden, 2004, p. 290). In a practical way, the aforementioned frames, cultures, or discourses transform individuals into 'targets', 'statistical data', or 'virtual reality' (see also: Der Derian, 2009; Gusterson, 1998).

In spite of their truly substantial contribution, three criticisms can be leveled at this second strand of literature. Firstly, at the empirical level, these studies are mostly concerned by the with nuclear weaponry (James Der Derian's book on virtual warfare, however, stands apart). The 'classical' or conventional dimensions of war(fare) are barely covered, whereas they play a fundamental role in international relations' history (among others because of the two World Wars). Secondly, both analyses of racism and of technical narratives remain based on national cases. They either focus on American soldiers, or German soldiers, or American nuclear experts, or on a comparison of French and German representations. None has really tackled the problem at the transnational level although it is known that military discourses and practices travel quite easily across national borders (Ralston, 1990). Thirdly, more importantly, these studies haven't questioned the links between 'macro' social structures, changes in military institutions, and the production of representations. Only the last two phenomena have been examined systematically. According to the scholarship so far, dehumanization can either be the product of an institutional culture; soldiers' representations; discursive frames operating at the organizational level; a Foucaldian regime of practices; anthropological rituals; discourses of a network of actors; or, the product of the rational conduct of bureaucracies. Scholars did not mean to negate the influence of the social structure but they rather put emphasis elsewhere. In this chapter, I propose to address these three shortcomings by focusing on conventional warfare, paying attention to the transnational dimension of the studied phenomenon, and mapping the structural forces responsible for the dissemination of the said strategic narrative.

HISTORICAL SOCIOLOGY INSPIRED BY SCIENCE AND TECHNOLOGY STUDIES

The argument of this text is that the emergence, dissemination, and continuity of the military cartographic narrative should be comprehended as the outcome of a complex social process that has to do with knowledge production, the institutional evolution of the armed forces, as well as changes of in the social, economic, and political structures in Europe (and to a lesser extent in the United States) after the medieval period. To put it differently, these representations became prevalent for two main reasons: (1) the social configuration was favorable to 'technical entrepreneurs' who developed and carried them out; (2) these entrepreneurs incorporated these cartographic representations in tactical, operational, strategic, and geopolitical-geostrategic discourses that pleased their powerful patrons (were they kings or commanding officers). All these elements are central to explain why and how the cartographic narrative that hushed up emotions became so prevalent.

Methodologically speaking, this approach is neither a Foucaldian genealogy nor a frame or discursive analysis but a historical sociologyical analysis inspired by research in Science and Technology Studies (STS) on the topic of weaponry and war (Adler, 1997; Latour, 1988; MacKenzie, 1990; Mort, 2001; Ritchie, 2010).[4] Its starting point is to question why and how some artefacts or knowledge succeed while others don't (the focus of this chapter is on knowledge only). Knowledge and representations are thus taken as a dependent variable. At a more theoretical level, STS scholars argue that the development of technical conceptions (in the domain of war and international security among others) depends on the combination of political, economic, organizational, and technical processes. Often, they stress that the emergence of technical conceptions results from the action of 'assemblages' of actors. They coined the term 'heterogeneous engineering' to qualify the action of these 'assemblages'. This approach furthermore confers the ability to study the effect of heterogeneous engineering projects transnationally. This is an important advantage in order to analyze the social processes responsible for the dissemination of the military cartographic narrative at the European level.

Historical sociological analyses that contribute to the STS research agenda do not aim at producing broad generalizations. STS scholars' ambition is rather to provide detailed historical reconstitutions of processes that led to the construction of representations. This scholarship is as much driven by the 'hows' as by the 'whys'. STS scholars are also interested in the articulations between local ('micro') and global ('macro') processes. For these reasons, their research usually requires a vast amount of empirical information. In some cases, STS scholars rely primarily on interviews, complemented by documents (see for example: MacKenzie, 1990). In other instances, they rely mainly on archives and published documents (Adler, 1997).

This chapter uses published documents. The empirical corpus was elaborated in three steps.[5] The first one consisted in locating and reading approximately a hundred secondary sources on the history of tactical, operational, strategic, and geopolitical-geostrategic thinking. Following this, a list of approximately one hundred most influential military treatises was established. The second step consisted in locating, reading, and analyzing these primary texts. Some of them were found on the Internet (among others on *Gallica*, the website of the French National Library). Others were consulted in a military library (the Belgian Ministry of Defence Central Library). Some texts were consulted in an academic library (the Namur University Moretus Plantin Library). A significant number of these treatises contained references to the cartographic narrative of war. In my previous research, this material was used to draw a 'genealogical tree' of the cartographic narrative (Illustration 7.1):

This tree illustrates how the cartographic narrative diffused itself in the strategic thinking from the end of the Middle Ages until today. In poststructuralist jargon, this tree represents a vast intertextual edifice that spanned over more than five centuries (Wasinski, 2011).

However, this previously published genealogical approach was relatively blind to the structural and material conditions of the narrative's emergence. In order to evaluate the importance of these factors it was necessary to go back to the literature accumulated during this previous research in order to gain additional information about the social background of the authors responsible for the production of the cartographic narrative. This information was complemented with books found in the literature more focused on the evolution of the states' structures in European history (Duby, 1973; Elias, 1983; Tilly, 1975; Weber, 1965)

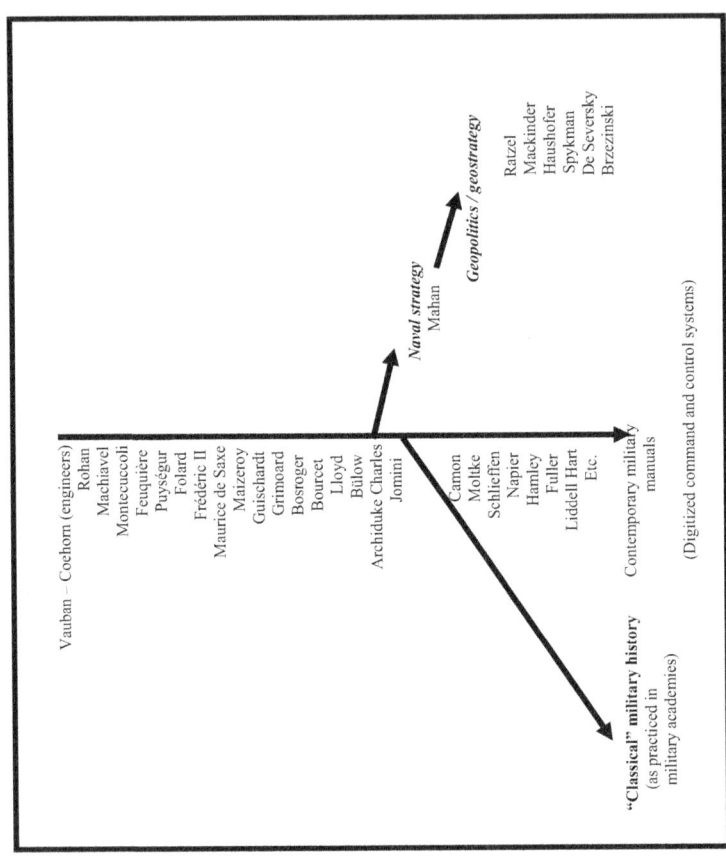

Illustration 7.1 The 'genealogical tree' of the military cartographic narrative

as well as that on the structural changes of armed forces (Adler, 1997; Kolko, 1994; Lynn, 1997; Pauwels, 2016). This last step was aimed at analyzing the structural dynamics the authors of the treatises were embedded in.

Emotions, Narrative, and Visibility

In this chapter, emotions are apprehended as a consequence of the way people experience (feel, perceive) reality (Boltanski, 2004; Boltanski & Thévenot, 2006; James, 1884, 2003). In turn, emotions can (when they are not fully repressed) trigger reactions (changes in behavior for example). The simplified sequence looks like this: reality → perception → emotion → reaction. Representations or Narratives can, however, influence emotions and, indirectly, reactions, by framing perceptions. Therefore, the may transform into: reality → narrative → perception → emotion → reaction.[6] In other words, narratives act as mediators between reality and perception. It is through their action on perceptions that they have an effect on emotions. As a consequence, socially constructed narratives participate in the regulation of emotions, be they 'emphatic' or 'heinous' ones. This chapter intends to analyze social structures generating narratives that condition emotions and their possible expression.

A link can be established between emotions and the issue pertaining to the framing and social (in)visibility of actors (Butler, 2010; Rancière, 2000; see also Delori in this volume). This link is even more striking if one considerations research focusesing on vision, as in Michel Foucault's work. Foucault is one of the first philosophers to have so clearly highlighted the connections between vision and power in his analysis of Bentham's panoptical prison design (Foucault, 1995). According to him, power rests on surveillance capacities (among others) which ensue from the use of devices intended to make individuals visible, or even 'readable' as a text. The panopticon is thus the core of a disciplinary gaze that transforms human beings into targets of political power. The philosopher Paul Virilio also investigated this. In his work, Virilio drew he draws attention to the importance of the equipments that breed war images (Virilio, 1994). He coined the concept of 'logistics of perception' in order to analyze devices (such as aerial cameras) used to picture war for both military–technical and propaganda purposes (Virilio, 1989). His ideas echoe those of Foucault on the panopticon. In an analysis of war cultures, poststructuralist scholar Michael J. Shapiro underlined that maps can also participate in this panoptical design. According to Shapiro, maps actually support resorting to military violence and prevent the development of a true encounter ethics (Shapiro, 1997). Recently, Antonius C.G.M. Robbens also referred to the emergence of a 'hostile gaze' to depict the dehumanizing effects of the night-vision systems used by soldiers in Vietnam and in Iraq (Robbens, 2013). In this regard, the panopticon would be operational around the clock.

This research points to the existence of institutionalized ways of looking (or gazing) at Others that, which either produce dehumanization through their transformation into objects (i.e. reification), dehumanization through sheer invisibilization, and/or dehumanization through their exclusion from the a given community. The ways Others are 'seen' by institutions and their members is the outcome of a narrative that neutralizes the expression of emphatic or heinous emotions toward them. These ideas are in line with the chapter's thesis regarding the production and stabilization of a (geo)strategic gaze. The main difference is that this chapter is not directly concerned with the detailed content of the narrative itself. Its objective is to study the structural conditions that which gave birth to the technical cartographic and dehumanizing imaginary. Another shortcoming of this chapter is that it has little to say about the ways actors on the field (i.e. soldiers in trenches) make sense of it (and, possibly, try to subvert it). A more anthropological investigation would be necessary to understand these dimensions (on this point, see: Croser, 2010). It is also important to note that this narrative is inextricably entwined with the rise of a strategic culture that put forward the quest for decisive battles (which culminate in the phenomenon of 'total warfare'). Lastly, this chapter does not consider the possible existence of a militarized and cartographic gaze outside of the Euro-Atlantic zone or in the Euro-Atlantic zone before the Middle Ages (e.g. during Antiquity). These questions are outside of the chapter's scope.

Engineers and Marginalized Military Theorists

In order to understand the emergence of the militarizedy gaze, it is necessary to step back in the history of Europe up to the Middle Ages. At that time, war(fare) mainly consisted of raids aimed at plundering (Duby, 1973; Reuter, 1985). European sovereigns did not only strive to defend themselves against enemies located outside of their kingdoms' boundaries.

They also had to face the danger of dissensions inside their own domains. They thus relied on raids to acquire wealth and territories, which they, in turn, used to buy the loyalty of their subordinates. As a consequence, war was not only a political activity but also an economic one. Obviously, this was a predatory system. That said, due to the weakness of sovereigns, most violent activities were not highly centralized, nor institutionally codified.

After centuries of this dynamic, it became difficult to find weakly defended territories to plunder (Duby, 1973). Unconquered faraway lands, for example in the East or in the Southeast of Europe, were not only distant but also unhospitable. Razzias in these areas were thus difficult to conduct for weak small medieval armies. Besides, a new economic process emerged in Europe. It was, among others, based on more intensive agricultural production. The medieval predatory system, upon which the sovereigns and their barons subsisted, was increasingly perceived as a nuisance to this new development. Some sovereigns nevertheless managed to reinforce their power in the changing context (Adler, 1997; Duffy, 1988; Elias, 1983; Lynn, 1997; Parrott, 2005; Tilly, 1975; Weber, 1965). Firstly, these sovereigns learned how to avoid relying excessively on high nobility for military support. On the contrary, skillful sovereigns strove to maintain them out of the military sphere, for example by incorporating them in to the (pacified) court society when they were financially weakened (because they were unable to repay debts they had contracted to maintain their standard of living). Secondly, sovereigns had a preference for officers coming from lower ranks of nobility and for members of the emerging *bourgeoisie* (despite attempts from the nobility to bar them access to commanding functions). Individuals from these two social groups were either socially and financially less independent and/or better educated than most of the barons. They made more docile and more efficient fighters, who agreed to follow military trainings and showed more respect for hierarchical rules. Thirdly, their armies consisted of provincial regiments of infantry and of companies of mercenaries from Switzerland, Germany, or on economically peripheral regions of Europe. Consequently, sovereigns were not only dependent on one social group for their protection against external enemies and internal threats. The Weberian monopoly of state violence progressively consolidated out of the capacity of the sovereign at manipulating the components of this assemblage. Basically, this amounted to a 'divide and rule' process. Ultimately, successful sovereigns took advantage of their strengthened position to impose the (centralized) fusion of their disparate forces. This in turn entailed the development of procedures and military knowledge (among other, publications on tactical rules). The combination of all these factors acted as a precondition for the strategic narrative in the making.

This picture would however be incomplete if it did not consider a specific group of this assemblage, i.e. the engineers (Blanchard, 1996; Duffy, 1979, 1985; Parker, 1996). Initially, most of them were from Italy. It is indeed in Italy, cradle of the Renaissance, that the best engineers were trained at the time. Among others, these engineers were specialists, especially in the field of fortifications. They developed a new type of fortress, more complex and capable of sustaining cannonballs. The Italian engineers soon offered their services to sovereigns throughout all over the European continent. Perceived with a certain distrust, because of their foreign origins, they were gradually replaced by national engineers. The range of their tasks also expanded in the process. Engineers still assisted the sovereigns in constructing protected borders, but they also conducted sieges and were responsible for army logistics. On the whole, they played an important role in the organization of armed forces. They contributed to strengthen sovereigns, who in turn helped them move up the social ladder. This (asymmetric) alliance between sovereigns and engineers was made possible because of nobility's relatively decreasing interest for military affairs. Thise emergence of the figure of the engineer in the European armed forces was the starting point for the development of the military gaze.

In a text he dedicated to Vauban, Henri Guerlac described the engineers as the true inventors of a science of war (Guerlac, 1986). The quantity of treatises written by military engineers (e.g. by Pierre Bourdin, Menno van Coehoorn, Jean Dubreuil, Albrecht Dürer, Alain Manesson Mallet, Nicolas Tartaglia, Sébastien Le Pestre Vauban, etc.) constitutes a testimony to this phenomenon (Pollak 1991). These texts, which focused on fortification building, were illustrated by numerous engravings (Picture 7.1).

Most often, these images were either plans or aesthetic drawings inspired by the model of the plan. The emergence of this type of representations were, among others, connected to the rediscovery of antique geometry (and its Euclidian rules) in the fields of arts and sciences during the Renaissance period. The new pictures participated in the transformation of the visual culture (Henderson, 1995; Panofsky, 1975). In the field of military knowledge, they actively supported the naturalization of the 'bird's' or 'god's eye view', i.e. the view of reality as seen from above, which quickly became a norm. It should also be underlined

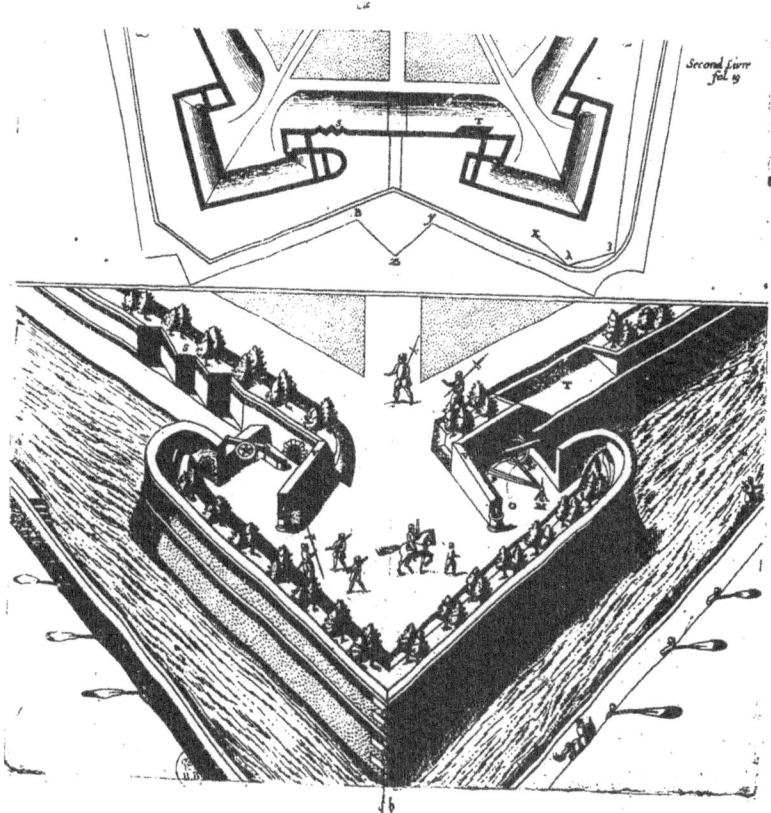

Picture 7.1 Seventeenth-century schematic illustration of a fortification. Source: Errard, Jean (1622). *La fortification démonstrée en réduicte en art*. Licence: Permission of the Bibliothèque nationale de France

that this way of seeing and picturing reality was mostly to apprehend the material universe.

This said, this change of visual culture affected the tactical military writers' community. During the sixteenth and seventeenth centuries, several waves of tactical textbooks were published in Europe (Colson, 1999; Gonzales de Leon, 1996; Kleinschmidt, 1999). They codified new tactical orders and military practices experimented by troops in Spain, the Netherlands, Sweden, and by Swiss and German mercenaries. These documents explained how to organize soldiers in lines and columns and make them cohesively move forward. They focused on technical details of the conduct of war within small units. These technical and tactical treatises, written by soldiers, were illustrated by 'bird's eye view' or 'god's eye view' of the orders of battle. They thus relied on and contributed to the dissemination of the visual culture developed by artists and engineers. This visual culture, in turn, contributed to a tradition of making emotions irrelevant in warfare (Picture 7.2).

Between the end of the seventeenth century and the beginning of the nineteenth century, these representations were used in a new category of military writings (Chagniot, 1997; Colson, 1999; Colson & Coutau-Bégarie, 2000; Duffy, 1988; Gat, 2002). Among others, these texts focused on battle orders of larger units. They also considered the problem of bringing these units on the battlefield in an advantageous position (on upper ground). Actually, these treatises formed a dense, but not monolithic, transnational intellectual edifice. This was the consequence of military debates that took place, during the eighteenth century, between the proponents of the column versus those in favor of the line. The authors of these treatises — such as Montecuccoli, Puységur, Feuquières, Folard, de Saxe, Guibert, Bülow, Lloyd, Jomini — had four things in common.

Firstly, several were not 'great captains'. Some were institutionally located at the periphery of the military institution (at least when they wrote their treatises). The individual trajectories of a few of them were also atypical, such as the one of the Swiss banker Jomini who joined for a while the Napoleonic armies. Most of them came from the bourgeoisie, the minor nobility, or were put aside for because their military opinions were considered too radical. Secondly, many of these authors were advocates of military efficiency. This drove them to support the quest for (decisive) battles. This went along with recommendations for the improvement of officer's technical skills (among others by a better military education) and greater centralization. In other words, these texts questioned the balance of forces within military institutions at the time. More centralization meant the reduction of nobility's prerogatives. This also helps us understand why military intellectuals were often situated on the fringe of institutions. Thirdly, these writers also used engravings of battlefields as seen from the sky to illustrate their works; authors such as Archduke Charles, Bülow, and Lloyd were even said to belong to a 'geometrical school' of strategic thought. Finally, they participated in the dissemination of the

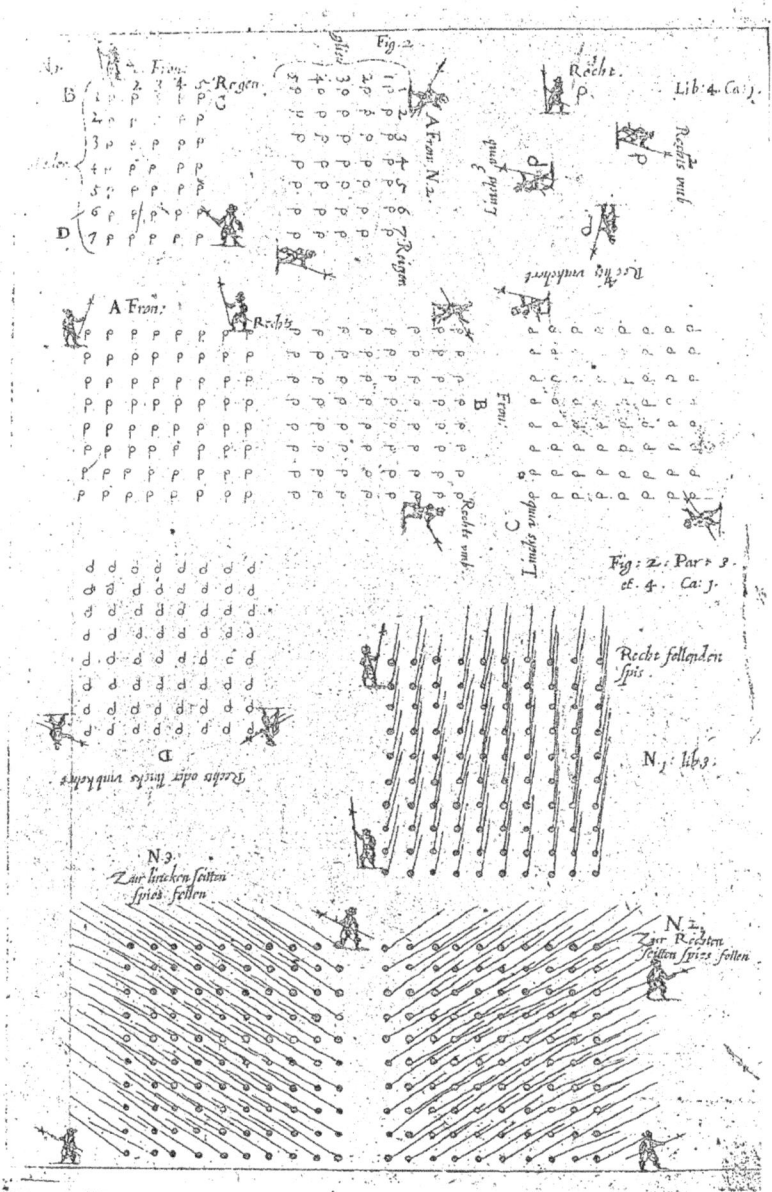

Picture 7.2 Seventeenth-century cartographic illustration of an infantry formation. Source: Wallhausen, Johann Jacobi von (1615)., *L'art militaire pour l'infanterie*. Paris: 63. Licence: Permission of the Bibliothèque nationale de France

visual culture of both engineers and tactical authors; however, their perspective was broader. The map-like images they used pictured vaster spaces, where large columns and lines of soldiers were deployed. These images confirmed the prevalence of the unemotional gaze in warfare (Picture 7.3).

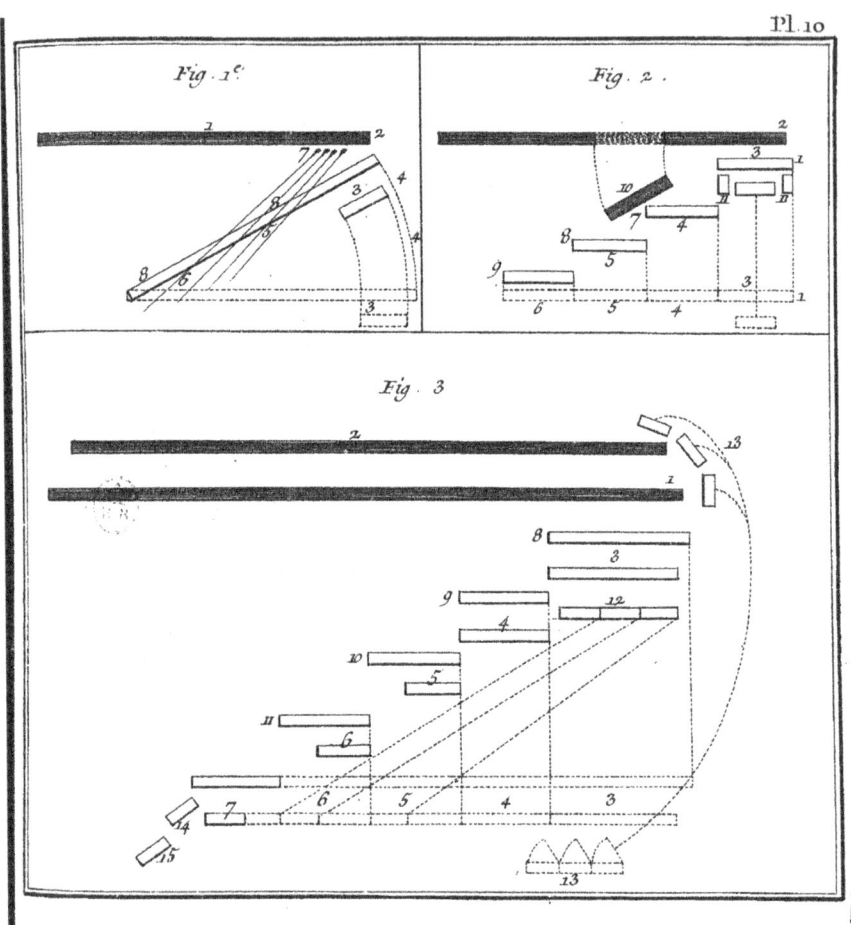

Picture 7.3 Eighteenth-century cartographic illustration of tactical battle movements. Source: Grimoard, Philippe-Henri de (1775). *Essai théorique et pratique sur les batailles*. Paris: 99. Licence: Permission of the Bibliothèque nationale de France

The Expansion of the Cartographic Gaze

During the nineteenth century, some of the ideas of the 'marginal' military theorists relating to the rationalization of armed forces and quest for efficiency were adopted. The geometrical and cartographic narrative of military violence, embodied in these theorists' writings, was strengthened in the process. To understand this phenomenon, one should not only focus on the inner workings of armed forces. Indeed, this great transformation was mostly the indirect result of the French Revolution, which was itself the consequence of a reshuffle of the 'domestic balance of power' between French social groups (Adler, 1997; Elias, 1983; Lynn, 1996; Pauwels, 2016). Before 1789, nobility made a point to block the social ascension of the bourgeoisie (among others, through bylaws forbidding the bourgeois to access certain functions). During the Revolution, the bourgeoisie allied with the people to the detriment of nobility. However, this assemblage did not last long. It was soon to be followed by a counterrevolutionary phase during the nineteenth century. This second assemblage was composed of a renewed alliance between nobility and the bourgeoisie at the expense of the rest of the population. In the alliance, trade and industry went to the bourgeoisie, whereas diplomacy and the armed forces remained in the hands of the nobility. This second assemblage was however not quite identical to the one prevalent during the *Ancien Régime* because, in the meantime, the bourgeoisie had grown stronger (it should also be noted that both groups were progressively merging through the intensification of inter-group weddings).

Those changes had a tremendous impact on the military field. First of all, the sidelining of nobility and the restriction of its privileges during the French Revolution made it possible to enforce radical reforms within armed forces. This institution became much more centralized. The reinforcement of institutional hierarchy made it easier to establish a unity of command and, as a consequence, to impose the quest for battles as a norm. This evolution put an end to the eighteenth-century tradition of maneuvering instead of fighting. From then on, without surprise, combats also became much more brutal (Lynn, 1996; Rothenberg, 1981). At the same time, the *de facto* technocratic ideal contained in the writings of the eighteenth-century thinkers became 'mainstream'. Among others, this ideal expressed itself with the development of new military schools intended for candidate-officers (such as Saint-Cyr or West Point).

Finally, technification and the development of military academies went hand in hand with the production of further military texts intended to teach officers how to fight efficiently. This phenomenon affected not only France but also Prussia (and later Germany), the United States, and Great Britain during the nineteenth century (Colson, 1993; Luvaas, 1964; Queloz, 2009). In summary, the sidelining of noble officers during the revolutionary era allowed the operational designs conceived at the margins of the institution during the eighteenth to get the upper hand in France before spreading in other European states and beyond the Atlantic Ocean.[7] These social evolutions supported the strengthening of the cartographic narrative of military violence. This narrative was not only used in theoretical treatises on the art of war. First, the cartographic narrative of war was also used during lectures on military history. Second, it was used during 'war games' (*Kriegspiel*) played by soldiers to analyze past battles and rehearse for future ones. Finally, it was applied during 'staff rides' conducted on historic sites of battlefields. In brief, this dehumanized and unemotional representation of war saturated the strategic discourse.

The new alliance between the *bourgeoisie* and nobility had another impact. The rise of the bourgeoisie was coterminous with the acceleration of the European and North American industrialization. This phenomenon had an influence in the field of military affairs (Echevarria, 2000; Ellis, 1986; Sampson, 1977). For example, the steam engine, a strong symbol of this process of industrialization, played an important role within armed forces. Ships and steam trains allowed armies to move more soldiers and war material faster and over greater distances. The industrialization had also an influence on the development of weapons. The industries produced more powerful artillery, more effective rifles, and machine guns. As it was shown during conflicts that took place outside of Europe (e.g. the American Civil War of 1861–1865 or the Russian–Japanese war of 1905), the introduction of these techniques had terrible effects on human lives (Travers, 1979). The general staffs' intellectual reaction, whose officers were often members of the aristocracy, turned out to be eminently conservative. It essentially consisted in developing war plans that transformed whole states, regions, or even parts of the European continent into operational zones that could be pictured cartographically (Bucholz, 1991; Kennedy, 1979; Zuber, 2002). Basically, it incrementally expanded the classical cartographic narrative inherited from the eighteenth century without really taking stock of the dramatic technological changes in the field of firepower. Even the First World War and its human consequences only marginally affected their operational and strategic designs based on the same cartographic narrative. On the Western front, operations were still being planned on maps by officers located in well-protected command centers, miles away from the frontline. The cartographic and dehumanizing narrative of war remained firmly entrenched among the officer corps all along the conflict. This relevance was also confirmed during the Second World War. Undeniably, armament was technically improved (among others, in the field of armored and air warfare) but the cartographic narrative of war continued to prevail in the operational planning. Even the introduction of nuclear armaments did not fundamentally alter this narrative. Although a new strategic discourse concentrating on the (not cartographic) notion of deterrence emerged, general staffs continued to think of military actions through cartographic representations during the Cold War (Ross, 1996). In short, whatever the extent of economic, social, and technical changes, emotions remained largely invisible in the field of warfare due to these representations.

Finally, the cartographic narrative can be found in the 'geopolitical' and 'geostrategic' discourses that appeared during the second part of the nineteenth century, became (in)famous during the Second World War, and circulated widely during the Cold War (Dodds & Atkinson, 2002; Raffestin, Loreno, & Pasteur, 1995). They were written by European or American authors like Friedrich Ratzel, Alfred Thayer Thayer Mahan, Halford J. Mackinder, Karl Haushofer, Alexander P. de Seversky, Karl Haushofer. After the Second World War, some of these ideas and representations were recycled in the United States, among others in popular magazines. Samuel P. Huntington's thesis on the 'clash of civilizations' as well as Thomas Barnetts' on the 'New Pentagon Map' stands as more recent, post-Cold War examples (Debrix, 2007). Initially, this knowledge was also the product of the alliance between the liberal bourgeoisie and the conservative aristocracy in Europe. They were supporting the nationalist's and imperialist's policies of their states (Picture 7.4).

Geopolitical texts also often endorse a militarist ideological vision (Lauterbach, 1944).[8] Actually, one of the common denominators of these writings is to symbolically transform empires and state borders into frontline through their borrowing of the strategic narrative to picture the world. Emotionally, these geopolitical discourses are different from the strictly military operational ones. Geopolitical pictures are aimed at rein-

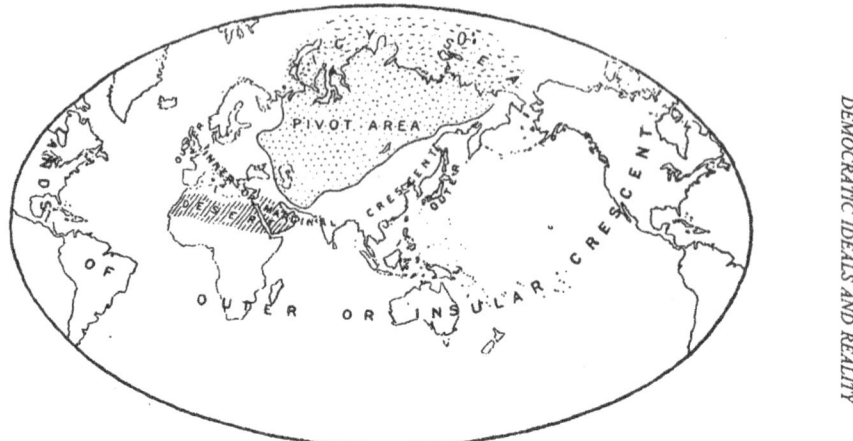

Picture 7.4 Twentieth-century geopolitical map 'The Natural Seats of Power'. Source: Mackinder, Sir Halford J. (1942), Democratic Ideals and Reality: A Study in the politics of reconstruction. Washington DC. National Defense University Press: 190.

forcing popular mobilization against an Other. They are used to generate 'negative' emotions, especially fear, for instance by picturing vast stretches of land in a 'threatening' red color.

Conclusion

The objective of this chapter was to show how historical-sociological tools of analysis can be used to understand why and how military cartographic narratives were used to shape collective emotions in warfare. Through dehumanized representations of warfare, 'Western' states have achieved the ability to control and manage emotions and transform them into a politically 'useful' instrument of state power. This argument relies on an ontological understanding of emotions as socially constructed phenomenon, which cannot be understood without analyzing historically contingent formations of state power and technological development. While in many current accounts the historicity of emotions remains a black box, I suggest borrowing from historical sociological tools used in the field of STS in order to trace the emergence of a technocentric representation of war. This approach helps detect continuities over long periods of time and focus on processes of transnational diffusion (and thus avoid 'methodological nationalism').

Empirically, the cartographic and dehumanizing narrative took form after the end of the Middle Ages. It was initially developed by Renaissance engineers and adopted by tactical and operational military writers at the fringe of the military institution. The changes introduced in the 'social balance of power' during the French Revolution were indirectly favorable to the reinforcement of this narrative. During the nineteenth century, ideological conservatism resulting from the alliance of the bourgeoisie and aristocracy made it possible for these representations to proliferate and become even more radical in the geopolitical-geostrategic domain. In the military field, these remained relevant during the twentieth century, as they did in the context of the Cold War.

The main lessons of this chapter is that macrostructural variables, such as historically specific configurations of state power and technological and organizational evolution, have an impact on emotions or their absence in international relations. In other words, I argue that emotions and/or their absence can be studied as a dependent variable that is changing over time. In the case at hand, the main drawback of the proposed historical sociological approach is that it says little about how soldiers on the ground actually justify (and possibly also contest) the conduct of war. In other words, it does not account for how 'effectively' the cartographic narrative might impact the emotional representations of individual soldiers. Another limit is the difficulty of generalizing beyond the chosen context: While the cartographic narrative seems to be closely related to the formation of the nation-state in Europe, further research might analyse whether it has also played an important role in other parts of the world.

Acknowledgments The author would like to address special thanks to Constance de Lannoy, Maéva Clément, and Eric Sangar for their kind assistance during the writing of this chapter.

Notes

1. The 'gaze' concept is hereafter borrowed from Priya Satia's book on British imperial warfare (2008). The historian evoked the construction of a coercive 'state gaze' by colonial agents and soldiers. Antoine Bousquet later coined the concept of 'martial gaze' (Bousquet, 2018).

2. Scholars from these fields analyzed 'images' and '(mis)perceptions' in international relations (Jervis, 1976; White, 1966). However, their research did not directly untangle the way knowledge production, emotions, and dehumanization are interwoven in conflict.
3. Historical research has nonetheless shown that links were forged between racist and technical dehumanizing narratives during both colonial wars and the Second World War (Hull, 2004; Russell, 1996; Satia, 2008; Sherry, 1989).
4. The whole range of STS's operational concepts could not be adopted and used in this short chapter. For more about them, see: Latour 1988.
5. Lack of space made it impossible to provide all references to these books and treatises in this chapter. More bibliographical information can be found in: Wasinski (2011).
6. In some instances, 'reaction' consists in actions aimed at transforming the narrative. In the field of military history, a good example is given by the Vietnam War. This conflict was first assessed by the Americans not as a local nationalist conflict but as a component of the war against communism, a narrative that has some emotional appeal in the United States. After the 1975 Communist victory, a new (and emotionally laden) narrative, based on the myth of the domestic 'stab in back' by Liberals, imposed itself about the conflict (Lembcke, 2000). This new narrative contributed to Ronald Reagan's accession to the presidency and helped justify, among others, its interventionist policy in Latin America in order to 'kick out the Vietnam syndrome'. To put it more schematically, a possible feedback loop can be drawn between 'reaction' and 'narrative'.
7. It should be stressed that officers of noble origin never completely left the armed forces. Rather, those who remained were inserted in a more binding institutional environment. Moreover, the *Restauration*, which took place after the end of the Napoleonic era, did not seriously question the military norm of efficiency that was imposed during the Revolutionary wars.
8. In France, *Hérodote* (founded by Yves Lacoste in 1976) constitutes an important exception. This periodical initially suggested an alternative geopolitics which was highly critical of the imperial projects.

References

Adler, K. (1997). *Engineering the Revolution. Arms and Enlightenment in France, 1763–1815*. Princeton: Princeton University Press.

Ashworth, T. (1968). The Sociology of Trench Warfare. *British Journal of Sociology*, 19(4), 407–423.

Bartov, O. (1991). *Hitler's Army. Soldiers, Nazis, and War in the Third Reich*. Oxford: Oxford University Press.

Bataille, G. (1991). *The Accursed Share* (Vol. 1). London: Zone Books.
Blanchard, A. (1996). *Vauban*. Paris: Fayard.
Boltanski, L. (2004). *La condition foetale. Une sociologie de l'engendrement et de l'avortement*. Paris: Gallimard.
Boltanski, L., & Thévenot, L. (2006). *On Justification. Economies of Worth*. Princeton: Princeton University Press.
Bousquet, A. (2018). *The Martial Gaze*. Minneapolis: University of Minnesota Press. (To Be Published).
Brown, K. (2008). "All They Understand Is Force": Debating Culture in Operation Iraqi Freedom. *American Anthropologist, 110*(4), 443–453.
Brown, K., & Lutz, F. (2007). Grunt Lit: The Participant-Observers of Empire. American Ethnologist. *American Ethnologist, 34*(2), 322–326.
Bucholz, A. (1991). *Moltke, Schlieffen, and Prussian War Planning*. New York: Berg.
Butler, J. (2010). *Frames of War. When Life Is Grievable?* Londres: Verso.
Buzzell, C. (2005). *My War. Killing Time in Iraq*. London: Corgi.
Cameron, C. M. (1994). *American Samurai. Myth, Imagination, and the Conduct of Battle in the First Marine Division, 1941–1951*. Cambridge: Cambridge University Press.
Chagniot, J. (1997). *Le chevalier de Folard. La stratégie de l'incertitude*. Monaco: Editions du Rocher.
Cohn, C. (1987). Sex and Death in the Rational World of Defense Intellectuals. *Signs, 12*(4), 687–718.
Colson, B. (1993). *La culture stratégique américaine. L'influence de Jomini*. Paris: Economica.
Colson, B. (1999). *L'Art de la guerre de Machiavel à Clausewitz*. Namur: Presses Universitaires de Namur.
Colson, B., & Coutau-Bégarie, H. (Eds.). (2000). *Pensée stratégique et humanisme. De la tactique des Anciens à l'éthique de la stratégie*. Paris: Economica.
Corbin, A. (1993). *The Village of Cannibals. Rage & Murder in France, 1870*. Harvard: Harvard University Press.
Croser, C. (2010). *The New Spatiality of Warfare. Operational Uncertainty and the US Military in Iraq*. London: Routledge.
Debrix, F. (2007). *Tabloid Terror. War, Culture, and Geopolitics*. London: Routledge.
Der Derian, J. (2009). *Virtuous War. Mapping the Military-Industrial-Media Entertainment Network*. New York and London: Routledge.
Dodds, K., & Atkinson, D. (Eds.). (2002). *Geopolitical Traditions. Critical Histories of a Century of Geopolitical Thought*. London: Routledge.
Doubler, M. D. (1994). *Closing with the Enemy. How GIs Fought the War in Europe, 1944–1945*. Lawrence: University Press of Kansas.
Dower, J. M. (1987). *War Without Mercy. Race and Power in the Pacific War*. New York: Pantheon.

Duby, G. (1973). *Guerriers et paysans: VIIe-XIIe siècles: Premier essor de l'économie européenne*. Paris: Gallimard.
Duffy, C. (1979). *Siege Warfare. The Fortress in the Early Modern World 1494–1660*. London: Routledge & Kagan Paul.
Duffy, C. (1985). *Fortress in the Age of Vauban and Frederick the Great 1660–1789*. London: Routledge & Kagan Paul.
Duffy, C. (1988). *The Military Experience in the Age of Reason*. New York: Atheneum.
Echevarria, A. J. (2000). *After Clausewitz. German Military Thinkers Before the Great War*. Lawrence: University Press of Kansas.
Eden, L. (2004). *Whole World on Fire. Organizations, Knowledge, and Nuclear Weapons Devastation*. Cornell: Cornell University Press.
Elias, N. (1983). *The Court Society*. New York: Pantheon.
Ellis, J. (1986). *The Social History of the Machine Gun*. Baltimore: The John Hopkins University Press.
Foucault, M. (1995). *Discipline and Punish. The Birth of the Prison*. New York: Vintage.
Gat, A. (2002). *A History of Military Thought from Enlightenment to the Cold War*. Oxford: Oxford University Press.
Goff, S. (2004). *Full Spectrum Disorder. The Military in the New American Century*. New York: Soft Skull.
Gonzales de Leon, F. (1996). "Doctors of the Military Discipline": Technical Expertise and the Paradigm of the Spanish Soldier in the Early Modern Period. *Sixteenth Century Journal, 27*(1), 61–85.
Guerlac, H. (1986). Vauban: The Impact of Science on War. In P. Paret (Ed.), *Makers of Modern Strategy from Machiavelli to the Nuclear Age* (pp. 64–90). Oxford: Clarendon Press.
Gusterson, H. (1998). *Nuclear Rites: A Weapon Laboratory at the End of the Cold War*. Berkeley: University of California Press.
Henderson, K. (1995). The Visual Culture of Engineers. In S. Leigh Star (Ed.), *The Cultures of Computing* (pp. 196–218). Oxford: Blackwell.
Hull, I. V. (2004). *Absolute Destruction. Military Culture and the Practices of War in Imperial Germany*. Ithaca and London: Cornell University Press.
James, W. (1884). What Is an Emotion? *Mind, 9*(34), 188–205.
James, W. (2003). *Essays in Radical Empiricism*. New York City: Dover.
Jeismann, M. (1997). *La patrie de l'ennemi. La notion d'ennemi national et la représentation de la nation en Allemagne et en France de 1792 à 1918*. Paris: CNRS Editions.
Jervis, R. (1976). *Perception and Misperception in International Politics*. Princeton: Princeton University Press.
Kennedy, P. M. (1979). *War Plans of the Great Powers, 1880–1914*. London: Allen & Unwin.
Kleinschmidt, H. (1999). Using the Gun: Manual Drill and the Proliferation of Portable Firearms. *The Journal of Military History, 63*(3), 160–170.

Kolko, G. (1994). *Century of War. Politics, Conflict, and Society Since 1914.* New York City: The New Press.
Latour, B. (1988). *Science in Action. How to Follow Scientists and Engineers Through Society.* Harvard: Harvard University Press.
Lauterbach, A. T. (1944). Militarism in the Western World: A Comparative Study. *Journal of the History of Ideas,* 5(4), 446–478.
LeBleu, J. (2009). *Long Rifle. A Sniper's Story in Iraq and Afghanistan.* Guilford: Lyons Press.
Lembcke, J. (2000). *The Spitting Image. Myth, Memory, and the Legacy of Vietnam.* New York: New York University Press.
Liulevicius, V. G. (2000). *War Land on the Eastern Front. Culture, National Identity, and German Occupation in World War I.* Cambridge: Cambridge University Press.
Luvaas, J. (1964). *The Education of an Army. British Military Thought, 1815–1840.* Chicago: Chicago University Press.
Lynn, J. (1996). *Bayonets of the Republic. Motivation and Tactics in the Army of the Revolutionary France, 1791–1794.* Boulder: Westview.
Lynn, J. (1997). *Giant of the Grand Siècle: The French Army, 1610–1715.* Cambridge: Cambridge University Press.
MacKenzie, D. (1990). *Inventing Accuracy. A Historical Sociology of Nuclear Missile Guidance.* Cambridge and London: MIT Press.
Meridale, C. (2005). *Ivan's War. The Red Army 1939–1945.* London: Faber and Faber.
Mort, M. (2001). *Building the Trident Network. A Study of the Enrolment of People, Knowledge, and Machines.* Cambridge: MIT Press.
Panofsky, E. (1975). *La perspective comme forme symbolique.* Paris: Minuit.
Parker, G. (1996). *The Military Revolution. Military Innovation and the Rise of the West, 1500–1800.* Cambridge: Cambridge University Press.
Parrott, D. (2005). Cultures of Combat in the Ancient Régime: Linear Warfare, Noble Values, and Entrepreneurship. *The International History Review,* 27(3), 518–533.
Pauwels, J. R. (2016). *The Great Class War 1914–1918.* Halifax: Lorimer.
Pollak, M. D. (1991). *Military Architecture Cartography & the Representation of the Early Modern European City. A Checklist of Treatises on Fortification in the Newberry Library.* Chicago: The Newberry Library.
Queloz, D. (2009). *De la manœuvre napoléonienne à l'offensive à outrance.* Paris: Economica.
Raffestin, C. (with Lopreno, D., Pasteur, Y.). 1995. *Géopolitique et histoire.* Lausanne and Paris: Payot.
Ralston, D. (1990). *Importing the European Army. The Introduction of European Military Techniques and Institutions in the Extra-European World, 1600–1914.* Chicago: University of Chicago Press.

Rancière, J. (2000). *Le partage du sensible. Esthétique et politique.* Paris: La Fabrique.
Renda, M. A. (2001). *Taking Haiti. Military Occupation & the Culture of U.S. Imperialism (1915–1940).* Chapel Hill and London: The University of North Carolina Press.
Reuter, T. (1985). Plunder and Tribute in the Carolingian Empire. *Transactions of the Royal Historical Society, 35,* 75–94.
Ritchie, N. (2010). Relinquishing Nuclear Weapons: Identities, Network and the British Bomb. *International Affairs, 86*(2), 465–487.
Robbens, A. C. G. M. (2013). The Hostile Gaze: Night Vision and the Immediation of Nocturnal Combat in Vietnam and Iraq. In N. L. Whitehead & S. Finnström (Eds.), *Virtual War and Magical Death: Technologies and Imaginaries for Terror and Killing* (pp. 132–151).
Ross, S. (1996). *American War Plan 1945–1950.* London: Frank Cass.
Rothenberg, G. E. (1981). *The Art of War in the Age of Napoleonic.* Bloomington: Indiana University Press.
Russell, E. P. (1996). "Speaking Annihilation": Mobilizing for War Against Human and Insect Enemies, 1914–1945. *Journal of American History, 82*(4), 1505–1529.
Sampson, A. (1977). *The Arms Bazaar. From Lebanon to Lockheed.* New York: Bantam Books.
Satia, P. (2008). *Spies in Arabia. The Great War and the Cultural Foundations of Britain's Covert Empire in the Middle East.* Oxford: Oxford University Press.
Shapiro, M. (1997). *Violent Cartographies. Mapping the Cultures of War.* Minneapolis and London: University of Minnesota Press.
Sherry, M. (1989). *The Rise of American Air Power. The Creation of Armageddon.* Yale: Yale University Press.
Sofsky, W. (2003). *Violence: Terrorism, Genocide, War.* London: Granta.
Tilly, C. (Ed.). (1975). *The Formation of the National State in Western Europe.* Princeton: Princeton University Press.
Travers, T. H. E. (1979). Technology, Tactics, and Morale: Jean de Bloch, the Boer War, and British Military Theory, 1900–1914. *Journal of Modern History, 51*(2), 264–286.
Vasquez, J. A. (1992). *The War Puzzle.* Cambridge: Cambridge University Press.
Virilio, P. (1989). *War and Cinema. The Logistics of Perception.* London: Verso.
Virilio, P. (1994). *Vision Machine: Perspectives.* Hoboken: John Wiley & Sons.
Wasinski, C. (2011). On Making War Possible. Soldiers, Strategy, and Military Grand Narrative. *Security Dialogue, 42*(1), 57–76.
Weber, M. (1965). *Politics as a Vocation.* Philadelphia: Fortress Press.
White, R. K. (1966). Misperception and the Vietnam War. *The Journal of Social Issues, XXII*(3), 1–169.
Zuber, T. (2002). *Inventing the Schlieffen Plan: German War Planning 1871–1914.* Oxford: Oxford University Press.

Christophe Wasinski is a lecturer in political science (International Relations) at the Université libre de Bruxelles (ULB) and a member of the research center *Recherche et Enseignement en Politique Internationale* (REPI). He is the author of "Rendre la guerre possible. La construction du sens commun stratégique" (P.I.E. Peter Lang, 2010). His articles were published in *Critiques, Cultures & Conflits, Etudes Internationales, International Political Sociology, Stratégique*, and *Security Dialogue*. He is currently heading a research program on 'frames of war' (funded by the Belgian National Research Funds, 2017–2019).

CHAPTER 8

Of Heroes and Cowards: A Computer-Based Analysis of Narratives Justifying the Use of Force

Eric Sangar, Maéva Clément, and Thomas Lindemann

INTRODUCTION

How do political leaders manufacture emotional consent around the use of force beyond the borders of their communities? This chapter discusses how a computer-assisted narrative analysis can be used to analyze and compare political discourses legitimizing the use of force. Our overall theoretical argument is that leaders shape collective emotions by using a specific narrative to bring societal consent over the use of force in international political conflict. We draw on research stressing how empathy and the rejection of violence correspond to individuals' 'natural' emotional state, acquired

---

E. Sangar (✉)
FNRS / University of Namur, Namur, Belgium

M. Clément
Helmut Schmidt University, Hamburg, Germany

T. Lindemann
University of Versailles-St Quentin, Versailles, France

Ecole Polytechnique, Palaiseau, France

as part of routine socialization processes in modern societies (Linklater, 2007, 2014). In this regard, the acceptance of the use of force by one's collective must be gained by political leaders in most contemporary societies. Political leaders do not achieve this by simply articulating rational interests but by producing narratives that target the emotions supporting this hindrance in order to alter or suppress them.

Our research builds on a specific understanding of emotions as social phenomena, experienced individually and/or collectively and shaped by intersubjective relationships as well as social structures. We thereby subscribe to an intersubjective ontology of emotions. Individuals learn how to 'feel' from significant others but also via the institutions of a given society or community. Yet this knowledge is not fixed once and for all; language and communication constantly (re)shape emotional knowledge and responses that individuals and collectives have learned in the past. Thus, to understand the formation and potential effects of emotions, it is not sufficient to analyze emotional impulses at the individual level, it requires studying cultural and political practices (Ahmed, 2004), which establish and subsequently change referential objects causing emotional stimuli.

Political leaders are known to mobilize community bonds by using specific emotional vocabularies that strengthen internal cohesion and identity (Koschut, 2014; Petersen, 2011). Beyond the practice of othering and the use of specific emotional vocabulary, we argue that political leaders use a complex narrative structure, combining specific characters and sequences, which plausibly stimulates the audience to perceive the use of force not only as necessary but, more importantly, as morally desirable. We call this recurring structure the 'hero-protector narrative'. We furthermore argue that this narrative is not Western-specific but present in societies and communities dominated by gender hierarchies that value hyper-masculinity.

This chapter is structured in three main sections. First, we conceptualize the emotional underpinning of those political narratives aimed at garnering support for action. We argue that the way the 'hero-protector narrative' is structured—around dichotomized roles and action sequences—incentivizes specific collective emotions, which in turn render the use of force morally desirable. In the second section, we present our methodological approach, starting with why we chose to develop a methodology centering on a computer-assisted narrative analysis, over other potential approaches. We argue that it combines the virtues of both qualitative, interpretative analysis and quantifiable coding. To operationalize our argument about the morphology of the 'hero-protector' narrative, we constructed narrative categories that partly draw on Propp's functional analysis of the narrative structures of fairy tales (2010), especially his fundamental distinction between narrative 'roles' and narrative 'sequences'. We explain how we selected the speeches and statements that were eventually coded and then detail the coding process. In the third section, we briefly present our empirical results obtained by using three quantitative indicators, and interpret commonalities and differences between the selected cases. The computer-assisted evaluation of the coding results enabled us to confirm the empirical validity of our argument but also to identify some noteworthy differences in the implementation of the hero-protector narrative by Bush and by bin Laden. Overall, our analysis confirms the presence of the 'hero-protector narrative' in statements by leaders aiming to justify the use of force. The conclusion summarizes the main advantages of and limits to our approach for researching emotions in discourses legitimizing the use of force in international political conflicts.

The 'Hero-Protector Narrative': A Conceptual Model to Understand the Manufacturing of Collective Emotions

Scholarship on conflict dynamics highlights that political leaders seeking to create support for the use of force have to handle both 'negative' and 'positive' aspects of emotions. Certain emotions have to be activated (Kaufman, 2001), while others have to be reduced or selectively channeled. Furthermore, emotional evaluations have to be linked to specific individuals and/or groups in order to justify violence. While the recognition of the enemy as a fellow human being has to be neutralized, compassion for suffering victims is a useful resource to reinforce the perceived need to resort to force. As Jasper emphasizes, compassion and outrage have to be stimulated simultaneously in order to garner support for action (Jasper, 2006, p. 23). In the following, we elaborate on the relationship between the emotions of compassion and anger, moral judgments and political narratives aimed at garnering support for action.

The Emotional Underpinning of the Collective Support for Action

Research in social psychology and philosophy has shown that the simultaneous presence of compassion and anger increase the probability of active interference in favor of perceived victims (Nussbaum, 1996, p. 28; Pronk, Olthof, & Goosens, 2016, p. 286). Compassion is stimulated by the perception of other actors' unjustified suffering and their inability to take action against this suffering; therefore, perceived innocence and weakness are seen to be essential attributes of objects of compassion (Ahmed, 2004, p. 192). Writing about the Western context, Ahmed further argues that compassion helps to identify an object that is in need of protection by a more powerful actor (2004, p. 22). The characterization of the object as 'deserving' compassion because of its weak and/or passive character is hereby essential.

The mobilization of compassion alone does not necessarily result in support for the use of force to punish the perpetrator—an alternative reaction could be to alleviate the victim's suffering, without physically harming the aggressor. So in order to elicit support for the use of force, sentiments of outrage—what we call here 'moral anger'—have to be activated, in that they serve as a "particularly powerful mobilizing force that motivates people to take and support risky, confrontational, and punitive actions" (Brader & Marcus, 2013, p. 179). Indeed, the perceived capability to punish the aggressor seems to be a pre-condition for the successful mobilization of anger (Lebow, 2010, p. 74). In turn, actors lacking resources required for effective punitive action or seeing themselves as 'weak' tend to reduce or even suppress anger, a finding confirmed by experimental psychology (Mackie, Devos, & Smith, 2000). But what is moral about anger? The perception of injustice often acts as a trigger for anger, which in turn favors the evaluation of a given situation as one that necessitates political action and mobilization (Thompson, 2006, p. 127). Emotions, moral judgments and motivations to act are thus intrinsically linked (Ugazio, Majdandžic, & Lamm, 2014, p. 159). The close relationship between moral perception, emotional stimulation, and support for political action is to be found not only at the level of the individual who directly experiences injustice, but also at the collective level, through intersubjective relationships and vicarious experience. In order to legitimize the use of force, politically efficient speech acts would thus require the *combined* activation of compassion—through the identification of a suffering, innocent victim—and moral anger—through the identification of an illegitimate aggressor—in order to overcome the audience's 'natural' resistance to the use of force.

Recent studies in neuroscience support the idea that compassion and moral anger can be stimulated through communicative processes (Greene

& Haidt, 2002, p. 518), a finding that in turn suggests the possibility of strategically manufacturing collective moral judgments. Rather than explicitly naming the emotions that they strive to elicit among the audience, we argue that political leaders engage in narratives whose *structures* aim at manufacturing emotional reactions among their target audience(s). Because the members of an audience want to avoid being accused of moral indifference, cowardice, or egoism, they cannot simply ignore a narrative of suffering that contains identifiable victims and perpetrators (Boltanski, 1993, pp. 38–44). Political narratives that undertake such clear narrative identifications are therefore able to stimulate collective mobilization around a common cause that is not defined by common material interests but by a shared moral purpose (Boltanski, 1993, pp. 53–56).

Furthermore, in order to manufacture emotional consent effectively, political narratives have to draw on discursive structures that are familiar to the audience and therefore likely to stimulate the desired emotional effect—independently of the narrative's veracity. In this regard, the 'hero-protector narrative' is a familiar narrative. It resonates with emotional contexts common to societies in which masculine virility is highly valued and reproduced by hegemonic mass culture (Evangelista, 2011). Scholars have long stressed the pervasiveness of melodramatic narratives "as a mode of popular culture that presents images and characters through hyperbolic, binary moralistic positions and arranges them within a plotline that restages the eternal battle between good and evil" (Anker, 2005, p. 23). We push this idea further and argue that, albeit cultural differences, political leaders looking to legitimize the use of force might build on a quite similar "emotional world" (Ling, 2014), bound toward the reproduction of patriarchal meanings and power relations. Indeed, as Ling points out, emotions are diverse, equivocal, and they "intersect cross-culturally as much as financial transactions and the flow of information" (2014, p. 581). In this regard, the 'hero protector narrative' might be found in very diverse cultural contexts and be the product of cross-pollination between Western and non-Western traditions.

The Structure of the 'Hero-Protector Narrative': Roles and Sequences

Our conceptualization of the 'hero-protector narrative' is largely inspired by (but not identical with) Propp's functional analysis of the narrative structures of fairy tales (2010). In particular, we rely on Propp's fundamental analytical distinction between narrative roles—recurrent characters involving a typical set of personality traits and repertoires of action—and narrative sequences—the arrangement of episodes constituting the specific structure common to all stories that share a similar narrative (such as a fairy tale).

The *narrative roles* characterizing the 'hero-protector narrative' rely on a double dichotomy. The first dichotomy rests on the stark contrast between the 'innocent victim' and the 'perverse aggressor'. Although the symbolizers of the 'innocent victim' might be culturally variable—for example ordinary peasants, workers, believers, newborns, children, young women and old people—they are always presented as helpless and/or suffering in dignity. In modern cultures, these attributes are recognized as worth being protected. At the opposite end, the figure of the perverse aggressor is often dehumanized, closer to animality than humanity. Even when the aggressor is perceived as *technically* human, it is generally portrayed as insensitive, ruthless, calculating, often psychopathic, and/or cruel by nature. In many modern cultural products, we find a total dissociation between the 'innocent victim' and the 'perverted aggressor' (Lukàcs, 1971). The latter is not capable of change; he/she is voluntarily and irremediably bad.

The second dichotomy is between the 'coward' and the 'hero-protector'. The 'coward' is often an intellectual and proves to be rhetorically skilled; at the same time, the coward can be more or less traitorous or simply be animated by excessive fear. This character typically speaks a lot but is afraid and helpless when confronted by others with a demand for concrete action. One of the emotional functions of the coward is to exploit the audiences' self-esteem, which rejects the coward's morally shameful behavior and seeks instead a morally 'honorable' self-identification. This is provided by the hero, who typically doesn't speak much, acts bravely and appears selfless. The essential feature of the hero is his/her role as a protector: he/she puts his/her material well-being and/or physical life at risk in order to protect the innocent victim (and its community) because this is the morally right choice. Very often, the hero-protector is associated with 'virile' qualities and reproduces a patriarchal discourse about society. In history, such representations were often associated with 'hubristic identities', "based on the leaders or the community's imagined exceptional qualities" (Lindemann, 2010, p. 32).

This double dichotomy serves to redirect compassion completely toward the innocent victim and stimulate moral anger. This is achieved, first, through the denial of the aggressor's moral integrity and capacity to redeem itself and, second, through the construction of the hero's legitimate cause, following the coward's inaction. Moral anger's function is to make audiences realize the need for the hero's intervention, even if this involves the use of force. Thus, the more the actions attributed to the narrative characters are differentiated and organized along the two axes 'perverse aggressor–innocent victim' (activation of morally charged anger and compassion) and 'hero–coward' (which offers the identification with a positive self-image vs. the negative counter-model), the more the narrative structure is framed for the emotional legitimization of the use of force.

Furthermore, the hero-protector narrative is structured around *narrative sequences*. The narrative's dramatized story of conflict features escalating sequences of illegitimate wrongdoings committed by a fundamentally unchanging 'aggressor' against the 'victim'. This narrative bears similarity with many classical forms of drama as it puts a current event into the context of a rising struggle between 'good' and 'evil' that started in the past, culminates in the present, and offers—when the hero fulfills his/her moral duty—the possibility of redemption and a better future (Alexander, 2004, pp. 551–552). In discourses legitimatizing the use of force, the audience's emotional reactions are thus reinforced by the construction of alternate sequences. In Bandura's words, this allows to "select from the chain of events a defensive act by the adversary and portray it as initiating provocation [...] By fixing the blame on others or on circumstances, not only are one's own injurious actions excusable, but one can feel self-righteous in the process" (1999, p. 203). The sequences of the 'hero-protector narrative' typically include an arc of suspense that portrays the present situation as a potentially cathartic turning point: the reactions to past aggressions were too 'weak' and thus enabled the aggressor to renew the aggression—but it is yet possible to do the right thing and confront the aggressor head-on. Consequently, the sequences provide a teleological temporal structure that suggests the current conflict as decisive and unavoidable: to be a hero requires to do the 'right thing', that is, use force, 'right now'.

In short, we argue that narratives seeking to legitimize the use of force have a structure that enables the stimulation of the emotions of compassion and anger while providing a positive, righteous, and morally idealized representation of the audience's collective self. Several typical characters and sequences characterize this narrative. Who exactly stands behind the 'perverse aggressor' or the 'innocent victim' is contingent—but not the formal structure of the plot. Conversely, we claim that this structure is not present to the same extent in political narratives that do not promote the use of force. Actors who do not seek to promote violence can afford to tell less dichotomic, more 'complicated' stories that may involve perspectives for negotiation or de-escalation, and perhaps even self-criticism. While the legitimation of violence requires portraying the adversary as essentially different, non-violent politics recognize the adversary on equal terms, differing only in terms of interests and/or values but not in their fundamentally human nature (Butler, 2010).

METHODOLOGICAL APPROACH: CAPTURING THE 'HERO-PROTECTOR NARRATIVE' USING COMPUTER-ASSISTED NARRATIVE ANALYSIS

How did we proceed methodologically to test our argument about the 'hero-protector narrative' as a specific, cross-cultural political narrative? Among the social sciences, research on narrative has been particularly flourishing in political psychology. What political-psychological approaches to narrative have in common is to consider our "engagement with the world of politics as fundamentally storied" (Hammack, 2014, p. 82). However, this common conceptual and epistemological position does not amount to a specific, codified methodology (Hammack & Pilecki, 2014). In the following, we thus present the specificities of the narrative methodology that we develop in this chapter and differentiate it from other qualitative and quantitative approaches to language. We then explain how we designed the narrative codebook to test our argument about the 'hero-protector narrative'. Finally, we summarize the data selection (political statements by four categories of leaders, in the context of the 2003 invasion of Iraq) and our coding procedure.

Developing a Computer-Assisted Narrative Approach

As an overall approach to language, narrative is in principle compatible with a range of methods. In the following, we reconstruct how we build our methodological approach, explaining the advantages and limits of the methods that we discarded along the way.

We briefly considered opting for content analysis. This particular method, defined by Neuendorf as "the systematic, objective, quantitative analysis of message characteristics" (Neuendorf, 2005, p. 1), relies on the identification of linguistic elements—such as specific words, visual elements, or grammatical patterns—that are easily and reliably identifiable across a large number of texts. Content analysis has the advantage of being easily scalable—that is, producing relatively reliable results even when a high number of documents and sometimes human coders are involved. Furthermore, commercial content-analytical tools sometimes offer pre-defined dictionaries for specific semantic fields, including emotions, which would enable an automated coding of expressions referring to emotions. Our argument stresses, however, that emotional content in speech acts is not always explicit. Indeed, we argued that emotions are rather suggested or 'activated' by specific narrative structures. A content-analytical approach that looks for individual, emotionally charged words would tend to treat narrative structures as mere factual statements. Narrative structures function in system, in relation to one another suggests specific moral, emotionally charged meanings. Reconstructing this meaning-making cannot be achieved when sentences are not coded in their context. Testing our argument about the 'hero-protector narrative' thus exceeds the capabilities of classical content analysis, as it does not capture the degree of semantic complexity of such narrative constructs.

In this regard, an alternative approach could have been discourse analysis. There are many definitions and practices associated with this approach but a basic understanding stresses three essential components:

> Discourse analysis is based on the premise that the words we choose to speak about something and the way in which they are spoken or written, shape the sense that can be made of the world and our experience of it. Discourse analysts are acutely conscious of the power of discourse and they consider our social and experiential worlds to be the product of our discursive construction of them. (Willig, 2014, pp. 341–342)

Discourse analysis is sensitive both to the contents of linguistic expression and to the way in which they are made as they refer to specific power relations. Because discourse analysis questions the construction of meaning, via the interaction of context and concrete linguistic utterings, it would fit our narrative approach better than content analysis. Methodological approaches to discourse in the social sciences have furthermore the normative ambition to uncover and criticize the ways in which power relations are built and stabilized through communication (Fairclough & Wodak, 1997). Consequently, they typically require the analysis of additional contextual data (such as institutional practices, material power distribution, and concrete actor strategies) and are well suited for explorative, case-study based research designs.

For our argument about the 'hero-protector narrative', discourse analysis would have been both over-ambitious and under-specified. Since we needed to analyze a certain number of statements in order to test the presence of the 'hero-protector narrative', it appeared unrealistic to engage in background research on the conditions in which each of the selected texts were produced. We had to assume that the political actors who publicly supported the use of force were sincere about it and wanted their audience to support their interpretation. In other words, our argument did not primarily aim to specify the power relations between speakers and audiences but to test whether there is one common narrative that powerful political actors use to stimulate collective emotions in in favor of the use of force as a legitimate course of action. Furthermore, because of its inherent complex analytical approach, linking discursive utterings and non-verbal, contextual parameters, classical discourse analysis is hard to apply coherently to a larger number of cases, and is therefore less suitable for cross-case comparison.

We needed therefore a methodology that enabled us to both be sensitive to 'meaning' in context *and* produce sufficiently high numbers of observations to support our claim about the specificity of discourses justifying the use of force. We designed an approach that combines the attention to narrative structures and hermeneutic interpretation of their meaning with the advantages of a computer-assisted qualitative data analysis. We summarized our approach under the term *computer-assisted narrative analysis*. To contrast it from other potential avenues of narrative inquiry, we stress the four main characteristics of our approach:

1. It is interested in a master narrative, which can be defined as "a cultural script about the meaning of social categories that exists in cultural artefacts and mass texts" (Hammack & Pilecki, 2014, p. 82). Though it would be interesting to analyze how the 'hero-protector narrative' resonates with individual, personal narratives, it is beyond the frame of our approach. To analyze how the use of force is legitimized in political narratives, we selected political speeches and statements, that is, official documents.
2. It is based on a deductive approach. We first conducted an inductive pre-study, insights of which were then formalized into a theoretical model, the 'hero-protector narrative' with its specific story form. This story form was then operationalized into a narrative codebook (see next section); from there, we proceeded deductively, that is, we conducted the analysis to see whether we find these narrative categories in the data.

3. It is primarily a formal analysis of narrative—albeit the narrative structures (roles and sequences) of our theoretical model are obviously theme-oriented—since our argument stresses the importance of the story's structure for emotional impact. Formal analysis does not mean that we engaged in micro-linguistics but that the analysis focused on the meaning of sequences within each text.
4. It is based on a codebook, which allowed for the quantification of the presence and extent of the 'hero-protector narrative' within the material. We used a coding software and its quantitative instruments, such as calculating the relative frequencies of specific narrative structures across the sampled material, in order to highlight similarities and differences between cases. Though allowing for some degree of quantification, this approach contrasts deeply both with purely quantitative (word-counting) approaches and with automated approaches to narrative analysis (Franzosi, 2010; Sudhahar, Franzosi, & Cristianini, 2011), as it neither aims to process very large corpora, nor to "automate the process of coding" (Sudhahar, Franzosi, & Cristianini, 2011, p. 64). In our approach, the researcher is merely assisted by a coding software, he/she creates the meaning-oriented categories of the codebook and his/her interpretation of meaning is essential to the manual coding process.

Our approach shares some similarities with qualitative content analysis, an emerging trend in IR research (Bennett, 2015), which relies on the coding of material according to a codebook. This method acknowledges that the coding of concepts requires contextual reading; coders are expected to code actual meaning conveyed by a linguistic structure, not simply its 'objective' manifestation. Similarly, our methodology involved a certain degree of interpretation—during the coding process—within the limits of our pre-defined narrative categories (story form), which aimed to increase the reliability of the coding.

Designing the Narrative Codebook

Narrative analysis has been developed prominently in literary studies, from the Russian formalists to the French structuralists (Barthes, 1977; Greimas, 1983; see also Toolan, 1988). We found great inspiration in Propp's work on the morphology of fairy tales (2010 [1968]). Propp's use of an abstract definition of constitutive narrative structures, including narrative characters and narrative sequences, seeks to determine how the storyline of a specific genre is constructed. This requires a basic amount of linguistic and cultural competency since the respective structures are not always explicit. For example, in a hypothetical culture in which non-violent action is commonly associated with heroism, a narrative character killing another would be most certainly perceived as a villain, even if the character's motives were morally defendable. In order to identify the (cross-cultural) presence of the 'hero-protector narrative', we thus extrapolated abstract definitions of key narrative characters and sequences that would have to be present. To do this, we did an inductive pre-study of pop-cultural artefacts forming the cultural context of the political speech acts that we were interested in. We identified recurring narrative patterns that matched some of the narrative structures borrowed from Propp's analytical framework. As a result of this inductive pre-study, we kept only four central narrative roles and five narrative sequences that we considered necessarily constitutive of the 'hero-protector narrative'. While the individual characters are clearly linked to gender hierarchies, they are not necessarily tied to a specific biological sex; we emphasize this point by using gender-neutral terms in the operational definitions. The resulting codebook is represented graphically in Fig. 8.1:

The next step was to elaborate abstract definitions that would allow to detect and classify the occurrences of these structures in political speech acts. This is how we operationalized the four ideal-typical characters of the 'hero-protector narrative':

1. The 'victim' is any (often collective) actor who remains passive during the narrative and is the target of the unprovoked, illegitimate aggression by the perverse aggressor.
2. The 'aggressor' is a perpetrator who pursues his/her advantage without any respect for the life and rights of others. The aggressor is typically portrayed as initiating acts of violence without prior provocation or legitimate cause and is often portrayed as 'perverse'.
3. The 'hero' is an actor who reacts to the illegitimate aggression out of a sense of moral obligation and not in the pursuit of egoistic interests. The hero sets out to eliminate the source of the aggression, even if this implies breaking moral rules that would apply in a legitimate normative order. In doing so, the hero puts his/her own material well-being or physical life at stake and is thus ready to sacrifice himself/herself in order to protect the victim. This stresses the difference between the hero and the 'coward'.

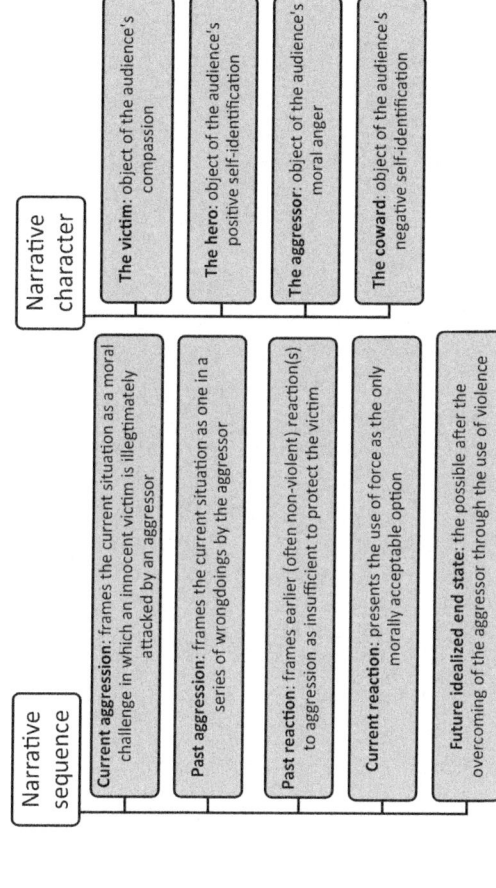

Fig. 8.1 Codebook design

4. The 'coward' is at the outset an actor who, despite having a moral responsibility toward the victim, does not do what is morally right out of fear for his/her life and material interest. Thus, the coward generally chooses the side of the materially strongest actor. As a result, the coward remains either passive during the aggression of the victim or even supports the aggressor. Because the coward does not do what would be morally right, he/she can become a legitimate target for the hero.

The 'hero-protector narrative' is also organized around specific action sequences—understood as a clearly observable episode that contains one element of the narrative climax. We operationalized these sequences as follows:

1. The first sequence is usually a current act of aggression against an innocent victim, shown allegedly from the victim's perspective. The audience's first spontaneous reaction is a combination of moral anger and compassion because the aggression happens without prior provocation by the victim or any other legitimate reason. The victim is unable to protect himself/herself, and this creates the moral necessity to intervene for anyone with a possibility to act.
2. The second sequence presents a former act of aggression, which can be considered a precedent to the extent that it happened in the more or less distant past. This sequence demonstrates the unchanging character of the aggressor and therefore his/her essentially cruel nature.
3. The third sequence often corresponds to the first (failed) attempt to protect the victim, which happened in the more or less distant past as a reaction to the chronologically first aggression; this sequence is often associated with a non-violent reaction that turned out to be ineffective.
4. The fourth sequence corresponds to the anticipated intervention of the 'hero-protector', who finally confronts the aggressor head on ('counteraction' in Propp's words). Here, the call for the use of force is contextualized as both 'necessary' (in terms of instrumental effectiveness) and 'good' (in terms of moral appropriateness and valorization). Only through the use of force can the hero change the course of events and eliminate the threat to the victim once and for all.
5. The final sequence often constitutes a normalization and de-dramatization. The dramatic tension is resolved and a better end state provides additional legitimacy to the use of force as a necessary and

morally appropriate means in order to restore the victim's dignity and return to 'normal life'.

In sum, the narrative codebook was operationalized around the abstract definition of roles and sequences in order to code the material without relying on personal pre-conceptions or the veracity of the political leaders' stories.

Selecting and Coding Speeches and Statements by Political Leaders in the Context of the 2003 Invasion of Iraq

What does our theoretical argument imply in terms of selecting material? First, our focus is on analyzing the way official political texts are crafted, in the form of the 'hero-protector narrative', not their reception within the target audience(s). We therefore selected textual material. Second, we argue that this narrative is used specifically in political discourses bent on legitimizing the use of force. Thus, we needed to compare speeches/statements made by political actors that sought to justify the use of force with speeches/statements made by actors who argued against it. Third, we claim that the 'hero-protector narrative' has a cross-cultural reach. This implies that we need to compare speeches/statements produced for audiences from different cultural backgrounds. Finally, when selecting appropriate speeches and statements for our empirical analysis, we had to exclude the possibility that different real-world events could influence the probability of choosing the 'hero-protector narrative'. We chose the 2003 invasion of Iraq as the common context for all selected texts. The debate on this war represented one of the most prominent and global controversies on the use of force (Ringmar, 2006). This controversy involved leaders and audiences from culturally and ideologically diverse backgrounds and involved the justification of the use of force by—among others—the US administration under George W. Bush and the then leading jihadist network *al-Qaeda*.

The selected material consists of 12 public statements—four prior, four during and four after the invasion of Iraq. Concretely, we chose speeches/statements by Osama bin Laden and George W. Bush (representing actors arguing for the use of force), as well as speeches/statements by the Muslim Association of Britain (MAB) and three US senators opposing the invasion of Iraq (representing actors who vocally opposed the use of force). By selecting actors who represented or claimed to represent, on one side, the

US nation and, on the other side, (parts of) the Islamic community of believers (*ummah*), the material contained texts produced for culturally diverse audiences. The main criterion for choosing specific statements was, besides their position on the timeline of the invasion, the length of the speeches/statements. These had to be long enough to, at least potentially, contain all the structures of the 'hero-protected narrative'. The concrete selection of speeches and statements is presented in Table 8.1.

In the following, the political actors who promoted the use of force within the context of the US-Iraq conflict are referred to as 'violent actors' and their speeches and statements on the legitimization of the use of force are shortened to 'violent discourses'. Conversely, the political actors who opposed the use of force are referred to as 'non-violent' and their speeches and statements as 'non-violent discourses'. We imported the 12 selected texts in the qualitative research software *Provalis QDAMiner*. This software provides all functionality of other qualitative coding software and offers advanced analytical tools for quantitative analysis—tools that enabled us to gain insights into the presence/absence of the 'hero-protector narrative' across the four cases.

Two independently working researchers coded all discourses in parallel, based on the narrative codebook. The coders were instructed not to rely

Table 8.1 Case selection

	Speeches and statements legitimizing the use of force	*Speeches and statements opposing the use of force*
U.S. political leaders	George W. Bush: "The Iraqi Threat", October 7, 2002; "End of Major Combat in Iraq", May 1, 2003; "Address One Year After Operation Iraqi Freedom", March 19, 2004.	US Senators: Sen. Barack Obama, "Speech Against the Iraq War", October 2, 2002; Sen. Robert Byrd, "Reckless Administration May Reap Disastrous Consequences", February 12, 2003; Sen. Edward Kennedy's speech on Iraq Policy, January 14, 2004.
Self-proclaimed representatives of the Islamic community	Osama bin Laden: "Message to Iraq", February 11, 2003; "Message to Iraqis and Americans", October 18, 2003; "Message to Europe", April 15, 2004.	Muslim Association of Britain: "Blair: Further Rubbing Salt into Our Wounds", November 13, 2002; "Muslim leaders' Declaration on Iraq", February 13, 2003; "A Day of Eid, Solidarity and Resolve for Muslims in Britain", February 4, 2003.

on their background knowledge but to code exclusively semantic meanings that could match the definitions of the narrative roles and sequences presented in the codebook. The basic coding units were 'units of meaning', that is, terms, sentences or a sequence of sentences that fit with one of the codebook definitions. In practice, coded narrative roles consisted mostly of individual terms or term combinations (such as 'treacherous US government', 'criminal dictator'), whereas narrative sequences consisted mostly of sentences or sentence combinations (such as "The Iraqi regime already used weapons of mass destruction against innocent civilians"). Passages that did not fit any of the codebook categories were not coded; as a result, in some texts, some passages were not coded.

After completion of the individual coding, the two researchers then mutually reviewed and harmonized their results. While such exchange among coders is usually not accepted in classical content analysis, because of the necessity for hermeneutic interpretation in qualitative content analysis it would not be helpful to calculate scores of intercoder reliability. Instead, we think that the intersubjective review of all coding results can

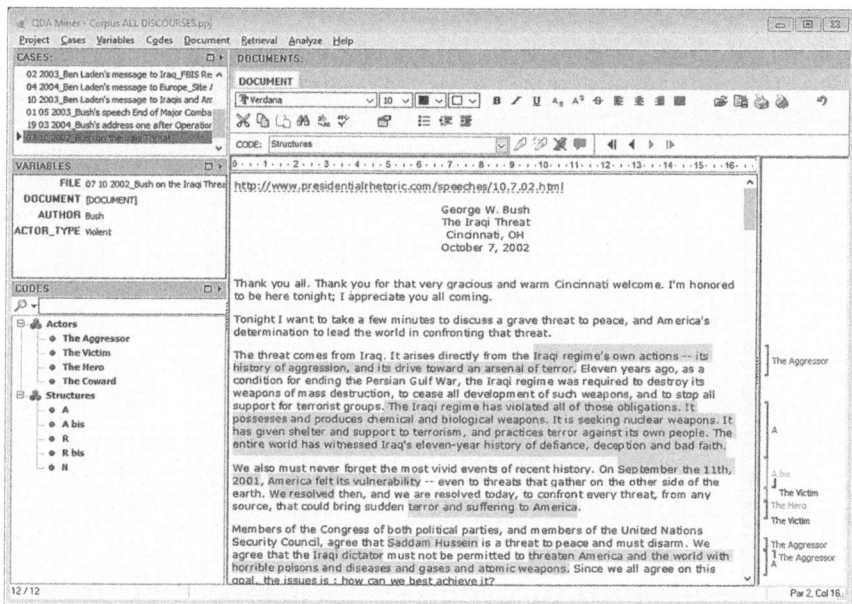

Fig. 8.2 Screenshot of coding software QDA Miner

increase their validity. The screenshot reproduced in Fig. 8.2 illustrates the software-based coding process[1].

In the following, we briefly discuss the results of this analysis and summarize the advantages and limits of our methodological approach.

INTERPRETATION OF THE EMPIRICAL RESULTS

To compare the four cases, the first indicator we used is the 'relative frequency of code' with regard to the 'violent discourses' and 'non-violent discourses'. Relative frequency here refers to the proportional share of a specific code among all coding results in a specific discourse category. For example, we find that 68.9% of all coded segments are contained in violent discourses, while only 31.1% of the coded segments were found in the non-violent discourses. This is already a basic quantitative hint toward plausibility of our argument. But it is necessary to differentiate along the individual roles and sequences of the 'hero-protector narrative'. When doing this, we observe a striking similarity in the relative frequencies of the key narrative roles and sequences in the speeches and statements produced by bin Laden and Bush. These narrative categories, while not completely absent, are distinctively less present in non-violent discourses. As figures 8.3 and 8.4 illustrate, the relative frequencies of the characteristic narrative elements are on average between two and three times higher in the group of 'violent discourses' than in the group of 'non-violent discourses'.

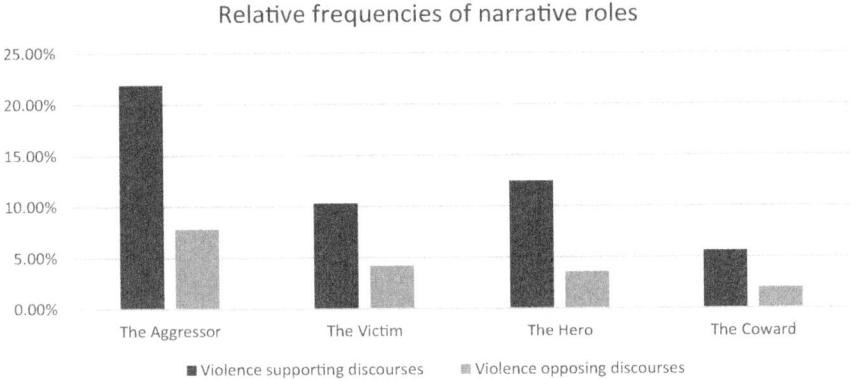

Fig. 8.3 Relative frequencies of narrative roles in violent versus non-violent discourses

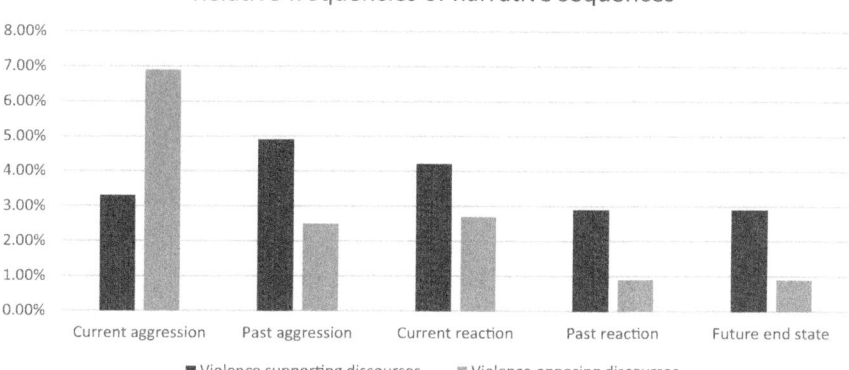

Fig. 8.4 Relative frequencies of narrative structures in violent versus non-violent discourses

Overall, we find that except for the sequence 'current aggression', all coded 'hero-protector' structures are significantly more associated with Bush's and bin Laden's speeches and statements. In non-violent discourses, the relative frequency of the sequence 'current act of aggression' is, however, higher than in violent discourses. Indeed, this sequence is the most frequently used sequence in non-violent discourses.

Confronted with this quantitative observation that ran contrary to our initial assumption, we analyzed the coded sequences once more in context. Fortunately, the used coding software enables easily locating of specific coding segments that belong to the same discourse categories. We found that non-violent discourses do not refrain from denouncing specific actions, such as the development of weapons of mass destruction, as illegitimate acts of aggression in the present. Furthermore, non-violent discourses spend much more time in analyzing their cause and characteristics and then developing an appropriate response. This greater emphasis on analysis inflates the number of sequences that are coded 'current aggression'. Conversely, in violent discourses, 'past aggression' sequences are proportionally more frequent than 'current aggression' sequences since the reference to historical precedents is essential to dramatize the story and justify the use of force as the last resort following a number of failed, non-violent reactions in the past. In other words, in discourses implementing the full 'hero-protector narrative', there is no need for analyzing the nature of the current aggression, since it is portrayed as occurring in a line of historical precedents (or, as in the case of Bush, analogies). This may confirm our assumption that it is less the nature of the current act of aggression but rather its historicity that serves as 'evidence' of the need for violence as the only effective and therefore morally appropriate reaction.

Keeping this in mind when looking at the speeches and statements by Bush and bin Laden once again, we find that flashbacks down a reconstructed memory lane are indeed plentiful, thus contributing to an arc of suspense, whose apogee is reached in the present-day context. In his Cincinnati speech, Bush links the threat posed by Hussein to the 9/11 attacks, hence narratively connecting Iraq with al-Qaeda terrorism (10/2002). Although this connection was not used in the more legalistic argumentation at the UN Security Council, it plays a major role in his speeches to a primarily US audience. Bin Laden also stresses previous US wrongdoings to argue that Bush and his allies are a 'huge evil on all humanity' that has to be stopped:

> Their fangs drip blood from the corpses of the children of Vietnam and Somalia and the children of Afghanistan and Iraq. (10/2003)

The second quantitative indicator we used consists in the co-occurrences of coded segments (narrative roles and sequences). Using *Provalis QDAMiner*, this was measured by retrieving the number of at least partly overlapping coding segments among the twelve analyzed statements. We find that both in Bush's and bin Laden's speeches and statements, the narrative role of the 'hero' typically overlaps with the narrative sequences of the 'past' and 'current' reactions, while the role of the 'aggressor' typically overlaps with sequences featuring 'past' and 'current' aggressions. The role of the 'victim' occurs in the 'current aggression' as well as in the

Table 8.2 Co-occurrences in speeches by Bush and bin Laden: absolute frequencies

Coding category	Current aggression	Past aggression	Future end state	Current reaction	Past reaction
The coward	1	1	0	2	1
The hero	0	5	3	15	5
The aggressor	15	25	1	8	9
The victim	8	7	8	2	1

'future end state' sequences but is consistently absent in all sequences presenting reactions to the aggression. Finally, the figure of 'the coward' appears in all sequences almost equally. Table 8.2 provides the full results of the co-occurrence analysis.

The four characters are found in the sequences corresponding to their distinctive roles, which reinforces their ideal-typical character. The more the characters are associated with the sequences in which they are expected to figure as the most prominent character, the more they are presented as unidimensional, and the easier it is for the narrative to elicit, among the audience, emotions associated with these characters. In this regard, the results show that the aggressor features typically in sequences describing acts of illegitimate aggression, while the hero takes center-stage in the sequence 'current reaction'.

It is worth noticing that the hero is less often co-occurring with the narrative sequence 'past reaction', a finding that is consistent with our model. Indeed, since the narrative argues that the past (and generally non-violent) reaction was not effective to protect the victim and eliminate the threat caused by the aggressor, the role of the 'hero' is correspondingly under-represented. This relatively 'non-heroic' past reaction contributes to explaining the recurrence of aggression and hence the moral urgency to strike hard to prevent further aggressions. It increases the necessity to use more 'effective'—that is, violent—means in the present, thus building up to a narrative crescendo.

Our analysis thus far confirms that the 'hero-protector narrative' is present in the discourses aiming to legitimize the use of force. Furthermore, it stresses how the combination and specific distribution of narrative roles in sequences have a motivational function and are linked to a specific course of action and bent on raising and maintaining support for the use of force. But what about our claim regarding the cross-cultural reach of our argument? For this purpose, we compared the coding results between the two 'violent actors'.

The third quantitative indicator, relative frequencies, confirms that both actors use the constitutive elements of the 'hero-protector narrative' comparably often. There are also subtle elements of divergence, as shown in Fig. 8.5.

The most striking differences can be found in the discursive importance of the future end state, as well as around the categories of the coward and the victim. Once again, the quantitative analysis enables us to see particular details of the material that our theoretical argument did not anticipate. Going back to the coded segments in question, we made the following observations.

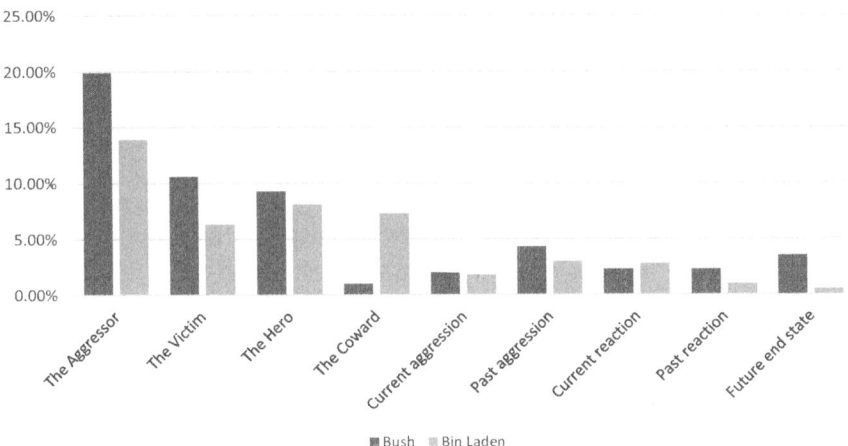

Fig. 8.5 Comparison of relative frequencies of coded segments between statements by Bush and bin Laden

The promise of an idealized future end state, which can be achieved for the victim as a result of the hero's action, features prominently in Bush's speeches, with the victim being predominantly identified as the Iraqi people. Bush emphasizes, for instance, that "the long captivity of Iraq will end, and an era of new hope will begin" (10/2002). He foresees the liberation of Iraqi minorities from oppression—"shar[ing] in the progress and prosperity of our time"—and argues that this will, in turn, secure the American nation and protect its freedom (10/2002). By contrast, this narrative sequence does not appear very often in bin Laden's speeches and statements. His elaborations on the future after the final "victory over the infidels" remain vague (10/2003). He argues rather abstractly that *jihad* will allow for the "victory to religion and establishing the state of Muslims", that is, the Caliphate (10/2003). This variation might refer to a more general feature of al-Qaeda's ideological discourse, which lays the emphasis on the intrinsic value of sacrifice for the greater good. Beyond references to restoring the historical *ummah*, al-Qaeda and its affiliated groups usually avoided concrete answers about rule under a future caliphate. The end state after victory against oppression is left to the imagination of the audience and only associated with vague promises of salvation (Clément, 2014). By contrast, typical 'Western' discourses generally portray the use of force as the 'least possible evil' that is required, according to a deontological moral logic, to achieve a greater political good, such as the restoration of order or the humanitarian protection of civilians (Weizman, 2011).

Another nuance to the common morphology of both narratives is bin Laden's extensive use of 'the coward' character, undoubtedly more recurrent than in Bush's speech acts. A certain amalgam between 'the aggressor' and 'the coward' distinguishes bin Laden's speech acts. Combining both characters is made easier by the simple dichotomy between believers and those who forfeited this status by helping non-believers. In bin Laden's discourse, the coward thus mainly corresponds to what he sees as the illegitimate leaders of the Muslim world, and to a minor extent to the US military, attacking a "small army of mujahidin" (02/2003). In Bush's discourse, on the other hand, the figure of the coward is euphemized. It is the negative version of the Self, that is, what the Self would become if it were not to act as its true Self. This is particularly noticeable in Bush's speech prior to the war in Iraq. Addressing the issue of inaction, he argues:

> The United Nations would betray the purpose of its founding, and prove irrelevant to the problems of our time. And through its inaction, the United States would resign itself to a future of fear. That is not the America I know. That is not the America I serve. (10/2002)

In the same vein, both discourses exhibit slight differences as to the figure of the victim. While often using the word "Iraq" in an undetermined way, Bush makes a strong difference between Iraqi civilians, whose characterization corresponds to the 'victim' category, and Saddam Hussein, whose attributes fit the 'aggressor' character. Compassion, in his discourse, is directed almost exclusively toward Iraqi civilians, while the American population is very rarely characterized in terms of fitting the role of the victim—to the exception of the victims of 9/11. Although bin Laden makes the difference between Western regimes and Western populations, there is no empathy expressed toward Western civilians; compassion is directed toward Muslim victims in general and Iraqi Muslims in particular. The comparison between both his and Bush's discourse suggests that 'the victim' might or might not belong to the in-group, thus providing valuable insights to further refine the codebook definitions.

Conclusion: Advantages and Limits of Our Approach

This chapter made the argument that there exists a common 'hero-protector narrative' used by leaders from diverse cultural backgrounds to justify the use of force. Consent to the use of force by the collective rests on the narrative's capacity to elicit specific collective emotions: compassion and moral anger. We argued that this is achieved through the very structure of the narrative. Methodologically, we have tested the empirical plausibility of this argument through a computer-assisted narrative analysis of political speeches and statements in the context of the Iraq War of 2003. Having manually coded a combination of narrative roles and sequences that are constitutive of the 'hero-protector narrative', the analysis produced both quantitative and qualitative evidence suggesting that this model represents indeed a cross-cultural technique to manufacture emotional consent in view of the collective use of force.

We think that our methodological approach has specific advantages compared to alternative approaches to research the emotional underpinning of narratives in international politics. A narrative approach as we proposed would enable IR researchers to look for structural characteristics and compare emotion narratives across contexts, at least with some basic linguistic background knowledge. It starts with an inductive, hermeneutic approach, then the elaboration of a pre-defined narrative codebook, which allows for systematic, manual coding with a degree of interpretation. The quantification of coding results helps, in turn, to detect empirical 'anomalies' that might remain unnoticed in a purely qualitative approach.

There are also limits to our approach. First, because human coding is an essential step, only a limited number of texts can be analyzed. This constrains the potential of producing 'hard' statistical correlations. Second, some might argue that the presence of a specific structure in master narratives might be secondary to the institutional orchestration and/or visual *mise en scène* of such narratives. In this regard, combining our formal narrative approach with a visual perspective represents a potentially fruitful endeavor. Third, our approach cannot account for the *effectiveness* of the 'hero-protector narrative'. In order to assess its influence on audiences, future research would need to access surveys and/or test the narrative on focus groups. However, this is a limit that concerns all analytical approaches to language and should not prevent researchers to create ways to account for its relationship to power.

Acknowledgments Parts of this chapter are based on the article "The "Hero-Protector Narrative": Manufacturing Emotional Consent for the Use of Force", published by the authors in the journal *Political Psychology*, available at http://onlinelibrary.wiley.com/resolve/doi?DOI=10.1111%2Fpops.12385. We thank the journal editors for their friendly permission to reuse some of the results presented in this article.

Notes

1. We used the letters A for 'aggression', A bis for 'aggression in the past', R for 'reaction', R bis for 'reaction in the past', and N for 'future end state', which correspond to the five narrative sequences.

References

Ahmed, S. (2004). *The Cultural Politics of Emotion*. New York: Routledge.
Alexander, J. C. (2004). Cultural Pragmatics: Social Performance Between Ritual and Strategy. *Sociological Theory, 22*(4), 527–573.
Anker, E. (2005). Villains, Victims and Heroes: Melodrama, Media, and September 11. *Journal of Communication, 55*(1), 22–37.
Bandura, A. (1999). Moral Disengagement in the Perpetration of Inhumanities. *Personality and Social Psychology Review, 3*(3), 193–209.
Barthes, R. (1977). Introduction to the Structural Analysis of Narratives. In R. Barthes & S. Heath (Eds.), *Image, Music, Text* (pp. 79–124). London: Fontana.
Bennett, A. (2015). Found in Translation: Combining Discourse Analysis with Computer Assisted Content Analysis. *Millennium – Journal of International Studies, 43*(3), 984–997.
Boltanski, L. (1993). *La souffrance à distance: morale humanitaire, médias et politique*. Paris: Editions Métailié.
Brader, T., & Marcus, G. E. (2013). Emotion and Political Psychology. In L. Huddy, D. O. Sears, & J. S. Levy (Eds.), *The Oxford Handbook of Political Psychology* (pp. 165–204). Oxford: Oxford University Press.
Butler, J. (2010). *Frames of War: When Is Life Grievable?* London and New York: Verso.
Clément, M. (2014). Al-Muhajiroun in the United Kingdom: The Role of International Non-recognition in Heightened Radicalization Dynamics. *Global Discourse, 4*(4), 428–443.
Evangelista, M. (2011). *Gender, Nationalism, and War: Conflict on the Movie Screen*. Cambridge and New York: Cambridge University Press.

Fairclough, N., & Wodak, R. (1997). Critical Discourse Analysis. In T. A. van Dijk (Ed.), *Discourse as Social Interaction* (pp. 258–284). London: Sage.
Franzosi, R. (2010). *Quantitative Narrative Analysis*. Thousand Oaks: Sage.
Greene, J., & Haidt, J. (2002). How (and Where) Does Moral Judgment Work? *Trends in Cognitive Sciences*, 6(12), 517–523.
Greimas, A. J. (1983). *Structural Semantics: An Attempt at a Method*. Lincoln: University of Nebraska Press.
Hammack, P. L. (2014). Mind, Story, Society: The Political Psychology of Narrative. In M. Hanne, W. D. Crano, & J. S. Mio (Eds.), *Warring with Words: Narrative and Metaphor in Politics* (pp. 51–77). New York: Psychology Press.
Hammack, P. L., & Pilecki, A. (2014). Methodological Approaches in Political Psychology: Discourse and Narrative. In P. Nesbitt-Larking, C. Kinnvall, T. Capelos, & H. Dekker (Eds.), *The Palgrave Handbook of Global Political Psychology* (pp. 72–89). London: Palgrave Macmillan.
Jasper, J. M. (2006). The Study of Emotion: An Introduction. In S. Clarke, P. Hoggett, & S. Thompson (Eds.), *Emotion, Politics and Society* (pp. 3–30). New York: Palgrave Macmillan.
Kaufman, S. J. (2001). *Modern Hatreds: The Symbolic Politics of Ethnic War*. New York: Cornell University Press.
Koschut, S. (2014). Emotional (Security) Communities: The Significance of Emotion Norms in Inter-allied Conflict Management. *Review of International Studies*, 40(3), 533–558.
Lebow, R. N. (2010). *Why Nations Fight: Past and Future Motives for War*. Cambridge: Cambridge University Press.
Lindemann, T. (2010). *Causes of War: The Struggle for Recognition*. Colchester: ECPR Press.
Ling, L. H. M. (2014). Decolonizing the International: Towards Multiple Emotional Worlds. *International Theory*, 6(3), 579–583.
Linklater, A. (2007). Distant Suffering and Cosmopolitan Obligations. *International Politics*, 44(1), 19–36.
Linklater, A. (2014). Anger and World Politics: How Collective Emotions Shift Over Time. *International Theory*, 6(3), 574–578.
Lukács, G. (1971). *The Theory of the Novel: A Historico-Philosophical Essay on the Forms of Great Epic Literature*. Cambridge, MA: MIT press.
Mackie, D. M., Devos, T., & Smith, E. R. (2000). Intergroup Emotions: Explaining Offensive Action Tendencies in an Intergroup Context. *Journal of Personality and Social Psychology*, 79(4), 602–616.
Neuendorf, K. A. (2005). *The Content Analysis Guidebook*. Thousand Oaks, CA: Sage.
Nussbaum, M. (1996). Compassion: The Basic Social Emotion. *Social Philosophy and Policy*, 13(1), 27–58.

Petersen, R. D. (Ed.). (2011). *Western Intervention in the Balkans: The Strategic Use of Emotion in Conflict*. Cambridge: Cambridge University Press.

Pronk, J., Olthof, T., & Goossens, F. A. (2016). Factors Influencing Interventions on Behalf of Victims of Bullying: A Counterfactual Approach to the Social Cognitions of Outsiders and Defenders. *The Journal of Early Adolescence*, 36(2), 267–291.

Propp, V. (2010 [1968]). *Morphology of the Folktale*. Austin: University of Texas Press.

Ringmar, E. (2006). Inter-texual Relations: The Quarrel Over the Iraq War as a Conflict Between Narrative Types. *Cooperation and Conflict*, 41(4), 403–421.

Sudhahar, S., Franzosi, R., & Cristianini, N. (2011). *Automating Quantitative Narrative Analysis of News Data*. Paper Presented at the WAPA Conference, 2nd Workshop on Applications of Pattern Analysis.

Thompson, S. (2006). Anger and the Struggle for Justice. In S. Clarke, P. Hoggett, & S. Thompson (Eds.), *Emotion, Politics and Society* (pp. 123–144). New York: Palgrave Macmillan.

Toolan, M. J. (1988). *Narrative: A Critical Linguistic Introduction*. London and New York: Routledge.

Ugazio, G., Majdandžic, J., & Lamm, C. (2014). Are Empathy and Morality Linked? In H. L. Maibom (Ed.), *Empathy and Morality* (pp. 155–171). Oxford: Oxford University Press.

Weizman, E. (2011). *The Least of All Possible Evils: Humanitarian Violence from Arendt to Gaza*. London and New York: Verso.

Willig, C. (2014). Discourses and Discourse Analysis. In U. Flick (Ed.), *The SAGE Handbook of Qualitative Data Analysis* (pp. 341–354). London: SAGE.

Eric Sangar is an FNRS Research Fellow at the University of Namur and a Research Associate at the Centre Emile Durkheim of Sciences Po Bordeaux. His personal research is currently focused on the theoretical and empirical links between collective memory, regimes of historicity and uses of history in contemporary armed conflicts. He holds a PhD from the European University Institute in Florence. His thesis entitled *Historical Experience: Burden or Bonus in Today's Wars?* was published in 2014. His research has been published in various journals in English, French and German, including the *Journal of Strategic Studies*, *Political Psychology* and *Contemporary Security Policy*.

Maéva Clément is a Research Associate and Teaching Fellow at the Institute of International Politics at the Helmut Schmidt University, Hamburg. She is a doctoral researcher in the Department of Political Science at the Goethe University, Frankfurt. Her research focuses on collective emotions, political violence, discursive and narrative methodology. In her thesis, she analyzes the role played by emotions in the turn to violence of several Islamist groups across Western Europe over the 2000s. She has previously published in *Political Psychology* and *Global Discourse*. She teaches courses on emotions in international politics, international relations theory, and peace and conflict studies at several universities in France and Germany.

Thomas Lindemann is Professor of Political Science at the Ecole Polytechnique (LinX Research Centre) and the University of Versailles Saint-Quentin. During the fall semester 2016–2017, he was Visiting Professor at Columbia University. He is the author of six books, including 'Causes of War' (ECPR Press 2010) and numerous articles published in *Political Psychology, International Political Sociology, International Relations, International Theory* and other leading journals. He has contributed to the introduction of the concept of recognition into the international relations discipline, with an emphasis on the antagonist and emotional aspects of the concept.

PART III

Discursive Agency and Emotions

CHAPTER 9

Moving Images and the Politics of Pity: A Multilevel Approach to the Interpretation of Images and Emotions

Gabi Schlag

Introduction

Over one million refugees crossed the Mediterranean Sea in 2015; more than 3500 died during their risky passage (IOM, 2017). This contemporary human tragedy became a face and a name on 2 September 2015: Alan (Aylan) Kurdi, a nearly three-year-old boy from Syria, his dead body washed ashore in Bodrum, Turkey. Twelve refugees, including Alan's brother Galip, and his mother Rehen, drowned that day. As citizens and academics, we are confronted with a vast number of moving, emotional, and affective images every day as the pictures of the dead Alan Kurdi illustrate. Lately but without surprise, both images and emotions have gained great attention in political science and international relations theory (IR) although studying images *and* emotions remains a challenge. Obviously, there is not one clear-cut answer to this challenge and, I'm convinced that there is no need for one methodology but many. In this chapter, I address

G. Schlag (✉)
Helmut-Schmidt-University, Hamburg, Germany

two questions in relation to this challenge. First, I reflect on the relation between images, emotions, and politics, with the aim to 'theorizing the process through which individual emotions become collective and political' (Bleiker & Hutchison, 2014, p. 492). Focusing on visual representations of emotions, I argue that images depicting moments of distress and misery can be both, powerful in the sense that they raise awareness and provoke emotional responses, and powerless in the sense that they depoliticize the suffering of others. Second, I sketch out a multilevel methodology that intends to capture and study emotions at different sites, including the image itself, its production, circulation, media(tiza)tion, audiencing, and intertextuality.

Emotions, Images, and Bodies: How Pictures Move Us

The power of images has never been more compelling than in today's digital age of globalized media channels and social networks. Images of war and violence, natural disasters, and human tragedies travel easily and often receive the attention and solidarity of a global audience (Heck & Schlag, 2013; Hutchison, 2014; Schlag, 2014). That images capture and represent emotions, or even provoke an affective response is nothing new. But how is it that some images move us? What concept of affect and emotion is implied here?

The study of emotions in IR has gained major attention in recent years, in particular, since Neta Crawford's article that was published in 2000. Key to these debates is the conviction that emotions are not (only) personal but collective (Mercer, 2014). As collective phenomena, emotions are regarded as political in the sense that they function as evaluative judgments and social bonds between community members (Fattah & Fierke, 2009, p. 70; Nussbaum 1996, p. 35). Emotions, however, have a history, too. How and 'why we feel the way we do' is a 'social and cultural process through which emotions are shaped in the first place' (Ahmed, 2014; Bleiker & Hutchison, 2014, p. 502).

Bleiker and Hutchison discuss several distinctions that have become influential in the study of emotions, including the differences between cognitive and affective as well as latent and emergent approaches (Bleiker & Hutchison, 2014, p. 492, 496). This is not the place to reiterate these debates. In my view, emotions matter as an individual, personal, *and* collective social phenomenon. Emotions are cognitive *and* bodily. Such a broad and inclusive understanding of emotions, however, implies that no single discipline or methodology is able to grasp the whole phenomenon. We are only able to see and describe a small brick of a fluid mosaic. As I will show later, a multilevel methodology that focuses on the intersubjective meaning-making of images is one way to study 'the concrete *processes* through which seemingly individual emotions either become or are at once public, social, collective and political' (Bleiker & Hutchison, 2014, p. 497; italics added), emphasizing that these processes unfold and connect at multiple levels of analysis.

As emotions matter at different levels of analysis and have to be interpreted, so do images. The image is itself an elusive, yet omnipresent phenomenon. The general notion of images, Mitchell explains, denotes 'any likeness, figure, motif, or form that appears in some medium or other' (Mitchell, 1984, 2005, p. xiii). An image is both, a medium and a mode of experience, communication, and knowledge making 'things' visible. As representations, images direct our attention to 'the language and imagery through which meanings are produced and disseminated in societies' (Bleiker, 2001; Hutchison, 2014, p. 4). In relation to emotions, though, images can be both, a representation and a driver. On the one hand, images are able to represent feelings of individuals and symbolize emotions of collectives. They make moments of distress and joy visible and knowledgeable. On the other hand, images sometimes unfold a special attraction not only to our mind but also to our heart. We all certainly know images that excite personal feelings of love and hate, but also collective emotions of fear and shame.

While it is obvious that images and emotions are somehow coupled, it is less clear why this might be the case and why this relation varies empirically. In his very last book *Camera Lucida*, Roland Barthes described the affective bond between a spectator and an image (a photography) as punctum: 'A photograph's punctum is that accident which pricks me' (Barthes, 1981, p. 27). Reflecting on the history of (artistic and religious) image making in Europe, one could argue that the emotional capacities derive from the mirroring qualities of pictures referring back to the Christian tradition of God's likeness (Belting, 2005).[1] This assumed and perceived likeness is even more apparent in secular photographs that depict actual people. We do not scratch out the face of a person on a photograph, although we know the difference between an image and what it shows (Mitchell, 2005, p. 31). It can be said that images work through their immediacy and ambiguity in a subtle, even mystical way (Hansen, 2011, pp. 55–56, 58). We are both fascinated and scared by images (Mitchell, 2005).

Understanding emotions, either on an individual or collective level, as already mediated through representations, questions how images represent emotions and how individuals and collectives express their emotions (differently) in relation to images, that is, when they look at, use or create images, become the focal points of research. As Bleiker & Hutchinson (2014, p. 506) pointedly write: 'All one can understand is the manner in which emotions are expressed and communicated'. That includes language as much as images.

INTERPRETING IMAGES AND EMOTIONS: A MULTILEVEL APPROACH

IR scholars have only recently addressed the methodological challenges of studying visuality (Schlag 2016; Andersen, Vuori, & Mutlu, 2015; Bleiker, 2015; Hansen, 2015, p. 277; Hutchison, 2014, p. 7). But as Bleiker writes, there is not one defining but multiple methods for studying images, how they are produced, what they mean and how they circulate (Bleiker, 2015, p. 873). Many scholars, including myself, share the constructivist commitment that images as representations produce intersubjective meaning and that these processes of meaning-making, then, can be interpreted in a systematic and reflective way.

Interpretive approaches are often defined in negative terms as a critique, even rejection of a positivist methodology (Neufeld, 1993). The plurality of interpretive approaches, though, shares an orientation toward the use of language and meaning-making understood as a social practice (Neufeld, 1993, p. 43; Yanow, 2006, p. xii). They 'put human meaning-making at the center of their concerns' (Yanow, 2006, p. xviii), either as a daily practice of humans self-interpreting the world or as a reflexive practice of academics interpreting other's interpretations of the world. Therefore, any interpretation is not only an individually but also an intersubjectively acknowledged practice that constitutes reality (Neufeld, 1993, p. 45), and these practices are powerful, too. Klotz and Lynch emphasize that meaning and meaning-making is always linked to the question 'how and why *certain* practices prevail in particular contexts' (Klotz & Lynch, 2007, p. 10; italics added). Hence, meaning-making is about power and often has powerful implications.

While interpretative approaches in IR, often associated with a constructivist and post-structuralist movement, have mainly focused on the use of language as a social and powerful practice, these basic propositions are also valid for visuals, how they are used to express meaning, how they are interpreted (differently) and how scholars are able to reconstruct these practices of meaning-making in a systematic, reflective, and critical way (Hansen, 2011, 2015; Schlag, 2016). While studying emotions and images within an interpretive paradigm, however, two challenges have to be faced: First, it is important to note that language and image work with different modalities. While postmodern linguistics and philosophers rightly argue that language does not mirror reality and that the relation between a signifier and the signified is artificial and abstract, images—in particular, photographs—attempt to have a natural and mimetic relation to the depicted reality. It is a defining characteristic of a photograph that a spectator is continually fascinated by its likeness (Kress & van Leeuwen, 2006, p. 8; Mitchell, 1984, pp. 521–524). Second, interpretation itself is a self-reflective process where personal feelings cannot be ignored. The choice and application of most methods depend on subjective factors, even methods themselves should be understood rather as performative and political than objective and neutral (Aradau & Hysmans, 2014). Thus, methods do not control our feelings and convictions as human beings but may help to explicate and reflect them (Bially Mattern, 2014). The aim, then, is to formulate conclusions that are accountable, open to criticism, and intersubjective.

Sites of Interpretation

My interpretative methodology focuses on representations of emotions, that is, how images represent emotions and how one or many people express their feelings, affects, and emotions in public, either verbally (e.g. talking and writing about emotions) or visually (e.g. creating and using visuals) in relation to the production, display, and circulation of an image.[2] As images and emotions are quite ambiguous phenomena, I argue that studying these processes requires a multilevel approach focusing on different sites of interpretation (Rose, 2016). At all of these sites, representations of emotions are important, as images are both a symbol of and a medium for communicating feelings and emotions.

By site of *production*, Gilian Rose refers to the circumstances under which an image is produced and how these circumstances might themselves produce effects. The differences between digital and analog media, for example, have fostered a debate on the manipulation and hyper-reality of images. Some scholars even argue that how an image is (technically) produced determines 'its form, meaning, and effect' (Rose, 2012, p. 20). The site of the *image* itself focuses on composition, style and the use of symbols (Rose, 2012, p. 27). Reading an image and its polyphonic meaning is to some extent comparable to learning a language, including its grammar, vocabularies, and practical usage (Kress & van Leeuwen, 2006). Thus, understanding an image requires knowledge not only of structural visual elements but also how they are (and have been) used differently. The site of *audiencing* directs our attention to a 'process by which a visual image has its meanings renegotiated, or even rejected, by particular audiences watching in specific circumstances' (Rose, 2012, p. 30). *Circulation*, as Rose writes in the fourth edition of her book, is certainly not a new phenomenon but its nature and quality have changed with the rise of digital images and digitized communication (Rose, 2016, p. 21). How images travel, change meaning in varying contexts, and how they might become part of a shared visual memory is relevant too.

The rapid development of digitization and the acceleration of circulation rates of images emphasize two sites Rose addresses only partly: the mediation/mediatization of politics and the intertextuality of images. By *mediation*, I refer to the fact that photographs are converted from one medium to another, for example, from mainstream news media (TV or print) to social media. This mediation is an important site of analysis because the production of an image continues when pictures travel from one medium to another (Andersen, 2012). Different contexts create different images, relating them to other modalities of communication—most notably, words. As the case of Alan Kurdi shows, the intersubjective meaning of images can change when photographs become re-mediated. *Mediatization*, by contrast, highlights the fact that life is mainly experienced via media. We recognize events far away because we see the pictures and hear the stories on TV, hence '[m]edia representations are crucial because all knowledge of political issues is unavoidable and inherently mediated' (Bleiker, Campbell, Hutchison, & Nicholson, 2013, p. 399).

Intertextuality, then, takes note of the fact that images not only circulate and transform but also refer to other images and might motivate the production of more images. There are many drawings, collages, cartoons, and graffiti that cite the original photograph of Alan Kurdi. These references are constitutive of the broader image because spectators understand the intertextual relation between the photograph and its artistic processing. Artistic citations might include a change of medium when, for example, activists and artists such as Ai WeiWei perform the motif of the dead boy at the shore (The Guardian, 2016).

Methods of Interpretation

Methods are neither representational nor value-neutral but performative and political (Aradau & Hysmans, 2014, p. 598). They are tools and their usefulness depends on the research questions we ask. Focusing on images, a pluralist approach to methods has been advocated by Bleiker (2015, pp. 877–879), including ethnographic methods, semiotics, content and discourse analysis, audience interviews, observation, and surveys. I have argued elsewhere that a combination of discourse analysis and iconology helps to study visuals in IR (Heck & Schlag, 2013; Schlag, 2016).[3] For emotions, the choice of methods and methodology is far more diverse as this volume demonstrates. A way to combine the study of emotions and images is to focus on the affective function of multimodal texts.

Multimodality 'is now a widely used term in the academic world', Carey Jewitt, Jeff Bezemer, & Kay O'Hallaron (2016, p. 1) write. In general, scholars created the term to 'highlight that people use multiple means of meaning-making' (Jewitt et al., 2016, p. 2). More specifically, multimodality refers to the fact that these means of meaning-making are not used separately but 'almost *always appear together*: image with writing, speech with gesture, math symbolism with writing and so forth' (Jewitt et al., 2016, p. 2). Thus, multimodal texts 'incorporate semiotic resources beyond verbal language' (Jancsary, Höllerer, & Meyer, 2016, p. 181). Modes refer to a variety of semiotic resources used for making-meaning, including images and moving images, writing, music, gesture, speech, and so on (Kress, 2010).[4] Modes have different functions and offer distinct potentialities and limits (Jewitt et al., 2016, p. 3). They certainly vary from context to context and how they are combined 'is governed by cultural and institutional rules' (Jancsary et al., 2016, p. 182).

It is, however, important to note that '*the* "multimodal method" cannot exist since the concrete form of analysis has to fit the particular research question, research context, and data' (Jancsary et al., 2016, p. 189). In general, a multimodal analysis explicates research steps many scholars already apply (although often in a rather implicit way) and that are well known in cultural studies: (1) Characterizing the genre, capturing the manifest and latent content and elements of a text, reconstructing the composition and its effects as well as (2) reconstructing and theorizing patterns of social meaning (Jancsary et al., 2016, pp. 191–201).

As emotions and how to study them are the major focus of this volume, multimodality helps to understand one (not the only) function that images have: representing, symbolizing, and evoking individual feelings and collective emotions that become political.

REPRESENTATIONS OF SHAME, GRIEF, AND PITY: SHOWING/ SEEING THE IMAGE OF A DEAD CHILD

When it comes to the movement of people, constructivists have mainly focused on how and why (forced) migration became securitized in liberal democracies in Europe, North America and Australia (Aradau, 2004; Bourbeau, 2011; Buzan, de Wilde, & Waever, 1998: Chap. 6). How media images shape perceptions of refugees and migrants, however, is only occasionally addressed. Bleiker, Campbell, Hutchison, and Nicholson, for example, show how emotional images of asylum seekers framed the political debate in Australia not as a humanitarian disaster but as a potential threat (Bleiker et al., 2013). This 'dehumanizing visual pattern' then, 'sets in place mechanisms of security and border control' instead of promoting humanitarian action and relief (Bleiker et al., 2013, p. 399).

If media representations influence how refugees and (forced) migration are socially constructed, it is important to understand the effects of such representations, that is, conceptualizing the processes whereby images and emotions become political. Using the outlined methodology, I will argue that already the content and form of the photograph is emotionally embedded. Then, I will show how expressions of feelings and emotions, in particular, shame and pity, by individuals became collective and political through the circulation, mediation/mediatization, and intertextuality of the photograph. A disclaimer is necessary here: Focusing on shame, grief, and pity is the result of an abductive research process (Friedrichs & Kratochwil, 2009, pp. 709–711); it is surely not an all-encompassing list of emotions we can study in relation to the picture of Alan Kurdi.[5] According to the Oxford dictionary (online), shame refers to '[a] painful feeling of humiliation or distress caused by the consciousness of wrong or foolish behaviour', grief is an '[i]ntense sorrow, especially caused by someone's death' and pity can be defined as '[t]he feeling of sorrow and compassion caused by the sufferings and misfortunes of others'. All these emotions are social as they constitute relations between people, co-constitutive because the distress of one person causes emotions of another person, and normative in the sense that people have learned how they should emotionally respond, for example, to the misfortune, even death, of a person.

The Site of Production: How It Feels to Take a Picture of a Dead Boy

Turkish journalist Nilüfer Demir took photographs on the morning of 2 September 2015 at the shore of Bodrum/Turkey, including pictures of a dead three-year-old boy. In an interview with CNN Turk, she explained that '[t]here was nothing left to do for him. There was nothing left to bring him back to life. [...]. There was nothing to do except take his photograph ... and that is exactly what I did. [...] I thought, "This is the only way I can express the scream of his silent body"' (cited in Griggs, 2015). This statement by Demir already hints at the strong affective responses to the picture and its motif. It shows a normative commitment that many journalists share when they are reporting and documenting crisis and conflicts. It might also show that the journalist's objectivity is rather a myth than a realistic practice.

The Site of the Image: How Death Becomes Visible

Two photographs have been widely published. The first photograph includes a clear composition where the lower third part exposes a dead boy, face-down into the sand, touching the water's edge with his head. His body is directed toward the sea. The other photograph depicts the moment when a Turkish police officer lifts the dead boy and carries him away. A close witness who documents the scene characterizes the point of view. While the first photograph shows no movement, the second photograph depicts an action.

As most photographs have been re-mastered and adopted to different media formats, the compositional proportions might vary. Most reproductions of the image stay with the medium long shot that allows a distant yet comprehensive view. Conventionally, the person(s) are centered and clearly mark the figurative and literal focal point of the images. The surrounding is also imaged giving the motif some general contextual knowledge (coastal side, beach, seawater). Nevertheless, the composition is very simple and minimalistic. The content is disturbing but clear: 'The photo of the drowned toddler stays. It is deadly calm: there are no sunken boats, exhausted crowds, or urgent situations at hand. There is a child on a beach in summer, who will never play again' (Ben-Ghiat, 2015).

Looking at the picture that shows only Alan Kurdi, we do not know the circumstances of his death, whether it was caused by accident or poses a crime. It also breaks a journalistic taboo as Hugh Pinney, vice president at Getty Images, says: 'a picture of a dead child is one of the golden rules of what you never publish' (cited in Laurent, 2015). No doubt, this taboo is regularly broken but the display of the picture provoked a lively debate on ethical standards of journalism (see below). Commentators have stressed that photographs of dead children had been taken in the weeks before but Alan Kurdi gained doubtful popularity because he looked more 'European' (Bouckaert, cited in Laurent, 2015). Some authors argue that the images of Alan Kurdi refer to the motif of a sleeping angle (Drainville, 2015) and to the motif of Pietà, the most iconic representation of empathy, commiseration, and lamentation in Christian art (Aulich, 2015).[6] Further references can be seen in the mythological idea of a deluge that is known in different cultures (Juneja & Schenk, 2014).

In general, images of dying or dead people strongly engage emotions showing people in situations of distress and evoking emotional responses by spectators (Zelizer, 2010). Today, many of these images are produced by citizens and distributed via social media networks (Andersen, 2012; Mortensen, 2011). Their display and proliferation, though, is regularly criticized and sometimes restricted by mainstream media through (informal) codes of conduct (Auchter, 2015; Friis, 2015). While images of suffering and death are highly affective, lacking contextual information often gives the impression that suffering comes from the outside, portraying an 'isolated victim awaiting external assistance' (Campbell, 2011, p. 8). Such images, then, have de-politicizing effects and are productive of 'colonial relations of power' (2011, p. 8), as Campbell has argued with reference to the visual representation of famine.

The photograph of Alan Kurdi illustrates that portraits of children are special. As a symbol, 'children are abstracted from culture and society, granted an innate innocence, seen to be dependent, requiring protection and having developmental potential' (Campbell, 2011, p. 9). Therefore, their suffering and death is particularly shocking, painful and often implies a call for action. Depictions of children are a well-known motif in the history of photojournalism. Think about the photo of Kim Phuc, a global icon of the Vietnam War, a photograph of a vulture staring at an emaciated child in Sudan, taken by Kevin Carter in 1993 and various pictures from the Israeli-Palestinian conflict of dead children (e.g. taken by Tyler Hicks in July 2014).

While images of children (and women) are typical motifs for showing humanitarian crisis and natural disasters, mainstream media often restricts the display of dead bodies. Such graphic images not only evoke grief and pity but also shame; being ashamed that a child has died. Such reactions of shame imply that the death of Alan Kurdi could have been prevented and that someone should be held accountable for it. We can see that the image, its motif, and genre, is already embedded in an affective frame constituting a relationship between the fate of Alan Kurdi and a spectator with her/his emotional reactions. It also illustrates the cultural and normative dimension of emotions since 'we' know (or have learned) how to respond to an image of a dead child.

The Site of Circulation: A Global Affective Community in the Making

The global circulation of the photographs showing Alan Kurdi 'relates to their status as portable physical artefacts' (Faulkner, 2015, p. 53). Digitization has accelerated the movement of images while the quantity of images steadily grows, thanks to common practices of taking and distributing pictures with a smart phone. The image of Alan Kurdi first appeared in an article by Turkish News Agency DHA showing 50 pictures of dead Syrian refugees that had been found on the shore of Bodrum in the morning. Four of them feature a little boy, who was identified later as Alan (often named Aylan) Kurdi. Two pictures of the series were widely published by mainstream and social media. The first photograph shows the dead Alan Kurdi, either facing the spectator or showing his back. The second image depicts the moment when Turkish police officer Mehmet Ciplak carries his dead body away.

Two hours later, the first picture with only Alan Kurdi's dead body appeared on twitter published by the Turkish journalist and activist Michelle Demichevitch. The image spread in the Middle East and then went viral when Human Rights Watch Director for Emergencies Peter Bouckaert, re-tweeted the picture of Alan Kurdi on twitter (D'Orazio, 2015). Writing about his intensions and feelings, whether to publish the photo or not, he said: 'It was not an easy decision to share a brutal image of a drowned child. But I care about these children as much as my own. Maybe if Europe's leaders did too, they would try to stem this ghastly spectacle' (Bouckaert, 2015).

The audience grew global when Washington Post correspondent Liz Sly shared her tweet (D'Orazio, 2015, pp. 12–14).[7] Many users, including politicians and representatives of NGOs and IOs, expressed their feelings in words and with emoticons, calling on political representatives to do something. But some followers also posted hostile comments (Thelwall, 2015). The following days, many meme and artistic responses were created and circulated via twitter, Facebook, and mainstream news (Vis, 2015; Ryan, 2015; see below on intertextuality). The hashtag #aylankurdi is active until today.

The Site of Media(tiza)tion: Framing the Repertoire of Emotions

The first non-Turkish newspaper that reports the story is the *British Daily Mail* online edition at 1:10 PM with the title 'Terrible fate of a tiny boy who symbolizes the desperation of thousands' (D'Orazio, 2015, p. 15). The next day, it is the front-page story of many newspapers worldwide although not all of them print a photo of Alan Kurdi. The intermodality of the photographs (as still images) changes, being now moved to a printed cover image, edited and linked to other images, stories—and in the case of twitter—emoticons. Through the 'remediation' by mainstream media, the image of Alan Kurdi becomes a global icon (Faulkner, 2015, p. 53).

With the beginning of journalistic framing of the image, the symbolic content starts to transform. While the photographs by Demir show a drowned toddler and a police officer carrying his dead body away, news headlines use the image as a symbol of a humanitarian disaster and the failure of the EU: 'Humanity washed ashore' (Gulf News), 'The reality—why Europe must act now' (The National), 'Unbearable' (Daily Mirror), 'The little victim of a growing crisis' (The Washington Post), 'Europe Divided' (The Times), 'Tiny victim of a human catastrophe' (Daily Mail), 'The shocking, cruel reality of Europe's refugee crisis' (The Guardian), 'Utan dünya!' ('World, be ashamed', Milliyet) and 'Dünyayi sarsti' ('Shocked world', Hürriyet).[8] While most Western media outlets used the image of Alan Kurdi as a symbol of a humanitarian tragedy, the Islamic State published it with the title 'The danger of abandoning Dārul-Islām' in its monthly magazine *Dabiq*. This display of the photograph is telling because it shows a contesting framing (although many readers might not conceive this frame as appropriate).

Through the emotional framing of media outlets, individual feelings and emotions become political. A statement by the editors of *The Independent* illustrates how this emotional framing gets a political twist: 'Some will feel we have overstepped the mark of common decency; a few will claim we have put emotion above rational debate. But the fact is this: abject people are dying and they need our help. If we cannot see that, then we have no right to look away from the consequences of inaction' (The Independent, 2015). *The Independent* initiated a political campaign that urged the British government to accept its fair share of refugees in the EU.

The Site of Audiencing: Emotions Without Consequences?

Audiencing includes comments by social network users that are closely linked to the circulation and mediatization of the images as well as to a public debate about political action. Users on twitter, for example, shared the picture of Alan Kurdi, often with emoticons and additional images (see below on intertextuality). Many commentators spoke and wrote about their personal feelings when they had seen the picture (crying, being speechless, shocked, feeling grief and anger, etc.). There are, however, also 'critical' tweets that question the story or accuse the parents of Alan Kurdi for being reckless and selfish. As Burns has shown, comments by politicians and citizens are comparable but following actions differed. While politicians mostly returned to the usual conduct of politics after some weeks, many people were mobilized and donated money, coordinated shelter for refugees or volunteered in other ways (Burns, 2015, p. 39). Further, many comments were expressed from the 'vantage point of a parent' (Burns, 2015, p. 39) stressing the affective and emotional relations between a child and an adult. This vantage point also iterates a hierarchical, yet empathic positioning Campbell has shown for the representation of famine that narrows the emotional repertoire to parents and their ability to feel and know what it means to lose a child.

In the UK, Chancellor George Osborne was the first member of the government who commented on the picture. During a factory visit, he said: 'There is no person who would not be very shocked by that picture—and I was very distressed when I saw it myself this morning—of that poor boy lying dead on the beach. […]. We know there is not a simple answer to this crisis. What you need to do is first of all tackle Isis and the criminal gangs who killed that boy' (cited in Wintour, 2015). It is interesting to note that Osborne expresses first his affective reaction and then imputes the Islamic State and smugglers to be responsible for Alan's death. Scottish first minister Nicola Sturgeon, instead, emphasized that the lives of refugees 'are the responsibility of all of us' calling upon Cameron 'to offer sanctuary to refugees who need our help' (cited in Wintour, 2015). Prime Minister Cameron said that he was moved by the picture too, but insisted that the UK already 'fulfills our moral responsibilities' in response to the refugee crisis (cited in Dathan, 2015). Asked by *The Independent*, he responded that the government is doing enough, although thousands had signed a petition created by the editors calling on the government to set quotas for taking in refugees. With this petition, the editors of *The Independent* pursued a political aim, namely changing restricted British migration politics.

In the United States, Senator John McCain displayed a close-up of the dead boy on the Senate floor and said in his 15-min-long statement: 'This image has haunted the world. But what should haunt us even more than the horror unfolding before our eyes are the thought that the United States will continue to do nothing meaningful about it' (cited in Tasch, 2015). He urged the US government to take in more refugees and to enhance its engagement in the Syrian conflict naming the crisis the 'greatest humanitarian tragedy of our times'. After the terror attacks in Paris three month later, though, many US politicians returned to the stereotypical link between refugees and terrorists (although not McCain).

As Alan Kurdi's aunt Tima is living in the Vancouver area, the story of his death was widely perceived in Canada and 'has [...] become an emotional issue in the Canadian election', The New York Times correspondent Ian Austen (2015) writes. Oppositional politicians, NGOs, and activists criticized the government for its refugee policies arguing that Canada was taking in fewer people from Syria than promised. The family of Alan Kurdi had applied for entry to Canada but their application was turned down due to incomplete documents.

Prime Minister Stephen Harper said that '[w]e had the same reaction, Laureen and I, as everybody else when we see the photo—it's heart-wrenching, it brings you right to your own family' (The Canadian Press, 2015). He added, though, that Canada should accept more refugees from Syria and should enhance its military action against the Islamic State, 'to fight the root cause of the problem' (cited in Austen, 2015). Immigration Minister Chris Alexander suspended his campaign saying that he was 'deeply saddened by that image'. In reaction to the story of the Kurdi family, Canada's refugee and migration policies became an essential topic of the election campaign. The opposition criticized the government for their words of condolence but lacking political action in order to remove legal obstacles for asylum seekers. After the elections in October, a new liberal government under its Prime Minister Justin Trudeau symbolically took in about 25,000 refugees from Syria (Kingsley & Timur, 2015).

The Site of Intertextuality/Mediality: Re-performing Images

Intertextual relations can be studied in various directions: on twitter where users posted artistic collages and illustrations, cartoons published in on- and offline media, graffiti in urban areas worldwide as well as sculptures and performances by activists and artists. Twitter users, for example, posted many artistic images and meme of Alan's original photograph (Faulkner, 2015; Ryan, 2015; Vis, 2015).[9] From 4 September 2015 onward, the original photograph of the dead boy had been replaced by artistic responses and user-generated variations (D'Orazio, 2015, p. 18). Mainstream media also included these images as well as screenshots of twitter posts in their online-reports. Accordingly, photographs of the young Alan laughing and playing were distributed as commemorates.

The French satirical magazine Charlie Hebdo printed a cover with cartoons referring to the story of Kurdi. Activists and artists, most prominently the Chinese artist Ai WeiWei, performed the motif and graffiti artists took up the motif of the boy as well. These intertextual and intermedial references demonstrate the iconic status of the image. Re-performances keep the image alive and become part of a collective memory (Picture 9.1).

CONCLUSION: WHAT CAN IMAGES AND EMOTIONS (NOT) DO—CHANGING POLITICS, FORMING COMMUNITIES?

In conclusion, I want to focus on two themes that seem to be important for further research on the relation between images, emotions, and politics: the power of graphic images for changing politics and the power of emotions for forming communities.

When graphic images are published by mainstream media, commentators commonly ask 'did it change politics?' Anne Burns (2015, p. 28) has argued 'that this assumed political function is cited in order to redeem the

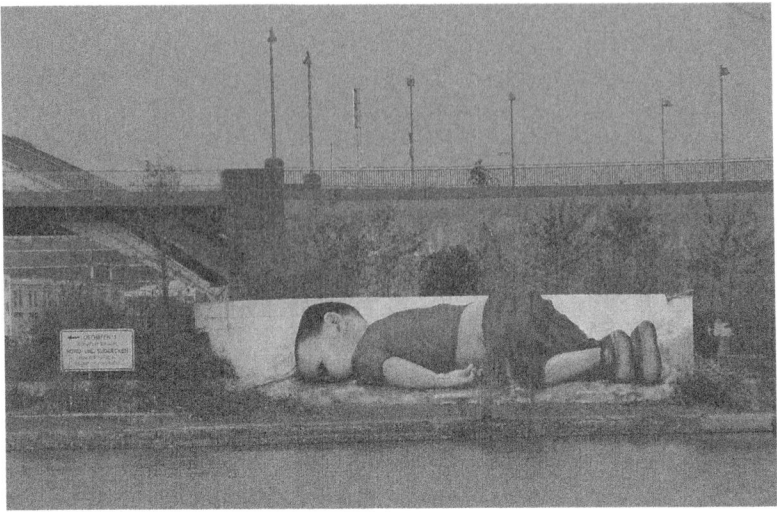

Picture 9.1 Graffiti Version of the Alan Kurdi picture, Frankfurt/Main. Source: Street art by Oguz Sen and Justus Becker, Frankfurt am Main, photographed by Frank C Müller; available under the Creative Commons Attribution-Share Alike 4.0 International license on Wikipedia Commons at https://commons.wikimedia.org/wiki/File:Mural_Ffm_Osthafen_01_(fcm).jpg

image's circulation'. Linking the publication of an image to its history-making power, it is acceptable to look at and share a photograph of a dead child assuming that it changes politics, she argues. The actual impact of images and emotions on politics, however, is even more complicated. Whether graphic images change history in the sense that they initiate a different kind of policies and provoke responsible action, depends on how 'we' use, see and sense visual representations of suffering, violence, and death. In the case of Alan Kurdi, the balance sheet is indecisive. On the one hand, the photographs made visible that thousands of refugees—men, women, and children—are dying during their risky passage to Europe. The photographs and their medi(ati)zation mobilized people and forced politicians to justify their policies to the public. On the other hand, the emotional framing of the photographs, either in mainstream or social media, had also de-politicizing effects. Emotions such as shame, grief, and pity might foster political mobilization but can also motivate a sensational spectatorship, a politics of pity *without* consequences (Chouliaraki, 2006).

The story of Alan Kurdi also illustrates how important emotions are for the formation of communities beyond the nation-state (Hutchison, 2014, 2016; Koschut, 2014). On the one hand, the fate of refugees, represented by a photograph of a dead boy, moved many people around the world. It created a fugitive public sphere where refugees became recognized as vulnerable subjects. People expressed their compassion with those who have greater misfortunes in life, constructing a kind of transnational solidarity. The immense response to the image at different sites shows how citizens, journalists, and politicians identify with the fate of displaced people and begin to take up responsibility. On the other hand, such representations are ambiguous reminding us of the gap between the represented and its representation as the very location of politics, Bleiker (2001, p. 510) writes. They show as much as they hide. As Hutchison (2014) argues for the Tsunami catastrophe in 2004, stereotypes and colonial imaginaries assisted the politics of pity similar to the display and reception of Alan Kurdi's image as I have intended to show. Emotions and images, then, might be a crucial, yet ambivalent bond that connects 'us' and 'them' across space and time.

Acknowledgments I would like to thank the editors, Maéva Clément and Eric Sangar, as well as Axel Heck, Hanna Pfeifer, and Katarina Ristic for helpful comments. All remaining errors and fallacies are my own.

Notes

1. I am absolutely aware that this depiction of a history is highly selective and Eurocentric. Visual histories and cultures indeed differ.
2. An immediate experience of someone's emotions and a visual documentation of a bodily sensation counts as a performance or representation of emotions. Due to a restricted access to relevant data, this dimension will not be discussed in this chapter.
3. For iconographic approaches to the relation between emotions and visuals, see Flam & Doerr (2015) and Falk (2015).
4. Note that Rose also refers to modes but in a different way (technological modality, compositional modality, social modality).
5. For example, shock and anger but also apathy and indifference.
6. Some artistic responses use the angel motif showing Alan Kurdi with wings or with the presence of an angel.
7. In retro, readers can find tweets under the Turkish hashtag #kiyiyavuraninsanlik and the English translation #HumanityWashedAshore.

8. For a collection of headlines, see Laurent (2015).
9. A selection of artistic responses is presented here: http://www.boredpanda.com/syrian-boy-drowned-mediterranean-tragedy-artists-respond-aylan-kurdi/.

References

Ahmed, S. (2014). *The Cultural Politics of Emotion* (2nd ed.). Edinburgh: Edinburgh University Press.

Andersen, R. S. (2012). REMEDIATING #IRANELECTION: Journalistic Strategies for Positioning Citizen-Made Snapshots and Text Bites from the 2009 Iranian Post-election Conflict. *Journalism Practice, 6*(3), 317–336.

Andersen, R. S., Vuori, J. A., & Mutlu, C. E. (2015). Visuality. In C. Aradau, J. Huysmans, A. Neal, & N. Voelkner (Eds.), *Critical Security Methods: New Frameworks for Analysis* (pp. 85–117). Abingdon and New York: Routledge.

Aradau, C. (2004). The Perverse Politics of Four-Letter Words: Risk and Pity in the Securitisation of Human Trafficking. *Millennium: Journal of International Studies, 33*(2), 251–277.

Aradau, C., & Hysmans, J. (2014). Critical Methods in International Relations: The Politics of Techniques, Devices and Acts. *European Journal of International Relations, 20*(3), 596–619.

Auchter, J. (2015). @GaddafisGhost: On the Popular Memoro-Politics of a Dead Dictator. *Journal for Cultural Research*, Online First. https://doi.org/10.1080/14797585.2015.1021994.

Aulich, J. (2015). The Life of Images: The Iconography of the Photograph of Alan Kurdi's Body and the Turkish Policeman. In F. Vis & O. Goriunova (Eds.), *The Iconic Image on Social Media: A Rapid Research Response to the Death of Aylan Kurdi*. Sheffield: Visual Social Media Lab.

Austen, I. (2015, September 3). Aylan Kurdi's Death Resonates in Canadian Election Campaign. *The New York Times*. Retrieved April 4, 2017, from http://www.nytimes.com/2015/09/04/world/americas/aylan-kurdis-death-raises-resonates-in-canadian-election-campaign.html

Barthes, R. (1981). *Camera Lucida: Reflections on Photography*. New York: Hill and Wang.

Belting, H. (2005). Image, Medium, Body: A New Approach to Iconology. *Critical Inquiry, 31*(2), 302–319.

Ben-Ghiat, R. (2015, September 3). Toddler's Image Stops Us in Our Tracks. *CNN Online*. Retrieved April 4, 2017, from http://edition.cnn.com/2015/09/03/opinions/ben--ghiat-toddler-picture-turkey/

Bially Mattern, J. (2014). On Being Convinced: An Emotional Epistemology of International Relations. *International Theory, 6*(3), 589–594.

Bleiker, R. (2001). The Aesthetic Turn in International Political Theory. *Millennium: Journal of International Studies, 30*(3), 509–533.

Bleiker, R. (2015). Pluralist Methods for Visual Global Politics. *Millennium: Journal of International Studies, 43*(3), 872–890.

Bleiker, R., Campbell, D., Hutchison, E., & Nicholson, X. (2013). The Visual Dehumanisation of Refugees. *Australian Journal of Political Science, 48*(4), 398–416.

Bleiker, R., & Hutchison, E. (2014). Theorizing Emotions in World Politics. *International Theory, 6*(3), 491–514.

Bouckaert, P. (2015, September 2). Dispatches: Why I Shared a Horrific Photo of a Drowned Syrian Child. *Human Rights Watch online*. Retrieved April 4, 2017, from https://www.hrw.org/news/2015/09/02/dispatches-why-i-shared-horrific-photo-drowned-syrian-child

Bourbeau, P. (2011). *The Securitization of Migration: A Study of Movement and Order*. Abingdon and New York: Routledge.

Burns, A. (2015). Discussion and Action: Political and Personal Responses to the Aylan Kurdi Images. In F. Vis & O. Goriunova (Eds.), *The Iconic Image on Social Media: A Rapid Research Response to the Death of Aylan Kurdi*. Sheffield: Visual Social Media Lab.

Buzan, B., de Wilde, J., & Waever, O. (1998). *Security: A New Framework for Analysis*. London: Boulder.

Campbell, D. (2011). The Iconography of Famine. In G. Batchen et al. (Eds.), *Picturing Atrocity: Reading Photographs in Crisis*. London: Reaktion Books.

Chouliaraki, L. (2006). *The Spectatorship of Suffering*. London et al.: SAGE.

D'Orazio, F. (2015). Journey of an Image: From a Beach in Bodrum to Twenty Million Screens Across the World. In F. Vis & O. Goriunova (Eds.), *The Iconic Image on Social Media: A Rapid Research Response to the Death of Aylan Kurdi*. Sheffield: Visual Social Media Lab.

Dathan, M. (2015, September 3). Aylan Kurdi: David Cameron Says He Felt 'Deeply Moved' by Images of Dead Syrian Boy but Gives No Details of Plans to Take in More Refugees. *The Independent*. Retrieved April 4, 2017, from http://www.independent.co.uk/news/uk/politics/aylan-kurdi-david-cameron-says-he-felt-deeply-moved-by-images-of-dead-syrian-boy-but-gives-no-10484641.html

Drainville, R. (2015). On the Iconology of Aylan Kurdi, Alone. In F. Vis & O. Goriunova (Eds.), *The Iconic Image on Social Media: A Rapid Research Response to the Death of Aylan Kurdi*. Sheffield: Visual Social Media Lab.

Falk, F. (2015). Evoking Emotions: The Visual Construction of Fear and Compassion. In H. Flam & J. Kleres (Eds.), *Methods of Exploring Emotions*. Abingdon and New York: Routledge.

Fattah, K., & Fierke, K. M. (2009). A Clash of Emotions: The Politics of Humiliation and Political Violence in the Middle East. *European Journal of International Relations, 15*(1), 67–93.

Faulkner, S. (2015). Aylan Kurdi and the Movability of Images. In F. Vis & O. Goriunova (Eds.), *The Iconic Image on Social Media: A Rapid Research Response to the Death of Aylan Kurdi.* Sheffield: Visual Social Media Lab.

Flam, H., & Doerr, N. (2015). Visuals and Emotions in Social Movements. In H. Flam & J. Kleres (Eds.), *Methods of Exploring Emotions.* Abingdon and New York: Routledge.

Friedrichs, J., & Kratochwil, F. (2009). On Acting and Knowing: How Pragmatism Can Advance International Relations Research and Methodology. *International Organization, 63*(4), 701.

Friis, S. M. (2015). 'Beyond Anything We Have Ever Seen': Beheading Videos and the Visibility of Violence in the War Against ISIS. *International Affairs, 91*(4), 725–746.

Griggs, B. (2015, September 3). Photographer Describes 'Scream' of Migrant Boy's 'Silent Body'. *CNN Online.* Retrieved April 4, 2017, from http://edition.cnn.com/2015/09/03/world/dead-migrant-boy-beach-photographer-nilufer-demir/

Hansen, L. (2011). Theorizing the Image for Security Studies: Visual Securitization and the Muhammad Cartoon Crisis. *European Journal of International Relations, 17*(1), 51–74.

Hansen, L. (2015). How Images Make World Politics: International Icons and the Case of Abu Ghraib. *Review of International Studies, 41*(2), 263–288.

Heck, A., & Schlag, G. (2013). Securitizing Images: The Female Body and the War in Afghanistan. *European Journal of International Relations, 19*(4), 891–913.

Hutchison, E. (2014). A Global Politics of Pity? Disaster Imagery and the Emotional Construction of Solidarity After the 2004 Asian Tsunami. *International Political Sociology, 8*(1), 1–19.

Hutchison, E. (2016). *Affective Communities in World Politics: Collective Emotions After Trauma.* Cambridge: Cambridge University Press.

IOM. (2017, March 8). Missing Migrants Project. Retrieved from http://missingmigrants.iom.int/latest-global-figures

Jancsary, D., Höllerer, M. A., & Meyer, R. E. (2016). Critical Analysis of Visual and Multimodal Texts. In R. Wodak & M. Meyer (Eds.), *Methods of Critical Discourse Studies.* London and New York: Sage.

Jewitt, C., Bezemer, J., & O'Hallaron, K. (2016). *Introducing Multimodality.* London and New York: Routledge.

Juneja, M., & Schenk, G. J. (2014). *Disaster as Image: Iconographies and Media Strategies Across Europe and Asia.* Regensburg: Schnell + Steiner.

Kingsley, P., & Timur S. (2015, December 31). Stories of 2015: How Alan Kurdi's Death Changed the World. *The Guardian.* Retrieved April 4, 2017, from https://www.theguardian.com/world/2015/dec/31/alan-kurdi-death-canada-refugee-policy-syria-boy-beach-turkey-photo

Klotz, A., & Lynch, C. (2007). *Strategies for Research in Constructivist International Relations*. Armonk and New York: ME Sharp.

Koschut, S. (2014). Emotional (Security) Communities: The Significance of Emotion Norms in Inter-allied Conflict Management. *Review of International Studies, 40*(3), 533–558.

Kress, G. R. (2010). *Multimodality: A Social Semiotic Approach to Contemporary Communication*. London and New York: Routledge.

Kress, G. R., & van Leeuwen, T. (2006). *Reading Images: The Grammar of Visual Design*. London and New York: Routledge.

Laurent, O. (2015, September 4). What the Image of Aylan Kurdi Says About the Power of Photography. *Time Online*. Retrieved April 4, 2017, from http://time.com/4022765/aylan-kurdi-photo/

Mercer, J. (2014). Feeling Like a State: Social Emotion and Identity. *International Theory, 6*(3), 515–535.

Mitchell, W. J. T. (1984). What Is an Image? *New Literary History, 15*(3), 503–537.

Mitchell, W. J. T. (2005). *What Do Pictures Want. The Lives and Loves of Images*. Chicago: The University of Chicago Press.

Mortensen, M. (2011). When Citizen Photojournalism Sets the News Agenda: Neda Agha Soltan as a Web 2.0 Icon of Postelection Unrest in Iran. *Global Media and Communication, 7*(1), 4–16.

Neufeld, M. (1993). Interpretation and the 'Science' of International Relations. *Review of International Studies, 19*(1), 39–61.

Nussbaum, M. (1996). Compassion: The Basic Social Emotion. *Social Philosophy and Policy, 13*(1), 27–58.

Rose, G. (2012). *Visual Methodologies. An Introduction to Researching with Visual Materials* (3rd ed.). Los Angeles et al.: SAGE.

Rose, G. (2016). *Visual Methodolgies. An Introduction to Researching Visual Materials* (4th ed.). Los Angeles et al.: SAGE.

Ryan, H. (2015). #KiyiyaVuranInsanlikik: Unpacking Artistic Responses to the Aylan Kurdi Images. In F. Vis & O. Goriunova (Eds.), *The Iconic Image on Social Media: A Rapid Research Response to the Death of Aylan Kurdi*. Sheffield: Visual Social Media Lab.

Schlag, G. (2014). A Buddha to Protect: Nargis and the Visual Politics of Security. In M. Juneja & G. J. Schenk (Eds.), *Disaster as Image: Iconographies and Media Strategies Across Europe and Asia* (pp. 137–146). Regensburg: Schnell + Steiner.

Schlag, G. (2016). Imaging Security: A Visual Methodology for Security Studies. In G. Schlag, J. Junk, & C. Daase (Eds.), *Transformations of Security Studies: Dialogues, Diversity and Discipline* (pp. 173–189). London and New York: Routledge.

Tasch, B. (2015, September 9). John McCain Displayed the Gut-Wrenching Photo of the Drowned Syrian Child on the Senate Floor to Urge US Action.

BusinessInsider. Retrieved April 4, 2017, from http://www.businessinsider.com/ap-mccain-displays-photo-of-dead-syrian-boy-on-senate-floor-2015-9?IR=T

The Canadian Press. (2015, September 3). Harper: Alan Kurdi Image Heartbreaking, But Doesn't Change Need To Fight ISIL. *Huffington Post*. Retrieved April 4, 2017, from http://www.huffingtonpost.ca/2015/09/03/aylan-kurdi_n_8084778.html

The Guardian. (2016, February 1). *Ai Weiwei Poses as Drowned Syrian Infant Refugee in 'Haunting' Photo*. Retrieved April 4, 2017, from https://www.theguardian.com/artanddesign/2016/feb/01/ai-weiwei-poses-as-drowned-syrian-infant-refugee-in-haunting-photo

The Independent. (2015, September 2). *Make Your Voice Heard: Sign The Independent's Petition to Welcome Refugees*. Retrieved April 4, 2017, from http://www.independent.co.uk/voices/editorials/make-your-voice-heard-sign-the-independents-petition-to-welcome-refugees-10483488.html

Thelwall, M. (2015). Undermining Aylan: Less Than Sympathetic International Responses. In F. Vis & O. Goriunova (Eds.), *The Iconic Image on Social Media: A Rapid Research Response to the Death of Aylan Kurdi*. Sheffield: Visual Social Media Lab.

Vis, F. (2015). Examining the Hundred Most Shared Images of Aylan Kurdi on Twitter. In F. Vis & O. Goriunova (Eds.), *The Iconic Image on Social Media: A Rapid Research Response to the Death of Aylan Kurdi*. Sheffield: Visual Social Media Lab.

Wintour, P. (2015, September 3). Osborne: We Must Tackle Isis and Gangs Who Killed Aylan Kurdi. *The Guardian*. Retrieved April 4, 2017, from https://www.theguardian.com/world/2015/sep/03/george-osborne-aylan-kurdi-syrian-boy-washed-up-on-beach-killed-by-isis

Yanow, D. (2006). Introduction. In D. Yanow & P. Schwartz-Shea (Eds.), *Interpretation and Methods: Empirical Research Methods and the Interpretive Turn*. London and New York: Routledge.

Zelizer, B. (2010). *About to Die: How News Images Move the Public*. Oxford: Oxford University Press.

Gabi Schlag is Research Associate and Lecturer at the Helmut Schmidt University/University of the Federal Armed Forces Hamburg, Germany. She holds a PhD from the Goethe-University, Frankfurt. She is the co-editor of *Transformations of Security Studies: Dialogues, Diversity and Discipline* (Routledge). Her work on visual security, military interventions, as well as discourses on European and transatlantic security and defense is published in journals such as the *European Journal of International Relations, Journal of International Relations and Development, Zeitschrift für Internationale Beziehungen*, and in several edited volumes such as *Uses of the West* (Cambridge University Press), *Theorizing NATO* (Routledge) and *Image as Disaster* (Schnell+Steiner).

CHAPTER 10

Political Emotions as Public Processes: Analyzing Transnational Ressentiments in Discourses

Reinhard Wolf

INTRODUCTION

In past decades, emotions have figured little in mainstream political science,[1] a field dominated by theories that privilege rational choice over other types of explanations. While this perspective has firmly aligned with anthropological assumptions that followed the *homo oeconomicus* model, it has also suited the narratives of political leaders who, when explaining their decisions, have emphasized their cool, objective reasoning rather than their personal moods or momentary feelings. Emotional explanations have thus suffered a dual disadvantage: they contravened the prevailing understanding of elite political behavior based on the calculation of long-term consequences—rather than on transitory emotions—and they were impeded by an absence of reported data concerning the leaders' "inner" emotional states.

Recent constructivist scholarship has challenged this neglect of emotions, both with respect to understanding human decision-making and

R. Wolf (✉)
Goethe University Frankfurt, Frankfurt, Germany

© The Author(s) 2018
M. Clément, E. Sangar (eds.), *Researching Emotions in International Relations*, Palgrave Studies in International Relations,
https://doi.org/10.1007/978-3-319-65575-8_10

regarding the ontological nature of emotions. It has set the "logic of appropriateness" against the "logic of consequence", while emphasizing the emotional underpinnings of norms and identities (Ross, 2006). It has also challenged the assumption that emotions are to be understood as private "inner states" that cannot be reliably accessed by social scientists. Some constructivist scholars (both within and beyond the field of international relations) argue that emotions are not the property of individual bodies but are irreducibly social "all the way down" (Barbalet, 1998; Bially Mattern, 2011). This bold ontological move opens an opportunity for entirely new research on emotions. An emphasis on the intersubjective quality of emotions frees researchers from their dependence on individuals' limited—and often unreliable—self-reporting of affective states.

This chapter follows a somewhat more conventional path. It does not subscribe to the notion that human emotions are entirely social and thus can always be fully apprehended by the study of human interactions. However, nor does it support the view that political emotions should primarily be seen as individuals' momentary inner states that fail to leave clear-cut traces in the public domain. Rather, it argues that many political emotions, due to their collective nature, can be intrinsically public and therefore can be readily identified using the established tools of discourse analysis (Crawford, 2014; Hutchison & Bleiker, 2014; Mercer, 2014).

I will demonstrate the methodological potential of discourse analysis in this particular field by drawing on the concept of political ressentiments. In contrast to "fleeting" anger, ressentiment is a long-term emotional orientation (Bar-Tal, Halperin, & de Rivera, 2007) that is developed and memorized in discourses that address the alleged moral deficiencies of that which is resented. To become political, ressentiment must be shared and sustained through language. Political ressentiment, by its very nature, is manifested and consolidated in texts: these, unlike "inner" emotional states, can be directly studied by scholars.

This chapter will first clarify its assumptions regarding human emotions before it describes, in greater detail, the complex nature of ressentiments. Upon that basis, it will then derive textual indicators for the presence of ressentiments among political actors. Hence, to use Todd Hall's classification, it attempts to demonstrate how discourse can indicate emotions actually experienced by a group of speakers, rather than just evoked within the addressed audience, or merely invoked by "…insert[ing] claims about emotional states into discourse…" (Hall, 2016). This is followed by a brief illustration analyzing the Greek government's discourse on German behavior during the climax of the sovereign debt crisis. The conclusion highlights the promise of investigating ressentiment discourses in international relations while also drawing attention to the limitations of my approach.

Assumptions Concerning the Ontological Nature of Emotions

The Cambridge Dictionary of Psychology defines an emotion as "...a transient, neurophysiological response to a stimulus that excites a coordinated system of bodily and mental responses that inform us about our relationship to the stimulus and prepare us to deal with it in some way" (Matsumoto, 2009, p. 179). Emotions can, therefore, be understood as somatic experiences, although they also involve cognitions that inform their subjects about their current situation. Moreover, by preparing the subject to respond to stimuli, emotions—unlike many other cognitions—entail an action tendency. Importantly, this perspective is compatible with the traditional notion that some emotions can be asocial private feelings (e.g., terror in the face of an approaching avalanche), while also accommodating the constructivist view that most human emotions intrinsically relate to a distinct social identity embedded in a distinctive cultural context (Mercer, 2014; Smith & Mackie, 2008).

Nevertheless, this general definition hardly answers the crucial question of what emotions *actually are*. If we conceive emotions as discrete entities, then we can attribute to them distinct causal effects (e.g., speech acts or other kinds of behavioral output). Accordingly, in order to study the causal consequences of emotions, researchers should prevent circular reasoning (identifying the presence of an emotion through its effects and explaining the observed effect with reference to the emotion) by establishing indicators for either the presence or the effects of specific emotions. If, however, researchers understand emotions as downright processes, it does not make sense to distinguish bodily and mental experiences from their effects—at the least, from those effects that are confined to action tendencies. In this case, they must be satisfied with identifying *reaction patterns*, which help them to comprehend why a given actor responds to a situation in a certain way.

This chapter subscribes to the view that emotions have an intrinsic process quality (Frijda, 2008, p. 74; Hall & Ross, 2015, p. 849; Mauss & Robinson, 2009, p. 229). The latter not only exists at the social level, where it is obvious that collective emotions are based on processes of contagion or communication. It also exists at the level of the individual subject, since emotions always involve the complex interplay of numerous brain and body processes.

This process perspective also appears more sensible due to the increasing realization that emotions are omnipresent in human affairs. There is a growing consensus that emotions are involved in all kinds of decisions, including those based on conscious calculations of costs and benefits (McDermott, 2004; Winter, 2014). Therefore, it makes little sense to investigate whether emotions were active in a certain decision or not. Rather, scholars need to explore which particular emotion(s) were involved in that decision; that is, they should try to identify different emotional processes, including cognition, somatic experience, action tendencies and, sometimes, actual decisions. As argued below, ressentiments are an ideal subject for such a research approach, as they are readily apparent in frequently observable patterns in texts and conversations. Political ressentiments are manifested in interrelated claims and demands that generate a web of meaning that is best apprehended through classic discourse analysis. Before describing these various indicators, it is therefore necessary to discuss ressentiment in greater detail.

THE NATURE OF RESSENTIMENT

A ressentiment may be described as a negative "emotional attitude" (Frijda, 2008, p. 73) about another's undeserved status. Due to this affective quality, ressentiments tend to be more stable and intense than other prejudices that may result merely from ignorance or simplifying cognitive heuristics.[2] This kind of negative stereotype is broadly based on the "emotional belief" (Mercer, 2010) that there is a mismatch between the object's (i.e., alter's) high *social* and low *moral* status (Oldmeadow & Fiske, 2012; Petersen, 2002, pp. 40–41). The resenting person or group (ego) *feels* that another enjoys more power and/or prestige than s/he actually deserves according to established norms and values (Barbalet, 1998; Feather, 2008; Feather & Nairn, 2005; Wilson & Davis, 2011, pp. 120–121). Thus Nietzsche, in his famous treatment of ressentiment in the *Genealogy of Morals*, describes the priests' attitude toward the nobility ("the knights") as a kind of self-righteous envy of the latter's dominant position (Nietzsche, 2008; Reginster, 1997; Scheler, 1994). Modern psychological studies have confirmed this conceptual link between resentment and perceived injustice: test subjects typically report feelings of resentment toward people they deem unworthy of success because they have achieved much with little effort. Moreover, resentment toward such people increased when the test subjects themselves had achieved limited success despite making great efforts (Feather & Nairn, 2005, p. 100).

Ressentiment promotes a variety of unfavorable perceptions and emotional reactions to its object. Like other unfavorable biases, ressentiment undermines trust, reduces confidence in the other party's competence, tends to increase fear, and makes dissociation from alter more attractive (Hilton & von Hippel, 1996). Additionally, ressentiment also "colors" perceptions in more specific ways: those resented are described as lacking in "warmth", thus seeming less trustworthy, less friendly, less moral and less sincere than others (Oldmeadow & Fiske, 2012). Moreover, ressentiment primes the resenter to experience (or re-experience) anger *vis-à-vis* the resented. As the latter is strongly associated with unfair behavior or hurtful experiences, resenting persons are inclined to ascribe illegitimate motives to alter. Hence, when interacting with alter, they will be more inclined to feel unfairly treated and thus more readily angered (Miller, 2001).

A key element of ressentiment is ego's awareness of its current impotence. For the moment, at least, ego lacks the means to resolve its anger by righting the perceived wrong. Even when feeling intensely wronged, s/he feels unable to administer instantaneous retribution. Ressentiment is thus grounded in the perception that another's social position is too high relative to their moral qualities *and* too secure to be immediately corrected (Scheler, 1994, Chap. 1). Often—and especially in international relations—this prominent social status is doubly frustrating for ego, contravening its standards of justice and obstructing the coveted corrective action.

This perceived impotence can result in these antagonistic attitudes persisting for a very long time (Meltzer & Musolf, 2002). As the desired redress must be postponed, ego remains conscious that there still is an "account" that needs to be settled. The resentful party will wait for an opportunity to eventually correct the perceived wrong (e.g., by "cutting down" alter in order to put it back into its deserved place; see Feather & Nairn, 2005; Feather & Sherman, 2002, p. 958). Consequently, ressentiment develops the typical quality of a simmering, smoldering feeling that distinguishes this emotion from "hot feelings" such as anger, rage and vengeance (Frijda, 2008, p. 73; Solomon, 1990, p. 265).[3]

Ressentiment can often grow considerably over time. Frequently, the frustration experienced about one's inability to rectify the original injustice becomes identified more closely with the object, with the result that negative feelings are increasingly associated with alter's character. Consequently, the bias against alter may become even more negative. Often the frustrated actors (e.g., Nietzsche's priests) will also attempt to win allies by persuading third parties of the moral shortcomings of alter. Or they will try to ensure that parts of their in-group do not forget about the account that still needs to be settled. This, too, should cause the resenting party to look for additional evidence and arguments to tarnish alter's reputation.

By its very nature, then, ressentiment is a highly social emotion that will readily manifest itself in discourses, especially at the intergroup level. Resenting parties tend to feel a particular need to express, propagate and justify their negative views about alter. Effectively tarnishing alter's moral status may lower alter's social status, which is the principal aim of ego. Such discourse might also win allies who might later support forceful attempts to cut down the object of resentment. In addition, the articulation of negative stereotypes also serves the subjective need to experience one's grudge as appropriate and justified (rather than viewing these feelings as a manifestation of one's envious or spiteful character). A consequence of these factors is that political resentments, especially at the group level, need to be articulated again and again, and be continuously (re)produced in public discourse. They entail a dynamic conversation about shared grievances and hopes for eventual retribution. This resentment narrative significantly shapes a group's identity and, by implication, its emotional attitudes toward its social environment (Mackie, Smith, & Ray, 2008; Smith & Mackie, 2008).

INDICATORS OF POLITICAL RESSENTIMENTS IN DISCOURSE

As previously noted, this chapter is based on the assumption that emotions, particularly social ones, have a distinct process quality. They are less "states" or "things" and more patterned responses to a specific stimulus. This ontology enables researchers to look for typical combinations of indicators that reveal a potential process. According to the definition cited above, the indicators of emotional processes might be observed in relation to three interrelated basic characteristics of emotions: cognition, bodily arousal and action tendencies. Before attempting to establish the presence of a concrete emotion in a particular case, scholars must explicate those distinct cognitions, bodily arousals, and action tendencies that characterize the emotional process (and preferably also the patterns that characterize alternative emotions). Moreover, in order to express the minimum conditions that demonstrate the involvement of an emotion, they should also try to distinguish between necessary constituents of the supposed emotional process and further components whose observation might provide supporting evidence. Given the somewhat amorphous nature of emotions, such a differentiation cannot result in identification of a precise "threshold". Nevertheless, scholars should at least aim for an approximate measure, lest they treat almost any discursive evidence as sufficient proof of a particular emotional process. This section will sketch the necessary and supportive indicators for the study of political ressentiments.

Given the fact that ressentiments are emotional *attitudes*, it is hardly surprising that their most accessible discursive indicators relate to the cognitive aspects of emotional processes. Resentful persons or groups see themselves confronted with an "unfair" but stable status hierarchy and therefore perceive a special need for allies or other kinds of supporters. In order to mobilize their support, they must try to convince these parties— be they bystanders or reluctant in-group members—of the legitimacy of their cause. They need to explain their grievances and must justify the means by which they seek to redress the "unfair" status. This is especially so for collective parties, such as nations. To establish the cognitive aspects of ressentiments, scholars can analyze ego's expressed views on status and the moral qualities it ascribes to alter. Researches need to be attentive to the following kinds of articulation (especially for the first four):

- Complaints about 'unfair' status shifts or about unjust obstructions of ego's social mobility
- An emphasis upon alter's unworthiness of its elevated status
- Negative stereotypes concerning alter's character, particularly essentializing stereotypes that try to explain alter's criticized behavior with reference to overall character rather than to momentary political circumstances
- Evidence of ego's awareness of its momentary impotence to correct an 'unfair' hierarchy of status
- Justifications of retributive measures taken against "unfair" status changes

- The ridicule of proponents of cooperation with alter as "naive" sympathizers who do not understand the latter's vile character
- Demands for special guarantees to minimize the risk of alter cheating in any proposed collaborative project

It is much more difficult to identify statements that could evidence bodily reactions involved in the feeling of a ressentiment. This is largely because ressentiments are not characterized as "hot" emotions, such as rage or hatred. While resentful parties may have experienced intense anger when the "unfair" status hierarchy was first established (e.g., by humiliating acts), somatic sensations eventually dissipate to the extent that momentary anger transmutes into an enduring ressentiment. However, this is not to say that, even at later stages of the process, bodily feelings have no part in the public posture of resenting actors. Such physical manifestations do leave traces in discourse, which can be detected through nuanced analysis. Notwithstanding its "cooler" nature, ressentiment should not be confused with sober, detached judgment on status asymmetries. Rather, it remains a grievance that agitates the resentful and affects their subjective well-being. While ressentiment may not involve full-scale anger, it does entail the latent sensation of moral indignation. Moreover, ressentiment primes actors to perceive (further) slights or other negative assessments of alter's behavior, and facilitates the activation of (renewed) anger in the face of events that others would consider of minor importance. Finally, a redress of the "unfair" status asymmetry should lead to positive sensations on the part of the aggrieved actor, which might well be publicly articulated. Consequently, evidence for bodily reactions might consist of the following:

- The use of emotionally loaded terms for describing the status asymmetry (e.g., "outrageous", "evil", "vile", "heinous")
- Drastic metaphors that convey the offensive character of the status asymmetry (e.g., "enslavement", "subjugation")
- Expressions of moral indignation or disgust toward alter's character (e.g., "oppressor", "opportunist", "monster", "criminal", "Satan")
- Satisfaction expressed about minor setbacks experienced by alter (*Schadenfreude*)
- Satisfaction expressed after retribution or successful diminution of alter[4]

The chief indicators of action tendencies relate to ego's aspiration to rectify the "unfair" hierarchy and to avoid anything that might (further) stabilize it. In particular, researchers could seek discursive links between negative representations of alter and demands for uncooperative policies. More importantly, those resentful will try to shape the wider public discourse (in the present case, the international discourse) in various ways that might hurt alter's status. In more private settings (e.g., confidential letters or cabinet meetings) they may also enjoy articulating imagined scenarios in which they are finally teaching alter the lessons it deserved all along (Petersen, 2002, pp. 49–50; Scott, 1990, pp. 8–9). Discursive evidence for action tendencies therefore include:

- Statements aimed at tarnishing the social or moral status of alter (in particular, accusations that seem farfetched)
- Principled calls for rectifying "unfair" status hierarchies regardless of the material costs
- Proposals for retributive actions against symbols of alter's elevated status
- Demands for an uncompromising stance in negotiations that are based on the premise that alter does not "deserve" any accommodation
- Expression of uncompromising stances toward alter that are justified by past negative experiences that are re-represented in a more biased (i.e., more negative) manner
- Articulation of revenge fantasies

Action tendencies of ressentiments may also be apparent through conspicuous gaps in the discourse; that is, by silent opposition against collaborative or conciliatory policies, indicated by a striking failure to discuss such measures. Specifically, resentful actors may fail to provide convincing reasons when they forgo opportunities to improve their material conditions. Among other things, they may tend to miss opportunities for cooperative projects involving alter because they do not trust it or because they want to avoid implicit recognition of alter's status.

Empirical Illustration: The Greek Government's Discourse on Germany's Role in the Sovereign Debt Crisis

To briefly illustrate my argument on the use of discourse analysis to uncover ressentiments, I draw on my research on status emotions in the Greek sovereign debt crisis (Wolf, 2016). In this ongoing project, I have largely confined myself to interpreting a complete sample of pertinent statements and official interviews that have been made by leading members of Greece's first SYRIZA administration and have been translated into English. Most of these documents were obtained by a manual search on the official websites of the prime minister and key cabinet members. In addition, I browsed left-wing blogs and internet pages for translated statements by SYRIZA leaders while they were still in opposition. Included in the corpus are the following kinds of texts:

- Election speeches and manifestos
- General addresses on the state of Greece and its economy
- Statements on Greece's position in Europe
- Statements on relations with Germany

Obviously, the constraint of English-language texts renders this undertaking somewhat challenging, for it seems likely that the Greek government is wary about making its most combative statements accessible to an international audience. I could partly compensate for this drawback by using additional statements cited in foreign language media and in research conducted by Greek colleagues. However, this cannot fully compensate for my inability to read the original Greek texts. Nevertheless, the translated texts alone comprise a corpus of roughly 300 pages and provide much useful material containing many explicit statements on Germany's role in the Greek crisis.

Occasionally, however, I shall also utilize representations that do not explicitly refer to Germany or its government, but rather to creditor countries in general, to foreign supporters of the bail-out memoranda, or to the so-called Troika (the IMF, the European Commission and the European Central Bank), which oversaw the implementation of the memoranda. This does not seem problematic because Greek politicians and citizens have come to view Germany as the paramount power that called the tunes within the group of creditors (Michailidou, 2016; Ntampoudi, 2014; Zafiropoulou, Theodosiou, Marini, & Papakonstantinou, 2015, pp. 48–52). In fact, negative attitudes toward Germany were largely a consequence of the view that Berlin had supposedly sidelined established decision-making procedures and imposed an authoritarian hegemony over the EU (Kotzias, 2016; Varoufakis, 2015a).[5] The finance minister of the first SYRIZA administration, Yanis Varoufakis, explained to an English newspaper immediately after his resignation that the Euro group was "completely and utterly" controlled by Germany (Varoufakis, 2015b). Greece thus faced a "Berlin-Frankfurt-Brussels directorate" (Varoufakis, 2014) that effectively demoted other European governments to obedient supporters of the German government. Germany was thus singled out as ultimately responsible for the austerity and indignity suffered by the Greek people. In the words used by SYRIZA leader and future Prime Minister Tsipras at a 2014 election rally, his compatriots had to choose between a "...Merkel Greece, or a Greece of dignity... A German Europe or a Europe of all people" (Tsipras, 2014b). When analyzing the government discourse for ressentiment-related cognition, arousals and action tendencies, I will also include some statements that merely imply Germany's responsibility.

The translated statements provide a clear picture of *cognitions* indicative of ressentiments. All types of constitutive ressentiment notions can be found throughout the texts, especially the fundamental assertion that Greece has been indefensibly relegated to a minor rank by a morally disqualified Germany. As the speakers repeatedly indicate, German policies in the debt crises have led to a situation where Greece is no longer an equal and respected member of the family of European nations. Rather, it has been subordinated to the role of a "silent butler" (Tsipras, 2014b). It has effectively been robbed of its national self-determination to which, as an EU member, it is entitled (Tsipras, 2015b, 2015g, 2015k). This humiliating (Tsipras, 2015c, 2015f; Varoufakis, 2014) demotion in status not only contradicts basic principles of European politics, but is also incompatible with Greece's specific place in European history as the most important national culture in Europe (Kotzias, 2015e) and the "birthplace of democracy" (Tsipras, 2015b, 2015c).

This dramatic status decline is largely described as a consequence of Germany's unforgiving application of superior economic power, which makes the situation so difficult to rectify through Greece's actions alone. The hierarchy has been "imposed" (Kotzias & Steinmeier, 2015; Tsipras, 2015k; Varoufakis, 2014) upon Greece by a "Berlin autocracy" that has thrown Greece into "debt bondage" (Varoufakis, 2014). Germany and its willing allies have subjected Greece to "blackmail" (Tsipras, 2015b, 2015c, 2015e, 2015f), "fiscal asphyxiation" (Tsipras, 2015b, 2015c, 2015f), and even to "fiscal waterboarding" (Varoufakis, 2012). In light of this stark asymmetry in raw power, redress of this situation is obviously very risky and costly for Greece.

Germany, on the other hand, now occupies an elevated position within Europe that does not reflect its international moral standing. In fact, its unethical conduct in the crisis implies that Germany has disqualified itself from a superior rank: it has violated crucial European norms (Tsipras, 2015k), has demonstrated racist attitudes toward Greek citizens (Kotzias, 2016, p. 47; Tsipras, 2015a; Varoufakis, 2015a), has used the debt crisis to make billions of euros at the expense of Greece and other indebted countries (Kotzias, 2015b, 2015d, 2016, p. 51), has deliberately transformed Greece into a debtor colony (Kotzias, 2016, p. 53; Tsipras, 2015f, 2015g) and, in the person of Chancellor Angela Merkel, is held responsible for "lies and evasions, killing both the peoples and the future of Europe" (Tsipras, 2014a).

On a number of occasions, prominent speakers have implied that this immoral conduct is more than just a temporary consequence of Germany's economic power. It is also linked to the country's past as an imperial power and international perpetrator. Thus, Varoufakis accused the "Berlin-Frankfurt-Brussels directorate" of engaging in a "full-swing" "Goebbels-like propaganda campaign" (Varoufakis, 2014). Similarly, foreign minister Kotzias perceives no difference between the thinking that was behind Imperial Germany's colonial projects in Africa and the notions that underlie Berlin's contemporary policies toward indebted European countries (Kotzias, 2016, p. 47). Likewise, Germany's alleged tendency to depict itself as a victim could already be observed during World War II (Kotzias, 2016, p. 51). Most strikingly, Kotzias sees Berlin's crisis policy in 2009–2010 as based on the belief that Germany could impose "…final solutions [*Endlösungen* in the German version] at the expense of Greece according to its own tradition" (Kotzias, 2016, p. 53). Unsurprisingly, Kotzias views Germany as a country that has a poor character and lacks both the maturity and the culture that it would need to act as a successful hegemon in Europe (Kotzias, 2016, p. 52).[6]

Some of the articulations quoted above already indicate the *emotional arousal* underlying them. Characterizing the creditors' actions as "killing", "blackmail", "fiscal waterboarding" or "financial asphyxiation" clearly represents them as abusive policies bound to arouse angry feelings. Similar is labeling such policies "brutal" (Tsipras, 2015d) or "barbarous" (Tsipras, 2015c, 2015k). Apart from such emotional terms, the speakers also use strong metaphors that evoke the offensive nature of the status hierarchy and its immediate causes. For instance, in addition to using the extreme metaphor of "final solutions", it has also been claimed that Greece serves as a "guinea pig" (Tsipras, 2015c) and as an "experimental austerity laboratory" (Tsipras, 2015h), that it is a nation in chains (Tsipras, 2015c) and is treated as a "pariah" (Kotzias, 2015a). Sometimes the creditors' behavior is also expressly categorized as an "insult" (Tsipras, 2015i), as "offensive" (Tsipras, 2015g), or as an intentional act of "humiliation" (Tsipras, 2015c; Varoufakis, 2014).

Circumstantial evidence of emotional arousal can likewise be inferred by examining ego representations that invoke the very high stakes of the confrontation. Rendering the choice before the nation as an alternative between a "Merkel Greece, or a Greece of dignity" (Tsipras, 2014b) is a case in point. Calling the country's dignity one of its "sacred and unnegotiable values" (Tsipras, 2015i, 2015k) is a further indicator of strong feelings, as are expressions connoting fierce patriotic struggles, such as "battle" and "war" (Tsipras, 2014b, 2015c, 2015e, 2015f, 2015g). ANEL leader Kammenos, soon to become defense minister in the first SYRIZA administration, perhaps most vividly expressed this sentiment in a campaign speech in January 2015: "We will never go as beggars on our knees to Merkel, we will go standing tall as Greeks do. The Greek people are fighting united to restore national sovereignty and dignity" (Squires, 2015).

Finally, in regard to *action tendencies*, the texts also show palpable signs of a desire for retribution and defiance, as well as reproachful articulations directed at domestic actors who argue for a more accommodating stance. The latter are not merely described as naïve fellow travelers who ignore "traps" laid out by creditors, but are labeled as "Quislings" who betray the nation (Varoufakis, 2014). As Kammenos declared in the above quote, genuine Greeks prefer to resist. They opt for "standing up to Merkel" (Tsipras, 2014b). One way to fight the unacceptable status asymmetry consists in tarnishing Germany's image and winning European allies. Linking contemporary Germany to its Nazi past serves this purpose. The same holds for public attempts to re-open the issue of German war reparations and an outstanding repayment of war loans that Germany had forced upon Greece during World War II. Stressing Greek demands for German reparations and repayments not only highlights the numerous atrocities of German occupation forces but also places Greece's current indebtedness into perspective—both by contrasting it to the greater sum allegedly owed by Germany (279 billion Euros; see Kolasa-Sikiaridi, 2016) and by stressing the far more benign origins of the Greek debt, which is aimed at putting the German government into an awkward position (Kotzias, 2015c; Tsipras, 2015j; Zafiropoulou et al., 2015, p. 82). Fantasies of revenge were also articulated by members of the SYRIZA administration. For instance, in March 2015, defense minister Kammenos threatened to use migrants and potential terrorists as a means of retaliation: "If they deal a blow to Greece, then they should know the migrants will get papers to go to Berlin. If Europe leaves us in the crisis, we will flood it with migrants, and it will be even worse for Berlin if, in that wave of millions of economic migrants, there will be some jihadists of the Islamic State too." Days before, foreign minister Kotzias had already told his EU colleagues that a Grexit would mean "…tens of millions of immigrants and thousands of jihadists" (Waterfield, 2015). However, when the refugee crisis escalated in the summer of 2015 and almost a million migrants entered Germany, there was no indication of the *Schadenfreude* that would be expected from an actor feeling ressentiment. However, this absence of evidence might be due to the fact that my material does not include untranslated statements exclusively directed at Greek audiences. More likely, *Schadenfreude* was not widely felt because the influx of refugees across the Turkish border also burdened an already weakened Greece, perhaps far more heavily than wealthy Germany.[7]

Conclusion

The illustration of recent Greek governmental attitudes toward Germany has demonstrated that the derived ressentiment indicators can be effectively applied to discern if texts demonstrate an integral pattern of cognitions, arousals, and action tendencies that are to be expected from resentful parties. Even this brief survey contains quite a number of striking representations of each of these three categories. Discourse analysis thus seems well suited to uncover the nuances and dynamics of shared emotional attitudes. That said, this empirical illustration could only demonstrate that ressentiments have been expressed by leading government officials. It could neither determine the intensity nor establish the relative weight of this emotion. Yet, gauging the degree of ressentiment seems quite feasible, provided that researchers can discern differences in the relative prevalence and intensity of relevant statements—perhaps by employing coding procedures often used in content analysis. For example, scholars could establish with some precision the waxing and waning of ressentiments by observing changes in the relative frequency and harshness of revenge fantasies or of complaints about unjust status hierarchies. To assess the relative importance of ressentiments, scholars would also have to seek evidence of other emotions that might affect or even counteract the influence of ressentiments. Thus, at the height of the Greek debt crisis, Kotzias and Varoufakis also occasionally voiced sympathy for Germany or Chancellor Merkel. Hence, to avoid confirmation bias, a more thorough analysis would also have to discuss statements that indicate the involvement of countervailing emotions— these might even rule out the experience of ressentiment. Thus, in the present case, there is important evidence suggesting that, at the height of the debt crisis, acute anger may have been even more prominent and influential than enduring ressentiments since, despite all odds, the SYRIZA government eventually opted for outright defiance. By calling for a national referendum on the creditors' demands and by campaigning for a negative vote (Οχι), the administration openly challenged Germany and other creditors. In doing so, it incurred great costs and even risked national disaster. This is an action tendency that better fits the anger pattern (Lerner & Keltner, 2001; van Kleef, de Dreu, & Manstead, 2004; van Kleef, van Dijk, Steinel, Harinck, & van Beest, 2008). For a few tense moments, ressentiment had arguably morphed into real wrath (Wolf, 2016). Thus, a nuanced understanding of the role of ressentiments can only be gained by giving due attention to other elements that might also affect a group's outlook and action tendencies.

That said, ressentiment is particularly worth studying as one of the clearest manifestations of emotion in public discourse. As this chapter has attempted to demonstrate, ressentiments should manifest themselves in numerous ways that are accessible to interpretive scholarship, but also to survey research, which would investigate the extent to which elite discourse resonates with the wider public.[8] While other emotions could similarly be studied with this pattern-matching approach, researchers should be mindful that different types of emotions may leave weaker traces in accessible discourses. For instance, "hot" emotions such as anger or joy tend to be of shorter duration and, perhaps, also more private and less articulated than ressentiment, national pride, collective gratitude, or fear. Hence, it might be more difficult to specify a sufficient number of observable indicators. However, such drawbacks could be compensated by supplementing discourse analysis with other approaches such as process tracing or opinion research.

Investigating ressentiments in greater detail holds particular promise for advancing our understanding of mutual escalations of nationalist discourses that may either encourage decision-makers or constrain their room for compromise. In particular, it might improve our analytical grasp of negative prejudices that impede international cooperation. These prejudices are often largely reduced to their cognitive dimensions. They are understood as consequences of misperceptions, "cognitive miser" heuristics, the fundamental attribution error, mental shortcuts, herd behavior, or of the personal need for cognitive consistency. This approach dominates many studies on anti-Americanism (e.g., Katzenstein & Keohane, 2006). Yet this focus on the cognitive dimension underrates the various ways in which the emotional side of resentment can affect the persistence and transformation of negative prejudices. For instance, the experience of ressentiment predisposes an actor through "emotional tags" to negative interpretations of actions and to angry reactions against the resented opponent, thus reinforcing negative stereotypes. Research into such discourses could, moreover, shed some light on the transformation of "hot" collective emotions, such as anger, into long-term emotional orientations like ressentiment or even hatred. On the other hand, prejudices caused by ressentiment might quickly disintegrate (or at least weaken) once the resented party suffers a sudden loss of status. Establishing the emotional basis of biases manifest in discourses therefore seems indispensable to enhance our knowledge of both the dynamics of prejudices and their motivational force.

Studying the dynamics and impacts of ressentiment should be especially useful in international systems that are undergoing profound shifts in the international distribution of social status. It also provides new insights into long-standing international status conflicts—such as the enduring rivalries between India and Pakistan or between the United States and Iran—that defy purely materialistic explanations. Other obvious subjects are Germany's anti-British resentment before and after World War I, and the widespread Asian resentment against Western imperialism (Aydin, 2007; Mishra, 2012). More recent cases include the anti-Americanism so prevalent in contemporary Chinese (Gries, 2004) and Russian nationalism, and Indian foreign policy, especially in the twentieth century. In these and many other instances, a better understanding of emotional factors can enhance an understanding of how antagonistic collective identities have endured. It provides a strong argument for the claim that collective identities are also emotional phenomena (Ross, 2006).

It is hoped that analyzing discourses of ressentiment would ultimately also be useful to decision-makers and diplomats who wish to promote international cooperation rather than conflict. At the very least, a closer examination of these texts and their productive power regarding national perspectives should make leaders more cautious before trying to enhance their countries' status—particularly, if they do so at the expense of another nation. It may also make them aware that negative short-term emotions may have enduring affective consequences that limit both the ability to learn, and to adjust policies when new opportunities for cooperation arise. A better understanding of the emotional underpinnings of negative prejudices could thus provide a far more realistic perspective on policy options that might enhance or diminish the prospects for solving regional or global problems.

Notes

1. This chapter partially draws upon Wolf (2015) and Wolf (forthcoming).
2. On such stabilizing effects of emotions, see (2012, pp. 82, 103); (2013, Chaps. 2, 3 and 4).
3. This temporal endurance is indeed a crucial element. Meltzer/Musolf reserve the French term "ressentiment" to this persistent feeling. I also use the English term, as it is widely understood as referring to a long-term emotion.
4. Here the first three types of indicators are of special importance, while the absence of the latter two does not rule the presence of ressentiments. After all, alter may not yet have experienced status diminution.
5. The 2016 book chapter referenced here is a condensed version of a book Kotzias (2013) had published in Greece. Unfortunately, there is no English version.
6. For additional elite references to parallels between contemporary German conduct and the Nazi era see also Michailidou (2016) and Zafiropoulou et al. (2015: 89–90).
7. For a government statement stressing both Greece's role as a "guardian of European culture" and its solidarity with "the [other] countries that are supporting the refugees, including Germany, Austria, Sweden and others", see Xydakis 2016.
8. In fact, polling data showed that anti-Germany stereotypes were very prominent in the Greek public (Katzikas 2015). On stereotypes in the Greek media discourse, see Tzogopoulas (2015).

References

Aydin, C. (2007). *The Politics of Anti-Westernism in Asia: Visions of World Order in Pan-Islamic and Pan-Asian Thought*. New York: Columbia University Press.

Barbalet, J. M. (1998). *Emotion, Social Theory, and Social Structure: A Macrosociological Approach*. Cambridge: Cambridge University Press.

Bar-Tal, D., Halperin, E., & de Rivera, J. (2007). Collective Emotions in Conflict Situations: Societal Implications. *Journal of Social Issues, 63*(2), 441–460.

Bially Mattern, J. (2011). A Practice Theory of Emotion for International Relations. In E. Adler & V. Pouliot (Eds.), *International Practices (Cambridge Studies in International Relations)* (Vol. 119, pp. 63–86). Cambridge: Cambridge University Press.

Crawford, N. C. (2014). Institutionalizing Passion in World Politics: Fear and Empathy. *International Theory, 6*(3), 535–557.

Feather, N. T. (2008). Effects of Observer's Own Status on Reactions to a High Achiever's Failure: Deservingness, Resentment, *Schadenfreude*, and Sympathy. *Australian Journal of Psychology, 60*(1), 31–43.

Feather, N. T., & Nairn, K. (2005). Resentment, Envy, Schadenfreude, and Sympathy: Effects of Own and Other's Deserved or Undeserved Status. *Australian Journal of Psychology, 57*(2), 87–102.

Feather, N. T., & Sherman, R. (2002). Envy, Resentment, *Schadenfreude*, and Sympathy: Reactions to Deserved and Undeserved Achievement and Subsequent Failure. *Personality and Social Psychology Bulletin, 28*(7), 953–961.

Frijda, N. H. (2008). The Psychologists' Point of View. In J. M. Haviland-Jones, L. F. Barrett, & M. Lewis (Eds.), *Handbook of Emotions* (3rd ed., pp. 68–87). New York: Guilford Press.

Gries, P. H. (2004). *China's New Nationalism: Pride, Politics, and Diplomacy. A Philip E. Lilienthal Book*. Berkeley, CA: University of California Press.

Haidt, J. (2013). *The Righteous Mind: Why Good People are Divided by Politics and Religion*. New York: Vintage Books.

Hall, T. H. (2016). "An Extremely Obnoxious and Illegal Case" Three Approaches to Emotion and Affect in the Aftermath of the Zhuhai Incident. Paper Presented at the Constructivist Emotion Research (CER) Workshop, April 8–9, Berlin.

Hall, T. H., & Ross, A. A. (2015). Affective Politics After 9/11. *International Organization, 69*(4), 847–879.

Hilton, J. L., & von Hippel, W. (1996). Stereotypes. *Annual Review of Psychology, 47*(1), 237–271.

Hutchison, E., & Bleiker, R. (2014). Theorizing Emotions in World Politics. *International Theory, 6*(3), 491–514.

Kahneman, D. (2012). *Thinking, Fast and Slow*. London: Penguin Books.

Katzenstein, P. J., & Keohane, R. O. (Eds.). (2006). *Anti-Americanisms in World Politics*. Ithaca: Cornell University Press.

Katzikas, D. (2015). Fragmentation and Exclusion: Understanding and Overcoming the Multiple Impacts of the European Crisis. Fragmex Papers. Retrieved September 4, 2017, from http://www.fragmex.eu/myfiles/Policyaper-on-Greek-Attitudes-and-Public-Discourses-on-Germany.pdf

Kolasa-Sikiaridi, K. (2016, August 18). Germany Still Refusing to Pay Billions of Euros in War Reparations to Greece. *GreekReporter*. Retrieved November 14,

2016, from http://greece.greekreporter.com/2016/08/18/germany-still-refusing-to-pay-billions-of-euros-in-war-reparations-to-greece/

Kotzias, N. (2013). *Ellada apoikia chreous: Eurōpaikē autokratoria kai germanikē prōtokathedria. Politikē – Oikonomia*. Athens: Anubis.

Kotzias, N. (2015a). Foreign Minister Kotzias' Interview on AMNA Web TV: February 1, 2015. Retrieved August 22, 2016, from http://www.mfa.gr/en/current-affairs/statements-speeches/foreign-minister-kotzias-interview-on-amna-web-tv.html

Kotzias, N. (2015b). Foreign Minister Kotzias' Interview with the German Daily Frankfurter Allgemeine Zeitung (29 May 2015. Retrieved August 22, 2016, from http://www.mfa.gr/en/current-affairs/statements-speeches/foreign-minister-kotzias-interview-with-the-german-daily-frankfurter-allgemeine-zeitung-faz-29-may-2015.html

Kotzias, N. (2015c). Foreign Minister Kotzias' Interview with the German Daily Süddeutsche Zeitung's Christiane Schlötzer (23 March 2015), Entitled "Greece's Foreign Minister: 'We Have to Find Another Path'": 23 March 2015. Retrieved August 22, 2016, from http://www.mfa.gr/en/current-affairs/statements-speeches/foreign-minister-kotzias-interview-with-the-german-daily-suddeutsche-zeitungs-christiane-schlotzer-23-march-2015-entitled-greeces-foreign-minister-we-have-to-find-another-path.html

Kotzias, N. (2015d). Foreign Minister Kotzias' Interview with the German Television Networks ARD and ZDF (Riga, 7 March 2015). Retrieved August 22, 2016, from http://www.mfa.gr/en/current-affairs/statements-speeches/foreign-minister-kotzias-interview-with-the-german-television-networks-ard-and-zdf-riga-march-2015.html

Kotzias, N. (2015e). Foreign Minister Kotzias' Interview with Theodoros Andreadis Syggelakis in Huffington Post Italia (3 April 2015), Entitled "Europe Needs to Realize that Syriza Is Not a Passing Phase". Retrieved August 22, 2016, from http://www.mfa.gr/en/current-affairs/statements-speeches/foreign-minister-kotzias-interview-with-theodoros-andreadis-syggelakis-in-huffington-post-italia-april-2015-entitled-europe-needs-to-realize-that-syriza-is-not-passing-phase.html

Kotzias, N. (2016). Schuldenkolonie Griechenland: Die EU als Imperium und Deutschlands Primat: Ein neuer Rahmen für die Interpretation der Krise in Südeuropa. In A. Agridopoulos & I. Papagiannopoulos (Eds.). *Griechenland im europäischen Kontext: Krise und Krisendiskurse* (pp. 39–65). Wiesbaden: Springer VS.

Kotzias, N., & Steinmeier F.-W. (2015). Joint Statements of Foreign Minister Kotzias and German Foreign Minister Frank-Walter Steinmeier in Berlin: February 11, 2015. Retrieved August 22, 2016, from http://www.mfa.gr/en/current-affairs/top-story/joint-statements-of-foreign-minister-kotzias-and-german-foreign-minister-frank-walter-steinmeier-in-berlin.html

Lerner, J. S., & Keltner, D. (2001). Fear, Anger, and Risk. *Journal of Personality and Social Psychology, 81*(1), 146–159.

Mackie, D. M., Smith, E. R., & Ray, D. G. (2008). Intergroup Emotions and Intergroup Relations. *Social and Personality Psychology Compass, 2*(5), 1866–1880.

Matsumoto, D. R. (Ed.). (2009). *The Cambridge Dictionary of Psychology.* Cambridge: Cambridge University Press.

Mauss, I. B., & Robinson, M. D. (2009). Measures of Emotion: A Review. *Cognition & Emotion, 23*(2), 209–237.

McDermott, R. (2004). The Feeling of Rationality: The Meaning of Neuroscientific Advances for Political Science. *Perspectives on Politics, 2*(4), 691–706.

Meltzer, B. N., & Musolf, G. R. (2002). Resentment and Ressentiment. *Sociological Inquiry, 72*(2), 240–255.

Mercer, J. (2010). Emotional Beliefs. *International Organization, 64*(1), 1–31.

Mercer, J. (2014). Feeling Like a State: Social Emotion and Identity. *International Theory, 6*(3), 515–535.

Michailidou, A. (2016). 'The Germans are Back': Euroscepticism and Anti-Germanism in Crisis-Stricken Greece. *National Identities, 19*(1), 1–18.

Miller, D. T. (2001). Disrespect and the Experience of Injustice. *Annual Review of Psychology, 52*(1), 527–553.

Mishra, P. (2012). *From the Ruins of Empire: The Revolt Against the West and the Remaking of Asia.* London and New York: Allen Lane.

Nietzsche, F. W. (2008). *On the Genealogy of Morals: A Polemic: By Way of Clarification and Supplement to My Last Book, Beyond Good and Evil* [Translated from the German]. Oxford: Oxford University Press.

Ntampoudi, I. (2014). The Eurozone Crisis and the Politics of Blaming: The Cases of Germany and Greece. *Political Perspectives, 8*(2), 1–20.

Oldmeadow, J. A., & Fiske, S. T. (2012). Contentment to Resentment: Variation in Stereotype Content Across Status Systems. *Analyses of Social Issues and Public Policy, 12*(1), 324–329.

Petersen, R. D. (2002). *Understanding Ethnic Violence: Fear, Hatred, and Resentment in Twentieth-Century Eastern Europe.* Cambridge: Cambridge University Press.

Reginster, B. (1997). Nietzsche on Ressentiment and Valuation. *Philosophy and Phenomenological Research, 57*(2), 281–305.

Ross, A. A. G. (2006). Coming in from the Cold: Constructivism and Emotions. *European Journal of International Relations, 12*(2), 197–222.

Scheler, M. (1994). *Ressentiment.* Milwaukee, WI: Marquette University Press.

Scott, J. C. (1990). *Domination and the Arts of Resistance: Hidden Transcripts.* New Haven, CT: Yale University Press.

Smith, E. R., & Mackie, D. M. (2008). Intergroup Emotions. In J. M. Haviland-Jones, L. F. Barrett, & M. Lewis (Eds.), *Handbook of Emotions* (3rd ed., pp. 428–439). New York: Guilford Press.

Solomon, R. C. (1990). *A Passion for Justice: Emotions and the Origin of the Social Contract*. Reading, MA: Addison-Wesley Pub. Co.
Squires, N. (2015). Greek Election: Who Are Independent Greeks? *The Telegraph*. 26 January 2015. Retrieved August 23, 2016, from http://www.telegraph.co.uk/news/worldnews/europe/greece/11369309/Greek-election-who-are-Independent-Greeks.html
Tsipras, A. (2014a). Interview Alexis Tsipras: "The Dilemma We Face on Election Day Throughout Europe Is Clear: Either with the Left or with Austerity": May 11, 2014. EuropeanLeft. Retrieved August 22, 2016, from http://www.european-left.org/node/2548
Tsipras, A. (2014b). Speech Delivered by Alexi Tsipras (Leader of SYRIZA, Thessaloniki, May 21, 2014). Retrieved August 22, 2016, from https://australiagreecesolidarity.wordpress.com/2014/05/22/syriza-leader-alexis-tsipras-addresses-thessaloniki/
Tsipras, A. (2015a). Give Us Six More Months, and We Will Be Another Country. Interview with *Stern*. 18 February 2015. Retrieved August 22, 2016, from http://www.stern.de/politik/ausland/interview-with-greek-primeminister-alexis-tsipras-give-us-six-more-months-and-we-will-be-another-country--5944522.html
Tsipras, A. (2015b). Prime Minister Alexis Tsipras' Address at the NO Rally in Syntagma Square: July 4, 2015. Retrieved August 16, 2016, from http://primeminister.gr/english/2015/07/04/prime-minister-alexis-tsipras-address-at-the-no-rally-in-syntagma-square/
Tsipras, A. (2015c). Prime Minister Alexis Tsipras' Address Concerning the Referendum to Be Held on the 5th of July: June 27, 2015. Retrieved August 16, 2016, from http://primeminister.gr/english/2015/06/27/prime-minister-alexis-tsipras-address-concerning-the-referendum-to-be-held-on-the-5th-of-july/
Tsipras, A. (2015d). Prime Minister Alexis Tsipras' Interview in *Corriere della Sera* Newspaper: June 9, 2015. Retrieved August 16, 2016, from http://primeminister.gr/english/2015/06/09/prime-minister-alexis-tsipras-interview-in-corriere-della-sera-newspaper/
Tsipras, A. (2015e). Prime Minister Alexis Tsipras' Speech in the Greek Parliament Concerning the Mandate to Conclude the Negotiation: July 11, 2015. Retrieved August 16, 2016, from http://primeminister.gr/english/2015/07/11/prime-minister-alexis-tsipras-speech/
Tsipras, A. (2015f). Prime Minister Alexis Tsipras' Speech in the Parliamentary Group of SYRIZA: June 17, 2015. Retrieved August 16, 2016, from http://primeminister.gr/english/2015/06/17/prime-minister-alexis-tsipras-speech-in-the-parliamentary-group-of-syriza/
Tsipras, A. (2015g). Prime Minister Alexis Tsipras' Speech to Parliament Regarding the July 5th Referendum: June 28, 2015. Retrieved August 16, 2016, from

http://primeminister.gr/english/2015/06/28/prime-minister-alexis-tsipras-speech-to-parliament-regarding-the-july-5th-referendum/

Tsipras, A. (2015h). Prime Minister Alexis Tsipras' Speech to the European Parliament: July 8, 2015. Retrieved August 16, 2016, from http://primeminister.gr/english/2015/07/08/prime-minister-alexis-tsipras-speech-to-the-european-parliament/

Tsipras, A. (2015i). Prime Minister Alexis Tsipras' Statement on the Latest Developments: June 28, 2015. Retrieved August 22, 2016, from http://primeminister.gr/english/2015/06/28/prime-minister-alexis-tsipras-statement-concerning-on-the-latest-developments/

Tsipras, A. (2015j). Prime Minister's A. Tsipras Speech in the Parliament During the Discussion Concerning the Reconstitution, Restructuring, and Upgrade of the Committee for the Pursuit of German Debts Owed to Greece: March 10, 2015. Retrieved August 16, 2016, from http://primeminister.gr/english/2015/03/10/greek-pms-a-tsipras-speech-in-the-parliament-during-the-discussion-concerning-the-reconstitution-restructuring-and-upgrade-of-the-committee-for-the-pursuit-of-german-debts-owed-to-greece/

Tsipras, A. (2015k). Primeminister's A. Tsipras Speech, During the Programmatic Statements of the Government: February 8, 2015. Retrieved August 16, 2016, from http://primeminister.gr/english/2015/02/08/primeministers-a-tsipras-speech-during-the-programmatic-statements-of-the-government/

Tzogopoulos, G. (2015). *Assessing the Image of Germany in the Greek Media: Visual Analysis of Greek Media Reports on the Role of Germany in the Greek Crisis*. Athens: Hellenic Foundation for European and Foreign Policy. Crisis Observatory Research Paper 18.

van Kleef, G. A., de Dreu, C. K. W., & Manstead, A. S. R. (2004). The Interpersonal Effects of Anger and Happiness in Negotiations. *Journal of Personality and Social Psychology, 86*(1), 57–76.

van Kleef, G., van Dijk, E., Steinel, W., Harinck, F., & van Beest, I. (2008). Anger in Social Conflict: Cross-Situational Comparisons and Suggestions for the Future. *Group Decision and Negotiation, 17*(1), 13–30.

Varoufakis, Y. (2012). Fiscal Waterboarding Versus Eurobonds: Misrepresenting the Latter to Effect the Former. Retrieved August 22, 2016, from https://yanisvaroufakis.eu/2012/05/24/fiscal-waterboarding-versus-eurobonds-misrepresenting-the-latter-to-effect-the-former/

Varoufakis, Y. (2014). Italy, Greece and Europe After the European Parliament Elections: An Interview with Alessandro Bianchi: June 1, 2014. Retrieved August 22, 2016, from https://yanisvaroufakis.eu/2014/06/01/italy-greece-and-europe-after-the-european-parliament-elections-an-interview-with-alessandro-bianchi/

Varoufakis, Y. (2015a). We Crossed a Lot of Our Red Lines: Interview with *Der Tagesspiegel*, June 9, 2015. Retrieved August 22, 2016, from http://www.tagesspiegel.de/weltspiegel/in-english/yanis-varoufakis-interview-we-crossed-a-lot-of-our-red-lines/11890142.html

Varoufakis, Y. (2015b). Yanis Varoufakis Full Transcript: Our Battle to Save Greece: Interview with *The New Satesman*, July 13, 2015. Retrieved August 22, 2016, from http://www.newstatesman.com/world-affairs/2015/07/yanis-varoufakis-full-transcript-our-battle-save-greece

Waterfield, B. (2015). Greece's Defence Minister Threatens to Send Migrants Including Jihadists to Western Europe. *The Telegraph*. 9 March 2015. Retrieved November 10, 2016, from http://www.telegraph.co.uk/news/worldnews/islamic-state/11459675/Greeces-defence-minister-threatens-to-send-migrants-including-jihadists-to-Western-Europe.html

Wilson, D. C., & Davis, D. W. (2011). Reexamining Racial Resentment: Conceptualization and Content. *The Annals of the American Academy of Political and Social Science*, 634(1), 117–133.

Winter, E. (2014). *Feeling Smart: Why Our Emotions Are More Rational than We Think*. New York: Public Affairs.

Wolf, R. (2015). Emotionen in den internationalen Beziehungen: Das Beispiel Ressentiments. In K.-R. Korte (Ed.). *Emotionen und Politik: Begründungen, Konzeptionen und Praxisfelder einer politikwissenschaftlichen Emotionsforschung* (pp. 187–212). Baden-Baden: Nomos.

Wolf, R. (2016). On Monday, Our National Humiliation Will Be Over. We Will Finish with Orders from Abroad": Status, Emotions, and the SYRIZA Government's Rhetoric in the Greek Sovereign Debt Crisis. Paper prepared for the Constructivist Emotions Research (CER) workshop, Berlin, 2-3 September 2016.

Wolf, R. forthcoming. Identifying Emotional Reactions to Status Deprivations in Discourse. *International Studies Review*.

Xydakis, N. (2016). Alternate FM Xydakis' Statement on the Refugee Issue, in Response to Statements from European Politicians: January 24, 2016. Retrieved April 5, 2017, from http://www.mfa.gr/en/current-affairs/statements-speeches/alternate-fm-xydakis-statement-on-the-refugee-issue-in-response-to-statements-from-european-politicians.html

Zafiropoulou, M., Theodosiou, A., Marini, I., & Papakonstantinou A. (2015). Discourse Analysis Report of Official and Political Documents for Greece: Public Discourse Analysis of the Greek Crisis: The Case of Greek Politicians' Perceptions of the Germans and Readers' Online Comments About Chancellor Merkel's Visits to Athens. Fragmex papers. Retrieved November 11, 2016, from http://www.fragmex.eu/myfiles/d2-1-Discourse-analysis-report-of-official-and-political-documents-for-Greece-ver2.pdf

Reinhard Wolf is Professor of International Relations in the Department of Political Science at Goethe University, Frankfurt, Germany. His current research focuses on the role of status, respect and emotions in international relations. Recent publications include *Respecting Foreign Peoples: The Limits of Moral Obligations*, in: *Journal of International Relations and Development* 19:1 (January 2016), 1–25; *Eclipsed by Clashing Titans? Europe and the Risks of US-Chinese Confrontation*, special issue of *European Foreign Affairs Review* 21 (2016) (co-edited with Sebastian Biba and Markus Liegl); and *Status and Emotions in Russian Foreign Policy*, special double-issue of *Communist and Post-Communist Studies* 47:3–4 (September-December 2014) (co-edited with Regina Heller and Tuomas Forsberg).

CHAPTER 11

Emotions and Time: Approaching Emotions Through a Fusion of Horizons

Clara Eroukhmanoff and Bernardo Teles Fazendeiro

America at its best is also courageous.... The enemies of liberty and our country should make no mistake: America remains engaged in the world, by history and by choice, shaping a balance of power that favours freedom.... America at its best is compassionate.

George W. Bush, 20 January 2001, Inaugural Address

In a single instant, we realized this will be a decisive decade in the history of liberty, that we've been called to a unique role in human events. Rarely has the world faced a choice more clear or consequential.

George. W. Bush, 29 January 2002, State of the Union Address

Time is no longer primarily a gulf to be bridged because it separates; it is actually the supportive ground of the course of events in which the present is rooted. Hence temporal distance is not something that must be

---

C. Eroukhmanoff (✉)
London South Bank University, London, United Kingdom

B. Teles Fazendeiro
Centro de Estudos Sociais, University of Coimbra, Coimbra, Portugal

© The Author(s) 2018
M. Clément, E. Sangar (eds.), *Researching Emotions in International Relations*, Palgrave Studies in International Relations, https://doi.org/10.1007/978-3-319-65575-8_11

> *overcome… In fact the important thing is to recognise temporal distance as a positive and productive condition enabling understanding.*
>
> Hans Gadamer (1989 [1960], p. 297)

Emotions seldom remain the same as time passes, but neither do they change completely nor remain disconnected to each other across time. Understanding the way in which emotional experiences intertwine helps us make sense of how political events are connected and whether they constitute a major break with the past. While experts and commentators on American politics argued that President G.W. Bush's initial foreign policy sought to isolate the United States from the outside world, a position that apparently changed after 9/11, the quotations above suggest otherwise. G.W. Bush's January 2001 inauguration speech reveals a number of appraisals about a compassionate and courageous America that struggles against enemies of freedom. Those appraisals set the scene for G. W. Bush's State of the Union address delivered five months after 9/11 in which he stated that America had now acquired a 'unique role' in the international arena. Seen through this prism, 9/11 did not radically change G. W. Bush's emotional appraisal, for his messianic and expansionist agenda was already present in the January 2001 inauguration speech; in other words, there was just as much continuity as change. Exploring emotional appraisals through time brings this claim forward. Or, using Hans Gadamer's terminology, continuity and change are unveiled when past and present *horizons* fuse.

A fusion of horizons is a process in which multiple temporal perspectives, arising from either different or similar traditions, are placed in dialogue with one another in order to foster a shared understanding. Though Gadamer's approach may often be applied to the study of texts and worldviews, we argue that it can also be transferred to the study of emotional appraisals in International Relations (IR). By emotional appraisals we mean the expressions by which certain communities are united, such as love of freedom or anger towards another (Koschut, 2014). Hence, this chapter speaks to Koschut's (2014) and Hochschild's (1979) concepts of 'emotion norms' and 'emotional communities' whereby communities are governed by a social structure of 'appropriate feelings' so as to create 'feeling rules' (p. 552). Feeling rules or emotional appraisals mark the boundaries by which one can feel adequate to express guilt, joy or anger with regard to a certain situation (Hochschild, 1979, p. 552).

For all the promise that may come from fusing different horizons of experience, there has been a reluctance to connect or fuse emotional appraisals across time, perhaps because of the assumption that emotions are inherently ephemeral (Crawford, 2000, p. 118). This chapter argues otherwise. Instead of taking emotions to be isolated experiences, we explore the extent to which they are intertwined across time, whereby time is a productive condition that enables understanding (Gadamer, 1989 [1960], p. 297). Understanding is thus 'to be thought of less as a subjective act than as participating in an event of tradition, a process of transmission in which past and present are constantly mediated' (Gadamer, 1989 [1960], p. 291). We suggest that by taking experience to be an evolving tradition, it is possible to unravel the complex relationships existing between emotional appraisals across time and the extent to which those experiences have changed or continued. An appreciation of time can thus open the methodological compass of the study of emotions. In order to apply Gadamer's fusion of horizons to the study of emotional appraisals, we turn to Stanley Fish's (1970) affective stylistics, a method which is concerned with texts and which takes the reader as an 'actively mediating presence.' We thus approach emotions from an interpretative or hermeneutical approach, focusing especially on language. To do so, the first section examines key challenges to the study of emotions, which we take to be the debate between the 'representational' and 'non-representational' bases of experience. The second section clarifies the ontological and epistemological foundations of our approach, laying the groundwork from which to build our methodology. Afterwards, we explore Gadamer's fusion of horizons and Fish's affective stylistics. Finally, we illustrate our methodological framework by examining G.W. Bush's two key speeches in 2001 and 2002.

The Methodological Challenge of the Emotional Turn: Between Non-representation and Representation

Emotions are part of who we are and what we do every day; we have all experienced emotions in some form or another (Zalewski, 2013, p. 133). As Crawford (2013, p. 121) suggests, they are 'everywhere.' A significant number of scholars now recognise that emotions are part of the logics of war, peace and conflict and that they should be explored thoroughly. Although mainstream IR theories have turned a blind-eye to the role of emotions in world politics (Reus-Smit, 2014, p. 568), often as a result of rationalist prejudices (Åhäll & Gregory, 2015a), an 'emotional turn' is now well under way. It has generated a wealth of publications concerned with war and politics (Åhäll & Gregory, 2015b), humiliation and political violence (Fattah & Fierke, 2009; Saurette, 2006), non-recognition and radicalisation dynamics (Clément, 2014), trust, empathy and the transformation of conflict (Head, 2012, 2016), trauma and affective communities (Hutchison, 2016), 'mixed' emotions (Ross, 2014), cultural politics (Ahmed, 2014), securitisation theory (Van Rythoven, 2015) and the security dilemma (Booth & Wheeler, 2007). Now that the role of emotions has gained a certain momentum in IR, turning to the question of how to study them is the next logical step.

Different contributions to IR and politics have looked at emotions in manifold perspectives. But, in doing so, they may sometimes neglect the ontological complexity of experience, suggesting—sometimes inadvertently—that only one aspect of emotion matters. Janice Bially Mattern (2011, pp. 66–67) alludes well to this problem:

> The field has solved the 'problem' of the elusive ontology of emotion by focusing instead on epistemology; *on the site or force through* which the emotional experience becomes known to those in its throes, and to researchers. The result is a literature organized around three broad analytics: those that emphasize the cognitive or intellectual dimensions of emotion; those that emphasize its physiological or affective dimensions; and those that emphasize the forces of the socio-cultural environment in which the emotional body is situated.

Any study of emotions is confronted by differences between what emotions are and how they ought to be researched. In this regard, emotions are often taken to be a specific type of experience: 'emotions are first of all subjective experiences that also have physiological, intersubjective, and cultural components' (Crawford, 2000, p. 125). Emotions are thus beset by a complex ontology to the extent that scholars do not always agree on how to approach them. There are those who take a more somatic understanding of emotions, seeing them as instinctive or unconscious, and those who emphasise a more cognitive perspective, likening them to subjective and intentional experiences (Åhäll & Gregory, 2013, p. 118). This divide can also be labelled as the representational versus non-representational debate. Either emotions require cognition, that is to say, some sort of reflected representation; or they are somehow non-representational, as if unconscious, unable to be fully categorised by way of language as events happen in real time (Prinz, 2007). At any rate, the debate between a representational and a non-representational understanding belongs to a much larger conversation about the study of movement and action more broadly. Scholars sympathetic to the practice turn in IR argue, for example, that social science has too often emphasised cognition and representation: 'conscious representations are emphasized to the detriment of background knowledge—the inarticulate know-how from which reflexive and intentional deliberation becomes possible' (Pouliot, 2008, p. 258). Potential incompatibilities notwithstanding, it is worth gauging some of these differences.

Insights from non-representational theory inform us that 'human life is based on and in movement' (Thrift, 2008, p. 5). Indeed, one of the main claims of a non-representational ontology, as conveyed by Nigel Thrift (2008, p. 176), is that 'emotions form a rich moral array through which and with which the world is thought and which can sense different things even though they cannot always be named.' Likewise, Andrew Ross (2014, p. 2) argues that 'standard emotional categories—such as hatred, anger, fear, joy, and empathy—are of limited usefulness when studying real-world social environments.' Textual and symbolic approaches downplay the visceral dimension of emotional experience and, according to Ty Solomon (2015, pp. 56–57), discourse-based approaches lead inevitably to a 'neglect of the body' and are for that reason remarkably *dis*embodied.

While the non-representationality of affect suggests that discursive representations do not fully account for bodily experience, we argue that emotions are nevertheless shaped by both representational and non-representational features. Further, although the differences between representational and non-representational experiences are important to detect, they are in no way incompatible. Jesse Prinz (2007, p. 65) appeals instead for what he calls 'embodied appraisal,' arguing that 'emotions are embodied, because they are somatic signals.' And yet, for Prinz (2007, 65), 'emotions are also appraisals, insofar as they represent concerns, as standard cognitive theories maintain.' One particular way to break away from the divide between the somatic and the cognitive, a divide that unhelpfully reifies the Cartesian split between mind and body, is to look at the collective and intersubjective understanding of emotions. A constructivist outlook argues that while emotions can be felt subjectively, the *expression* of emotions is in relation to others, in a language that others understand (Fattah & Fierke, 2009, p. 70). In this neo-Wittgensteinian view, emotions do not stand alone, but rather depend on a shared understanding of the meaning of objects and practices (Fattah & Fierke, 2009, p. 70). This implies that appropriate expressions of emotions 'are shaped as much by context and socialisation as neurology' (Fierke, 2015, p. 43). The dependence on customs and past interactions highlights the social foundations of emotions or a 'social emotionology.' Drawing from Stearns and Stearns, Fierke (2015, p. 46) argues that 'through the process of socialisation, the emotionology of a culture influences how the individual experiences emotions.' In other words, 'emotionology' allows us to look at norms and how actors are emotionally invested towards them, experiences which are represented (though not exclusively) by language. As shown below, it is precisely that element of representation which permits us to look at emotional appraisals through time and to turn to Gadamer's approach. Although emotions spring from a somatic, almost non-representational experience, they can still be studied with recourse to language.

From Ontology to Methodology: Appraisals and Emotional Temporality

Emotional appraisals are 'essential to an emotion's identity' (Prinz, 2007, p. 51). Because we judge certain objects, however unconsciously, we can discuss and label, the feelings and the reactions of others to particular ideas, events, objects, and so on. Put differently, the fact that emotions can be identified allows us to understand methodologically *what* changed and continued through time. Appraisals, which rely in part on a cognitive experience, are but one part of emotional experience. By appraisal, we follow Jessie Prinz's (2007, p. 51) definition:

> A representation of an organism/environment relation that bears on wellbeing. Call such a relation a 'concern.' Anger, for instance, involves an appraisal of threat or offense. Fear involves an appraisal of danger. Sadness involves an appraisal of loss. Offenses, dangers, and losses are all matters of concern.

Hence, we agree with Simon Koschut (2014, p. 545) that emotions can be regarded as 'moral judgments that reflect an intellectual appraisal of present expectations and past experience,' although we maintain that this is but one side of the whole spectrum of emotional experience. The focus on emotional appraisals has the benefit of bringing to the fore the emotional 'norms communicated through language,' such as the objects, symbols and political positions one hates or loves through time (Koschut, 2014, p. 544). And yet, given the limits of language, a pluralist understanding of emotional experience is essential. It is for that reason that some scholars refer to an entire *array* of emotional experiences in the course of studying particular events. For instance, when approaching violence, war and trauma, Roland Bleiker and Emma Hutchison (2015, p. 515) speak of a 'whole spectrum of emotions—not only anger and fear for instance, but also empathy compassion and wonder.' The first step towards studying emotions through time is thus to admit that those experiences are inherently complex and never entirely represented by one single category. Bearing that caveat in mind, there is then the issue of connecting those appraisals through time.

Emotions as Temporal Experiences: Fusing Horizons

We turn hereby to the hermeneutic philosophy of Hans-Georg Gadamer to conceptualise how emotions, as experiences, flow and are entangled through time. While this may seem intuitive, emotions can sometimes be regarded as fleeting and ephemeral experiences, something that appears just as quickly as it disappears (Crawford, 2015, p. xii). Though this is not necessarily the predominant view of emotions, not least because several scholars underscore the lasting effects of humiliation and traumatic experience (Fattah and Fierke, 2009; Hutchison, 2016; Saurette, 2006), our approach highlights precisely the strong relationship between continuity and change in the sense that emotional appraisals are far from being isolated experiences in time. Indeed, they have temporal effects that last beyond their initial manifestation and articulation. To understand how emotional appraisals are connected, it is best to visit Gadamer's notion of evolving tradition. Taking experience to be a tradition that is changing through time is, for Gadamer, the first step towards accounting for and raising awareness of how the past and present are intricately connected. It makes little sense to interpret human experiences, even more so events, if the past is ignored.

The past is made present because we are all conditioned by a horizon. The past influences us not so much because one is consciously aware of continuity, that is of the extent to which our previous choices conditioned our future, but because we make use of historical symbols and language to make sense of the present (Gadamer, 1972, pp. 237–238). According to Gadamer (1989 [1960], p. 301), individuals are often in a situation that is structured by a horizon: 'we define the concept of "situation" by saying that it represents a standpoint that limits the possibility of vision. Hence an essential part of the concept of "situation" is the concept of "horizon."' Thus, to avoid the restrictions that our own horizons place upon us, Gadamer (1989 [1960], p. 367) argues for their fusion across distinct moments in time, a fusion that allows us to 'regain the concepts of a past in such a way that they also include our own comprehension of them.'

Gadamer's concept of a fusion of horizons—and in our case of emotional appraisals—dispels the assumption that emotions are experiences that seem to appear only in isolated moments in time. Experience is still interpreted in light of past concepts, appraisals and symbols. No new language or mode of expression is suddenly brought to the fore; rather the event is likely to be interpreted with recourse to several concepts rooted in the past. That said, appealing for an awareness of 'tradition' is not to suggest that change is impossible, nor to claim that all understanding must necessarily be conservative or otherwise incapable of sensing change. Rather what Gadamer (1989 [1960], pp. 276–280) means by tradition is the historical 'situatedness' of experience. In the course of understanding, the interpreter is limited by his or her prejudices and fore-meanings but, as Hoy (2012, p. 109) suggests 'what counts [for Gadamer] as the tradition is always revisable. Tradition therefore is not necessarily reactionary, but it can be radicalized as well.'

The limits of a horizon and the nature of tradition suggest that emotional appraisals need to be contextualised in light of their past. And yet, Gadamer's perspective has consequences not only for how we interpret the emotional appraisals of others but also for how we position ourselves as interpreters; for 'a person who is trying to understand is exposed to distraction from fore-meanings that are not borne out by the things themselves' (Gadamer, 1989 [1960], p. 280). As we come to terms with the experiences of others, we too—however indirectly—are projecting our own 'fore'-meanings upon their experiences. The historical 'situatedness' of all experience implies that no single event is likely to be interpreted in like manner, but it is not an appeal to relativism. As already noted, all interpretations are conditioned by a set of historical concepts, words, symbols and habits that are more or less transferable among speakers or else no communication would be possible. Whether a group of interpreters may or may not empathise with a leader's speech, such as G.W Bush's declarations before and after 9/11, one is nevertheless subject to the constraints of language in the sense that all the interpreters will more or less agree on the meaning of the words, particular gestures and emotional appraisals. What may be subject to dispute, however, is precisely the element that is shaped by our 'fore'-meanings, such as the emphasis that one gives to one particular appraisal or another, or the extent to which one considers this or that expression to be sincere, over-stated or insignificant. In any case, accounting for those 'fore'-meanings remains an important task, for it contextualises the role of the past in our own personal interpretations and just how much they are the product of a historical context.

Overall, analysing emotional appraisals requires a fusion of horizons. A fusion of horizons allows researchers to go beyond their own horizon, by creating an alternative one. This new horizon is not new in the sense of escaping previous horizons, but novel in proposing a new understanding of those emotional appraisals. One cannot totally escape previous horizons, since those horizons partly constitute the new horizon. Therefore, the task of fusing horizons needs to be developed reflexively, since the past influences not only the subjects of one's inquiry, but also ourselves as interpreters. We turn therefore to Stanley Fish's affective stylistics, a method that does justice to Gadamer's fusion of horizons.

APPLYING STANLEY FISH'S AFFECTIVE STYLISTICS TO EMOTIONAL EXPERIENCES THROUGH TIME

Though less concerned with ontology, Fish's approach is by and large compatible with the broader temporal claims invoked by Gadamer. It offers a way of locating and juxtaposing distinct emotional appraisals across time. Contrary to approaches to art criticism which analyse texts without considering their effects on experience, Fish's method underscores the need to imagine an 'idealised reader' who constructs and understands the flow of continuous, as well as changing, experience (Fish, 1970, p. 45). An idealised reader has the semantic competence to make sense of the words spoken. When reading a sentence, an idealised reader draws on his internalised repertoire of words and thus on his particular horizon and 'fore-meanings.' Because of the historical situatedness of experience, an idealised reader is never an objective observer standing outside of the world and the emotional appraisals he/she interprets. Yet, an idealised reader does neither interpret emotional appraisals from a purely subjective standpoint whereby his interpretation only belongs to and is understood by him. As Gadamer (2012, p. 109) points out, 'the fact that one can never depart too far from linguistic conventions is clearly basic to the life of language: he who speaks a private language understood by no one else, does not speak at all.' Therefore, the idealised reader is he/she who has the semantic capability to understand the meaning of the sentence and who is also reflexive of his own fore-meanings when interpreting the sentence.

To this end, Fish (1970, p. 125) begins by noting the advantages of his method with recourse to a verse from John Milton's *Paradise Lost*:

> Nor did they not perceive the evil plight.

Fish appeals to the experience of the reader by exploring the effects of the sentence on the reader, rather than merely asking what the sentence means: 'And what the sentence does is give the reader something and then take it away, drawing him on the with the unredeemed promise of its return' (1970, p. 125).[1] Put differently, if we are to look solely at the meaning of the sentence, the rules of English grammar offer little room for doubt: the double negative—the 'nor' and the 'not'—cancel each other out, and so the statement can easily be rejigged to 'they did perceive the evil plight.' The meaning is thus quickly conveyed, even if this reductive approach is scarcely appropriate. Further, proceeding in this way ignores the underlying temporal experience of reading:

> But however satisfactory this may be in terms of the internal logical of grammatical utterances (And even in those terms there are problems), it has nothing to do with the logic of the reading experience, or, I would insist, with its meaning. That experience is a temporal one, and in the course of it the two negatives combine not to produce an affirmative, but to prevent the reader from making the simple (declarative) sense which would be the goal of a logical analysis. To clean the line up is to take from it its more prominent and important effect—the suspension of the reader between the alternatives its syntax momentarily offers. (Fish, 1970, p. 126)

In order to capture the experience by which the statement is characterised, one needs to ask what is actually being done and, more important, look at how an emotional appraisal—followed by all subsequent appraisals—flows through time: 'essentially what the method does is slow down the reading experience so that "events" one does not notice in normal time, but which do occur, are brought before our analytical attention' (Fish, 1970, p. 128). This technique imposes a 'great burden on the analyst, who in his observation on any one moment in reading must take into account all that has happened' (Fish, 1970, p. 27).

Fish's method suggests that statements need to be read slowly and chronologically in order to detect the relationships between experiences and expectations. A statement in the past, like when reading the first page of a book, may indicate some sort of emotional appraisal, one which will have to be related to a later section of that book. In short, all these experiences need to be organised chronologically, related to each other, and read not only for their meaning but also for the emotions to which they are giving rise. As noted by Fish, the statement 'Nor did they not perceive the evil plight' has not only a direct meaning, easily decipherable by the rules of grammar, but also an emotional dimension that appeals to the reader, reflecting the narrator's attempt to suspend and highlight the problem of evil.

Table 11.1 summarises the main tenets of Fish's affective stylistics and the extent to which it is compatible with Gadamer's fusion of horizons.

Table 11.1 Applying affective stylistics to the study of emotional appraisals

Steps in order	Task
1. Chronology	Organise texts chronologically, starting from the oldest to the newest.
2. Slow reading	Slow reading in order to detect emotional appraisals that are articulated by specific symbols, such as slogans, ideas and words.
3. Unravel the pluralist understanding of an emotional appraisal	Avoid as much as possible to reduce the emotional appraisal to one single category, such as love or hate, but detect, with recourse to the surrounding context, whether other emotions are implied, such as, hope, despair, and so on.
4. Fuse emotional norm appraisals	• Relate emotional appraisals about the same object to each other, detecting whether changes about those judgements occurred or whether they continued through time. • In case of change, infer how the emotional appraisal of the past related to the more recent appraisal, and thus which emotions and events may have partially constituted the more recent evaluation. For example: hope in the past may open up disappointment by virtue of how new events shatter past expectations.

We use it, however, as a means by which to interpret emotional appraisals across time.

Building on Fish, the first task is to place the emotional appraisals in chronological order. It is then important to read the text slowly in order to look for symbols—which can be ideas, words or slogans—and the extent to which people are 'emotionally attached to them' (Koschut, 2014, p. 589). For instance, a statement such as 'I love America' reflects an emotional judgement about a specific object, in this case America. Instead of simply 'translating' the meaning of texts, it is necessary, according to Fish (1970, p. 149) to see that 'in any linguistic experience we are internalising attitudes and emotions.' These emotions can be located within particular norms. In the case of 'I love America', love may represent an appraisal about an adherence to the nation-state or a deep affection for an imagined community. By slowing down the process of reading, we also decelerate the speed of contagion by reflecting on the emotions generated by the speeches. Lastly, it is important to fuse those distinct emotional appraisals, detecting whether they changed or continued, including how events and past evaluations constituted the new emotional appraisal. We illustrate this method in the next section.

Case Study

We look mainly at two speeches preceding and following the Al Qaeda attacks of 11 September 2001, otherwise known as '9/11'. We choose 9/11 as it has often been represented as a temporal rupture that radically changed the architecture of world politics (Kennedy-Pipe & Rengger, 2006, p. 540). Some in fact maintain that there was an 'American experience before 9/11,' and a different one after 9/11 (Rogers, 2012). Others suggested that, although most individuals returned to approximate normalcy in the few months following the attacks, it was nevertheless a distinct kind of normalcy (Gaddis, 2004, pp. 4–5). If these claims are to be confirmed, we should be able to notice a radical change in the emotional norms evoked by G.W. Bush after September 2001. That said, statements made by G.W. Bush (29 January 2002) often seem to confirm the notion that a radical rupture did take place. Shortly after the attacks, G.W. Bush declared that he was speaking outside of the 'normal course of events,' that the United States '*awakened* to danger' (29 January 2002) and that thousands of lives *suddenly* ended' (11 January 2001). Yet, some scholars now agree that the 'shifts' governing world politics after 9/11 were only *symptomatic* of existing tendencies, rather than *caused* by 9/11 (Kennedy-Pipe and Rengger, 2006, p. 546). Further, Holland (2013, p. 93) rightly points out that the construction of '9/11' as both a 'crisis' and a 'somatic marker' was the first step towards legitimising the War on Terror.

In any case, we are interested mostly in accounting for the view that American foreign policy changed substantially after 9/11. The United States was often perceived to be pursuing an isolationist policy under G.W. Bush until 9/11, the latter of which 'forced' Washington to play a more prominent role in international politics. Indeed, before 9/11, G.W. Bush was criticised for his 'go-it-alone' style of defence (Plate 23/07/2001), moving America towards isolationism (Buzbee 28/08/2001). His 'America first' attitude apparently also led him to eschew international treaties like the Anti-Ballistic Missile Treaty or the Kyoto Protocol (Chung 22 January 2001). But if isolationism was in effect the sole course of American policy, the resurgence of interventionism would surely help reinforce the idea that 9/11 led not only to serious rupture in world politics, but also to a major change in United States' foreign policy. We take issue with the latter point of view. By fusing horizons, and thus looking at G.W. Bush's emotional appraisals through time, it is possible to find an underlying sense of continuity in the way the United States' government was positioning itself in the international arena. The aims of compassionate protectionism and of hating and responding to tyranny were in fact invoked prior to 9/11 and these appraisals persisted thereafter.

Chronology

In order to underscore continuity, we focus on the emotional appraisals invoked in two key speeches made by President G.W. Bush before and after 9/11. We selected his inauguration speech, delivered on 20 January 2001 as it provides an idea of how the Bush administration positioned the United States as an actor in the international system. The second speech is the State of the Union address of 29 January 2002, approximately four months after 9/11. By following our method, we organise and analyse the speeches chronologically, not only to study how they are connected but also to understand how prior emotional appraisals constituted subsequent events. This approach allows us to seize the role of emotions in constructing new security narratives as well as grasp their evolution *in* and *across* time. Moreover, by emphasising active reading, Fish's method forces us to reflect on how emotional symbols or slogans affect 'us.' In other words, affective cues have effects that can prepare the audience to be receptive to certain messages in the future.

Slow Reading

After organising the speeches chronologically, we discern the emotional appraisals of 2001 and of 2002 by slowing down our reading. This activity is meant to increase the conscious and cognitive part of interpretation. This 'strategy of decertainising' or 'disorientation' is however progressive: the reader first commits him or herself (the first time less than consciously) to the assertion of the sentence. Afterwards, he or she has to undergo a change which makes the text less uncertain, as one goes back and forth between words (Fish, 1970, pp. 124–125). At the beginning of each sentence, the idealised reader formulates expectations about how the sentence will end. These expectations do not emerge 'naturally' or out of the text itself, but reflect the fore-meanings of the idealised reader, which are situated within a particular time and space. This calls to the reflexivity of the interpreter in the activity of 'slow reading,' by recognising that expectations about the sentence are not objective but derive from the previous knowledges shared by interpreter and his or her community. Not every interpreter's expectations will therefore be the same, for we are limited, to some extent, by our own horizon. Hence, when using the possessive pronoun 'we' in the analysis below, we are aware that 'we' represents the researcher's epistemological tradition. Yet again, this interpretation is not completely subjective, since it rests on language and language is not a private practice. The conclusions drawn in this analysis are thus bound to a 'cultural emotionology,' in other words, bound to a particular social community sharing several epistemological, if not linguistic, conventions.

To take an example from G.W. Bush's 2001 speech:

> All who live in tyranny and hopelessness can know: the United States will not ignore your oppression, or excuse your oppressors. When you stand for your liberty, we will stand with you.

Here, we commit ourselves to reading the first part of the sentence. We are thus prepared for several constructions:

> All who live in tyranny and hopelessness can know, that *you should* (express dissent).

> All who live in tyranny and hopelessness can know, that *you are* (friends of America).
> All who live in tyranny and hopelessness can know, that *you will* (be free).

Upon stating the first part of the sentence, the symbols 'tyranny' and 'hopelessness' provoke a sense of discomfort and empathy towards 'all who live' under such conditions. The following words 'the United States will not' tell us that our expectations were misconceived, thereby reducing our certainty. Moreover, the subject has changed from 'all who live' to 'the United States.' It is not 'all who live' who will change their own conditions of living, but the United States, which has now acquired a paramount role in the transformation of 'all who live.' We go forward in the hope that we will find an explanation for our misapprehension: 'the United States will not ignore your oppression,' relieving the early experience of discomfort caused by the symbols of 'tyranny' and 'hopelessness'. 'All who live' are now being heard and their conditions will change by virtue of United States' compassion. We are now not only open to the idea that the United States should help 'all who live under tyranny and hopelessness', but we demand that this be done. Yet, upon reading the next sentence: 'When you stand for your liberty, we will stand with you,' we are again disorientated. The compassion of the United States comes with a condition; 'when' here stands as a proviso upon which the suffering of 'all who live' will be alleviated.

We proceed in this manner chronologically wherever emotional appraisals are found, precisely to detect how the speaker is positioning him or herself as time passes. We can therefore proceed to another statement from G.W. Bush's 2002 speech:

> The last time we met in this chamber, the mothers and daughters of Afghanistan were captives in their own homes, forbidden from working or going to school. Today women are free, and are part of Afghanistan's new government.

We read this sentence by noting that G.W. Bush is now speaking after 9/11. In this light, we are inclined to make several inferences:

> The last time we met in this chamber, *we were* (in a state of shock).
> The last time we met in this chamber, *we awakened* (to danger).
> The last time we met in this chamber, *we were attacked* (on 9/11).

The next five words 'the mothers and daughters of Afghanistan' induce emotional uncertainty, pleading for a resolution. We are now actively looking for an explanation, rather than merely 'following an argument along a well lighted path' (Fish, 1970, p. 124). Again, the subject changes from 'we' to 'the mothers and daughters of Afghanistan,' thereby connecting 'our' conditions to the 'mothers and daughters of Afghanistan.' More precisely, American lives, which have been shattered by the attacks, share a similar experience to the mothers and daughters of Afghanistan, a gendered experience of life that is threatened. By contrast, American lives are separated from Afghan men. As such, we are feeling empathy and compassion towards 'American lives' and the 'mothers and daughters of Afghanistan,' but not towards Afghan men.

We proceed to the next statement that they 'were captive in their own homes, forbidden from working or going to school.' We are compelled to feel disgust and horror at the sight of mothers and daughters being captive. Here, 'Afghan mothers and daughters' do not share the same experience as American mothers and daughters, for American women are free to go to school and work. While directing the reader towards disgust and horror, 'we' also feel a sense of relief since the 'we' of America is better off than 'Afghan mothers and daughters.' The connection between Afghan mothers and daughters and American lives becomes clearer: American lives can provide solace to Afghan women and daughters, an appraisal of reassurance which is satisfied by the next sentence: 'Today women are free, and are part of Afghanistan's new government.'

Unravelling the Pluralist Understanding of Emotional Appraisals

On the whole, the utterances examined in 2001 and 2002 generate the following emotional appraisals in chronological order: compassion, then empathy, then fear, then despair disgust, then horror and finally relief. On top of that, what is important to detect is not merely a single category, like 'love,' 'hate,' or 'anger', but words that have emotional resonance within a cultural emotionology. In that sense, emotion norms are 'moral judgements of appropriate behaviour' (Koschut 2014, p. 534). Although the word 'free' may not be classified as an emotion, the concept of 'freedom' has emotional resonance in the 'West' that helps constitute it as an emotion norm. Although G.W Bush clearly referred to the emotional symbols of 'hopelessness,' the two speeches were loaded with other moral judgements about American lives as well as the lives of Afghan daughters and mothers. In this sense, ideas of 'liberty' stand hand in hand with emotions of joy, contentedness and satisfaction. By contrast, 'tyranny' and hopelessness' provoke horror, fear and empathy insofar as they are attached to collective norms about what life is and ought to be. To that effect, feelings of compassion and empathy towards Afghan daughters and mothers are vested in an imaginary encounter with American lives, both of which have witnessed the destruction caused by Afghan men. In that respect, Americans share a common experience with people who are oppressed, in this case Afghan mothers and daughters. More importantly, emotions of profound dislike for tyranny, expressed in 2001 before the attacks on the World Trade Center and the Pentagon, were well echoed in 2002. A fusion of horizons allows us to unravel these connections.

Fusing Emotional Norm Appraisals

Fusing emotional appraisals helps us capture the sense of change as well as continuity at two different moments in time. It contextualises the underlying tradition by which events are interpreted. On the one hand, the case study highlights that feelings of disgust, horror and anger were invoked towards authoritarian countries in 2001, appropriated in 2002, and later directed towards the Afghan government and Afghan men more generally. 9/11 was a novel event, but the appraisal against tyranny was not. On the other hand, empathy and compassion were all expressed in favour of oppressed peoples in 2001, which were then embodied by Afghan mothers and daughters in 2002. Thus, in 2001 *and* 2002, the United States continued to demonstrate its commitment to relieving oppressed peoples (Fig. 11.1).

Contrary to the claim that 9/11 'changed everything,' the fusion reveals continuity. The emotional norms espoused in 2001 not only informed but also set the scene for the unique role of the United States in the post-9/11 world. Moreover, by looking at the relations between utterances through time, one is able to see how the emotions are in fact interconnected. For instance, one would not be able to experience relief upon hearing 'today women are free' if the sense of shock, horror and disgust had not been evoked prior to that statement. Likewise, it would be difficult for the listener to experience compassion at the conditions of 'Afghan mothers and daughters' if he or she had had not been compelled to feel empathy for 'all who live under tyranny and hopelessness.' In short,

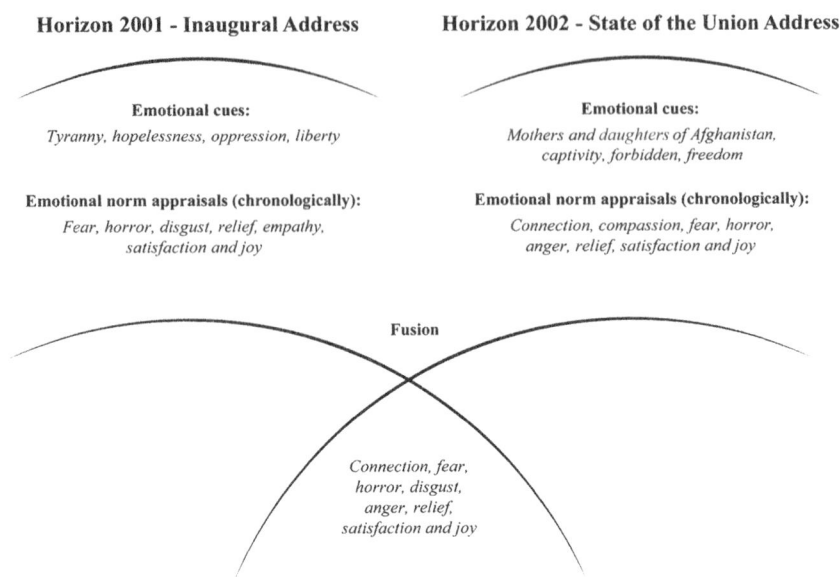

Fig. 11.1 Illustration of the fusion of emotional appraisals

a fusion of horizons allows us to connect moments that are temporally spread far apart as well as locate the intricate connections between appraisals as they are happening in time. Overall, the tradition of emotional appraisals put forth before 9/11 also manifested after the attack. Even if the direction of those appraisals was narrowed down, in this case to Afghanistan, that change—though relevant—hardly implies a significant alteration. The key emotional appraisals of the Bush administration, focused primarily on seeking compassion for the oppressed, not only persisted thereafter but were reinforced by 9/11.

Conclusion

This chapter developed a hermeneutical approach to the study of emotions through the use of Gadamer's fusion of horizons. Looking at the connections between emotional appraisals helps us dispel the idea that emotions are single-time occurrences that bear no connections with the past. There is by contrast an underlying tradition that underpins the way in which actors act and react to particular events. Methodologically, an approach that fuses distinct horizons of experience enables to question the extent to which certain emotional appraisals are novel. We do not contend in this regard that 9/11 was a shocking experience for most if not all Americans. And yet, this tells us little about the meaning which it subsequently acquired and the effects it engendered thereafter. We showed that all the emotions of compassion, empathy, fear and hate that sprung from 9/11 were not isolated incidents. Rather, past emotional appraisals persisted while others helped constitute the experiences after 9/11. The chronological setting and our ability to detect those intertwined experiences are thus crucial, and a fusion of horizons allows precisely to account for those connections.

Apart from these advantages, however, our approach is limited to one facet of emotional experience. Indeed, it concentrates mainly on the representational—in particular, the appraisal—dimension of emotions. It does not, therefore, do justice to the whole array of emotional experience, such as bodily reactions, movements or unconscious reflections. One could, of course, argue that these parts of experience are also temporally constituted, but our method is derived from an epistemology that was directed towards the study of language and the effects thereof. Gadamer's approach has been applied mainly to historical texts and Fish's affective stylistics to the study of literature. In any case, we find that their approaches are not limited to the study of history, nor to the aesthetic domain. Instead, we agree with Bleiker and Hutchison (2008, p. 130) that we should complement existing social sciences methods with other 'modes of inquiry stemming from the humanities.' On top of that, there may be some skepticism towards the position of the 'idealised reader' and the limits imposed by our own horizons. However, their fusion is precisely meant to foster new understandings by placing horizons in dialogue with one another. The 'new' horizon is not new in terms of removing the researcher's fore-meanings, but is new in the sense of generating an approach that is influenced by two horizons. Further, making reflexivity integral to this methodological approach allows researchers to become aware of their own assumptions. In so doing, it encourages us to question our own emotional experiences, but also opens the possibility for creativity, as we become aware of how our own horizons and those of others prompt a new understanding of experience.

Overall, this chapter puts forth a methodology for the study emotions in world politics. By adopting a temporal lens, we hope that it also contributes to wider debates in IR about the influence and problem of time

(Hom, 2010, 2016; Hutchings, 2008; Jarvis, 2008; Solomon, 2014). Further studies of emotions and time could thus benefit from connecting our emotional appraisals not only to political and ethical norms, such as notions of appropriate behavior, but also to underlying ideas about the way in which time is constituted. We find much promise within these approaches, not least because it would help link promising and ongoing areas of inquiry in IR. It is safe to say that the complex relations between time, experience and emotion are now being taken seriously within the domain of politics, and our chapter takes, we hope, one small step in that direction.

Notes

1. One could argue that the distinction drawn by Stanley Fish between 'what a sentence means' and what a 'sentence does' resonates with part of John Austin's speech act theory. Austin distinguishes between the locution, the act *of* saying something, the illocution, the act *in* saying something and the perlocutionary effect, the consequential effects of the word on the hearer, where the success of the first two make a sound utterance, conform to a specific grammar, whilst the last provokes effects on the hearer or reader. In *How to do things with words*, Austin argues that words are performative through these three acts. In effect, for Austin (2008, p. 130) 'to say something *is* to do something, or *in* saying something we do something, and even *by* saying something we do something.' Hence, substituting the question 'what does this sentence mean?' with 'what does this sentence do?', as Fish suggests, emphasises the effects of the text on the audience and thus the perlocutionary effect of speech.

References

Åhäll, L., & Gregory, T. (2015a). Introduction. In L. Åhäll & T. Gregory (Eds.), *Emotions, Politics and War* (pp. 1–14). Oxon: Routledge.

Åhäll, L., & Gregory, T. (Eds.). (2015b). *Emotions, Politics and War*. Oxon: Routledge.

Åhäll, L. A., & Gregory, T. A. (2013). Security, Emotions, Affect. *Critical Studies on Security, 1*(1), 117–120. https://doi.org/10.1080/21624887.2013.790217.

Ahmed, S. (2014). *The Cultural Politics of Emotion* (2nd ed.). Edinburgh: Edinburgh University Press.

Bleiker, R., & Hutchison, E. (2008). Fear No More: Emotions and World Politics. *Review of International Studies, 34*(1), 115–135. https://doi.org/10.1017/S0260210508007821.

Booth, K., & Wheeler, N. (2007). *The Security Dilemma: Fear, Cooperation and Trust in World Politic.* London: Palgrave Macmillan.

Clément, M. (2014). Al-Muhajiroun in the United Kingdom: The Role of International Non-recognition in Heightened Radicalization Dynamics. *Global Discourse, 4*(4), 428–443. https://doi.org/10.1080/23269995.2014.918306.

Crawford, N. C. (2000). The Passion of World Politics: Propositions on Emotion and Emotional Relationships. *International Security, 24*(4), 116–156.

Crawford, N. C. (2013). Emotions and International Security: *Cave! Hic Libido. Critical Studies on Security, 1*(1), 121–123. https://doi.org/10.1080/21624887.2013.790218.

Fattah, K., & Fierke, K. M. (2009). A Clash of Emotions: The Politics of Humiliation and Political Violence in the Middle East. *European Journal of International Relations, 15*(1), 67–93. https://doi.org/10.1177/1354066108100053.

Fish, S. (1970). Literature in the Reader: Affective Stylistics. *New Literary History, 2*(1), 123–162.

Gadamer, H.-G. (1989 [1960]). *Truth and Method* (J. Weinsheimer & D. G. Marshall, Trans. 2nd Revisited ed.). London and New York: Continuum.

Head, N. (2012). Transforming Conflict: Trust, Empathy, and Dialogue. *International Journal of Peace Studies, 17*(2), 33–55.

Head, N. (2016). A Politics of Empathy: Encounters with Empathy in Israel and Palestine. *Review of International Studies, 42*(1), 95–113. https://doi.org/10.1017/S0260210515000108.

Hoy, D. C. (2012). *The Time of Our Lives: A Critical History of Temporality.* Massachusetts: MIT Press.

Hutchison, E. (2016). *Affective Communities in World Politics: Collective Emotions after Trauma.* Cambridge: Cambridge University Press.

Jarvis, L. (2008). Times of Terror: Writing Temporality into the War on Terror. *Critical Studies on Terrorism, 1*(2), 245–262. https://doi.org/10.1080/17539150802184637.

Koschut, S. (2014). Emotional (Security) Communities: The Significance of Emotion Norms in Interallied Conflict Management. *Review of International Studies, 40*(3), 533–558. https://doi.org/10.1017/S0260210513000375.

Mattern, J. B. (2011). A Practice Theory of Emotion for International Relations. In E. Adler & V. Pouliot (Eds.), *International Practices* (pp. 63–86). Cambdrige: Cambridge University Press.

Pouliot, V. (2008). The Logic of Practicality: A Theory of Practice of Security Communities. *International Organization, 62*(2), 257–288.

Prinz, J. (2007). *The Emotional Construction of Morals.* Oxford: Oxford University Press.

Reus-Smit, C. (2014). Emotions and the Social. *International Theory (Forum), 6*(3), 568–574. https://doi.org/10.1017/S1752971914000281.

Rogers, P. (2012). Global Terrorism. In M. Cox & D. Stokes (Eds.), *US Foreign Policy* (2nd ed., pp. 335–350). New York: Oxford University Press.
Ross, A. G. (2014). *Mixed Emotions: Beyond Fear and Hatred in International Conflict.* Chicago: The University of Chicago Press.
Saurette, P. (2006). You Dissin Me? Humiliation and Post 9/11 Global Politics. *Review of International Studies, 32*(3), 495–522. https://doi.org/10.1017/S0260210506007133.
Solomon, T. (2014). Time and Subjectivity in World Politics. *International Studies Quarterly, 58*(4), 671–681. https://doi.org/10.1111/isqu.12091.
Thrift, N. (2008). *Non-Representational Theory: Space, Politics, Affect.* Oxon: Routledge.
Ty, S. (2015). Embodiment, Emotions, and Materialism in International Relations. In L. Åhäll & T. Gregory (Eds.), *Emotions, War and Politics* (pp. 56–68). Oxon: Routledge.
Van Rythoven, E. (2015). *Learning to Feel, Learning to Fear? Emotions, Imaginaries, and Limits of the Politics of Securitization* (pp. 1–18). *Security Dialogue*: Security Dialogue. https://doi.org/10.1177/0967010615574766.
Zalewski, M. (2013). Theorizing Emotion: Affective Borders in Homeland. *Critical Studies on Security, 1*(1), 133–135.

Clara Eroukhmanoff is a Lecturer in International Relations at London South Bank University. Her research expertise is located at the intersection of critical security studies and the visual and emotion turns. She has published in *International Studies Review* and *Critical Studies on Terrorism* and is currently working on her monograph entitled 'The securitization of Islam post-9/11: indirect speech acts and emotions' with Manchester University Press.

Bernardo Teles Fazendeiro is a post-doctoral researcher at Centro de Estudos Sociais at the University of Coimbra, Portugal, specialising in interpretivist International Relations, Role theory and Post-Soviet politics. He has published in *International Affairs, Central Asian Survey* and *International Studies Review*. His book on Uzbekistan's foreign policy is to be published by Routledge in 2017.

CHAPTER 12

Speaking from the Heart: Emotion Discourse Analysis in International Relations

Simon Koschut

INTRODUCTION

The study of emotion discourse in International Relations (IR) involves a project that seeks to systematically integrate emotions within discourse analysis. It is argued here that the inclusion of emotions as an additional category of analysis for intersubjectivity allows further questions and that, so far, the extended scope of meanings that emerge from the integration of emotions within discourse analysis remains largely untapped in IR. When studying emotion and discourse, it is necessary to differentiate between two dimensions (Abu-Lughod & Lutz, 1990, p. 10). The *discourse on emotions* relates to the way emotions are talked about scientifically or in everyday parlay. It defines the way we ontologically and epistemologically conceive of emotions as being rational/irrational, biological/cultural, personal/social, or spontaneous/strategic. *Emotion discourse*, by contrast, refers to the assumption that discourses have some affective content or effect (Edwards, 1997, p. 170). Emotion discourse is concerned with how actors talk about emotions and how they employ emotion categories when talking about subjects, events, or social relations. Emotion discourse can

S. Koschut (✉)
Free University Berlin, Berlin, Germany

be strategically used to construct social hierarchies by, for example, assigning praise or blame to actions or attributes and by verbally contrasting various emotions with alternative emotion categories within the discursive construction of reality. Theoretically, such an understanding views emotions as socially constructed representations of meaning that are linked to conceptions of identity and power.

Studies involving the discourse-emotion nexus have in recent years been among the most active and interesting areas contributing to the 'emotional turn' in IR as one of the most promising developments in the field (Ahäll & Gregory, 2015; Bially Mattern, 2011; Edkins, 2003; Fierke, 2013; Hutchison, 2016; Koschut, 2017; Leep, 2010; Ross, 2014; Solomon, 2015; Van Rythoven, 2015; Wilcox, 2015). That said, there has been strikingly little elaboration of appropriate methods and criteria for studying emotion discourse, understood as the words, phrases, narratives, expressions, and representations that in some way symbolically refer to emotion and anything that is visual such as photographs, artwork, and images. This raises an important methodological question: If the power of language includes an affective dimension then the question is how can researchers analytically extract the emotion potential and emotionalizing effects built into political discourse?

Emotion Discourse Analysis

In a step towards fostering methodological engagement and dialogue on this issue, I propose a framework for empirical research on emotion discourse in world politics. Precisely, the idea is to explore how the ways in which discourse evokes, reveals, and engages emotions can speak to larger questions in IR. The goal is to go beyond the 'emotions matter' approach of the first wave of emotion scholarship in IR to offer more specific ways to integrate the consideration of emotion into existing research, particularly that of a constructivist vein.[1] A social constructivist perspective emphasizes the importance of the intersubjective and sociocultural character of emotions (Averill, 1980; Harré, 1986). In line with this view, it is argued here that emotions involve institutionalized responses that allow political actors to participate in world politics using specific meaning structure or as Fattah and Fierke (2009, p. 70) put it, 'emotions (are) socially meaningful expressions, which depend on shared customs, uses and institutions'. In short, a social constructivist perspective argues that emotions are cultural products that owe their meaning and purpose to learnt social rules.

Why is it necessary to adapt discourse analysis in IR to the study of emotion? Emotions play an important role in language-based processes at the international level. Take the example of 'naming and shaming': If language power is able to inflict social suffering (the loss of social status or ontological insecurity) upon agents, such discursive identity constructions implicate an affective dimension. For, if an actor can be shamed into changing its behaviour through non-physical power, it must *feel* the negative social implications of such power in order to be persuaded or forced into compliance. Otherwise, these discursive mechanisms would be useless. If emotions underpin the meanings within and effects of discourses, they need to be identified and made accountable for based on empirical research. Such an undertaking not only speaks to emotion research in IR but also promises new insights and tools for the study of discourse in international politics (see, e.g. Campbell, 1992; Der Derian & Shapiro, 1989; Diez, 2001; Epstein, 2008; Hansen, 2006; Milliken, 1999; Weldes & Saco, 1996; Zehfuss, 2002). Due to analytical clarity and limited space, I focus on the textual dimension of discourse in this chapter. I am not concerned here with the non-verbal and visual dimension of discourse although I recognize that this is an important area of research (see, e.g. Bleiker, 2009; Hansen, 2011).

The notion of integrating emotions within discourse analysis put forward here is based on two interrelated questions: Why study emotions through discourse? How can we study emotions through discourse? Concerning the first question, I argue that textual and verbal utterances provide us with a promising way to make emotions empirically accessible for researchers. One of the main challenges of emotion research (as flagged by the editors in the introduction) is that, due to their subjective nature, we have neither direct access to emotional states and intentions nor can we empirically retrieve the emotional reception and experience of agents. As Harré (1986, p. 4) notes, emotions constitute an 'ontological illusion', in the sense that 'there is an abstract and detachable "it" upon which research can be directed'. The problem of the subjective ontology of emotion can be resolved, however, by shifting the analytical focus from their internal phenomenological perception and appraisal by individuals to their representational and intersubjective articulation and communication within social spheres. One way to study emotions as intersubjective representations, and thus gain access to their social meanings, is through their explication in discourse. This chapter takes discourses, 'framings of meaning and lenses of interpretation' (Hansen, 2006, p. 7), as a point of entry for the study of emotion.

That said, discourse scholarship in IR hardly offers systematic approaches for analysing the emotion potential and emotionalization effects of texts (Bleiker & Hutchison, 2014). Regarding the second question, I argue that it is thus essential to develop specific methodological criteria for the empirical study of emotions via speech acts. More specifically, I propose three criteria that the study of emotion discourse must answer to, which revolve around (1) selecting appropriate texts, (2) mapping the verbal expression of emotions (emotion potential of texts), and (3) interpreting and contextualizing their political effects (emotionalization effects of texts).

First, researchers need to be aware of the fact that different types of texts or genres may contain and reveal various emotions in very different ways. Hence, the selection of appropriate texts for the research question under study involves a careful searching and mixing of different textual sources to prepare the ground for empirical analysis.

Second, the study of emotion discourse requires research strategies and tools to trace the expressions of emotions through the emotion potential of texts. Discourse analysis typically involves at least two dimensions of textual features. On the one hand, researchers need to pay close attention to the micro-structure of texts (particular words and linguistic concepts such as metaphors or euphemisms) and interpret their scope of meaning and usage in a particular discourse (Chilton, 1996; Straehle, Weiss, Wodak, Muntigl, & Sedlak, 1999). On the other hand, discourse analysis aims not solely on partial fixations of meaningful words and expressions but instead attempts to uncover larger patterns or structures within and among discourses that serve as systems of meanings at the macro-level of texts (Derrida, 1978, Connolly, 1983). By combining these two dimensions, researchers may identify and make explicit what kind of emotional meanings are linked to exactly which textual elements or structures.

Finally, and most importantly, researchers need to answer the 'so what' question of what the emotion potential of texts essentially helps us explain or understand. I refer to this as the emotionalizing effects of texts. This need not imply a causal relationship in any strict sense but rather the sociopolitical implications of analysing emotions in discourse, what doing so can reveal, or what significance it can carry. Emotional expressions arguably represent an important link between the discursively constructed identities of subjects, on the one hand, and the power exerted through discourses, on the other hand. Beyond this very general assumption, however, researchers need to empirically show what the emotions built into discourse actually 'do' in terms of, for example, revelation of the speaker's motives and attitudes, recognition of audience reception and responses, construction of power relationships and hierarchies, or stimulating certain performances and behaviour. These three criteria—selecting texts, mapping expressions, and interpreting effects—translate into three consecutive steps to conduct an emotion discourse analysis (EDA) that is specified and empirically illustrated in the following sections.

Step One: Developing Research Questions and Making Text Selections

The point of departure for any EDA is to compile a dossier of sources produced by the actor(s) under study. The focus should be on emotions that are either explicitly expressed or tacitly implied over a range of sources and within or across a coherent time period. This may include a variety of textual sources, including (but not limited to) official statements (speeches, press releases, parliamentary debates), legal texts (treaties, conventions, agreements), biographical texts (diaries, autobiographies, personal notes), media texts (newspaper articles, interviews, editorials), and even popular culture (poems, novels, songs). While the selection of texts ultimately depends on the research question, there are some things to consider when studying the emotions within these texts.

To begin with, one would assume that the more formal and official the character of the text the more implicit and circumscribed emotional expressions are likely to be. Hence, a biographical text or a poem is more likely to contain more explicit and outspoken emotional statements than say a legal text. That, however, should not mislead researchers to conclude that legal texts do not contain emotional meanings at all, only that these are concealed behind legal prose and style. It is widely recognized that legal cultures are not emotion-free spaces but deeply intertwined with emotional norms, rules, experience, and expectations (Nussbaum, 2003; Posner, 1999). In some cases, legal texts may, for example, even prescribe specific emotions, such as the legal practice of duelling, which is based on the concept of honour. Still, some texts in international politics may be more emotionally 'loaded' than others. A clever way to conduct an EDA is thus to combine different textual genres to get a more comprehensive picture of and better access to the emotions involved.

The researcher should then search for a small number of canonical texts by charismatic authorities that may serve as emotional 'landmarks' (Laclau & Mouffe, 1985). Such landmark texts usually involve foundational or transformative moments or crises during which emotions are likely to be more prevalent and outspoken. This is not to say that emotions cannot be studied under 'normal' circumstances. Rather, the focus on foundational or transformative moments represents a pragmatic move to study emotions at times when they become most acutely visible (Crawford, 2000, p. 130; Ross, 2006, p. 211). Moreover, dramatic events challenge and often transform established emotional attachments and meanings, which arguably make them more relevant to the study of emotion discourse (Bleiker & Hutchison, 2008, p. 129).

While the initial focus on a small number of texts from dramatic and uprooting points in time may be necessary from a research perspective, it nevertheless creates problems for the study of emotion discourse. As I have pointed out elsewhere, the focus on charismatic authorities delimits the study to the emotional expressions of a particular group of people, which may or may not be representative of a larger collective (Koschut, 2016). This selection bias needs to be addressed, either by delimiting the research question or by extending the data material. A more sophisticated way to do this would be to develop a theory for why the emotional expressions by charismatic authorities are worth looking at, for example, by pointing to their accentuated social status and power within groups. Here, the question of intertextuality becomes crucial. Intertextuality highlights the interconnections and cross-links between different texts in building authority and constructing identities (Der Derian & Shapiro, 1989; Kristeva, 1980). Emotional intertextuality refers to the way emotional expressions are quoted, appropriated, or criticized within and against other texts. Emotions rarely reside in a single text or are unique in their way of expression. Emotions often relate to similar emotions expressed in other culture-specific and/or historical discourses and narratives as well as involve specific considerations and memories of sociocultural contexts and spatial embedding of previous speech acts and their emotional impact (e.g. pride in national achievements). This may help identifying resonating discourses and hence justify focusing on them.

Another problem results from the temporal framing of texts. Emotional expressions during crises are likely to be very different from those expressed during more stable periods. For example, in the aftermath of 9/11, the Cuban government temporally abandoned its previous antagonistic rhetoric vis-à-vis the United States in favour of official expressions of sympathy and condolence (Hall, 2015, p. 171). It is thus sometimes necessary to extend or at least consider the time frame beyond a period of crisis. Finally, the meaning of emotions themselves is highly contingent on their historical and cultural embedding. For example, the philosophers of the Enlightenment employed the term 'passion' when referring to the emotions, which has very little to do with the modern usage of the word 'passion'. It is thus important to include a larger text-based analysis from the relevant time period under study as well as secondary sources to confirm or disconfirm the findings and/or to detect changes in emotional meanings and expressions.

Step Two: Mapping the Emotion Potential of Texts

The second step concentrates on the analysis of the emotion potential of texts and how identities of Self and Other are discursively connected to specific emotional expressions. The research strategy chosen here concentrates on the analysis of the emotion potential of discourse. The main purpose of mapping emotions within texts in this way is to analytically separate the descriptive meaning of written words from their connotative emotional meaning (Abu-Lughod & Lutz, 1990, p. 5). From a methodological perspective, researchers need to show *what kind* of emotional meanings are linked to exactly *which* textual components to fully grasp the emotion potential and, subsequently, the emotionalizing effects of texts (see step three). For example, one might be able to make a good case that Ronald Reagan's 'Evil-Empire-speech' was an emotionalized speech act, characterized by an aggressive, hard-line stance towards the former Soviet Union. But that hardly answers the question of what kind of textual items actually make such a discursive performance emotional. A key assumption of social constructivism is that emotions are linked to identities rooted in sociocultural structures. In addition to establishing the frequencies of specific emotion terms and words through a simple word count, the analysis needs to observe which emotions are the most fundamental and prevalent to their styles of expression and sense of Self and Other, respectively. This dimension concerns whether emotions refer to the self-image of a group or the outside image of other groups. It differentiates between those emotion categories, which are both inwards and reserved for members of a group, on the one hand, and those emotion categories that are directed outwards (Hutchison, 2016; Koschut, 2014). For example, membership in prestigious international 'clubs' (e.g. the G7 or 'the world of democracies') is often linked to emotions of pride and self-esteem for the in-group ('proud Self'), on the one hand, and emotions of contempt and inferiority towards particular out-groups ('disgusting Other'), on the other hand (Leep, 2010, p. 335). Conversely, some groups may display emotions of sympathy towards likeminded others. Accounting for the large range of linguistic features that serve to express emotion, it is helpful to distinguish between at least four ways of communicating emotions in discourse: emotion terms, connotations, metaphors, as well as comparisons and analogies.

First, emotional meaning may be conveyed explicitly by establishing a direct reference to an emotional feeling through emotion terms. With nouns like *fear, anger, love, hate, pride, shame*, verbs like *to fear, to love, and to hate*, and adjectives like *afraid, loving, hateful, and angry* or adverbs like *sadly*, and *regrettably*, words refer directly to emotions. It is necessary and important, however, to keep in mind the lexical and semantic variation of emotion terms in and among different languages and cultures. Some emotion concepts are so unique in their cultural meaning that they cannot be translated into English at all, such as the German schadenfreude or the Japanese emotion term 'amae'. Hence, some emotions get 'lost in translation', and researchers should be fully aware of this by gaining a considerable degree of cultural and historical background knowledge.

Second, emotional meanings may be communicated implicitly through connotations. An emotional connotation contains a context-invariant value judgement or opinion that conveys the emotional attitude of the speaker (Schwarz-Friesel, 2013). Certain words are affectively 'loaded' in the sense that their semantic utterance is linked to emotional meaning. Some affective items such as *genocide, terrorist, rogue state, outlaw, and massacre* often carry a negative appeal because they refer indirectly to specific emotion concepts of disapproval such as anger, contempt, or even hate (though some may also take pride in being labelled a 'terrorist' or 'outlaw'). By contrast, other emotional connotations with a more positive appeal such as *peaceful, freedom fighter, hero, honest broker, and responsible member of the international community* typically indicate emotional connotations of admiration such as pride, joy, or sympathy. Further, the emotional value expressed in texts can be raised or lowered by linguistic markers of duration and intensity. Speaking of the 'horror of an *endless* conflict' or the '*never-ending* fear of nuclear war', for example, adds a temporal dimension to an emotional connotation like *horror* or an emotion term like *fear*, thereby communicating the enduring presence of an emotional disposition. With regard to intensity, verbal means such as *very, utterly, somewhat, lightly, deeply, heavily, and exceedingly* denote a high or low level of emotional intensity, respectively. Conversely, words may be stripped off their negative emotional connotations by the speaker, for example, by coding them as *ethnic cleansing* instead of *genocide* or *collateral damage* in order to trivialize the killing of innocent civilians. Needless to say, the meanings resulting from emotional connotations are often sociocultural constructs and may thus resonate differently from culture to culture. Conversely, it is equally important to read the silence: which emotional terms and connotations are avoided in which contexts and towards which subjects?

Finally, a typical characteristic of affective language is that it is highly figurative. Bleiker (2009), for example, shows how the metaphor of *balance of power* produces emotional poetic images. Figures of speech, particularly metaphors, comparisons, and analogies, play an important role in encoding emotional expressions. An emotion metaphor is a symbolic speech act, which is supposed to illustrate an emotional state (Kövecses, 2000; Wierzbicka, 1999). Metaphors are usually employed to express emotions that are difficult to articulate. Emotional comparisons and analogies construct comparative categories by either employing historical references that are widely known and shared and thus evoke similar emotional responses ('He is the greatest war criminal since Adolf Hitler') or by conceptualizing emotional expressions through mental imagery. For example, comparisons such as *feel like in heaven, problem from hell, dark abyss*, and *beacon of democracy* conceptualize emotions through the image of light and darkness, which many people associate with moral hope and mortal fear, respectively.

Step Three: Interpreting and Contextualizing the Emotionalization Effects of Texts

This move shifts attention to larger and interdependent textual structures as a motivational resource to show that emotions are not only expressed by a speaker but are simultaneously received through emotional encodings by an audience to produce social effects. As Hansen (2006, p. 30) writes, 'contextualized discourse analysis combines the analysis of how texts seek to create stability with analysis of whether these constructions are being accepted or contested within the political and public domain'. The researcher's task here is to situate emotional expressions within the sociocultural context. This means that the analytical focus moves from tracing the meaning of single or multiple emotion words to interpreting and contextualizing their meaning and effects by looking at how these expressions are directed at and resonate with particular audiences. Since discourse is intersubjective and iterative, part of the way we access its emotionality is by observing the tone and content of its reception in a given context. More importantly, the analysis needs to explicitly state how emotional expressions have implications for social behaviour and social relations. Even though the prevailing assumption among mainstream constructivists in IR is that social norms and ideas are 'a property of intentional actors that generate motivational and behavioural dispositions' (Wendt, 1999, p. 224), it is questionable to claim that ideas and knowledge have a motivational force of their own. Simply knowing about 'self' and 'other' may influence thought processes and mind-sets but it does not necessarily motivate to act in a certain way. It is when one gets angry at the 'Other' that one feels inclined to seek revenge and embark on retaliatory acts. Likewise, if one sympathizes with members of a group, one will likely be more trustful and behave in a conciliatory way towards that group. Cognition that lacks emotional input fails to produce a sense of obligation or loyalty necessary for collective action. Conversely, emotion that lacks cognition has no object, so there is nothing to get angry or sympathetic about. In short, it is the socio-psychological link between these cognitive and emotional categories that constitutes a motivational resource for social mobilization and intersubjectivity.

One way of interpreting emotionalizing effects in discourse is to look for cases of emotional Othering in the social construction of identities. Social identity not only involves cognitive commitments in terms of knowing to belong to a particular group but, crucially, also entails emotional attachments in terms of the connection one feels towards other people, sensitivity to their opinions, feelings, and expectations. As Tajfel (1981, p. 255) underlines, social identity is 'that part of the individual's self concept which derives from his knowledge of his membership of a social group (or groups) together with the value and emotional significance attached to membership'. Analysing the way emotional expressions refer to 'the Other' in discourses is to search for the construction of chains of connotations between words or pairs of concepts and their emotional meaning, which are often reproduced via polarizing speech acts. As Campbell (1992, p. 89) suggests, 'the "barbarian" invoked connotations (…) is energized by moral concerns (…); these moral concerns naturalize the self (…) by estranging the other (…). Each has its own emotional valence (…) the combined valuations of which constitute a position of being occupied by any one of a number of identities'. For example, the social construction of an 'Aryan identity' in Nazi Germany was deeply rooted in the collective establishment and experience of ritualized and institutionalized emotions of pride and confidence in the German *Herrenvolk* (e.g. evident during the infamous Nuremberg rallies) accompanied by the projection of collective feelings of contempt and disgust towards the Jewish Other. It is important to remember, however, that there is rarely a single Self/Other dichotomy but rather different degrees of Otherness in discourse. It is thus necessary to show 'how the Other is situated within a web of identities rather than in a simple Self-Other duality' (Hansen, 2006, p. 36).

Besides Othering, there are many more ways to study the emotionalizing effects of discourse. These include, for example, intertextuality (interconnection and cross-links of emotional meanings between different texts), performativity (deliberate emotional construction of subjects), or interpellation (identification with ideological emotional states). All of this suggests that there exist collective standards about what to feel and how to express emotions in discourse. Hochschild (1979), for example, develops the idea of 'feeling rules' that determines what emotions are considered to be good or bad in a given social group. Reddy (2001) argues that emotional expressions such as emotional talk and gestures are 'performative speech acts' that possess a transformative character in social relationships. A group's ways of feeling are thus shaped by the group's moral order located within dominant cultural frames in two ways. The first is a set of felt attachments that constitutes a particular political community with felt value. The second is a means of reward and discipline by confirming or withholding social belonging to that political community. Both are interrelated: Attachment generates a sense of belonging which, in turn, constructs a certain type of power relationship. These ways of feeling may impact on social performance in terms of identity construction and conformity to group pressure. This takes place through properly performed and standardized verbal and gestural emotional expressions that ultimately draw the community members closer together (Koschut, 2014). From this point of view, values, beliefs, and norms are represented through ritualized symbols and images (such as flags, heroes, shrines, battlefields, or institutions) as well as speech acts that are capable of arousing synchronized emotions in and among individual members. For example, national and transnational 'cultural totems' like the American Stars and Stripes or the Black Banner of Islamic State 'can move people' to affectively identify with a collective entity and reproduce its underlying power relationships and social hierarchies.

Empirical Illustration: NATO's Emotional Construction of Russia as the 'Radical Other'

The methodological framework developed above is empirically illustrated using the conflict between NATO and Russia over the annexation of the Crimean peninsula. The case is chosen to offer an empirical window into the emotional undergirding of inter-group discourse. Its purpose is to give the reader a more detailed empirical account of the emotion potential and emotionalization effects of a particular discourse at the international level. Specifically, I look at how NATO's construction of Russia as the 'radical Other' during the Crimean crisis was significantly underpinned by emotional meanings, resulting in the suspension of most of NATO's cooperation with Russia and a reconstruction of Russian identity from being a partner of the West to becoming a pariah state.

Text Selection

As pointed out above, a fruitful way to study emotion discourse is to initially focus on a small number of texts from dramatic and uprooting points in time, involving charismatic authorities that carry significance for particular audiences. Due to limited space and for illustrative purposes, I put the analytical focus on the study of a single, exemplary text. The text that I have chosen is an official press release by NATO, issued on 1 April 2014.[2] Why did I choose this particular text? The press release includes a statement by the foreign ministers of NATO member states following their meeting in Brussels, the first such meeting after the Russian annexation of the Crimean peninsula. In this statement, NATO member states articulate their position pertaining to the Crimean crisis, which makes the text a formidable source to study how NATO members constructed Russian identity in international politics. Furthermore, the fact that this statement was adopted by all NATO members makes it a representative sample of NATO discourse as opposed to, for example, a statement by a single member state. As I argue, NATO constructed Russia as the 'radical Other' during the Crimean crisis, thus emphasizing social distance, status lowering, and moral deviance vis-à-vis Moscow. This is empirically significant because it differs fundamentally from previous discourse in which NATO depicts its relationship with Russia in much more amicable terms. For example, as the NATO -Russia Founding Act of 1997 states:

> NATO and Russia do not consider each other as adversaries. They share the goal of overcoming the vestiges of earlier confrontation and competition and of strengthening mutual trust and cooperation. (...) They intend to develop, on the basis of common interest, reciprocity and transparency a strong, stable and enduring partnership.[3]

In addition to an analysis of the emotions underpinning this process of constructing Russia as the 'radical Other', I consult additional sources and the political context surrounding the event.

Mapping Emotional Expressions

If emotions underpin the meanings and effects of the NATO discourse, they need to be identified and made accountable for based on empirical research. The study of emotion discourse in IR involves a project that seeks to systematically integrate emotions within discourse analysis. The goal is to identify a way to examine affective connotations and emotion categories that come to the fore in discourses. In this section, this is done by mapping the textual components that create emotional (inter)subjectivity between NATO and Russia. For reasons of analytical clarity and space limitation, I confine the empirical analysis to relatively simple emotion terms and connotations rather than more complex metaphors and comparisons/analogies as well as to the immediate implications of NATO's discourse for its member state leaders rather than its reception among wider audiences.

Below, I highlight the emotional expressions in the text in *italics* and denote their meaning using a short commentary in cling squares, focusing on the parts of the statement that explicitly deals with Russia. One may perhaps find the insertions and interjections in the text as a subjectively informed reading of the text. Yet, the insertions and interjections add considerable strength to the analysis rather than constituting a weakness or lack of rigor. The insertions written in the text have the merits of making the assumed emotional meanings of relevant textual components more explicit and transparent to the reader. Nevertheless, this represents my own subjective reading of the text, and I am certainly not claiming that this analysis constitutes the only way of emotionally reading the text. By making the emotion potential of the text explicit and transparent via text insertion, the reader may either ascribe to my particular reading of the text or reach an alternative conclusion and, in the latter case, may wish to empirically challenge the analysis put forward here.

In early March 2014, tensions increased between NATO and Russia as a result of the Ukrainian crisis and Russia's move to annex of Crimea. The following emergency session of the UN Security Council only served to underline fundamental differences over Ukraine's territorial integrity and sovereignty. On 1 April 2014, NATO foreign ministers gathered for the first time since the Russian occupation of Crimea had touched off one of the worst crisis in NATO -Russian relations after the end of the Cold War. As a result of the meeting, NATO foreign ministers suspended all practical cooperation with Russia, issuing the following statement to justify its reaction:

> We, the Foreign Ministers of NATO, are
> *united* [emotional reference to mutual sympathy/we-feeling]
> in our
> *condemnation* [intensification of the prior 'we-feeling' by contrasting it with a negative emotion encoding of anger and projection of guilt/blame on an outsider]
> of Russia's
> *illegal* [emotional expression of anger for breaking a taboo]
> military intervention in Ukraine and Russia's
> *violation* [emotional reference to a perceived moral breach]
> of Ukraine's sovereignty and territorial integrity. We
> *do not recognize* [withholding respect]
> Russia's
> *illegal and illegitimate* [repeated and extended emotional expression of anger for breaking a taboo]
> attempt to
> *annex* [intensification of the emotional expression of anger by making explicit the perception of unlawfully taking possession of something]
> Crimea. We
> *urge* [emotional expression of hope/desire]
> Russia to take immediate steps, as set out in the statement by the NATO-Ukraine Commission, to return to compliance with international law and its international obligations and responsibilities, and to engage immediately in a
> *genuine* [emotional reference to honesty and truthfulness]

dialogue towards a political and diplomatic solution that
respects [specific categorization of a positive emotion through an emotion term]
international law and Ukraine's internationally recognized borders. We support the deployment of an OSCE monitoring mission to Ukraine.

Our goal of a Euro-Atlantic region
whole, free, and at peace [indirect emotional reference to shared sympathy and pride/joy about NATO's 'way of life']
has not changed, but has been
fundamentally challenged [emotional expression of intense anger/annoyance] by Russia.
(…)
Over the past twenty years, NATO has consistently worked for
closer cooperation [reference to previous sympathy/emotional intimacy]
and
trust [specific categorization of a positive emotion through an emotion term]
with Russia. However, Russia has
violated [emotional expression of disappointment, dishonour, and disrespect: 'They have taken advantage of our trust and sympathy and deceived us']
international law and has acted in contradiction with the principles and commitments in the Euro-Atlantic Partnership Council Basic Document, the NATO-Russia Founding Act, and the Rome Declaration. It has
gravely breached [intense emotional expression of serious betrayal: 'This is a stab in the back!']
the
trust [specific categorization of a positive emotion through an emotion term]
upon which our cooperation must be based.
(…)
As stated by our Heads of State and Government at the Chicago Summit in 2012, NATO is based on
solidarity, Alliance cohesion, and the indivisibility [unity of feeling/'we-feeling' and mutual support/sympathy within a group: 'Nothing stands between us!']
of our security. In the current situation, the Alliance has already taken steps to demonstrate
solidarity [repeated expression of 'we-feeling']

and strengthen its ability to anticipate and respond quickly to any challenges to Alliance security. We will continue to provide appropriate
reinforcement and visible assurance of NATO's cohesion [repeated unity of feeling and mutual caring/sympathy]
and
commitment [expression of an emotional state of being dedicated to a common cause/activity; emotional pledge to honour a joint obligation]
to
deterrence [outward projection of fear in order to discourage outsiders from doing harm]
and collective defence against any
threat of aggression [emotional expression of fear/worry because of a possible danger of inflicting bodily harm, pain and physical suffering]
to the Alliance.

Most conventional discourse analyses would take this affective content for granted without making it explicit. The analytical focus on emotion employed in this case seeks to correct this imbalance and extends discourse analysis by proposing a framework for empirical research on emotion discourse in international politics. The goal is to identify a way to specifically examine emotional expressions that come to the fore in these discourses. The next step is to study their implications.

Interpreting and Contextualizing Emotionalization Effects

Having identified emotional expressions and meanings in the text, the final step is to analytically structure these meanings to gain insights pertaining to their sociopolitical implications. This is based on the assumption that NATO members do not express emotions randomly or spontaneously but as part of a carefully crafted script or narrative that seeks to discursively construct intersubjectivity between NATO and Russia in a particular way. In other words, we need to search for a 'structure of feeling'—a set of emotions that show a regular pattern—built into the text that constrains and compels the affective experience among NATO members on the inside (as the text producer) and Russia on the outside (as the primary audience), thereby constituting a power relationship (Williams, 1961, p. 47). How do emotions underpin and structure this insider/outsider dualism?

The discourse clearly (re)constructs the relationship between NATO and Russia as, once again, rooted in antagonistic identities of the Cold

War by constructing radically different categories of 'Self' and 'Other' and 'us' and 'them'. This represents a sharp discursive shift from previous NATO statements, such as one from March 2012: 'NATO and Russia are not adversaries or enemies. We are committed to being strategic partners and we are working on it together'.[4] A mere two years later, NATO's identity is constructed as the in-group, based on shared values (liberalism, democracy) in a peaceful transatlantic space. Russia, by contrast, is constructed as the out-group, challenging and violating the values of the in-group through its actions in the Ukraine and, as a consequence, threatening the peaceful order and 'way of life' of the transatlantic area. These antagonistic identities establish an insider/outsider dualism that draws a psychological line between NATO and Russia. The identity politics behind this construction of antagonistic intersubjectivity is reinforced by NATO's Secretary General Anders Fogh Rasmussen, who sets the tone in his remarks to NATO's foreign ministers, shortly before their meeting on 1 April: 'NATO's open door policy (…) erase(d) many of the painful dividing lines on our continent. (…) The crisis in Ukraine risks creating new dividing lines'.[5] This is what a conventional discourse analysis might come up with.

However, such a conventional discourse analysis, while compelling, arguably draws only a partial picture of the identity politics at play here. The antagonistic identities linked to the insider-outsider dualism between NATO and Russia are not only discursively constructed through cognitive knowledge about 'us' and 'them' but are simultaneously underpinned by corresponding emotions of sympathy for 'us' and anger towards 'them'.

In the case of NATO and Russia, the sympathy/anger dualism arguably constitutes the discursive structure of feeling that facilitates group cohesion among NATO member state leaders on the inside as well as social distance vis-à-vis Russia on the outside through emotional Othering. This can be empirically traced, for example, in the statement by NATO foreign ministers on Russia when they stand 'united in our condemnation of Russia's illegal military intervention in Ukraine and Russia's violation of Ukraine's sovereignty and territorial integrity'. Here, an implicit emotional reference to mutual sympathy between NATO members ('united') is contrasted to the divisive acts by Russia that are accompanied by emotional expressions of anger ('condemnation', 'illegal', and 'violation'). Another example is the juxtaposition between, on the one hand, the transatlantic area that aims to be 'whole, free, and at peace' which again implies unity, belonging, and mutual sympathy among NATO members and, on the other hand, emotional expressions of anger at Russia for 'fundamentally challenging' this goal. One can find similar sympathy/anger dualisms in several other places in the text. Emotion words and terms that denote sympathy, such as 'closer cooperation', 'trust', 'solidarity', 'Alliance cohesion', 'indivisibility', or 'assurance', and emotion words that imply anger, such as 'condemnation', 'violation', 'illegal and illegitimate', 'gravely breached', or 'threat of aggression', are placed in stark contrast to each other and thus underpin an emotionally attuned cognitive separation between the 'in-group' and the 'out-group', and 'us' and 'them'. Importantly, this has behavioural implications and motivates collective action, as NATO enhanced its air policing in the Baltic States, deployed AWACS aircraft to improve surveillance of Poland and Romania, and increased its naval presence in the Black Sea following the meeting.

This, of course, is not to say that anger and sympathy are the only emotions present in the NATO discourse. Anger and sympathy are viewed here as 'master emotions' in this particular discourse because they structure the social meanings and effects of the discourse and thus set the collective standard of emotional expression in this particular case. Other emotional expressions can be measured against this standard: Further emotional expressions either relate to (and thus reinforce) the insider/outsider dualism underpinned by sympathy/anger or seek to moderate it (and thus leave a potential back door open should Russia wish to seek reconciliation with NATO). Concerning the first category, member states express emotions that relate to anger. For example, speaking of Russian actions as a 'threat of aggression' implies fear that harm or pain may be inflicted upon NATO. A similar expression can be found in the remarks by Anders Fogh Rasmussen quoted above when he mentions the 'painful dividing lines' that may return in Europe due to Russian behaviour. How are pain, harm, and fear related to anger? Anger is often a response to pain. Anger often occurs when people do not feel well, feel threatened, or experience loss. Fear can also be a driver of anger, particularly whenever fear is related to the feelings of a group: The fear that my group gets treated badly makes me angry, and so anger is there to protect me from my fears (Linklater, 2011). Regarding the second category, NATO discourse employs alternative emotional expressions such as hope and desire that appear to express NATO's plea for reconciliation. For example, when NATO foreign ministers 'urge Russia to take immediate steps (...) to return to compliance', 'engage in a genuine dialogue', and 'respect international law', they are effectively building an emotional bridge to smooth the way for Russia for future cooperation. A similar speech act of bridge building through hope and desire can also be found in the inaugural remarks by NATO's secretary general minutes before of the foreign ministers meeting: 'We continue to urge Russia to pull back its troops; live up to its international obligations and engage in a constructive dialogue with Ukraine'.[6]

To sum up, the discourse constructs the relationship between NATO and Russia as rooted in antagonistic identities by constructing cognitive categories of 'Self' and 'Other' and 'us' and 'them'. These antagonistic cognitive identities are simultaneously underpinned by corresponding emotional expressions of 'sympathy' and 'anger' that motivate certain types of behaviour (solidarity with the in-group/hostility towards the out-group), thereby establishing and reproducing an insider/outsider dualism. This dualism, however, is not total. There are also mixed signs that display an emotional desire for reconciliation.

Conclusion

This chapter concludes by reflecting on some of the gains and limits of integrating emotions within discourse analysis, specifically speaking to the significance, originality, and limitations of the use of EDA as a method of data collection. In addition to outlining the specific value of the analysis for our understanding of identity and power relations, I identify three sets of concerns that researchers need to address when employing discourse analysis to trace emotions and that speak to some of the methodological challenges outlined in the introduction to this volume. The chapter concludes by tentatively exploring possible synergies and cross-links with other methodological approaches such as process tracing and narrative analysis.

The idea of using EDA to construct the emotional representation of social reality adds to our understanding of discourses in IR because it allows researchers to examine questions that are not amendable in conventional discourse analysis. It underlines the need to adapt traditional methods in IR to make them more sensitive to emotions. Emotions are no more private than language and their expression, and effects within political spheres add explanatory value to the construction of cognitive meanings and identities. Moreover, EDA develops insights into the social nature of feelings that are not easily accessible by traditional interpretive methods and aims to trace the powerful effects of emotional expressions in discourse and how this might change over time. As with any method, there are certain limitations attached to using EDA as a data collection tool. While these limitations do not negate the usefulness of EDA, they need to be acknowledged in order for future researchers to identify strategies that can potentially ameliorate these difficulties.

One difficulty concerns the wide range of phenomena that potentially fall into the category of emotions, such as short-term bodily reactions, undifferentiated moods and sensations, affects, feeling states, or relatively stable emotional dispositions. This relates to the problem of temporality flagged by the editors. How can we differentiate analytically between these different phenomena simply by studying texts? The short and unsatisfactory answer is we cannot (at least not by looking at a small selection of texts). The best we can do is to search for possible indicators that may be able to approximate the type of affective phenomena in texts and discourses and triangulate between different sources, for example, by conducting interviews with relevant decision makers or by watching video footage (if available) to trace the tone and facial expression of speaker and audience over time.

A second concern relates to the difficulty of analytically separating the individual level from the collective level of emotional expression. For example, when NATO's Secretary General speaks about 'painful dividing lines', is he referring to his own subjective feeling of bodily pain or to the collective feeling of pain experienced by NATO as a body politic? From a social constructivist perspective, the straightforward answer would be that culturally influenced patterns of emotions impact deep inside people as they are socialized into communities. Hence, the link between emotion and language is necessarily a social one. Neither emotion researchers nor observers use 'emotional x-ray machines' (Wilce, 2009, p. 25). EDA claims no access to the inner emotional world of human beings but targets their intersubjective expression and collective representation within social spheres. While this may come at the risk of homogenizing the emotions of groups, it nevertheless offers generalizable patterns that allow researchers to study intergroup dynamics in world politics.

Finally, the goal of identifying generalizable patterns of emotion discourse necessitates the construction of ideal-type emotional categories for analytical purposes. This does not negate the fact that emotions constitute a mixed, and oftentimes messy, object of inquiry. While emotions are indeed fluid and shifting, EDA argues that they also display a high degree of attachment and entanglement resulting in relatively stable patterns of emotional meanings and webs of interconnections. Emotional meanings overlap with, mutually influence, and conflict with other emotional meanings. Importantly, emotions can also change and vary significantly in their historical meaning and sociocultural expression. In my view, the crucial factor is to determine the dominant emotion meanings by which hierarchies and identities are underpinned relative to other, less prevalent emotion meanings. In short, emotions have a powerful effect on the constitution of social reality by framing what is possible and what is not.

While EDA adds considerable strength to traditional discursive methods, it also allows for possible synergies and cross-links with other methodological approaches such as process tracing and narrative analysis. Since narrative analysis equally emphasizes the historical, cultural, and social contextualization of language, the way emotions impact on, enrich, and enable certain narratives to 'stick' with audiences as well as how emotions become the subject of storytelling can be easily combined with EDA (Kleres, 2010). For example, in the case above, NATO discourse was arguably embedded in a larger narrative of separation and difference rooted in historical conceptions of Russia as the 'semibarbarian state' that, despite its material power and social adaptations, could not be fully ascribed 'great power status' by the established European great powers (Neumann, 2014, p. 102). Furthermore, EDA may also be combined with process tracing, particularly if the aim of the researcher is to trace the effects of emotion words on socialization and learning processes of certain actors over time. In the end, EDA provides an original and innovative methodological framework to analyse the significance and implications of emotions in world politics.

Acknowledgements Research for this chapter has been generously funded by the German Research Council (DFG) as part of the research project *Constructivist Emotion Research (Grant number: KO-4078/3-1)*.

Notes

1. I owe this point to Todd Hall.
2. Statement by NATO foreign ministers on Russia, Press Release (2014) 062, 1 April 2014, http://www.nato.int/cps/en/natohq/news_108501.htm.
3. Founding Act on Mutual Relations, Cooperation and Security between NATO and the Russian Federation, 27 May 1997, http://www.nato.int/cps/en/natohq/official_texts_25468.htm.

4. Remarks by NATO Secretary General Anders Fogh Rasmussen at a press conference with Moscow-based journalists, 26 March 2012, http://www.nato.int/cps/en/natohq/opinions_85625.htm?selectedLocale=en.
5. Remarks by NATO Secretary General Anders Fogh Rasmussen at the ceremony to mark the NATO enlargement anniversaries, 1 April 2014, http://www.nato.int/cps/en/natolive/opinions_108509.htm.
6. Doorstep statement by NATO Secretary General Anders Fogh Rasmussen at the start of the NATO foreign ministers meeting, 1 April 2014, http://www.nato.int/cps/en/natolive/opinions_108502.htm.

References

Abu-Lughod, L., & Lutz, C. A. (1990). Introduction. In C. A. Lutz & L. Abu-Lughod (Eds.), *Language and the Politics of Emotions* (pp. 1–23). Cambridge: Cambridge University Press.

Ahäll, L., & Gregory, T. (Eds.). (2015). *Emotion, Politics, and War*. New York: Routledge.

Averill, J. R. (1980). A Constructivist View of Emotion. In R. Plutchik & H. Kellerman (Eds.), *Emotion: Theory, Research and Experience: Vol. I. Theories of Emotion* (pp. 305–339). New York: Academic Press.

Bially Mattern, J. (2011). A Practice Theory of Emotion for International Relations. In E. Adler & V. Pouliot (Eds.), *International Practices* (pp. 63–86). Cambridge: Cambridge University Press.

Bleiker, R. (2009). *Aesthetics and World Politics*. New York: Palgrave Macmillan.

Bleiker, R., & Hutchison, E. (2008). Fear No More. Emotions and World Politics. *Review of International Studies, 34*, 115–135.

Bleiker, R., & Hutchison, E. (2014). Theorizing Emotions in World Politics. *International Theory, 6*(3), 491–514.

Campbell, D. (1992). *Writing Security*. Minneapolis: University of Minnesota Press.

Chilton, P. (1996). *Security Metaphors: Cold War Discourse from Containment to Common House*. New York: Peter Lang.

Connolly, W. E. (1983). *The Terms of Politial Discourse*. Princeton: Princeton University Press.

Crawford, N. C. (2000). The Passion of World Politics. Propositions on Emotion and Emotional Relationships. *International Security, 24*(4), 116–156.

Der Derian, J., & Shapiro, M. J. (1989). *International/Intertextual Relations: Postmodern Readings of World Politics*. Lexington, MA: Lexington.

Derrida, J. (1978). *Writing and Difference*. Chicago: Chicago University Press.

Diez, T. (2001). Europe as a Discursive Battleground. Discourse Analysis and European Integration Studies. *Cooperation and Conflict, 36*(1), 5–38.

Edkins, J. (2003). *Trauma and the Memory of Politics*. Cambridge: Cambridge University Press.
Edwards, D. (1997). *Discourse and Cognition*. London: Sage.
Epstein, C. (2008). *The Power of Words in International Relations: Birth of an Anti-whaling Discourse*. Cambridge, MA: MIT Press.
Fattah, K., & Fierke, K. M. (2009). A Clash of Emotions: The Politics of Humiliation and Political Violence in the Middle East. *European Journal of International Relations, 15*(1), 67–93.
Fierke, K. M. (2013). *Political Self Sacrifice. Agency, Body and Emotion in International Relations*. Cambridge: Cambridge University Press.
Hall, T. H. (2015). *Emotional Diplomacy*. Ithaca: Cornell University Press.
Hansen, L. (2006). *Security as Practice: Discourse Analysis and the Bosnian War*. London: Routledge.
Hansen, L. (2011). Theorizing the Image for Security Studies: Visual Securitization and the Muhammad Cartoon Crisis. *European Journal of International Relations, 17*(1), 51–74.
Harré, R. (1986). An Outline of the Social Constructionist Viewpoint. In R. Harré (Ed.), *The Social Construction of Emotions* (pp. 2–14). Oxford: Blackwell.
Hochschild, A. R. (1979). Emotion Work, Feeling Rules and Social Structure. *American Journal of Sociology, 85*, 551–575.
Hutchison, E. (2016). *Affective Communities in World Politics*. Cambridge: Cambridge University Press.
Kleres, J. (2010). Emotions and Narrative Analysis: A Methodological Approach. *Journal for the Theory of Social Behaviour, 41*(2), 182–202.
Koschut, S. (2014). Emotional (Security) Communities: The Significance of Emotion Norms in Inter-allied Conflict Management. *Review of International Studies, 40*(3), 533–558.
Koschut, S. (2016). The Structure of Feeling: Emotion Culture and National Self-Sacrifice. *Millennium – Journal of International Studies, 45*(2), 174–192.
Koschut, S. (2017). The Power of (Emotion) Words: On the Importance of Emotions for Social Constructivist Discourse Analysis in IR. *Journal of International Relations and Development* (Online first).
Kövecses, Z. (2000). *Metaphor and Emotion*. Cambridge: Cambridge University Press.
Kristeva, J. (1980). *Desire in Language: A Semiotic Approach to Literature and Art*. New York: Columbia University Press.
Laclau, E., & Mouffe, C. (1985). *Hegemony and Socialist Strategy*. London: Verso.
Leep, M. C. (2010). The Affective Production of Others. United States Policy Towards the Israeli-Palestinian Conflict. *Cooperation and Conflict, 45*(3), 331–352.
Linklater, A. (2011). *The Problem of Harm in World Politics*. Cambridge: Cambridge University Press.

Milliken, J. (1999). The Study of Discourse in International Relations. *European Journal of International Relations, 5*(2), 225–254.

Neumann, I. B. (2014). Status Is Cultural Durkheimian Poles and Weberian Russians Seek Great-Power Status. In D. W. Larson, T. V. Paul, & W. C. Wohlforth (Eds.), *Status in World Politics*. Cambridge: Cambridge University Press.

Nussbaum, M. (2003). *Upheavals of Thought. The Intelligence of Emotions*. Cambridge: Cambridge University Press.

Posner, R. A. (1999). Emotion Versus Emotionalism in Law. In S. A. Bandes (Ed.), *The Passions of Law* (pp. 309–329). New York: New York University Press.

Reddy, W. M. (2001). *The Navigation of Feeling: A Framework for the History of Emotions*. Cambridge: Cambridge University Press.

Ross, A. (2006). Coming in from the Cold. Constructivism and Emotions. *European Journal of International Relations, 12*(2), 197–222.

Ross, A. (2014). *Mixed Emotions. Beyond Fear and Hatred in International Conflict*. Chicago, IL: Chicago University Press.

Schwarz-Friesel, M. (2013). *Sprache und Emotion*. Tübingen and Basel: UTB.

Solomon, T. (2015). *The Politics of Subjectivity in American Foreign Policy Discourses*. Ann Arbor, MI: University of Michigan Press.

Straehle, C., Weiss, G., Wodak, R., Muntigl, P., & Sedlak, M. (1999). Struggle as Metaphor in European Union Discourses on Unemployment. *Discourse & Society, 10*(1), 67–99.

Tajfel, H. (1981). *Human Groups and Social Categories*. Cambridge: Cambridge University Press.

Van Rythoven, E. (2015). Learning to Feel, Learning to Fear? Emotions, Imaginaries, and Limits in the Politics of Securitization. *Security Dialogue, 46*(5), 458–475.

Weldes, J., & Saco, D. (1996). Making State Action Possible: The United States and the Discursive Construction of "The Cuban Problem", 1960–1994. *Millennium, 25*(2), 361–398.

Wendt, A. (1999). *Social Theory of International Politics*. Cambridge: Cambridge University Press.

Wierzbicka, A. (1999). *Emotions Across Languages and Cultures*. Cambridge: Cambridge University Press.

Wilce, J. M. (2009). *Language and Emotion*. Cambridge: Cambridge University Press.

Wilcox, L. B. (2015). *Bodies of Violence*. Oxford: Oxford University Press.

Williams, R. (1961). *The Long Revolution*. Westport: Greenwood.

Zehfuss, M. (2002). *Constructivism in International Relations: The Politics of Reality*. Cambridge: Cambridge University Press.

Simon Koschut is Visiting Professor in International Relations and European Integration at the Otto Suhr Institute at the Free University Berlin. Previously, he was a Fritz Thyssen Fellow at the Weatherhead Center for International Affairs at Harvard University and Assistant Professor at the University of Erlangen-Nürnberg. He has published in numerous peer-reviewed journals, including *Review of International Studies*, *Millennium*, *Journal of International Relations and Development*, *Cambridge Review of International Affairs*, and *Cooperation and Conflict*. He is the author of *Friendship and International Relations* (with Andrea Oelsner, 2014) and *Normative Change and Security Community Disintegration: Undoing Peace* (2016). He leads a research consortium on *Constructivist Emotion Research* that deals with the power of emotion discourse in international politics.

CHAPTER 13

Grasping the Role of Emotions in IR via Qualitative Content Analysis and Visual Analysis

Sybille Reinke de Buitrago

INTRODUCTION

The chapter inquires into the role of emotions in discursive constructions of self and other in International Relations (IR). It analyses how Iran is constructed in US security policy discourse vis-à-vis the US self, by conducting a qualitative content analysis of US policy and strategy documents, complemented by a visual analysis of cartoons in US media that picture Iran, the Iranian leadership and US-Iranian relations. A particular focus lies on the developments leading up to and following right after the 2015 nuclear agreement with Iran.[1] Doing so, the chapter considers the role of US national identity in constructions of Iran and the link between national identity and emotions, that is, in which instances there is an emotional footprint in or emotional framing of articulations—be it text or visuals—regarding the self's national identity and regarding the self versus the

---

S.R. de Buitrago (✉)
Institute for Peace Research and Security Policy, University of Hamburg, Hamburg, Germany

Institute for Peace and Theology, Hamburg, Germany

© The Author(s) 2018
M. Clément, E. Sangar (eds.), *Researching Emotions in International Relations*, Palgrave Studies in International Relations, https://doi.org/10.1007/978-3-319-65575-8_13

other. National identity may be seen as describing a given political community with institutions, rights and duties in a historic and defined territory, with shared myths and memories, and a given way to comprehend and define the self (Smith, 1991, p. 9 ff.). A national identity is differentiated from something other in order to exist. It requires the production of difference, which may also include the creation of otherness (Holland, 2014, p. 203). National identity, and the understanding of how the self differs to and relates with others—how self and other are constructed, is also formed in narratives on and experiences with the other (see also Neumann, 1999). Likewise, political behaviour towards the other is shaped by self-other constructions and the particular emotional content. Paying attention to the emotional factor and to specific emotions can tell us much about how US discourse constructs Iran, the underlying motivations and the plausible effects on relations. The chapter thus hopes to contribute specific insights to the debate on the role of emotions in IR, in particular on the identity-emotion nexus, how to methodologically grasp emotions in discourse, and how methods can be fruitfully combined.

The combination of the two selected methods gives the researcher not only multiple tools and perspectives with which to inquire into the topic. Together, the qualitative content analysis and the visual analysis filter out from policy and strategy documents specific articulations on how US discourse constructs self and other and which emotional framing is present. As cartoons are more pointed in what they represent and how, the emotional appeal can be grasped. With cartoons illustrating societal thinking and decision-makers being part of society, there exists a link between decision-maker representations and cartoons' meaning. The triangulation can also strengthen the validity of results. The chapter proceeds as follows: it elaborates the theoretical and methodological approach; illustrates the results of the empirical application; and offers implications regarding the changes in US discourse, the continuing mistrust, and efforts to re-build relations, as well as regarding methodology and further research needs.

Theoretical and Methodological Approach

The Issue of Subjectivity in Designing Research on Emotions

Underlying the applied theoretical and methodological approach are particular epistemological and methodological considerations, such as that knowledge about social phenomena, and about emotions, cannot be directly accessed. The premise is that we see and understand the social world with our particular views of self and other, which are formed in experiences with the other(s) and through our culturally shaped filters (see, e.g. Harré & Sammut, 2013, pp. 26–28; May, 2013, pp. 72–73). These views include biases and subjectivities. Also researchers are subjective, as pointed out (see, e.g. Ulbert, 2005, pp. 24, 27), in terms of following a particular research interest, making certain interpretations, and applying their cultural lens. The approach to gaining knowledge should then also include the reflection by the researcher about approaching a given topic. This, we may argue, also encompasses a critical angle where gained insights can serve as partial basis for critiquing existing knowledge, power structures and resulting policy. To deal with researcher subjectivity, methodological tools are useful. When working with a qualitative content analysis, the researcher has at the disposal a systematic, theory-led method, and can further document the research process, and triangulate (see also Mayring, 2003, pp. 42–44; Ulbert, 2005, p. 27). A visual analysis is likely more subjective, that is, the researcher may easily also react emotionally to images viewed. In fact, scholars (Holland, 2007, pp. 196, 201, 207–208) see researchers as not detached and thus emotionally affected in their work, but argue that emotions actually add to the understanding of what is researched. This author agrees that subjectivity cannot be completely avoided and proposes to reduce it by approaching the research interest of emotional framings with the help of a systematically built and theory-led category construct (for more on studying emotions via textual and visual analysis, see further below).

Emotions

Emotions are seen here ontologically as integral part of human thinking, perception/interpretation and behaviour, meaning that emotions are closely linked with identity formation and expression, social processes, (political) decision-making and the shaping of self-other relations. Since the emotional turn in IR, scholars (e.g. Bleiker & Hutchison, 2008; Crawford, 2000; Wolf, 2011, 2012) have highlighted emotions as considerable factor impacting political behaviour and international interaction. Holland (2007) sees emotions as essential in knowledge production, too. How to soundly grasp emotions conceptually and methodologically is still evolving though. For example, as Hutchison and Bleiker (2014, p. 491 ff.) state, how emotions gain political relevance and impact should be a focus in research. They recommend to apply a macro-micro angle, focusing both on the impact of emotions vis-à-vis identity, understanding and behaviour, and on the process of particular emotions becoming socially and politically relevant.

Through emotions we define ourselves in light of collective identities, make decisions based on norms and morals, and even act as states towards other states (Fierke, 2012, p. 93; Haidt, 2013). The sharing of emotions within a group shapes the views of self and other, a dynamic that allows the in-group to differentiate itself from out-groups (Sasley, 2011, p. 457) and, thus, to construct the self vis-à-vis others with a particular national identity. Also, interstate relations are shaped by emotions. Scholars have shown that a given state tends to be seen as the source of the felt emotions towards that state (Ahmed, 2004, p. 11; Leep, 2010, pp. 332–335). Furthermore, at the state level there can be an amplification of emotions, making emotional reactions towards another state more intense (Wolf, 2011, p. 118). This seems to apply particularly to (views of) enmity, as is illustrated in the case study. Thus, the focus on self-other constructions provides a unique perspective for examining how interstate relations are defined and shaped in light of the understanding of the self, (particular) others, certain issues and developments, and seen-as-appropriate policy needs. Constructing self and other can also involve processes of othering, where another state becomes the key or even radical other, which shapes self-other relations in a typically negative manner (Neumann, 1999).

Another important aspect that deserves mention is emotionalisation. When the understanding of a particular context or situation is emotionalised, its emotional content and intensity are increased; we may see emotionalisation as both adding an emotional framing or strengthening an existing one and as intensifying present emotions. Especially conflicts allow for emotionalisation, in that they provide fertile ground and give room for emotionalising the contested issue(s) as well as self and other. Simplifications or simplified portrayals of the situation by those involved or having interests in it are often found. Political actors may also have stakes in such simplifications and apply these to benefit their political agendas. Emotionalising the situation and the involved issues and actors adds weight to the claims made. For example, the highlighting of threats and dangers regarding another state or a change in relations with that state may evoke certain reactions, including those that are desired by the claimant. At the same time, emotionalisation has its costs. In the articulation of threats and dangers, scholars (Agnew & Muscarà, 2012; Holland, 2014;

Neumann, 1999) highlight the discursively created boundaries between self and other in processes of othering and their long-lasting effects on perception and interpretation, as well as on behaviour and relations. While there is little research on the particular link between emotions and othering (see for example Hansen, 2006; Holland, 2014; Neumann, 1999), considering emotions in IR adds a perspective to understand how self and other relate, and how political developments and applied policy impact relations.

Uncovering Meaning and Emotions

To assess meaning regarding self and other, and the emotional content, we may consider the meaning expressed in text and images. Useful textual sources are policy and strategy documents. These offer insights on the strategic orientations and objectives of a country, thereby expressing views on the own role in global affairs vis-à-vis another state, and visions to shape interstate relations and the international system. Views of various other states include different ascriptions to and constructions of these others. National security policy documents, for example published by IPU/DCAF (2005, p. 33), illustrate the particular approach of a government to provide security, the specific understanding of security, perceived threats and dangers to the self, as well as security interests and preferred and pursued policy means. Such documents thereby express relations of the self to various others as well as the varying intensities of threat to the self, making them fruitful for uncovering meaning and emotions in discursive self-other constructions.

Also, images express meaning. The visual turn in IR and the research on visuality (see, e.g. Bleiker, 2009; Hansen, 2015) focus on visuals' impact on people and their actions via motivating certain emotions in certain portrayals and representations. Images are a useful source for the researcher on emotion due to their illustration of the condensed essence of a particular view of a topic and its emotional frame; studying images complements this easy-to-grasp essence to results of lengthy text analysis. Images tend to be remembered better or quicker than pure text. Cartoons, as one type of visual and typically composed of one image or a series of images, are also a focus in IR scholarship (see, e.g. Dodds, 2010; Manzo, 2012). Images/visuals can inform about existing representations of self and other in IR, and about a particular geopolitical outlook (MacDonald, Dodds, & Hughes, 2010).[2] Regarding political issues represented in visuals, Baudrilliard sees the border between reality and illusion blurring in today's media age and argues that representation in media is required to make political events real (2002, p. 30). This becomes visible in political struggles and contestation being couched in and referring to cultural myths and narratives that give statements shared meaning (Bronfen, 2006, p. 23).

Cartoons, and other popular culture media, express widely shared geopolitical representations, and political leaders utilise such references to connect with an audience. The creators of cartoons also highlight or build relations between viewers and situations. Effective cartoons provoke the viewer, but since they are culture-specific they can suggest different interpretations (Dodds, 2010, pp. 114–119; Hughes, 2007, p. 987). Cartoons resonate with the viewers' feelings regarding a particular issue and/or actor entity; the contextual knowledge required to understand a cartoon is typically provided by mainstream sources such as public media. That cartoons are taken serious by those who are being portrayed and/or criticised is illustrated by events following the publication of Mohammad cartoons in the Danish *Jyllands-Posten*, or by images shown by the French *Charlie Hebdo*. Cartoons, therefore, have an implicit, at times explicit, political dimension. Even though it is not decision-makers of a country that issue cartoons, but journalists and caricaturists, they all come from the same society and thus at least partly share a cultural, social and political outlook regarding self and other. Cartoons can express critical views of self and other, and of their relation. Cartoons allow one to pinpoint issues in an ironical or mocking manner, they may contest certain other portrayals and their inherent understandings, and they evoke emotions. Dodds (2010, p. 114), for example, argues that visuals can illustrate conceptions of regions such as the Middle East as dangerous, in turn suggesting apparent dangers or threats to the US or Americans. Hansen (2011, p. 53 f.) thus calls for considering such images and any linked text, along with policy discourse the image might refer to.

The chapter conducts a qualitative content analysis of key US policy and strategy documents and of statements by US decision-makers regarding Iran and the Iranian leadership, especially those relating to the Iranian nuclear program. Additionally, the visual analysis considers cartoons in US media picturing Iran, the Iranian leadership and US-Iranian relations. Cartoons were selected based on the media's circulation being significant, such as national circulation for newspapers, and of thematic relevance; an Internet search was conducted to identify newspapers with national circulation and other media sources with relevant cartoons (using the keywords: cartoons, images, US, Iran, Iranian regime, Iranian nuclear agreement/deal). We may assume that cartoons in media with national circulation have a large reception. Cartoons provide insights on the popular sharing of representations in official documents.

The benefits of mixing qualitative content analysis with a visual analysis reside in the combination of perspectives on different content type and depth, and different emotional appeal. The visual analysis is considered complementary due to a smaller sample of cartoons and the stated greater subjectivity involved in interpreting them. The more detailed statements in policy and strategy documents can be fruitfully compared with and complemented by cartoons' content and expressed meaning. Since cartoons tend to offer more pointed representations and are not smoothed out, they appeal more directly to emotions. They are meant to evoke emotions, and they can be highly charged with emotions. The additional consideration of cartoons thus adds value when aiming to understand and research the role of emotions in IR. As cartoons arguably express a part of societal thinking, of which national decision-makers are a part, we may assume some link between representations by decision-makers and what is expressed in cartoons. The limits and caveats of mixing these methods come from their different nature regarding source, author, scope, and context of creation. Their difference as to depth and explanatory potential, including with regards to cartoons needing more interpretation influenced by the viewer's subjectivity, can be a limit. There may also be distinct underlying assumptions. The analysis will show if this actually presents a problem that cannot be overcome. It seems that the benefits of such an approach outweigh the potential weaknesses. Mixing different methods brings value due to triangulation being generally beneficial for adding validity and depth to understanding. Flick (2003, p. 311 ff.), for example, argues for triangulation increasing validity, objectivity and knowledge.

Qualitative Content Analysis

By using qualitative content analysis, this contribution analyses communication content, the given social and political context and the particular perspectives of actors as speakers, in a replicable manner (see also Bortz &

Döring, 2005, p. 329). Qualitative content analysis is an empirical, systematic and theory-led method that examines recorded and fixed symbolic material to study a particular society's communication. As a method of inference, it allows conclusions about aspects such as the speakers' understanding and motivations regarding a topic (Behnke, Baur, & Behnke, 2006, p. 339; Mayring, 2003, p. 12). It thereby enables the researcher to grasp the emotional content and framing in representations of a particular other, namely Iran and the Iranian leadership.

Following a specific research interest and drawing on Mayring's summarising technique of qualitative content analysis (2003), the author reduced text in policy and strategy documents via abstraction to a manageable amount that mirrored the original. In order to abstract text passages in a systematic manner, deductive categories were developed based on the research interest of how Iran is represented in US discourse, and on surveyed literature. The research interest in how Iran is in security matters portrayed as friend, rival or threat; the relevance to the self-understanding; made arguments; and the emotional framing were used to formulate the following deductive categories:

- US constructions of the self, and national identity
- US constructions of Iran
- US articulations regarding self and other in relation
- articulated threats and challenges to US national security
- articulated threats and challenges to US national security interests abroad
- articulated security needs
- articulated emotions and emotional representations of Iran, the Iranian leadership and US-Iranian relations

The author coded the text material qualitatively; coding units were parts of sentence, so that content could be sufficiently grasped. Since the deductive categories proved fairly comprehensive, no additional (inductive) categories were formulated.[3] Filtering and categorising text via categories enabled the author to abstract text, reduce text material, crystallise relevant information, and make structural connections and systematic comparisons as basis for interpretation. Documents analysed include policy and strategy documents, presidential remarks and speeches, speeches by other administration officials, senator and representative statements, as well as think tank papers. The author selected documents based on a systematic search on administration, ministerial, congressional and think tank websites (with the keywords: Iran, Iranian regime, Iranian nuclear agreement/deal, US -Iranian relations). Documents had to be longer than a few sentences and thus exclude short press statements; researchers are called upon to decide at what length and substance a document is included in an analysis. Results of the qualitative content analysis were grouped after all material was coded.

As a general pattern in discourse, the author observed a debate on how threatening Iran actually was; this debate cut across the political spectrum in the US, although the threat was 'painted' as more severe on the Republican side. Another pattern relates to views before and after the nuclear agreement on July 14, 2015: documents from before clearly construct Iran as threatening, documents afterwards express a somewhat weakened threat. In addition, documents of the executive under Obama showed a general softening in language towards Iran. Almost all documents express US fears of a nuclear-armed and irrational Iran. Other topics in documents were the usefulness of sanctions, Iranian sponsorship of terrorism and the issue of trust/mistrust.

Visual Analysis

As stated farther above, the author conducted an Internet search for relevant cartoons with the following keywords: cartoons, images, US, USA, Iran, Iranian regime, Iranian nuclear agreement/deal. In total, 12 cartoons were pre-selected based on clarity of what is presented and ease of understanding (it is admitted that another researcher may have selected some other cartoons, depending on knowledge of and own ideas regarding the topic, but it is also supposed that the content portrayed would be similar). Five particularly telling cartoons are discussed in detail further below. Cartoons were analytically approached for their degree and elements of condensation (reducing complexity), repetition (increasing effectiveness), dramatisation (provoking), exaggeration (changing understanding of something) and caricature of leading personalities, as well as for the policy needs expressed (see also Dodds, 2010, p. 118; 2007). The expressions about self and other, intentions and motivations for action, character ascriptions and the emotional amplification were considered, such as in cartoons depicting national decision-makers (see also Hughes, 2007, pp. 976–978, 989).

As cartoons often are coloured, considering the colouring gives us another tool to assess cartoons and their emotional content; colours may be seen as additional, important dimension of visual meaning. As Andersen, Vuori and Guillaume (2015, pp. 441–442) state, colours have a performative function via the significations and associations we give them, acting as shorthand when we (want to) communicate. Emotional content is further expressed in discourse regarding the behaviour of the other and (assumed/interpreted) motivations for specific behaviour, as well as in character ascriptions made to the other. Attending to self-descriptions also adds insights on the particular aspects involved in US self-other constructions vis-à-vis Iran.

Based on the above stated elements and functions of cartoons, especially by Dodds (2010, 2007) and Hughes (2007), and the research interest here, the visual analysis proceeded with defining categories to grasp visual content, its meaning and the emotional framing regarding the US self and Iranian other. The approach combines deductive and inductive categories to grasp both the more explicit portrayals and the implicit framing, for example via colour use (researchers will need to adjust their design according to their research interest). The categories are:

- description of what is shown, theme
- portrayals of political leaders of the US and Iran
- portrayals of US-Iranian relations, and of similarities and contrasts
- portrayals of threats/dangers
- portrayals of needed policy by the US
- repetitions (among cartoons)
- aspects of dramatisation/exaggeration
- emotions expressed
- emotions evoked by researcher (affect felt)
- stylistic means, including colour use

Attention was also paid to expressions of similarities/equations and oppositions/dichotomies regarding self and other. In particular, those cartoons that were created right around the Iranian nuclear agreement were analyzed in depth; those published in the 2000s were considered for context. Cartoons were then viewed/coded using the defined categories; for each cartoon, ideas/interpretations were retrieved per category, as well as additional thoughts. During the analysis, a number of themes fitting with the above-mentioned aspects and categories came to the fore, in particular the reduced complexity, repetition of certain meanings (such as deception by Iran, or naivety of the US), dramatisation/exaggeration of some items by oversizing certain elements (such as Iranian nuclear means of power), and the caricature of leaders (such as Obama). Results of the visual analysis support the pattern of US mistrust of Iran, and added the view of a naive, weaker US and Iran posing as powerful, challenging state; regarding the latter, cartoonists apparently aimed to ridicule the US seemingly budging to Iran's tough stance and trusting Iranian regime on its words, despite its breaking of committments in the past. Cartoons thus illustrate a perception of US-Iranian dichotomy in aims and power. The use of red colour helped to dramatise certain elements in cartoons, and to paint a picture of danger. In particular, colour use, expressed humour and some of the oversized elements evoked emotions in the author despite her researcher position; attempting to analyse cartoons as objectively as possible though, it was helpful to look at cartoons several times, note own feelings and then proceed with the analysis. The author concludes that a visual analysis (in particular of cartoons) is both interesting and amusing and can add essential additional insights to a text analysis.

The US Self and the Iranian Other in US Discourse: Empirical Discussion

Overall, the analysis illustrates the construction of a dangerous Iranian other. Before the nuclear agreement, Iran and the Iranian leadership were portrayed as the evil other that threatens the US and the world with its nuclear program, along side sponsoring terrorism and regional destabilisation; afterwards, discourse showed more diversity in constructions and includes views of Iran as possible partner for the US and the world.

The *qualitative content analysis* has brought to light a pattern of expressed US fears regarding a potentially nuclear-armed Iran, present in nearly all analysed documents. To understand why a nuclear-armed Iran would present such a grave threat, the discursive context must be considered. Before the agreement, Iran was portrayed as hostile, aggressive, radical, misleading, insincere, terror-sponsoring, as regional destabiliser, international outcast, and declared enemy of the US and Israel—clearly, Iran was the dangerous and threatening other. Iran was said to have ignored and rejected respective UN resolutions and non-proliferation treaties. Fears of a nuclear-armed Iran have even led to calls for US surgical strikes against suspected Iranian nuclear facilities; debated were somewhat unspecific warnings of needing to prevent an Iranian nuclear bomb versus the potentially enormous effects of a military strike for regional and global stability (Fisher, 2013; Kroenig, 2012; USIP, 2011; Weighing, 2012).

Sanctions were another hard policy tool to respond to the perceived Iranian threat. Implemented sanctions against Iran, and the value of increasing sanctions or threatening to do so, were continually discussed. Some argued that the sanctions' great political and financial costs would bring Iran to the negotiation table (Cordesman, 2014; Obama, 2013), others doubted sanction effectiveness (Beinart, 2015; Gladstone, 2013). With sanctions having increased the cost of Iranian actions, they were counted among the factors that contributed to a changed Iranian position. Another considered factors was the change in Iranian leadership.

A further issue is the US construction of Iran as a sponsor of terrorism, radicalism and extremism. Iran is accused of intentionally destabilising the region to benefit own power interests (Fisher, 2013; US Department of State, 2014, 2012). Regarding the region, Iran's declared hostility against Israel is considered highly destabilising and of great concern; the US also sees Iran as acting against US regional interests (Cordesman, 2014) and misleading the world. Opposite we find the construction of the good, responsible and internationally supported US, acting to promote a stable and secure Middle East. For example, US officials are portrayed to have increased pressure upon the Iranian leadership only slowly in order to promote positive change in Iran (USIP, 2011).

When Obama entered the White House in 2009, US discourse towards Iran showed fewer dichotomies in the constructions of self and other. He emphasised the need for diplomacy to motivate positive change in Iran and for activating Iran's nascent reform movement. Yet, also under Obama's two administrations, the construction of Iran as threatening and destabilising actor that must be globally integrated remained (Obama, 2013; White House, 2013, pp. 4, 8); the US did still engage in othering Iran. But when Iran's president, Rouhani, offered dialogue in 2013, Obama took the opportunity, recognised Iranian goodwill (Obama, 2013) and thus added a positive element to the US construction of Iran. Yet, Iran was still called upon to prove its goodwill regarding its nuclear program (ibid). US discourse expressed continuous mistrust of the Iranian leadership—another pattern in US discourse—with many reminders of Iran having broken past commitments.

After the beginning of dialogue at the end of 2013, US discourse was split on the issue of trusting Iran. A large part, including Obama and his administration officials, highlighted the dialogue as positive development (Kerry, 2014), which even led to the re-opening of the US embassy in Tehran after 36 years. Supporters of dialogue saw in it a strengthening of US security, and great value for regional stability and global peace (White House, 2015a, 2015b). No alternatives were seen when viewing Iran's activities and potential realistically (Beinart, 2015). Critics of a dialogue with Iran mistrusted the Iranian leadership's sincerity. Criticism of the agreement centred on allowing Iran to keep thousands of centrifuges and continue some enrichment, on imposing only time limited restrictions, on inspections being pre-announced and on lacking guarantees for Iranian compliance (Mascaro, 2015). Especially US Republicans were adamantly opposed to any deal with Iran, speaking of a cheating and untrustworthy Iran (Hatch, 2015a, 2015b; Lane, 2015). Critics among Democrats warned of an Iranian leadership unwilling to moderate behaviour, and criticized the agreement's complexity and loopholes, legitimising Iran to pursue its nuclear arms program and lacking safeguards (Alexander, 2015; Burr, 2015; Schumer, 2015). Altogether, the qualitative content analysis has shown a significant shift in US discourse: Iran and its leadership are articulated as threat, but as lesser one. Instead of the extremist and dangerous US other only, Iran is now also linked with some positive elements; yet strong mistrust continues.

The *visual analysis* has even more clearly illustrated a strong US mistrust of the Iranian leadership and intentions for the peaceful settlement on the nuclear issue. The US was pictured as naive versus a strong-positioned and uncompromising Iran, alluding to imbalanced relations. An example is a 2015 cartoon picturing US Secretary of State Kerry and Iranian president, Rouhani, in a frame entitled 'US-Iran Framework'; outside that frame we see Rouhani sitting on a nuclear bomb (Varvel, 2015). Kerry is happily smiling, Rouhani not. The cartoon implies hidden intentions of the Iranian leadership, and Iran not wanting to give up its nuclear weapons plans. The image expresses a naive US, and thus imbalanced US-Iranian relations; Kerry's and Rouhani's different facial expressions strengthen this. The nuclear bomb, outside the framework, presents a clear danger that is controlled by Iran; dramatisation is used to make the point. Viewers are led to believe that Iran is more powerful and thus threatening.

Similarly, another cartoon criticizes the US for trusting Rouhani on his word. It shows Abraham Lincoln, representing the US, looking satisfactorily at the mobile phone with a photograph sent by Rouhani who took a selfie of his face but not the nuclear bomb he is sitting on. The message reads 'See? No Nukes! [Smiley]' (Koterba, 2015). Iranian leaders are portrayed as deceiving, and the US as overly trusting, weak and/or naive.

The claimed power imbalance between the US and Iran, and the Iranian threat, are portrayed pointedly in cartoon that shows a threatening Iranian leader screaming 'Death to America' before the agreement, and afterwards still screaming the same, only with a nuclear bomb and a large bag of US Dollars (McKee, 2015). The money and the bomb imply an Iran unhindered in building nuclear weapons but now equipped with more resources to do so. The strong facial expressions, the screaming and the reddish background exaggerate the threat and evoke alarming feelings. The colour of red is associated with danger and serves to increase the threat's intensity. Iran is shown as able to threaten the US and the US as giving in.

Another cartoon consists of two images (Vaidyanathan, 2015, cartoon by Gary Varvel). The first shows Kerry holding an olive branch at Rouhani, saying 'We are extending an olive branch to you, if you disarm'. Rouhani looks hesitantly. The second shows Kerry looking surprised at his cut-off arm with the olive branch on the floor; Rouhani is walking away with an oversized saber. Kerry's olive branch and Rouhani's saber, and the act of cutting off an arm, express imbalanced US-Iranian relations. Kerry's surprise illustrates US naivety. Rouhani rejecting the olive branch and walking away from Kerry express Iranian unwillingness to cooperate with the US. The oversized saber, almost as large as Rouhani, may present an exaggerated Iranian hard-power approach.

Another two-image cartoon ridicules Obama's red line (Foden, 2015). The first image shows Obama drawing with an oversized red marker a solid and clearly visible red line, entitled 'Hard red line'; Rouhani, standing behind, says 'No'. The second image shows Obama drawing with a light pink marker a hardly visible light pink line, entitled 'Fuzzy pink line'; Rouhani says 'I can live with that'. We see a bent-down Obama capitulating before Rouhani. Implied, here, are a strong Iran that can dictate its terms to the US, and an unprincipled Obama. The use of red colour again has the performative function of distinguishing and communicating what to do and what not. The change from red to light pink suggests diminishing clarity and distinction, and implies a line that may be crossed much easier.

Cartoons thus repeatedly express the theme of the US mistrusting Iran/the Iranian leadership, as well as Iran misleading the US by still keeping the nuclear bomb and rejecting US offers. The US is shown as giving in and being naive towards Iran. Iran is shown as not earnestly interested in cooperation. The aspect of imbalanced relations is thereby re-stated.

Implications

Future US-Iranian Relations

The noticeable shift in US security policy discourse, as demonstrated by the results of the qualitative content analysis, constructs Iran as a lesser threat starting in 2015/2016. Iran and the Iranian leadership have moved from the aggressive, extremist, dangerous and threatening other to a still threatening other that is, however, also a possible partner. Iran is now also linked to some positive elements. Yet, despite the new US-Iranian dialogue and the first steps of cooperation, there is still significant mistrust of the Iranian leadership expressed in US discourse, and othering of Iran still takes place. The analysis of cartoons has added a pointed and emotional picture regarding a deceiving, powerful and armed Iran versus a naive US. Iranian intentions are viewed critically, and there are hints at perceived hidden intentions to still build nuclear arms. The comparison of available cartoons published around the time of negotiations showed that most cartoons expressed these views. In light of the discursive shift shown by the qualitative content analysis above, there is therefore a debate shaped by remarkably diverging views, including a nascent split between the official discourse and the general public.

While constructions of Iran have become more nuanced, continued views of a threatening and cheating Iranian other and further existing mistrust hamper balanced US-Iranian relations. Negative character ascriptions to and negative emotions towards the other are interlinked and mutually confirming. In addition, we may consider the US self's need for emotional stability. When views of Iran as key threatening other, after having informed decision-makers for over three decades, are challenged by new developments, there is likely an incentive to maintain views. A completely new picture of Iran and the Iranian leadership may challenge the US self identity, and alternative views may have difficulty to become accepted. There is still a large opposition to the agreement, likely motivated by continuing mistrust. Those that favour a hard line against Iran may also actively emotionalise discourse and link negative emotions to Iran, the agreement and improved relations. Resulting constructions and the linked emotions develop their own force, inform interaction, and become part of multi-layered institutional structures. This is why heavily emotionalised discourse and policy are difficult to overcome.

Building positive US-Iranian relations may be facilitated by what White (1998, p. 122; 1984, p. 160) calls realistic empathy that serves as corrective to harmful misperceptions. Together with an understanding of emotions as something shared, hostility may be reduced and relations improved. Since emotions are something that we experience physically and bodily, the emotional component in relations seems important. Working to enable trust via positive interactions may reassure the self and help to overcome mistrust. Placing relations on a larger basis by extending them to the societies may stabilise positive change. Also, the healing of relations is significant. Recent work on emotions in US security policy towards Iran discusses the aspect and function of healing relations (Reinke de Buitrago, 2016). In light of the new US administration under President Donald Trump, however, US-Iranian relations may worsen again, and the nuclear agreement is at risk.

Methodological Implications: The Value of Combining Analyses of Different Scope, Focus and Depth

Implications relate to the combination of the two analytical methods. In order to better understand the impact of (distinct) emotions on perception, discourse and international relations, it seems highly useful to further strengthen methodological tools and refine existing methods for precise application. During the conduct of this analysis, it has become clear that the combination of the two methods is a fruitful endeavour by adding perspectives to approach emotions in IR for a deeper understanding. Although the applied methods differ in scope, focus and depth, they complement each other. Qualitative content analysis generates rich details and uncovers discursive claims, which in turn can inform policymaking; visual analysis identifies additional 'sticky' aspects of an interstate relationship by putting the emphasis on public views on specific issues that are reproduced using means of exaggeration and dramatisation.

A challenging matter is the linking of the two analyses. They differ in nature with regards to the context that is available to study the perceptions of a particular issue. Thus, when looking at a document as part of qualitative content analysis, the researcher typically has much more surrounding context; cartoons stand as they are, with little context or none that is immediatly available for analysis. To bring the results of each method in contact and compare them, the researcher needs to zig-zag between the particular insights of each and shift back and forth between different scopes, foci and depths, ideally thus producing a completed mosaic that provides a richer understanding. Interlinking insights from policy and strategy documents and from cartoons requires considering wider policy discourse and context, as well as particular issues and viewpoints together. To deal with potential hurdles of combining both methods, possibly arising from their different scope, focus and depth, it has proven useful for the researcher to maintain solid awareness of the different nature of sources. For other researchers interested in this combination of method, it would be important to have sufficient sources of text and cartoons; not all subject matters in IR are frequently covered by cartoons. Both methods are also highly interpretive, and with researchers being subjective, care must be taken to minimise co-constructions influenced by own biases resulting from socialization in a specific educational environment or a specific national culture. Another challenge, or limit, is the interpretation of cartoons from countries of which the researcher lacks cultural knowledge. This also applies to text sources; having lived in the country whose material is analysed seems helpful. In further developing this combined methodological approach, it seems significant to concentrate on building robust and differentiated categories that can be applied to all results to enable easier comparison.

It is concluded that used in combination, visual analysis is complementary and insightful. The combination has allowed the researcher to illustrate a popular reproduction of enmity and threat perceptions; representations by security policy decision-makers resonate in wider society via popular media and journalists' representations. The construction of enmity towards Iran thus exceeds what is stated in policy documents, implying that US-Iranian relations are not only shaped by conflicting interests but also by emotions that are re-produced and activated by journalists. This implies for media a quite active role in the shaping of perceptions of another state and relations with that state. Combining the two methods therefore offers potential for other studies of interstate relations and cases of threat/enemy construction.

From the analysis, a number of avenues for further research have become clear. One of them relates to the above-stated active role of media. How active a role media can play in influencing national politics regarding international/transnational issues has been illustrated (see Reinke de Buitrago, 2014). But finding out about national media concretely contribute to the shaping of interstate relations is of further interest. Research on the role of emotions in IR needs to further specify the dynamics of how the self's emotions towards and (cognitive) perceptions of the other influence each other. An interesting question to answer would be how a perception of another state as more positive/less threatening, resulting from changing political circumstances, can stimulate more positive emotions, and which other factors are needed for such a development. Of further interest would be what may be called emotional interdependencies, that is, how self and other are emotionally dependent on each other and how a change in the external environment may affect this interdependence. More research also seems to be needed on particular emotions and their possibly distinct impact. Thus, we should inquire into the difference between various emotions and how this difference plays out in perceptions of self and other.

Notes

1. The Iranian nuclear agreement, the Joint Comprehensive Plan of Action (JCPOA), was signed by Iran, the five permanent UN Security Council members (China, France, Russia, UK and US), Germany, and the EU on July 14, 2015 in Vienna.
2. For a review of the nexus between geopolitics and visual culture, see Hughes (2007).
3. Inductive categories may be formed when deductive categories prove too large or when the analysis yields new content beyond the already existing categories.

References

Agnew, J., & Muscarà, L. (2012). *Making Political Geography*. Lanham, MD: Rowman & Littlefield Publishers, Inc.

Ahmed, S. (2004). *The Cultural Politics of Emotion*. New York: Routledge.

Alexander, L. (2015, August 28). *Alexander Announces Opposition to President Obama's Nuclear Agreement with Iran*. Retrieved May 18, 2016, from http://www.alexander.senate.gov/public/index.cfm/pressreleases?ID=b5ab24fc-c80c-412a-9160-19b3bf6e5026

Andersen, R. S., Vuori, J. A., & Guillaume, X. (2015). Chromatology of Security: Introducing Colours to Visual Security Studies. *Security Dialogue, 46*(5), 440–457.

Baudrilliard, J. (2002). *Screened Out*. London: Verso.

Behnke, J., Baur, N., & Behnke, N. (2006). *Empirische Methoden der Politikwissenschaft*. Paderborn: Verlag Ferdinand Schöningh.

Beinart, P. (2015, July 14). Why the Iran Deal Makes Obama's Critics So Angry. *The Atlantic*. Retrieved May 18, 2016, from http://www.theatlantic.com/international/archive/2015/07/iran-nuclear-deal-obama/398450/

Bleiker, R. (2009). *Aesthetics and World Politics*. Basingstoke: Macmillan.
Bleiker, R., & Hutchison, E. (2008). Fear No More: Emotions and World Politics. *Review of International Studies, 34*, 115–135.
Bortz, J., & Döring, N. (2005). *Forschungsmethoden und Evaluation* (3rd ed.). Heidelberg: Springer Medizin Verlag.
Bronfen, E. (2006). Reality Check. Image Affects and Cultural Memory. *Differences, 17*(1), 20–46.
Burr, R. (2015, August 5). *Burr on Iran Deal: American People Aren't Buying into Bad Deal*. Retrieved May 18, 2016, from https://www.burr.senate.gov/press/releases/burr-on-iran-deal-american-people-arent-buying-into-bad-deal
Cordesman, A. (2014). *U.S. Strategy and Added Sanctions on Iran: The Role of the Administration and Congress in a 'Good Cop, Bad Cop' Approach*. Washington, DC: CSIS.
Crawford, N. (2000). The Passion of World Politics: Propositions on Emotion and Emotional Relationships. *International Security, 24*(2), 116–156.
Dodds, K. (2007). Steve Bell's Eye: Cartoons, Geopolitics and the Visualization of the 'War on Terror'. *Security Dialogue, 38*(2), 157–177.
Dodds, K. (2010). Popular Geopolitics and Cartoons: Representing Power Relations, Repetition and Resistance. *Critical African Studies, 2*(4), 1–19.
Fierke, K. (2012). *Political Self-Sacrifice: Agency, Body and Emotion in International Relations*. Cambridge: Cambridge University Press.
Fisher, M. (2013, September 24). Obama's Speech to the United National on Syria, Iran and War. *The Washington Post*. Retrieved January 3, 2016, from http://www.washingtonpost.com/blogs/worldviews/wp/2013/09/24/read-full-text-of-obamas-speech-to-the-united-nations-on-syria-iran-and-war/
Flick, U. (2003). Triangulation in der qualitativen Forschung. In U. Flick, E. v. Kardoff, & I. Steinke (Eds.), *Qualitative Forschung: Ein Handbuch* (pp. 309–318). Reinbek: Rowohlt Taschenbuch Verlag.
Foden, G. (2015). *Obama's Fuzzy Pink Line*. Cartoon. Retrieved May 25, 2016, from https://www.cartoonstock.com/newscartoons/directory/r/red_line.asp
Gladstone, R. (2013, January 10). Iran Finding Some Ways to Evade Sanctions, Treasury Department Says. *International New York Times*. Retrieved May 18, 2016, from http://www.nytimes.com/2013/01/11/world/middleeast/iran-finding-ways-to-circumvent-sanctions-treasury-department-says.html?_r=0
Haidt, J. (2013). *The Righteous Mind. Why Good People Are Divided by Politics and Religion*. New York: Random House.
Hansen, L. (2006). *Security as Practice: Discourse Analysis and the Bosnian War*. Oxon: Routledge.
Hansen, L. (2011). Theorizing the Image for Security Studies. Visual Securitization and the Muhammad Cartoon Crisis. *European Journal of International Relations, 17*(1), 51–74.
Hansen, L. (2015). How Images Make World Politics: International Icons and the Case of Abu Ghraib. *Review of International Studies, 41*(2), 263–288.

Harré, R., & Sammut, G. (2013). What Lies Between? In G. Sammut, P. Daanen, & F. M. Moghaddam (Eds.), *Understanding Self and Others: Explorations in Intersubjectivity and Interobjectivity* (pp. 15–30). London and New York: Routledge.

Hatch, O. (2015a, June 22). *Hatch: The Stakes Are Too High to Act as If Iran Is a Trustworthy Partner.* Retrieved May 18, 2016, from http://www.hatch.senate.gov/public/index.cfm/2015/6/hatch-the-stakes-are-too-high-to-act-as-if-iran-is-a-trustworthy-partner

Hatch, O. (2015b, September 15). Why the Iran Deal Makes War More Likely. *The Washington Times.* Retrieved May 18, 2016, from http://www.washingtontimes.com/news/2015/sep/15/iran-deal-why-the-iran-deal-makes-war-more-likely/

Holland, J. (2007). Emotions and Research. *International Journal of Social Research Methodology, 10*(3), 195–209.

Holland, J. (2014). The Elusive Essence of Evil: Constructing Otherness in the Coalition of the Willing. In D. Pisoiu (Ed.), *Arguing Counter-Terrorism. New Perspectives* (pp. 201–220). Abingdon, Oxon and New York: Routledge.

Hughes, R. (2007). Through the Looking Blast: Geopolitics and Visual Culture. *Geography Compass, 1*(5), 976–994.

Hutchison, E., & Bleiker, R. (2014). Theorizing Emotions in World Politics. *International Theory, 6*(3), 491–514.

IPU/DCAF. (2005). *Parlamentarische Aufsicht über den Sicherheitssektor: Prinzipien, Mechanismen und Praktiken.* Geneva: Inter-Parliamentary Union and Geneva Centre for the Democratic Control of Armed Forces.

Kerry, J. (2014, February 1). U.S. Speech at Munich Conference on Security, Diplomacy Issues. Retrieved January 3, 2016, from http://iipdigital.usembassy.gov/st/english/texttrans/2014/02/20140201292176.html?CP.rss=true#axzz2s6gU1ouN

Koterba, J. (2015). Cartoon. The Choices Program, Teaching with the News, The Iran Nuclear Deal. Under Link: Political Cartoons Powerpoint, Brown University, Providence, RI. Retrieved May 24, 2016, from http://www.choices.edu/resources/twtn/twtn-iran-cartoon

Kroenig, M. (2012). Time to Attack Iran. Why a Strike Is the Least Bad Option. *Foreign Affairs, 91*(1), 76–86. Retrieved January 3, 2016, from https://www.foreignaffairs.com/articles/middle-east/2012-01-01/time-attack-iran

Lane, S. (2015, July 14). Ted Cruz and John Cornyn Are Not Happy with Iran Deal. *The Dallas Morning News.* Retrieved May 18, 2016, from http://trailblazersblog.dallasnews.com/2015/07/ted-cruz-john-cornyn-iran-nuclear-deal.html/

Leep, M. C. (2010). The Affective Production of Others: United States Policy Towards the Israeli-Palestinian Conflict. *Cooperation and Conflict, 45*(3), 331–352.

MacDonald, F., Dodds, K., & Hughes, R. (Eds.). (2010). *Observant States: Geopolitics and Visual Culture.* London: I.B. Tauris.

Manzo, K. (2012). Earthworks: The Geopolitical Visions of Climate Change Cartoons. *Political Geography, 31*(8), 481–494.

Mascaro, L. (2015, July 14). The Talking – And Arguing – Points of the Iran Nuclear Deal. *Los Angeles Times.* Retrieved May 18, 2016, from http://www.latimes.com/world/middleeast/la-fg-iran-vulnerabilities-20150715-story.html

May, V. (2013). *Connecting Self to Society. Belonging in a Changing World.* Houndmills: Palgrave Macmillan.

Mayring, P. (2003). *Qualitative Inhaltsanalyse: Grundlagen und Techniken* (8th ed.). Weinheim und Basel: Beltz Verlag.

McKee, R. (2015). Cartoon. The Choices Program, Teaching with the News, The Iran Nuclear Deal. Under Link: Political Cartoons Powerpoint, Brown University, Providence, RI. Retrieved May 24, 2016, from http://www.choices.edu/resources/twtn/twtn-iran-cartoon

Neumann, I. B. (Ed.). (1999). *Uses of the Other. "The East" in European Identity Formation.* Manchester: Manchester University Press.

Obama, B. (2013, November 23). *Statement by the President on First Step Agreement on Iran's Nuclear Program.* The White House. Retrieved May 18, 2016, from http://www.whitehouse.gov/the-press-office/2013/11/23/statement-president-first-step-agreement-irans-nuclear-program

Reinke de Buitrago, S. (2014). Jihadist Terrorism in Europe: What Role for Media? In D. Pisoiu (Ed.), *Arguing Counterterrorism: New Perspectives* (pp. 160–180). London and New York: Routledge.

Reinke de Buitrago, S. (2016). The Role of Emotions in US Security Policy Towards Iran. *Global Affairs, 2*(2), 155–164. https://doi.org/10.1080/23340460.2016.1164975.

Sasley, B. (2011). Theorizing States' Emotions. *International Studies Review, 13*(3), 452–476.

Schumer, C. (2015, September 15). Iran Won't Change Its Ways Under This Deal. *The Washington Times.* Retrieved May 18, 2016, from http://www.washingtontimes.com/news/2015/sep/15/iran-deal-schumer-iran-wont-change-its-ways-under-/

Smith, A. D. (1991). *National Identity.* London: Penguin Books.

U.S. Department of State. (2012). *Country Reports on Terrorism 2012.* Washington, DC: U.S. Department of State.

U.S. Department of State. (2014). *Country Reports on Terrorism 2014.* Washington, DC: U.S. Department of State.

Ulbert, C. (2005). Konstruktivistische Analysen der internationalen Politik: Theoretische Ansätze und methodische Herangehensweisen. In C. Ulbert & C. Weller (Eds.), *Konstruktivistische Analysen der internationalen Politik* (pp. 9–34). Wiesbaden: VS Verlag für Sozialwissenschaften.

USIP. (2011, November 22). *Speech by National Security Advisor Tom Donilon.* Retrieved January 3, 2016, from http://iranprimer.usip.org/blog/2011/nov/22/speech-national-security-advisor-tom-donilon

Vaidyanathan, R. (2015, July 16). Iran-US Relations: Nine Cartoons Tell the Story. Cartoon by G. Varvel. *BBC News*, Washington, DC. Retrieved January 2016, from http://www.bbc.com/news/magazine-33531598

Varvel, G. (2015). Cartoon, US-Iran Framework. *The Week*. Retrieved May 11, 2016, from http://theweek.com/cartoons/548347/political-cartoon-world-kerry-iran-nuclear-deal

Weighing Benefits and Costs of Military Action Against Iran. (2012). The Iran Project. New York. Retrieved May 18, 2016, from https://www.wilsoncenter.org/sites/default/files/IranReport_091112_FINAL.pdf

White House. (2013). *National Security Strategy.* Retrieved January 3, 2016, from http://www.utexas.edu/lbj/sites/default/files/file/news/National%20Security%20Strategy%202013%20%28Final%20Draft%29.pdf

White House. (2015a, July 14). *Statement by the President on Iran.* Retrieved January 3, 2016, from https://www.whitehouse.gov/the-press-office/2015/07/14/statement-president-iran

White House. (2015b, August 5). *Remarks by the President on the Iran Nuclear Deal.* Washington, DC: American University. Retrieved May 18, 2016, from https://www.whitehouse.gov/the-press-office/2015/08/05/remarks-president-iran-nuclear-deal

White, R. K. (1984). *Fearful Warriors: A Psychological Profile of U.S.-Soviet Relations.* New York: Free Press.

White, R. K. (1998). American Acts of Force: Results and Misperceptions. *Peace and Conflict: Journal of Peace Psychology, 4*(2), 93–128.

Wolf, R. (2011). Respect and Disrespect in International Politics: The Significance of Status Recognition. *International Theory, 3*(1), 105–142.

Wolf, R. (2012). Der 'emotional turn' in den IB: Plädoyer für eine theoretische Überwindung methodischer Engführung. *Zeitschrift für Außen- und Sicherheitspolitik, 5*(4), 605–624.

Sybille Reinke de Buitrago is a researcher at the Institute for Peace Research and Security Policy at the University of Hamburg (IFSH) and the Institute for Peace and Theology (ITHF), Germany. Her research focuses on international relations, peace and conflict resolution and security policy. Her recent publications include "The Meaning of Borders for National Identity and State Authority" in *Border Politics: Defining Spaces of Governance and Forms of Transgression* (eds. C. Günay and N. Witjes, 2017); "Threats of a Different Kind: China and Russia in U.S. Security Policy Discourse", in *S+F Sicherheit & Frieden/Security & Peace* (2016); "The Role of Emotions in U.S. Security Policy towards Iran", *Global Affairs* (2016); and "Self-Other Constructions, Difference and Threat: U.S. and Arab 'Othering' of Iran" in *Regional Insecurity After the Arab Uprisings* (ed. E. Monier, 2015). She lectures at the Leuphana University in Lüneburg, Germany.

CHAPTER 14

Methods and Methodologies for the Study of Emotions in World Politics

Roland Bleiker and Emma Hutchison

INTRODUCTION

Emotions are central to world politics. They lie at the core of key political phenomena, from war to humanitarian emergencies and from diplomatic negotiations to financial crisis. Take the example of terrorism: the reason why people engage in terrorist attacks is often deeply emotional, as are the public and political reactions to them. It is impossible to understand the design and impact of the terrorist attacks of 11 September 2001 without the deeply emotional nature of the event. As Erik Ringmar (Chap. 2) puts it: "take away the emotions and there will be little international politics left."

While central to world politics, emotions have paradoxically been largely absent from scholarly approaches to international relations. Or so at least argue several contributors to this volume. Reinhard Wolf (Chap. 10) points out that "for decades emotions have hardly figured in mainstream political science." Clara Eroukhmanoff and Bernardo Teles Fazendeiro (Chap. 11) highlight that "IR theories have turned a blind eye to the role of emotions in world politics." Ringmar (Chap. 2) writes of how "international politics is next to always analysed in rationalistic terms," stressing

R. Bleiker (✉) • E. Hutchison
School of Political Science and International Studies, University of Queensland, Brisbane, Australia

© The Author(s) 2018
M. Clément, E. Sangar (eds.), *Researching Emotions in International Relations*, Palgrave Studies in International Relations, https://doi.org/10.1007/978-3-319-65575-8_14

the need to look at the "psychological processes" that shape the outlook of politicians. In a similar vein, we read that "friendship as an emotional bond between individual political actors ... receives little to no attention" (van Hoef, Chap. 3) or that "most specialists are reluctant to study the role of emotions in contemporary Western wars" (Delori, Chap. 6; also Wasinski, Chap. 7).

International relations scholarship has, indeed, come fairly late to the study of emotions. But it is important not to underestimate the work that has been done already. There exists a lot more scholarship on emotions and world politics than commonly assumed, so much so that one can say that an "emotional turn ... is now well underway in IR" (Eroukhmanoff and Teles Fazendeiro, Chap. 11). Over the past two decades, a vibrant body of literature has engaged the politics of emotions in countless different realms, from war to diplomacy and from alliance politics to humanitarian crises.[1] Take just one example: the emotional predispositions and bonds that develop between political leaders. Studies in political psychology and foreign policy were among the first international relations approaches to take emotions seriously. Emerging in the 1970s, the respective contributions explored the relationship between emotion and reason in the process of decision-making. They opposed the assumption that decisions are taken on the basis of "classical rationality," stressing, instead, that leaders have often no choice but to draw upon ideas and insights that may involve "the emotional rather than the calculating part of the brain" (Hill, 2003, p. 116; see also Marcus, 2002, pp. 221–250; Jervis, Lebow, & Stein, 1985). More recent work draws on neuroscience and other literatures to explore how emotions shape face-to-face diplomacy (for instance, Holmes, 2013). Add to this that historians have for long examined how heads of state and other decision-makers are influenced by the emotional context in which they grew up, think and operate (for recent examples see Costigliola, 2012; Keys, 2011).

While there is a rich and vibrant body of knowledge on emotions and world politics, and while we need more serious and sustained engagements with this literature, there is one gap that stands out in particular: the relative absence of methodological debates. Maéva Clément and Eric Sangar (Chap. 1) rightly highlight this problem and the need to address it. The dilemma is particularly well captured by Audrey Reeves (Chap. 5), who compellingly shows how traditional methodological approaches offered not much help to understand the kind of affective political experiences she was trying to investigate.

The challenge is considerable and has been identified by two influential pioneers of the research on emotions and world politics: Neta Crawford and Jonathan Mercer. Crawford (2000, p. 118) recognizes that the inherently "ephemeral" nature of emotions poses major "methodological concerns." Because emotions are "deeply internal," it is difficult isolate them or distinguish what a "genuine" emotion may indeed be. Mercer (1996, p. 1) too worries that "emotion is hard to define, hard to operationalize, hard to measure, and hard to isolate from other factors." For most scholars emotions simply seem, as Paul Saurette (2006, p. 504) puts it, "impossibly fuzzy." Quantifying emotions is difficult. Labelling and measuring them, even in qualitative terms, is also a delicate process. We can try to verbalize our emotions yet often words fail to convey the full extent of what we feel inside. Or so it seems at first sight. Emotions appear to exist unconsciously, even unknowingly, deep in the recesses of an individual's mind and body. For an international relations scholar working with prevailing methodological frameworks, investigations into emotions therefore seem to result in research that is speculative or tenuous at best.

At the same time, the methodological challenges associated with studying emotions are not as unusual as it seems at first sight. Janice Bially-Mattern (2014, pp. 589–594) convincingly points out that emotions are in fact no more and no less "fuzzy" than many other well-established and much studied phenomena in international relations, such as interests, identity, ideology or even anarchy. None of these and many other concepts can be easily quantified and yet they have been central to theoretical and empirical inquiries. Renee Jeffery (2014b, pp. 584–589), as a result, proposes a shift away the traditional preference of methodological observation and search instead for experimental ways of appreciating the political roles of emotions. Perhaps the issue, then, has less to do with the allegedly elusive nature of emotions and more to do with to the traditionally limited methodological scope of disciplinary international relations.

The purpose of our concluding remarks is to address some of these challenges. We engage the chapters in this book and we offer suggestions in parallel—or, rather, in reinforcement of—the six key points that Clément and Sangar (Chap. 1) flagged at the outset. In doing so, we draw on and expand some of our previous work (most notably Bleiker 2014, 2015; Bleiker & Butler, 2016; Bleiker & Hutchison, 2007, 2008; Hutchison, 2014, 2016; Hutchison & Bleiker, 2008, 2014, 2015). We proceed in three steps.

We first engage an issue that was outlined in the introduction (Clément and Sangar, Chap. 1) and comes up regularly through the book: the challenge of defining feelings, emotions and affect. We do so not to arrive at a definitive statement, but to highlight that definitional issues, and in particular the relationship between emotions and affect, are intimately linked with some of the key methodological questions that Clément and Sangar flagged: that we need to understand how emotions work across different levels of analysis, from individual to collective ones; that emotions are inherently social, cultural and political; and that emotions shift and change with time and across space.

Second, we recognize the need to take into account methodological contributions from existing social scientific work in international relations. But, at the same time, and more importantly, we highlight the need to go beyond social scientific analyses and, in particular, beyond methods that rely on more traditional cause-effect models. Here, we highlight the usefulness of Jacques Rancière's concept of the distribution of the sensible: of understanding how collective emotions frame what is and is not logical, rational, sensible and thus politically relevant, possible and desirable (Rancière, 2004).

Third, we stress that such an approach to analysing political emotions requires creativity and methodological pluralism. Emotions work in exceptionally complex ways. No single method could possibly account for their political significance and influence. The chapters in this volume emphasize the need to draw on a range of different methods, from semi-structured interviews to discourse analysis, autoethnography, content analysis and semiotics, among others. To validate such a broad and diverse range of methods, we need an epistemological framework that eschews the need to arrive at overarching models and, instead, appreciates the pluralism and creativity and perhaps even elusiveness that resides in each particular approach. Such a framework requires reflections on both method and methodological issues: that is, we need to discuss not only the tools needed to investigate the political roles of emotions but also the epistemological status attributed to these tools.

DEFINING FEELINGS, EMOTIONS AND AFFECT: POLITICAL AND METHODOLOGICAL IMPLICATIONS

Several chapters in this volume highlight the difficulties involved with defining emotions. Clément and Sangar (Chap. 1) mention how efforts to pinpoint the nature of emotions are "highly contested and at times particularly fuzzy." Ringmar laments that the "vocabulary of affect is hopelessly confused" and there is little agreement on how related terms are used or, indeed, how they should be employed.

We engage these discussions here by highlighting how scholars differentiate phenomenologically between feelings, emotions and affect. We do so not to settle definitional disputes but to highlight how the struggle to understand what emotions are goes to their very political core: it highlights that emotions in all their guises, as distinguishable emotions as well as more non-conscious feelings and affects, work at different levels—from the individual to the collective—and that they are always more than just personal reactions or expressions.

Most international relations scholars use the term "emotion" loosely, as a broad umbrella term to denote a range of different phenomena. We do so too in this chapter. But some scholars also draw a clear distinction between emotions and feelings. Mercer (2014) refers to feelings as "a conscious awareness that one is experiencing an emotion." Crawford (2000, p. 125) sees emotions as "inner states that individuals describe to others as feeling." But both Mercer and Crawford go further and stress the need to capture the social dimensions at stake. This is why Crawford (2014) highlights how emotions—individual and subjective as they might be—are also always intertwined with pre-existing social, cultural and political contexts. Mercer's very notion of "social emotion" underlines this point too, for it captures how emotions become intersubjective when they relate to something social that people care about, whether it is power, status or justice.

Reflecting on the distinction between emotions and feelings might therefore help us appreciate the connections between bodily based phenomena and the processes through which emotions are communicated to others. While feelings may emerge from within the body, they are at the same time central to the politics of emotions. Feelings are internal in that they are felt within bodies, yet they are in a sense external as well. Mercer (2014) put it this way: bodies cause emotions but emotions cannot be ontologically reduced to the body. Even though we experience emotion emerging from our bodies, feelings are formed and structured within particular social and cultural environments (Lutz, 1988). They are constituted in relation to culturally specific traditions, such as language, habits and memories. This is why Sangar, Clément and Lindemann (Chap. 8) stress the need to "conceive emotions as social phenomena" that can shape political attitude to a range of phenomena, including war. Likewise, this is why Wolf (Chap. 10) believes that "emotions are intrinsically public and therefore can be well established by analysing social discourse." Karin Fierke (2014) goes one step further, stressing that individual expressions of emotions "should not ultimately be the focus of social and political analysis at the international level." This is the case, she argues, because individual emotions are less significant for understanding global politics than the emotions that surround political phenomena.

The distinction between emotions and affect brings out socio-political issues in an even more pertinent way. In some disciplines, such as geography, this distinction is so intensely debated that scholars differentiate between "emotional geography" and "affective geography" (see Thien, 2005; Thrift, 2004). Emotions are seen as personal and often conscious feelings that have social meaning and political consequences. Related phenomena can in this way be identified and assessed. Affective dynamics, by contrast, are viewed as much broader phenomena that exist both before and beyond consciousness: they are a wide range of non-reflective and subconscious bodily sensations, such as mood, intuition, temperament, attachment, disposition and even memory. In an investigation of the politics and potentials of museums to illuminate the human costs of war, Audrey Reeves (Chap. 5) insightfully outlines the consequences of these emotions-affect distinctions for international relations scholarship (see also Eznack, 2011, 2013; Holmes, 2013; Ross, 2006, p. 199; Sasley, 2010).

The difference between emotion and affect pivots around the issue of representation (see Pile, 2010, pp. 6–10; Reeves, Chap. 5; Eroukhmanoff and Teles Fazendeiro, Chap. 11). Those who theorize affect consider the phenomena as inexpressible: it cannot be analysed through representations. The study of affect thus opposes attempts to understand specific, seemingly individualized emotions and moves towards an approach that studies how particular feelings, sentiments and emotions together act as a type of collective social force (Thrift, 2004, p. 60; see also Protevi, 2009). Affect in this sense is "performative": it enables understandings of how emotional flows both act upon individuals and in doing so enact particular socio-political norms and behaviours. Emotional geographers disagree with many of the charges made against them. They argue that since emotions can only be understood through representations, it is crucial to understand the respective practices (see also Bondi, 2005; Eroukhmanoff and Teles Fazendeiro, Chap. 11; Reeves, Chap. 5; Thien, 2005; for a useful critical discussion of the affect/emotion discussion, see Leys, 2011).

To use the term "affect" is thus to make a shift from isolating specific emotions to the more general recognition that emotion, feeling and sensations combined generate often unconscious and unreflective affective dispositions that connect and transcend individuals (Massumi, 2002, pp. 27–28, 217; Thrift, 2004, p. 60). As Ringmar (Chap. 2) puts it: "everything is couched in terms of affect." In this sense, affect is always social and always "intertwined across time" (Eroukhmanoff and Teles Fazendeiro, Chap. 11). This position also resonates with international relations research. For Janice Bially-Mattern (2014), the task of singling out certain emotions, such as anger (see Heller, Chap. 4) becomes problematic as soon as one recognizes, as most scholars meanwhile do, that emotions and cognition are intrinsically interwoven and thus, by extension, hard to keep conceptually separate. For Ross (2014, pp. 2, 17–19) too, anger, fear or other emotions are socially constructed and somewhat arbitrary categories that are not really able to capture the rich complexities of how affective energies work and circulate between political actors and communities.

Affect can then provide the conceptual tools to understand how a broad range of psycho-social predispositions produce or mediate political emotions. Recent research by Lucile Eznack (2013) illustrates the issues at stake. She shows how historically cultivated affective dispositions—both positive and negative—can temper or exacerbate hostilities between nation-states and in doing so influence the nature of ensuing state behaviour. Juxtaposing US anger towards Britain in the 1956 Suez Crisis with that focused towards the Soviet Union during the 1979–1980 Afghanistan intervention, Eznack shows how anger at an ally/friend and an adversary/enemy alters according to the pre-existing affective dimensions of their relations.

Definitional disputes can never be settled. Nor can concepts ever capture the far more elusive realities they seek to define. This is why we consciously use the broad term "emotion." But conceptual disputes provide a way into understanding the substantive issues at stake, particularly the processes through which feelings, emotions and affect are both individual and collective. There is fairly widespread agreement that emotions are not only shaped by historical and socio-cultural factors but also, and in turn, play a key role in constituting collective identities and the type of political values and practices associated with them. But figuring out suitable methodological approaches for studying these collective emotions is, of course, a far more difficult and contestable task.

Understanding the Politics of Emotions Beyond Social Scientific Models

Most methodological approaches to the study of emotions in international relations are social science driven and, while useful, not enough to understand the collective dimension of emotions. Some of most systematic methodological debates so far have been carried out in political psychology and focus on quantitative approaches. They deal, for instance, with the emotional predispositions of leaders and samples of the population (Marcus, 2002, pp. 235–236; Small, Learner & Fischhoff, 2006). Neuroscientific inquiries have also generated important methodological advances, particularly with regard to the use of experiments, be they laboratory, survey or field based. These studies can make more reliable statements on issues of cause and effect that qualitative emotions methods may be hard-pressed to do (see Jeffery, 2014b; McDermott, 2011).

While experiments and other quantitatively measurable methods can yield important insights, there are nonetheless limits to how much they can assess. Two such methodological limits stand out.

First, scholars can only measure how people physiologically or behaviourally react or what they say they feel. In addition, the respective methods often focus on individuals and small groups, which do not operate at the same level and in the same way as larger collectives. Indeed, if the methodological challenges are significant when investigating individual or interpersonal emotional dynamics they are far greater when it comes to analysing emotions at the level of large collectives, such as in national and transnational spheres. States, for instance, have no biological mechanisms and thus cannot experience emotions directly. How, then, can the behaviour of states be shaped by emotions?

Second, traditional social scientific notions of causality are limited in their ability to capture the political impact of collective emotions. Take an example from the topic that Sybille Reinke de Buitrago (Chap. 13) and Gabi Schlag (Chap. 9) engage: the links between images, emotions and politics. The emotional dimensions of images rarely cause political events, at least not in a linear way. This is the case even in instances where impact is obvious. Consider the debates on the use of torture in the war against terror. As early as the summer of 2003, it was publicly known—in part through reports from Amnesty International—that US troops were using torture techniques when interrogating prisoners in Iraq. There was, however, little public interest or discussion about the issue. Domestic and international outrage only emerged in the spring of 2004, in direct response to graphic photographs of US torture at the Abu Ghraib prison facilities. The intensely emotional images of torture managed to trigger major public discussions in a way that "mere" words could not. But to attribute causality here is far from straightforward. This is even more the case with instances where impact is more diffuse, though equally clear. No method can, for instance, retrace the causal or even the constitutive links between the highly emotional visual representations of 9/11, the emergence of a discourse of evil and the ensuing war on terror. And yet, hardly anybody would question that images and emotions were key parts of the nature and impact of 9/11. Indeed, the very attack was designed for maximum visual and emotional impact. It was meant to do much more than kill physical bodies: the idea was to create a spectacle that can circulate visually and instil fear.

Rather than speaking of linear causality here, one might use terms like "discursive causality" (Hansen, 2006, p. 26) or "discursive agency" (Bleiker, 2000, p. 208). Doing so illuminates how emotions often work inaudibly but powerfully; over time and across space, by slowly entrenching—or gradually challenging—how we feel, view, think of the sociopolitical worked around us. Ringmar (Chap. 2) speaks of the "felt sense," of how feelings influence both cognitive thoughts and broader political phenomena.

Understanding how emotions work in such indirect ways poses inevitable methodological challenges. But they can be addressed and overcome. One of the most useful ways of doing so has been advanced by Jacques Rancière. He speaks of the "distribution of the sensible," that is, of how in any given society and at any given time, there are boundaries between what can be felt and not, thought and not and, as a result, between what is politically possible and not. These boundaries are arbitrarily but often accepted self-evidently as common sense (Rancière, 2004, p. 13; see also Rockhill, 2009, pp. 199–200). Collective emotions are, in this sense, highly political insofar as they can either entrench existing configurations of sensing, seeing and thinking, or indeed, they can challenge them. The boundaries between what is sensible and not sometimes shift rapidly, as in the case of torture debates, but mostly they evolve gradually as the visual world—and other representational stimuli—around us evolves.

Multidisciplinary Methods for the Study of Political Emotions

Broadening our understanding of how emotions work politically inevitably also entails broadening the methodological framework we use to study emotions. Rather than relying on social science methods alone, we should complement them with modes of inquiry stemming from the sciences and the humanities. The latter, for instance, consist of methods applied in, say, ethnography, architecture, art history, musicology and media studies.

Only a multitude of methods can attempt to stitch together the intricate and non-linear processes through which emotions shape the political. Different methods illuminate different dimensions of the links between emotion and politics. An adequate appreciation of the political issues at stake is thus likely to emerge only from combining a broad range of methods. The chapters in this volume offer an impressive illustration of such an approach. The tools employed here include phenomenology and psychoanalysis (Ringmar), content analysis (Heller; de Buitrago), semi-structured interviews (Delori), autoethnography (Reeves), discourse analysis (Wolf; Koschut), narrative analysis (Sangar, Clément and Lindemann), audience observation (Schlag); hermeneutics (Eroukhmanoff and Teles Fazendeiro).

Relying on such a broad set of methods for the study of political emotions seems commonsensical. In fact, many method scholars acknowledge the need for pluralism and recognize that, by extension, their own approach is a "necessary but not sufficient methodology" (Van Leeuwen & Jewitt, 2004, p. 5). A content analysis, for instance, can identify important patterns but say nothing about the political impact of emotions, just as a survey experiment can gauge relative impact but offer no knowledge of the origin or nature of links between emotions and politics. This is why critical methods scholars argue against analytically separating sensory domains (Mason & Davies, 2009, pp. 600–601). While commonsensical in principle, the actual application of a multidisciplinary approach to the study of emotions in world politics is far more complex and difficult.

Only very few researchers possess the methodological skills to navigate across the wide range of methods necessary to assess the complexity of the links between emotions and politics. Scholars who employ, say, discourse analysis rarely have the skills to conduct large-scale quantitative surveys. Likewise, researchers who do lab experiments are not usually equipped to conduct a semiology.

These practical challenges to multidisciplinary research are significant but can be overcome. Extra training can provide scholars with the skills needed to employ a wider range of methods. Some of the chapters in this volume offer fantastic examples of how this can be done successfully. Take the two chapters that deal with the links between emotions, images and politics. Schlag (Chap. 9) flags how a multitude of methods, from discourse analysis to iconology, can be applied across multiple visual sites and modalities: from the construction of an image to its content to its political receptions (see Rose, 2008). Buitrago (Chap. 13), likewise, employs content and visual analysis to great effect, arguing that zigzagging between them better captures "the complex nature of emotions and their various expressions and channels."

A further challenge to interdisciplinary work on emotions is linked to a deeply entrenched antagonistic dualism that continues to separate those advocating qualitative and quantitative methods. The divide between these traditions is enforced not only by different methodological trainings, but also by a range of epistemological assumptions that seem to make genuine cross-method inquiries difficult. Quantitative methods tend to be associated with positivist epistemologies while qualitative approaches are meant to be post-positivist in nature. This is neither accurate nor useful but, instead, and as Clément and Sangar (Chap. 1) point out, leads to a "path dependency" that boxes them into "specific ways of collecting and analysing." There is no reason why, for instance, discourse analysis could not be combined with quantitative survey experiments. Only through such unusual methodological combinations can we hope to understand the politics of emotions across their origin, history, meaning and causality.

Towards a Pluralist Epistemological Framework

The biggest challenge to a truly pluralist approach to the study emotions and politics is not of a practical but of an epistemological nature. To use methods as diverse as discourse analysis and quantitative surveys can only be done if each of these methods is given the chance to work according to its own logic. A genuinely interdisciplinary and pluralistic approach needs to abandon the idea that all methods have to operate according to the same rules and standards of evidence.

To advance such a proposition is to go against the grain of much of the philosophy of knowledge that drives the social sciences. Manuel De Landa

(2006, pp. 10–11) refers here to totalizing forms of knowledge. In such systems, each component has to behave according to an overall logic that structures the movement of parts. To make sense and fit in, each methodological component of this system has to operate according to the same principles: those of testable hypotheses. Methods that do not fit these criteria are seen as unscientific and illegitimate. This is the logic of aiming for "generalizable" findings that test "causal relationships" (Heller, Chap. 4). The aim here is to avoid "arbitrary and unsystematic" methods, such as discourse analysis, and, instead, aim for studies of emotions that can deliver a "more systematic comparative picture of time and space, with systematic comparative elements and a more longitudinal perspective that can show what 'constitute' really entails" (Heller, Chap. 4).

Our suggestions fundamentally depart from such propositions. We argue for a heterogeneous combination of seemingly incompatible methods. Expressed in other words, multiple methods should be used even if, or precisely because, they are not compatible with each other. We draw on assemblage theory and the concept of rhizomes (Deleuze & Guattari, 1996) to defend an approach that we believe is both necessary and controversial: necessary because it is the most convincing way to understand the complex links between emotions and politics; controversial because doing so breaks with deeply entrenched social scientific conventions that require each methodological component to behave according to the same coherent overall logic (De Landa, 2006, pp. 10–11).

Assemblages are an alternative to totalities. They offer a conceptual base for multidisciplinary and methodologically reflective research. This is the case because assemblages, according to De Landa (2006, pp. 10–11), are structured by relations of exteriority: the properties and behaviour of its components neither have to explain the whole nor fit into its overall logic. Heterogeneity is a key feature here, for each component is both linked and autonomous. De Buitrago (Chap. 13) appropriately speaks of completing a "mosaic" of knowledge. Even Heller (Chap. 4), who pushes for more generalizable proportions, recognizes that "the influence of emotions is filled with spontaneous expressions of strong emotional subjectivity."

When we pursue such inquiries into the politics of emotions we could speak of "messy methods" (Aradau & Huysmans, 2014, p. 607; Law & Urry, 2004, p. 390). But messy here does not mean that individual inquiries cannot be, at the same time, meticulous, thorough and systematic. Discourse analysis, for instance, does not necessarily need to be "arbitrary and unsystematic" (Heller, Chap. 4), but can be carried out in as precise a manner as any other method (see Koschut, Chap. 12; Dunne & Neumann, 2016; Hansen, 2006). The key is to recognize that the criteria by which methodologies operate are not seen as being independent of their specific purpose.

Once we recognize these issues, methods cannot be employed or understood without a proper engagement with methodologies. This point has already been underlined by scholars working on critical approaches to methods in politics and international relations. John Law and John Urry (2004, p. 397), Lene Hansen (2006, p. ixi), Linda Tuhiwai Smith (2012, p. ix), Patrick Jackson (2011, p. 25), Michael Shapiro (2003, 2013) as well as Claudia Aradau and Jef Huysmans (2014, p. 598) all stress that methods—that is, the tools we use to embark on research—are inevitably intertwined with the strategies that these methods employ and the context within which they are carried out. The task of methodologies is to challenge the idea of methods as neutral techniques and to reflect upon the choices and implications that they embody (see Clément and Sangar, Chap. 1). Implied—and at time explicitly articulated—in these positions is the idea that one can embark on systematic and rigorous research even while one accepts that there are several and at times even incompatible models of doing so. Although still fairly controversial in international relations, such critical positions on methodology are not new. They have long been debated in the philosophy of science or in quantum and complexity theory. Consider, just as an example, how Paul Feyerabend (2002, pp. 1, 18, 160) argued decades ago that the numerous procedures that make up the sciences have no common structure and that, as a result, "successful research does not obey general standards; it relies now on one trick, now on another." He presents the violation of existing basic rules as the very process through which science progresses—not towards a new and better paradigm, but towards recognition that science, and the methods it applies, is always incomplete and bound by its social context.

Conclusion

Drawing on the chapters in this volume, we have tried to outline a multidisciplinary and pluralist framework for the study of emotions in world politics. To do so requires combining work on methods (techniques, practices) with reflections on methodologies (epistemological reflections on the potentials and limits of these techniques and practices).

We argued that what is needed is not a systematic theory of emotions, an attempt to fix the parameters of knowledge once and for all, but a more open-ended search for the type of scholarly and political sensibility that could conceptualize the influence of emotions even where and when it is not immediately apparent. Numerous intangible but nevertheless important political dimensions of emotions can be appreciated only if scholars accept that insight cannot necessarily produce certainty, or at least not the type of knowledge that is objective, measurable and falsifiable. Accepting that knowledge about emotions is inevitably partial and contingent does not mean we cannot evaluate interdisciplinary and pluralist research. The key is to recognize that insights into the politics of emotions should not be evaluated by some a priori standard of reference, but by their ability to generate new and valuable perspectives on political puzzles. This process is neither radical nor unique to the task of assessing ephemeral phenomena, such as emotions. It applies just as much to the domain of reason. Quentin Skinner is one of numerous scholars who stress how our judgement of what is reasonable depends not on some prior set of objective criteria, but on the concepts we employ to describe what we see or experience as rational (Skinner, 2002, pp. 4, 44). For instance, if examinations of fear can provide us with explanations of political behaviour that would not have been possible through other forms of inquiry, then they have made a contribution to knowledge, even though the so-generated insight may remain contestable and, ultimately, un-provable.

Once the logic of totality is forgone, the possibilities for investigating the significance of emotions in world politics open up. It becomes possible to combine seemingly incompatible methods, from ethnographies to semiologies, surveys and interviews to discourse and content analyses. The logics according to which they operate do not necessarily have to be the same, nor do they have to add up to one coherent whole, for it is precisely through such creative openness that we can hope to capture the complex ways emotions are intertwined with world politics.

Notes

1. See, for instance, Åhäll and Gregory, 2015; Bially Mattern, 2011; Booth and Wheeler, 2007; Callahan, 2004; Edkins, 2003; Eznack, 2011 and 2013; Fierke, 2013; Hall, 2011; Holmes, 2015; Jeffery, 2014a; Koschut, 2014; Mercer, 2005, 2010; Petersen, 2002; Ross, 2014; Sasley, 2011; Saurette, 2006; Solomon, 2012; Tuathail, 2003.

References

Åhäll, L., & Gregory, T. (Eds.). (2015). *Emotions, Politics and War*. Abingdon: Routledge.

Aradau, C., & Huysmans, J. (2014). Critical Methods in International Relations: The Politics of Techniques, Devices and Acts. *European Journal of International Relations, 20*(3), 596–619.

Bially Mattern, J. (2011). A Practice Theory of Emotion for International Relations. In E. Adler & V. Pouliot (Eds.), *International Practices* (pp. 63–86). Cambridge: Cambridge University Press.

Bially-Mattern, J. (2014). On Being Convinced: An Emotional Epistemology of International Relations. *International Theory, 6*(3), 589–594.

Bleiker, R. (2000). *Popular Dissent, Human Agency and Global Politics*. Cambridge: Cambridge University Press.

Bleiker, R. (2014). Visual Assemblages: From Causality to Conditions of Possibility. In M. Acuto & S. Curtis (Eds.), *Reassembling International Theory: Assemblage Thinking and International Relations* (pp. 75–82). London: Palgrave.

Bleiker, R. (2015). Pluralist Methods for Visual Global Politics. *Millennium: Journal of International Studies, 43*(3), 872–890.

Bleiker, R., & Butler, S. (2016). Radical Dreaming: Indigenous Art and Cultural Diplomacy. *International Political Sociology, 10*(1), 56–74.

Bleiker R., & Hutchison E. (2007). Understanding Emotions in World Politics: Reflections on Method. *Working Paper No 5*, Department of International Relations, Australian National University.

Bleiker, R., & Hutchison, E. (2008). Fear No More: Emotions and World Politics. *Review of International Studies, 34*(S1), 115–135.

Bondi, L. (2005). Making Connections and Thinking Through Emotions: Between Geography and Psychotherapy. *Transactions of the Institute for British Geographers, 30*, 433–448.

Booth, K., & Wheeler, N. J. (2007). *The Security Dilemma: Fear, Cooperation, and Trust in World Politics*. Basingstoke: Palgrave.

Callahan, W. A. (2004). National Insecurities: Humiliation, Salvation and Chinese Nationalism. *Alternatives: Global, Local, Political, 29*(2), 199–218.

Costigliola, F. (2012). *Roosevelt's Lost Alliances: How Personal Politics Helped Start the Cold War*. Princeton: Princeton University Press.

Crawford, N. C. (2000). The Passion of World Politics: Propositions on Emotions and Emotional Relationships. *International Security, 24*(4), 116–136.

Crawford, N. C. (2014). Instituionalizing Passion in World Politics: Fear and Empathy. *International Theory, 6*(3), 535–557.

De Landa, M. (2006). *A New Philosophy of Society: Assemblage Theory and Social Complexity*. London: Continuum.

Deleuze, G., & Guattari, F. (1996). *A Thousand Plateaus: Capitalism and Schizophrenia* (B. Massumi, Trans.). London: The Athlone Press.

Dunne, K., & Neumann, I. B. (2016). *Undertaking Discourse Analysis for Social Research*. Ann Arbor: University of Michigan Press.

Edkins, J. (2003). *Trauma and the Memory of Politics*. Cambridge: Cambridge University Press.

Eznack, L. (2011). Crises as Signals of Strength: The Significance of Affect in Close Allies' Relationships. *Security Studies, 20*(2), 238–265.

Eznack, L. (2013). The Mood Was Grave: Affective Dispositions and States' Anger-Related Behaviour. *Contemporary Security Policy, 34*(3).

Feyerabend, P. (2002). *Against Method* (3rd ed.). London: Verso.

Fierke, K. M. (2013). *Political Self-Sacrifice: Agency, Body and Emotion in International Relations*. Cambridge: Cambridge University Press.

Fierke, K. M. (2014). Emotions and Intentionality. *International Theory, 6*(3), 563–567.

Hall, T. H. (2011). We Will Not Swallow This Bitter Fruit: Theorizing the Diplomacy of Anger. *Security Studies, 20*(4), 521–555.

Hansen, L. (2006). *Security as Practice: Discourse Analysis and the Bosnian War*. New York: Routledge.

Hill, C. (2003). *The Changing Politics of Foreign Policy*. Houndmills: Palgrave.

Holmes, M. (2013). The Force of Face-to-Face Diplomacy: Mirror Neurons and the Problem of Intentions. *International Organizations, 67*(4), 829–861.

Holmes, M. (2015). Believing This and Alieving That: Theorizing Affect and Intuitions in International Politics. *International Studies Quarterly, 59*(4), 706–720.

Hutchison, E. (2014). A Global Politics of Pity? Disaster Imagery and the Emotional Construction of Solidarity After the 2004 Asian Tsunami. *International Political Sociology, 8*(1), 1–19.

Hutchison, E. (2016). *Affective Communities in World Politics: Collective Emotions After Trauma*. Cambridge: Cambridge University Press.

Hutchison, E., & Bleiker, R. (2008). Emotions in the War on Terror. In A. J. Bellamy, R. Bleiker, S. E. Davies, & R. Devetak (Eds.), *Security and the War on Terror* (pp. 57–70). London: Routledge.

Hutchison, E., & Bleiker, R. (2014). Theorizing Emotions in World Politics. *International Theory, 6*(3), 491–514.

Hutchison, E., & Bleiker, R. (2015). Grief and the Transformation of Collective Emotions After War. In L. Åhäll & T. Gregory (Eds.), *Emotions, Politics and War* (pp. 210–222). London: Routledge.

Jackson, P. T. (2011). *The Conduct of Inquiry in International Relations*. London: Routledge.

Jeffery, R. (2014a). *Reason and Emotion in International Ethics*. Cambridge: Cambridge University Press.

Jeffery, R. (2014b). The Promise and Problems of the Neuroscientific Approach to Emotions. *International Theory, 6*(3), 584–589.

Jervis, R., Lebow, R. N., & Stein, J. G. (1985). *Psychology and Deterrence*. Baltimore: John Hopkins University Press.

Keys, B. (2011). Henry Kissinger: The Emotional Statesman. *Diplomatic History, 35*(4), 587–609.

Koschut, S. (2014). Emotional (Security) Communities: The Significance of Emotion Norms in Inter-Allied Conflict Management. *Review of International Studies, 40*(3), 553–558.

Law, J., & Urry, J. (2004). Enacting the Social. *Economy and Society, 33*(3), 390–410.

Leys, R. (2011). The Turn to Affect: A Critique. *Critical Inquiry, 37*(3), 434–472.

Lutz, C. A. (1988). *Unnatural Emotions: Everyday Sentiments on a Micronesian Atoll and Their Challenge to Western Theory.* Chicago: University of Chicago Press.

Marcus, G. E. (2002). Emotions in Politics. *Annual Review of Political Science, 3,* 221–250.

Mason, J., & Davies, K. (2009). Coming to Our Senses? A Critical Approach to Sensory Methodology. *Qualitative Research, 9*(5), 587–603.

Massumi, B. (2002). *Parables for the Virtual: Movement, Affect, Sensation.* Durham: Duke University Press.

McDermott, R. (2011). New Directions for Experimental Work in International Relations. *International Studies Quarterly, 55*(2), 503–520.

Mercer, J. (1996). Approaching Emotion in International Politics. Annual Meeting of the International Studies Association, April 25, San Diego, California.

Mercer, J. (2005). Rationality and Psychology in International Politics. *International Organization, 59*(1), 77–106.

Mercer, J. (2010). Emotional Beliefs. *International Organization, 64*(1), 1–31.

Mercer, J. (2014). Feeling Like a State: Social Emotions and Identity. *International Theory, 6*(3), 515–535.

Petersen, R. D. (2002). *Understanding Ethnic Violence: Fear, Hatred and Resentment in Twentieth Century Eastern Europe.* Cambridge: Cambridge University Press.

Pile, S. (2010). Emotions and Affect in Recent Human Geography. *Transactions of the Institute for British Geographers, 35,* 5–20.

Protevi, J. (2009). *Political Affect: Connecting the Social and the Somantic.* Minneapolis: University of Minnesota Press.

Rancière, J. (2004). *The Politics of Aesthetics, Translated and Introduction by Gabriel Rockhill.* London and New York: Continuum.

Rockhill, G. (2009). The Politics of Aesthetics: Political History and the Hermeneutics of Art. In G. Rockhill (Ed.), *Jacques Rancière* (pp. 195–215). Durham: Duke University Press.

Rose, G. (2008). *Visual Methodologies: An Introduction to the Interpretation of Visual Methods.* London: Sage.

Ross, A. A. G. (2006). Coming in From the Cold: Emotions and Constructivism. *European Journal of International Relations, 12*(2), 197–222.

Ross, A. A. G. (2014). *Mixed Emotions: Beyond Hatred in International Conflict.* Chicago: Chicago University Press.

Sasley, B. (2010). Affective Attachments and Foreign Policy: Israel and the 1993 Oslo Accords. *European Journal of International Relations, 16*(4), 687–709.

Sasley, B. (2011). Theorizing States' Emotions. *International Studies Review*, *13*(3), 453–476.
Saurette, P. (2006). You Dissin Me? Humiliation and Post 9/11 Global Politics. *Review of International Studies, 32*(3), 495–522.
Shapiro, M. J. (2003). *Methods and Nations: Cultural Governance and the Indigenous Subject.* New York: Routledge.
Shapiro, M. J. (2013). *Studies in Trans-disciplinary Method: After the Aesthetic Turn.* New York: Routledge.
Skinner, Q. (2002). *Vision of Politics, Vol. 1, Regarding Methods.* Cambridge: Cambridge University Press.
Small, D. A., Lerner, J. S., & Fischhoff, B. (2006). Emotion Priming and Attributions for Terrorism: Americans' Reactions in a National Field Experiment. *Political Psychology, 27*(2), 289–298.
Smith, L. T. (2012). *Decolonizing Methodologies: Research and Indigenous Peoples.* London: Zed Books.
Solomon, T. (2012). 'I Wasn't Angry Because I Couldn't Believe It Was Happening: Affect and Discourse in Response to 9/11. *Review of International Studies, 38*(4), 907–928.
Thien, D. (2005). After or Beyond Feeling? A Consideration of Affect and Emotion in Geography. *Area, 37*(4), 450–456.
Thrift, N. (2004). Intensities of Feeling: Towards a Spatial Politics of Affect. *Geogrfiska Annaler: Series B, 86*(1), 57–78.
Tuathail, G. Ó. (2003). "Just Out Looking For a Fight": American Affect and the Invasion of Iraq. *Antipode, 35*(5), 856–870.
Van Leeuwen, T., & Jewitt, C. (Eds.). (2004). *The Handbook of Visual Analysis.* London: Sage.

Roland Bleiker is Professor of International Relations at the University of Queensland, where he coordinates an interdisciplinary research programme on Visual Politics. Recent publications include *Divided Korea: Toward a Culture of Reconciliation* (2005/2008), *Aesthetics and World Politics* (2009/2012) and, as co-editor with Emma Hutchison, a forum on "Emotions and World Politics" in International Theory (Vol 3/2014). Bleiker's new book *Visual Global Politics* is forthcoming with Routledge in 2018.

Emma Hutchison is Research Fellow in the School of Political Science and International Studies at the University of Queensland. Her work focuses on emotions and trauma in world politics, particularly in relation to security, humanitarianism and international aid. She has published in numerous academic journals. Her book *Affective Communities in World Politics: Collective Emotions After Trauma* was published with Cambridge University Press in 2016.

Index[1]

NUMBERS & SYMBOLS
9/11, 6, 21, 109, 132, 134, 198, 201, 256, 263, 266, 267, 269, 271, 273, 282, 333

A
Abu Ghraib, 333
Action tendencies, 20, 78, 79, 85, 92, 233, 234, 237–239, 241, 243–245
Affective disposition, 80, 94, 110, 331
Affective experiences, 111, 114, 122, 292
Affective states, 5, 34, 92, 232
Affective stylistics, 17, 21, 257, 263, 265, 273
Afghanistan, 21, 115, 132, 135, 136, 138, 140, 141, 154, 198, 269, 270, 272, 331
Agency, 52, 57, 66, 67, 76, 121, 333
Air power, 133, 136
Alliance politics, 326
American foreign policy, 267
Analogies, 87, 198, 284, 285, 289
Ancien Régime, 167
Anger, 6, 10, 18, 20, 41, 55, 77–95, 181, 182, 184, 185, 192, 202, 221, 232, 235, 236, 238, 245, 246, 256, 259–261, 270, 271, 284, 290, 291, 293–295, 331
Animals, 36, 41, 42, 154
Anti-Americanism, 246
Anti-positivist, 52
Anxiety, 33, 120, 153
Architecture, 11, 19, 23, 109, 114–117, 122, 266, 334
Arendt, Hannah, 131, 135, 136, 142, 146
Assemblages, 156, 161, 162, 167, 336

[1] Note: Page numbers followed by "n" refer to notes.

Attitudes, 24, 78, 80, 85, 117, 118, 153, 167, 234, 235, 240, 242, 244, 266, 267, 281, 329
Audiences, 87, 89, 113, 120, 180, 182–185, 188, 192–194, 198–200, 202, 210, 214, 215, 220, 232, 240, 244, 268, 274n1, 281, 285, 286, 288, 289, 292, 296, 297, 308, 334
Audiencing, 210, 214, 221
Auschwitz, 85, 107
Australia, 216
Authenticity, 9, 11
Autobiographies, 58, 152, 281
Auto-ethnography, 19, 103–123
Awareness, 5, 35, 110, 210, 235, 237, 261, 262, 319, 329
Awe, 41, 116, 117

B

Barthes, Roland, 189, 211
Behavioral, 5, 41, 79–81, 84–86, 233
Bin Laden, Osama, 147n10, 181, 193, 196–198, 200, 201
Biographies, 58
Blair, Tony, 43, 44
Blame, 78, 185, 278, 290
Bodily awareness, 35
Bodily experiences, 12
Bodily reactions, 19, 238, 273, 296
Bodily sensations, 5, 225n2, 330
Bourgeoisie, 161, 164, 167–169, 171
Brain, 34, 234, 326
Brexit, 43, 44
Bureaucratic violence, 131, 134, 135, 142
Bush, Barbara, 54
Bush, George H. W., 54
Bush, George W., 43, 44, 54, 134, 181, 193, 196–198, 200, 201, 256, 257, 262, 266–270
Butler, Judith, 19, 130–133, 135, 136, 139, 159, 186, 327

C

Cameron, David, 222
Cartography, 19, 20, 152–154, 156–158, 160, 165–171
Cartoons, 21, 24, 152, 214, 223, 303, 304, 307–309, 311–313, 315–319
Causality, 332, 333, 335
Causal relationships, 9, 280, 336
Centrality, 91, 136
Charlie Hebdo, 223, 308
Cheney, Dick, 43
Choreography, 113
Churchill, Winston S., 18, 51, 123n1
Circulation, 24, 105, 108, 115, 121, 152, 210, 213, 214, 216, 219–221, 224, 308
Classes, 9, 22, 33, 104, 109, 118, 120
CNN, 217
Codebook, 83, 88, 90, 186, 188–196, 201, 202
Cognitions, 10, 20, 40, 233, 234, 236, 237, 241, 244, 258, 259, 286, 331
Cold War, 3, 83, 93, 115, 136, 140, 169, 171, 290, 292, 293
Collateral damage, 138, 141, 143, 285
Colonialism, 61, 171n1, 172n3, 218, 225, 242
Colours, 112, 113, 312, 313, 316
Comparatives approach, 95
Compassion, 19, 20, 131–133, 135, 137, 145, 181, 182, 184, 185, 192, 201, 202, 217, 225, 256, 261, 267, 269–273
Complaints, 237, 244
Complexities, 9, 12, 107, 187, 258, 311, 313, 315, 331, 334, 337

Computer-assisted analysis, 17, 179, 180, 186, 188
Conflicts, 3, 4, 46, 57, 60, 64, 65, 80, 83, 94, 95, 118, 152–154, 168, 169, 172n2, 172n6, 179, 181, 185, 194, 217, 219, 222, 246, 257, 258, 284, 288, 297, 306
Connotations, 85, 284–286, 289
Consciousness, 5, 81, 95, 110, 216, 330
Constructivism, 75, 283
Consumption, 109, 117, 119, 120
Contempt, 41, 284, 287
Contextualization, 297
Conventional warfare, 155
Cooperation, 79, 80, 92, 238, 245–247, 288–291, 294, 295, 317
Critical realism, 53, 55, 66

D

Debt crisis, 20, 233, 239
Decision-making, 4, 16, 18, 22, 53, 81, 95, 231, 240, 305, 326
Deductive categories, 84, 310, 320n3
Dehumanization, 152, 154–156, 160
Deleuze, Gilles, 105, 336
Depression, 39
Despair, 107, 108, 265, 270
Differentiation, 4, 23, 80, 237
Dilemmas, 57–59, 62, 65, 66, 113, 134, 258, 326
Diplomacy, 89, 105, 121, 167, 326
Discourse analysis, 7, 17, 18, 20, 21, 23, 24, 75, 88, 114, 187, 188, 215, 232, 234, 239, 244, 245, 277, 328, 334–336
Disgust, 41, 153, 238, 270, 271, 287
Distress, 117, 210, 211, 216–218, 221
Document-coding ratio, 91
Dramatization, 87

E

Embodied emotions, 34, 259
Embodiment, 111
Emergent properties, 55, 57–59, 64–67
Emotional appraisals, 24, 256, 257, 260–272, 274
Emotional attitudes, 20, 93, 234, 236, 237, 244, 284
Emotional consent, 179, 183, 202, 203
Emotional framing, 221, 224, 303–306, 310, 312
Emotional intensity, 285
Emotional interdependencies, 320
Emotionalization, 92, 280, 285, 288, 292
Emotional meanings, 24, 280, 281, 283, 284, 286–289, 297
Emotional norms, 266, 271, 272, 281
Emotional predispositions, 326, 332
Emotional processes, 234, 236, 237
Emotional stability, 317
Emotion discourse, 17, 21, 24, 277–297
Emotion term, 283–285, 289, 291
Emotive pattern, 81, 93
Empathy, 179, 201, 218, 221, 258, 259, 261, 262, 269–271, 273, 318
Engineers, 160–166
Enmity, 3, 22, 67, 69, 306, 319
Epistemology, 1, 4, 10, 14, 15, 20, 21, 75, 104, 107, 129, 186, 257, 258, 268, 273, 277, 304, 328, 335–337
Equality, 57–59, 65, 91
Ethnography, 10, 110, 111, 119, 215, 334, 338
Eulogy, 54
Evaluative judgments, 210
Everyday, 19, 87, 105, 109, 120, 277

Exaggeration, 311–313, 318
Experiences, 5, 12, 13, 15, 19, 22, 23, 34, 35, 37, 40, 42, 43, 54, 57, 79, 81, 87, 93, 96, 103–107, 110–114, 117–122, 131, 132, 134, 135, 137, 138, 140, 146, 159, 180, 182, 187, 211, 214, 225n2, 232, 233, 235, 236, 238, 239, 245, 246, 247n4, 256–266, 269–271, 273, 274, 279, 281, 287, 292, 294, 296, 304, 305, 318, 326, 329, 332, 338
Experiments, 7, 25n2, 163, 182, 242, 327, 332, 334, 335
Extrinsic, 77, 92

F
Facebook, 220
Fairy tales, 181, 183, 184, 189
Falkland, 118
Fear, 3, 6, 20, 33, 39, 41, 45, 61, 63, 105, 153, 170, 184, 192, 201, 211, 235, 245, 259–261, 270, 273, 284, 285, 292, 294, 311, 313, 331, 333, 338
Feeling, 5, 6, 9, 13, 18, 23, 24, 34–40, 43, 44, 56, 77–79, 81, 82, 85–87, 92, 107, 112, 129, 130, 132, 145, 146n2, 153, 211, 213, 216, 219–221, 231, 233, 235, 236, 238, 242–244, 247n3, 256, 260, 270, 271, 284, 286, 287, 290–296, 308, 313, 316, 328–331, 333
Felt sense, 22, 35–46, 333
Feminism, 111, 112, 119
Feyerabend, Paul, 337
Film, 112
Fish, Stanley, 21, 257, 263–268, 270, 273, 274n1

Focusing, 14, 18, 20, 21, 34, 39, 40, 42, 46, 67, 112, 122, 155, 210, 213, 215, 216, 257, 258, 282, 289, 306
Foreign policy analysis, 3, 67
Foucault, Michel, 108, 111, 130–132, 140, 159
Frames, 5, 7, 11, 19, 23, 35, 84, 90, 92, 114, 119, 130, 132–134, 136–145, 152, 155, 156, 185, 188, 216, 219, 221, 283, 307, 315, 328
Frames of war, 130, 132, 133, 136, 139, 145
France, 44, 120, 136, 163, 165, 166, 168, 172n8, 320n1
French Revolution, 167, 171
Friends, 54, 57–62, 64, 65, 68, 69, 119, 269, 310, 331
Friendship, 3, 18, 22, 51, 326

G
Gadamer, Hans-Georg, 21, 256, 257, 260–265, 272, 273
Game Theory, 57
Gaze, 111
Gendlin, Eugene, 18, 33–46
Generalizability, 8, 9
Genocides, 108, 117, 129, 134, 284, 285
Genuine emotion, 327
Geography, 330
Germany, 20, 60, 161, 168, 239–246, 247n7, 320n1
Getty Images, 218
Good practice, 7
Gorbachev, Mikhail, 53, 54
Gorbachev, Raisa, 54
Governmentality, 4

Great Britian, 18, 52, 53, 61–65, 67, 105, 109, 116–120, 136, 146n3, 168, 171n1, 221, 222, 320n1, 331
Greece, 240–244, 247n7
Grief, 216, 219, 221, 224
Grievable life, 133

H

Habits, 6, 36, 37, 40, 44, 81, 262, 329
Hall, Tod H., 4, 55, 56, 81, 232, 233, 283, 297n1, 338n1
Haraway, Donna, 111
Harper, Stephen, 222
Hates, 33, 130, 131, 142, 145, 211, 261, 265, 270, 273, 284
Hatred, 3, 20, 133, 134, 145, 153, 238, 246, 259
Heritage, 105, 112, 120–122
Hermeneutics, 19, 24, 52, 57, 66, 195, 202, 261, 334
Heterogeneity, 336
Historical sociology, 156–159
Holocaust, 106, 116–118
Homogeneity, 12, 296
Hopes, 39, 42, 122, 200, 236, 246, 265, 269, 273, 274, 285, 290, 294, 295, 304, 335, 338
Hopkins, Harry, 62
Horizons, fusion of, 21
Humanitarian action, 216
Humanitarian crises, 219, 326
Humanitarian wars, 134, 135
Human Rights Watch, 219
Human shield, 139
Humiliation, 13, 44, 216, 243, 258, 261
Hypotheses, 336

I

Identity, 6, 21, 43, 76, 78, 81, 82, 91, 95, 105, 180, 184, 232, 233, 236, 246, 260, 278–280, 282, 283, 286–288, 292, 293, 295, 297, 303, 305, 306, 317, 327, 331
Illiberal war, 116
Imperialism, 65, 169, 171n1, 172n8, 242, 246
India, 246
Indifference, 131, 133–135, 140, 183
Inductive categories, 90, 96n1, 188, 190, 202, 310, 320n3
Inner state, 5, 232, 329
Innocence, 45, 133, 135, 182, 184, 185, 192, 195, 218, 285
Institutionalization, 6, 11, 12, 16, 18–20, 82, 152, 155, 156, 160, 161, 164, 167, 172n7, 187, 202, 215, 278, 287, 317
INTEGRUM, 88, 90
Inter-coder reliability, 89, 90, 96
Interests, 1, 2, 11, 14, 15, 18–20, 38, 43, 46, 52, 55, 68, 80, 81, 83, 84, 92, 95, 112, 120, 131, 132, 145, 157, 162, 180, 183, 186, 188, 190, 192, 278, 289, 305–307, 310, 312, 314, 317, 319, 320, 327, 333
Intermediary level, 53, 56, 67, 68
Interpellation, 287
Interpretative approaches, 11, 14, 18, 19, 35, 51–69, 75–77, 95, 108, 112, 132, 138, 144, 145, 180, 181, 188, 189, 195–202, 209, 245, 246, 261–264, 266, 268, 271, 280, 281, 285–288, 292–295, 305, 307–310, 312, 319
Interpretative Political Science (IPS), 52, 53, 55–59, 65–68

Interpretivist analysis, 52, 53, 56, 138
Interstate relations, 306, 307, 319
Intersubjective meaning, 211, 212, 214
Intersubjectivity, 5, 18, 82, 114, 130, 142, 180, 182, 195, 212, 213, 232, 258, 259, 277–279, 286, 292, 293, 296, 329
Intertextuality, 157, 210, 214–216, 220, 221, 223, 282, 287
Interviews, 2, 11, 19, 89, 111, 112, 131, 136–141, 145, 152, 157, 215, 217, 240, 281, 296, 328, 334, 338
IPS, *see* Interpretative Political Science
Iran, 21, 246, 303, 304, 308–319, 320n1
Iranian nuclear agreement, 309, 311, 312
Iranian nuclear program, 308
Iraq, 20, 43–45, 118, 132, 136, 142, 143, 152, 154, 160, 186, 193–196, 198, 200, 201, 332
Iraq War, 115, 202
Islamic State, 136, 220, 222, 244, 288
Isolationism, 117, 267
Israeli-Palestinian conflict, 219

J
Jealousy, 41
Jihad, 45, 138, 140, 143, 193, 200, 244
John McCain, 222
Joy, 10, 41, 105, 117, 134, 138, 211, 234, 239, 245, 256, 259, 271, 284, 291
Just War, 109, 117

K
Kerry, John, 315, 316
Knowledge, 2, 8, 9, 13, 36, 39, 85, 93, 108, 111–113, 118, 154, 156, 162, 169, 172n2, 180, 195, 202, 211, 214, 218, 259, 268, 284, 286, 293, 304, 305, 308, 309, 311, 319, 326, 334–336, 338
Kohl, Helmut, 54, 58, 59
Kosovo, 18, 77, 83, 88, 89, 91–93, 134, 136
Kurdi, Alan, 20, 209, 214, 216, 218–225

L
Learning curve, 94–95
Lesser evil, 134, 135, 142, 144
Liberal war, 19, 114–118, 121, 122
Libya, 135, 136, 140, 141, 146n3
Ljubljana, 54
Loneliness, 107, 108
Longitudinal analysis, 76, 95, 336
Love, 33, 117, 256, 261, 265, 266, 270, 284

M
Mali, 136
Mandela, Nelson, 44
Master emotions, 288
McCain, John, 222
Media representations, 214, 216, 303, 308, 309, 319
Mediation, 214, 216
Mediatization, 214, 216, 221
Memoirs, 58
Memorials, 61, 62, 105, 109, 119, 120, 130
Memories, 6, 36, 37, 39, 85, 96, 105, 110, 130, 198, 214, 223, 282, 304, 329, 330
Messy methods, 336
Metaphors, 18, 37, 38, 44, 85, 87, 107, 116, 132, 238, 242, 280, 284, 285, 289

Middle Ages, 154, 157, 160, 171
Military cultures, 155
Military maps, 152, 160
Military organization, 137, 144
Misfortunes, 217, 225
Mistrust, 304, 311, 313–318
Mitterrand, François, 54, 58, 59
Mixed emotions, 10, 258
Mobility, 23, 122, 237
Mood, 6, 34, 108, 112, 116, 231, 296, 330
Moralization, 92
Moral obligations, 55, 58, 60, 63, 65, 68, 190
Moral status, 234, 236, 239
Moral technologies, 136
Movement, 23, 47n1, 107–110, 112, 113, 119, 122, 166, 213, 216, 217, 219, 259, 273, 314, 336
Multi-disciplinary, 334–337
Multi-level methodology, 210, 211
Multimodal analysis, 17, 24, 215
Multimodality, 215, 216
Multiple methods, 11, 212, 336
Museum, 19, 103, 330

N
Naming and shaming, 279
Narrative analysis, 17, 23, 180, 186, 295, 297, 334
National identity, 105, 303, 304, 306, 310
Nationalism, 246
NATO, *see* North Atlantic Treaty Organization
NATO-Russia Founding Act, 291
NCV, *see* Non-Combatant Casualty Cut-Off Value
Negative emotions, 20, 52, 55, 67, 77, 135, 153, 154, 170, 317

Neoliberalism, 3, 120
Neurosciences, 7, 12, 36, 182, 326
Neutralization, 20, 135, 153
The New York Times, 216
Nietzsche, Friedrich, 132, 234, 236
Nineteenth century (XIXth century), 164, 167–169, 171
Nobility, 161, 162, 164, 167, 168, 234
Non-Combatant Casualty Cut-Off Value (NCV), 142–144
Non-representational, 107, 257–260
Norms, 4, 33, 91, 95, 162, 167, 172n7, 232, 234, 242, 256, 260, 261, 266, 270, 271, 274, 286, 287, 306, 330
North Atlantic Treaty Organization (NATO), 21, 77, 83, 89, 90, 92, 93, 95, 134, 135, 288–297, 297n2, 298n4, 298n6

O
Obama, Barack, 136, 194, 311, 313, 314, 316
Official speech, 77, 88
Organizational frames, 155
Orientalism, 137
Osborne, George, 221, 222
Othering, 180, 286, 287, 293, 306, 307, 314, 317
Otherness, 287, 304

P
Pakistan, 246
Partners, 115, 121
Partnership, 54, 60, 62, 64, 289, 291
Path dependency, 2, 335
Patriarchy, 12, 183, 184
Personal relations, 52, 63

350   INDEX

Phenomenological psychology, 34
Phenomenology, 34, 35, 45, 334
Photographs, 116, 118, 211, 213–220, 223–225, 278, 315, 333
Physiology, 5, 41, 78, 258
Pictures, 20, 76, 91–93, 95, 109, 152, 159, 162, 169, 209–212, 214, 216–219, 221, 224, 241, 281, 293, 303, 313, 317, 336
Pity, 131, 209–225
Pluralism, 328, 334
Political leaders, 19–21, 56, 179–181, 183, 193, 194, 231, 308, 312
Political psychology, 4, 7, 186, 326, 332
Political values, 331
Positive peace, 55
Positivism, 57
Post structuralism, 108, 109, 116, 157, 213
Practices, 4, 7, 11, 14, 34, 40, 56–59, 80, 81, 94, 96, 108, 118, 132–134, 136–138, 142, 152, 155, 163, 180, 187, 195, 212, 213, 217, 219, 259, 260, 268, 281, 330, 331, 337
Precognitive, 34
Prejudices, 234, 245–247, 258, 262
Pride, 3, 245, 282, 284, 287, 291
Prinz, Jesse, 259, 260
Process tracing, 2, 58, 68, 95, 245, 295, 297
Proust, Marcel, 36
Psychoanalysis, 10, 334
Psychotherapies, 34
PTSD, 138, 139
Putin, Vladimir, 54, 83

Q
QDA Miner, 194, 195, 198
Qualitative content analysis, 18, 21, 75–96, 189, 303–320
Qualitative methods, 14, 332, 335
Quantification, 9, 189, 202
Quantitative methods, 14, 335

R
Racist violence, 130, 131, 134, 135
Rage, 236, 238
Rationality, 3, 152, 154, 326
Rationalization, 152, 167
Readiness potential, 41, 42
Reciprocity, 57, 58, 60, 289
Recognition, 3, 43, 79, 91, 92, 153, 181, 239, 281, 331, 337
Reconciliation, 13, 46, 54, 94, 294, 295
Reflexivity, 4, 9, 19, 66, 118, 140, 268, 273
Refugees, 117, 209, 216, 219, 221–225, 244, 247n7
Reification, 145, 155, 160
Reliability, 14, 18, 22, 189, 195
Renaissance, 162
Representational, 215, 257–259, 273, 279, 333
Resentments, 13, 20, 79–81, 85, 92–96, 235, 236, 246
Resonance, 4, 270
Respect, 46, 61, 81, 96, 133, 141, 143, 147n10, 161, 190, 231, 241, 271, 283, 285, 290, 291, 294, 313, 326, 330, 332
Ressentiment, 20, 231–247
Retribution, 235, 236, 238, 243
Revenge, 44, 81, 153, 239, 243, 244, 286
Rhizomes, 336
Rhodes, R. A. W., 52, 56–59, 66–68
Roosevelt, Eleanor, 62
Roosevelt, Franklin D., 18, 51, 52, 60, 68
Rouhani, Hassan, 314–316
Routines, 36, 42, 155

Rules of Engagement, 137, 143, 144
Russia, 18, 21, 77, 78, 82–84, 86, 88–92, 96, 288–295, 297, 297n2, 320n1
Russian Foreign Policy, 75
Russian-Georgian war, 77, 83, 88, 91, 92, 94

S

Sadness, 41, 105, 116, 117, 260
Sampling, 88, 90
Sanctions, 311, 314
Satisfaction, 44, 238, 271
Schadenfreude, 238, 244, 284
Science and Technology Studies (STS), 156–159, 170
Search key, 88, 90
Self and other, 283, 303–308, 310–312, 314, 320
Self-esteem, 95, 184, 284
Semantic patterns, 75, 76, 91
Semiotics, 18, 132, 145, 215, 328
Sensing, 6, 11, 25n1, 35–46, 52, 53, 61, 76, 95, 110–113, 120, 130, 131, 134, 138, 139, 141, 142, 144, 145, 146n6, 160, 167, 187, 190, 210, 217, 224, 233, 234, 256, 259, 261–264, 267, 269–271, 273, 279, 280, 283, 284, 286, 287, 329, 330, 333, 336
Shame, 44, 120, 211, 216, 217, 219, 224, 279, 284
Shock, 218, 221, 269, 271, 273
Simplifications, 85, 87, 306
Site of audiencing, 221–223
Site of image, 210, 214
Site of production, 210, 213, 217
Social bonds, 210
Social capital, 3
Social disposition, 138

Social media, 11, 123, 214, 218, 219, 224
Social Network Analysis, 57
Social status, 91, 95, 235, 236, 246, 279, 282
Somatic experience, 233, 234
Sounds, 38, 46, 110, 112, 115, 122, 274n1
Soviet Union, 61, 64, 283, 331
Spaces, 6, 10, 11, 40, 54, 56, 76, 103, 104, 106–110, 112, 113, 115–117, 121, 122, 129, 166, 172n5, 225, 268, 279, 288, 289, 293, 328, 333, 336
Speakers, 82–85, 89, 90, 92, 93, 96, 107, 188, 232, 241, 242, 262, 269, 281, 284, 285, 296, 309
Spectator, 211, 213, 214, 218, 219
Speech acts, 20, 182, 187, 190, 201, 233, 274n1, 280, 282, 283, 285–287, 295
Staging of affect, 109, 112, 114, 116, 118, 120, 121
State behavior, 77–82, 331
Status, 4, 76–84, 88, 91, 92, 96, 107, 121, 201, 219, 223, 234, 237–239, 241, 242, 244, 246, 247, 247n4, 288, 297, 328, 329
Status asymmetry, 93, 238, 243
Status conflicts, 77–79, 83, 84, 95, 246
Status deprivation, 77, 81, 83
Status emotions, 239
Stereotypes, 20, 85, 93, 225, 234, 236, 237, 246, 247n8
Stimulus, 77, 81, 233, 236
Strategic gaze, 19, 151–171
Sturgeon, Nicola, 222
Subjectivity, 85, 119, 120, 304, 305, 309, 336
Sudan, 219
Suez Crisis, 53, 64, 65, 68, 331

Suffering, 117, 131, 132, 134, 137, 139, 181–184, 210, 217, 218, 224, 231, 241, 246, 269, 279, 292
Surprise, 41, 55, 92, 167, 209, 316
Surveys, 2, 35, 111, 202, 215, 245, 310, 332, 334, 335, 338
Symbolic capital, 120
Sympathy, 3, 55, 131, 245, 283, 284, 290–295
Syria, 45, 95, 209, 222, 223
Syriza, 20, 240, 241, 243, 245

T
Taboo, 218, 290
Teaching, 3, 8, 14, 55, 129, 152, 168, 239
Technostrategic discourse, 155
Terrorism, 133, 144, 198, 313, 314, 325
Threat construction, 311, 313–317, 319, 320
Threat perceptions, 319
Times, 5, 6, 10, 11, 13, 20, 23, 24, 35, 40–42, 54, 61, 62, 76, 77, 83, 89, 90, 93, 104, 115, 120, 122, 141, 142, 153, 160, 162, 164, 171, 184, 196, 197, 200, 201, 220, 222, 225, 235, 236, 281–283, 288, 290, 296, 297, 306, 308, 313, 315, 317, 327, 328, 331, 333, 336, 337
Tobruk, 62, 63, 65, 67
Torture, 134, 332, 333
Totality, 338
Tourism, 104, 120, 121
Traditions, 8–10, 14, 34, 35, 52, 55, 57, 58, 66–68, 77, 84, 96, 110–112, 154, 164, 167, 183, 211, 233, 242, 256, 257, 261, 262, 268, 271, 272, 295, 297, 326–329, 332, 335
Transparency, 7, 9, 289
Trauma, 13, 137, 138, 258, 261
Travelogue, 107
Triangulation, 11, 114, 304, 309
TripAdvisor, 19, 114
Triumph, 41
Trudeau, Justin, 223
Trump, Donald, 43–45, 318
Trust, 235, 239, 258, 289, 291, 294, 311, 318
Tsipras, Alexis, 241–243
Turkey, 209, 217
Twentieth-century/XXth century, 170, 171, 246
Twitter, 219, 220, 223

U
Ukraine, 95, 290, 291, 293, 295
Unintended consequences, 57–60, 64, 65, 68
United Kingdom, *see* Great Britain
United States (U. S.), 90, 136, 142, 154, 156, 168, 169, 172n6, 201, 222, 246, 256, 266–269, 271, 283
U.S.-Iranian relations, 303, 308, 310–312, 315, 317–319

V
Validity, 14, 113, 181, 196, 304, 309
Variable, 9, 88, 143, 154, 156, 171, 184
Vengeance, 236
Verbalizations, 38, 84
Verdun, 54
Video, 112, 122, 123, 144, 296
Vietnam War, 172n6, 219
Virility, 183

Visual analysis, 10, 13, 20, 21, 303–305, 308, 309, 311–313, 315, 319, 335
Visual representations, 210, 218, 224, 333

W
War on terror, 139, 140, 267
Washington Post, 220
Weber, Max, 57, 138, 157, 161
Western way of war, 130, 133, 136, 138, 142

World War I/First World War, 105, 115, 117, 119, 130, 169, 246
World War II/Second World War, 65, 93, 108, 115–117, 119, 146n6, 155, 169, 172n3, 242, 243

Y
Yalta Conference, 61

Z
Zedong, Mao, 44

Printed in Great Britain
by Amazon